Art Sex Music

Cosey Fanni Tutti

FABER & FABER

This edition first published in the UK in 2017
by Faber & Faber Ltd, Bloomsbury House,
74–77 Great Russell Street, London WC1B 3DA
First published in the USA in 2017

Typeset by Reality Premedia Services Pvt. Ltd.
Printed in the UK by CPI Group (UK) Ltd, Croydon CR0 4YY

A CIP record for this book
is available from the British Library

ISBN 978–0–571–32851–2
Limited edition ISBN 978–0–571–32853–6

2 4 6 8 10 9 7 5 3

Dedicated to Chris – my heartbeat

List of Illustrations

Author's Note

As I was researching for an exhibition, going through some of my old diaries to fact-check, I got totally distracted and drawn into my past and ended up reading for hours. I finally closed the diaries and put them back in the cupboard, all chronologically lined up, like my story in waiting. I knew at that moment what form my book would take. If I was going to enter the lion's den of my past, it would be by using my diaries as my primary source. They offered an unblinkered view into my mindset of that time, and I could avoid the misty goggles of retrospection. The diaries evoked strong feelings of extreme happiness, my spirited passionate self, and the not-so-good feelings of dark sadness and pain. It was a revelatory process and they provided exactly what I needed – albeit a harsh and definitely not rose-tinted view of my past.

1

'Yours was a difficult birth,' my mother told me. I was born with my left elbow bent and my fist firmly wedged against my chin like Rodin's *The Thinker*. Then she added, with a smile, 'You've been difficult ever since.'

The name chosen was Christopher; it was expected I would be a boy – but I wasn't. The name was then changed to Christine and a middle name, Carol, added, which became my given name . . . alongside nicknames Tuppence, Sputnik, Caz, and later names of Cosmosis, Scarlet and Cosey. So many names – but only one 'me'.

Just before the stroke of midnight on 4 November 1951, Hedon Road Maternity Hospital, sandwiched between a cemetery on one side and Hull Prison on the other. So began the first twenty-one years of my life living in the port of Kingston upon Hull – then the most violent city in England. It was buzzing with energy and an expectancy of a better life after the devastation wreaked upon it, and its people, by World War II. The fishing and manufacturing industries were thriving, employment was at a healthy level, and the slum clearance and building of new homes fostered a spirit of positive change.

With such high hopes of prosperity while surrounded by post-war dereliction, a pervading sense of self-survival, and a confrontational and uncompromising attitude, it's no wonder people were often at loggerheads for one reason or another. But the serious violence centred around drunkenness and conflict between the trawlermen, sailors, Teddy boys, mods, skinheads and Hells Angels. Everyone gave a wide berth to the trawlermen, who we called Fisher Kids. When they came back from a fishing trip laden with a fat wage packet, they'd drop off some cash to their families, don their pale-blue, double-vented 'Fisher Kid' suits and head straight for the pubs to get legless and fight. They were hard drinkers, like the dockers and sailors, but their distinctive suits made them stand out a mile. We'd avoid them, not just crossing the road but dodging out of sight completely. That was my environment and I loved it.

~

I was about three years old, sitting in my pushchair with Mum pushing me, my Grandma Rarity at her side and my sister, Pam, holding on to the pram. The sun was shining. I was in a cotton summer dress and overwhelmed by a profound feeling of happiness, warmth and love, smiling as I looked up at the beaming faces all gazing down at me. That first experience of loving oneness proved key to my knowing what love should feel like. That fundamental emotional benchmark, set at such an early age, meant that I also recognised when things didn't feel right or measure up.

Significantly, I was not in the company of any of my dad's family at such a joyous moment. Grandma Rarity was the mother of my mum's first husband, Donald, an RAF pilot. They had married in 1941, during World War II, but he went missing in action the very next year. Mum was heartbroken and Grandma devastated, as Donald was her only child and she'd already lost her husband after just seven years of marriage. Mum was like a daughter to her, and Grandma like a surrogate mother to Mum (who had lost her own mother in 1939). Me and my sister became the much-loved grandchildren Grandma never had, visiting her in Nuneaton for weeks at a time. My dad seemed resentful of the closeness we shared. He never came with us and kept Grandma at a distance.

Pam had arrived first, in 1950, which is why expectations were high that I would be a boy. Consequently we were both a disappointment to my dad from the start. He'd decorated the children's room with toy-soldier wallpaper in preparation for his son's arrival. We often wondered why our bedroom had boys' wallpaper, but just accepted it. He finally repapered our room when we were about ten years old, and the soldiers were replaced by red roses. I wasn't impressed, and kind of missed (and preferred) the soldiers.

So there I was, Christine, not Christopher, but Dad always called me by my second name, Carol, or my nicknames Tuppence or Sputnik. If I was in trouble, or to show his contempt for me, he'd call me Christine, almost spitting the word at me. All the various names he had for me – my sister was only ever called versions of Pamela – were like code names for his moods, and I soon realised this and responded according to the one he used.

My mum always called me Carol, loved me no matter what I did (I was a bit of a hellion), smiled and laughed so much with us when Dad wasn't around, and sang as she went about the house. Her warmth and loving tenderness were in direct contrast to Dad's cold detachment. When he worked night shifts, I'd cuddle up with Mum in their big bed and drift off to sleep. I'd sit at her feet by the fire, watching TV, and she'd stroke my hair for hours – unless my dad was around.

Those affectionate moments between me and Mum were often spoiled by Dad walking into the room and fracturing the calm atmosphere with a brusque 'Get up off the floor' – as if speaking to a dog. I only recall one time that he held me in his arms, when I was about six years old. I'd had some teeth out and was still groggy from the gas so he had to carry me into the house. It wasn't a gesture of affection, but I convinced myself that he loved me nevertheless because he held me safe in his arms, and because he bought me a bar of chocolate. Not totally appropriate when I had a mouth full of bleeding gums and couldn't eat anything.

Mum married Dad in 1948; she was his elder by six years. They lived with Mum's father in Wadham Grove, Hull, until they were rehoused to Staveley Road, on the spanking-new Bilton Grange council estate, about five miles from the town centre. My parents' jobs meant we were one of just a few professional families amongst the coal men, factory workers and dockers in our road. The Scott family lived next door to us. Mr Scott, a burly but gentle docker, would painlessly pull my loose baby teeth out for me and give me a penny. The Scott family weren't there long and the Smith family, with their eight children, moved in. That brought a batch of new friends to play with – and Mrs Smith's freshly baked bread. The smell from the oven was amazing and she'd invite me in and give me a hot bread roll dripping with melted butter. Our neighbours on the other side, the Goodriches, were different. They were more middle-class and had an immaculate house and garden and a shiny car. Owning a car was rare. I can only recall four cars ever being parked in our road. Elaine Goodrich became one of my best friends. We slept in adjacent bedrooms and would knock on the wall to signal to each other to lean out and talk through our open windows, exchanging comics swung across on lengths of string or wool.

The Bilton Grange Estate was built as part of the post-war house-building programme. Being the third-biggest port in the UK, Hull was the second-most-bombed city, so a massive rebuild was essential to replace the homes damaged or destroyed. The new estate I lived on had a shopping parade, a library, a park and even a cinema, the Berkeley. That arrived just in time for me to go to children's Saturday

4

cinema and watch classics such as *Flash Gordon*, *The Lone Ranger* and *The Three Stooges* and to take part in yo-yo competitions. But me and my best friend, Les Maull, mainly got up to no good as soon as the lights went out. We'd throw our lolly sticks and rolled-up sweet wrappers at the screen, then crawl along the wooden floor sticky with melted ice cream, ice lollies and abandoned grungy sweets, making our way between the rows of seats, shouting and laughing, to create a game of Chase with the ushers until we burst out of the fire exit or got thrown out.

Even with a purpose-built park, me and my friends preferred to play where our parents told us not to, on a place called 'the Dump'. I'd often go there, find an isolated spot at the back of the hills and hide in the long grass and bushes and sit alone daydreaming. I loved the smells and the tranquillity. I owned that place; time and thoughts could venture anywhere without interruption or judgement. I was (and still am) prone to wandering off into my own thoughts. My father would yell, 'Wake up, Dolly Daydream!' I hated that abrupt awakening. But there, on the Dump, nestled safely in nature, I was happy. I could let my imagination roam free and it was all the more potent because it was a place I shouldn't be. My chosen idyll for tranquil moments, where I felt safe and at peace, was in fact a blanket of weeds and wild flowers that camouflaged the remnants of lost lives and destroyed hopes and dreams. I didn't know it was an old rubbish dump full of debris from the war, heaps of gravestones, bricks and glass from bombed buildings. To us, the Dump was just a place that had great hills to slide down on sheets of cardboard gathered from the back of the shops en route. The hills we loved so much had been formed from the mass of post-war rubble being cleared in the centre to create a running track and cinder cycle track – everything scooped to the edges like a huge ring donut and covered in mud and grass. We didn't use the running tracks; we preferred to climb the mounds of rubble, playing Hide and Seek or Cowboys and Indians with pretend horses galloping up and down the undulating humps and bumps of buried detritus. I always insisted on being an Indian squaw because, from what I saw in films, they were feisty fighters who rode their horses like men did, and I wanted to be in the thick of the action.

It was to the Dump that we all went when I 'found' a five-pound note in the house. My dad used to lose change from his pockets down the side of our old sofa and chairs, and I'd go round tapping the underneath to see if I could hear any money rattling. My little hands could get right down under the lining. When I found the five-pound note tucked away, I was beyond excited. I had a momentary waver of 'Should I . . .?', then I took it to Les and his sisters and we all made a unanimous and very wise decision to spend it all on cakes and sweets. We sat and ate our hoard, hidden from view in the long grass of the Dump.

The sheer destruction caused by the bombing of Hull meant that bombed-out buildings were everywhere me and my friends wandered as children. Those bomb sites, which held such fascination for me, were our playgrounds and we'd fantasise about the people who had once lived there. Toys, pianos, kitchens left almost intact, the tattered wallpaper on one remaining wall of a house complete with fireplace, half a staircase, or a small piece of bedroom floor hanging precariously . . . I don't know how any of us escaped injury clambering up rickety steps and across broken floorboards.

There was a lot of fighting on our estate, and in his own way Dad may have wanted to toughen me up. He succeeded because, by the age of ten, I was proud that I could defend myself against anyone in my class, boy or girl, and more on the estate. You had to be able to stand your ground or you'd get hurt. As word got around, people kept their distance and I didn't often get any bother.

Disagreements were dealt with there and then and you moved on, often remaining friends. When an older girl beat me, my dad sent me round to her house armed with a pair of garden shears. She was twice my age and size. Crazy. Nevertheless, I had no option but to go round under orders from Dad. He stood at the end of our path and watched to make sure I did as I was told. I knocked on the door, surprise-punched her when she answered, and screamed at her that if she ever touched me again I'd be back and have her with the garden shears. That's Hull for you.

Being a post-war baby also meant that my formative years involved a tacit acceptance (and dread) of death from incurable illnesses. The NHS had only just come into being, in 1948. Scarlet fever, measles, German measles, mumps and whooping cough were all commonplace and had their fatalities. Both me and my sister succumbed to all of them. But Pam tended to be more sickly than me and also contracted glandular fever and pneumonia. I was protective towards her because she seemed so vulnerable, shy, and not as full-on as me, so I'd often fight for her even though she was fifteen months older. Tonsillitis was so common that tonsillectomy was recommended for those who had repeat attacks. We were keen to undergo it after finding out that part of the recovery was eating jelly and ice cream. We weren't so eager after we heard a few children had died during the surgery.

But it was the word 'cancer' that everyone feared the most. A girl at my infant school died of cancer. She was called Elizabeth and played Mary in the nativity play one Christmas, then never came back to school. We all knew she was dying – we were told in assembly – and we'd walk past her house every day, to and from school, feeling sad for her but being too young to fully understand what dying really meant. Mainly because we were told in assembly that she'd go to 'heaven' and would be happy.

I was about ten years old when my mother got breast cancer. She and the family assumed that, like her mother, she would probably die from it, the general consensus being that cancer killed you slowly and painfully. So when I heard the news, Grandma and Elizabeth immediately came to mind, and dark thoughts that I was going to lose my mother. Mum had what they'd now call a lumpectomy and I remember her lying in bed crying because she thought the lump had come back, and Dad trying to console and reassure her that everything would be all right. Thankfully she made a full recovery.

My paternal grandfather was not so blessed. He died of bone cancer just a few years later. I remember being taken to see him in hospital, not realising that my 'outing' was a last goodbye. It was a bright sunny day, I was all dressed up and, as instructed, standing outside awaiting permission to enter. The hospital was Victorian, old red brick, with tall windows, austere. The cancer ward Grand-dad was in smelled of what I imagined decaying bodies must smell like. It made me nauseous. Then I saw my granddad, who was now yellow, lying in what looked like a huge bed of white linen, all tucked in nice and tidy. But the bed wasn't huge: it was him who was so small. He'd wasted away to a skeleton of his former self. He was such a kind-hearted, quiet man, and as I looked at him and we exchanged smiles, I was struggling to make sense of how something invisible could have such dreadful effects. It was around this time that my dad gave up smoking. Everyone we knew who had cancer was a smoker. People knew smoking was bad for you. Cigarettes were called 'coffin nails', and when referring to smokers' cough people would often light-heartedly say, 'It's not the coughing that buries you: it's the coffin they carry you off in.'

My first day at Bilton Grange Infant School is still vivid in my memory. The huge hall smelled of polish and disinfectant and was full of silent children all sat cross-legged on the wooden floor, with brown-card name tags hung round our necks on bits of string. I wasn't nervous about going to school because Pam was already there and me and Les started school together. We had curious childhood habits. We'd eat mud, coal, flowers and clover leaves, and now we proceeded to eat the wax crayons we were given at school. The purple crayons seemed the most tasty and we'd have to ask for replacements suspiciously often. It was just a short walk to school from our house and I'd meet friends along the way, droves of us chattering away as we crossed the road under the supervision of the crossing warden, our happy 'lollipop lady', Mrs Stephenson.

Halfway through my junior school a new family moved into our street, about four doors away from me. They piqued my curiosity, not because there were so many children – that was normal – but because all the girls had their golden blonde hair styled into beautiful glossy ringlets. I got to know Margaret, who was my age, and I'd call for her on the way to school. I was always invited into their kitchen. The floor was bare concrete – no rug, nothing. I'd never been in a house that was so spartan. I knew about being poor and hard-up but this was poverty. It was most definitely not, however, a joyless place. It was warm and welcoming and heaving with children surrounding their mother as she sat busily getting them ready for the day. All the girls had sections of their hair bound in pieces of old cotton rags, which stuck out at funny angles or dangled down like thick strips of multicoloured twisted rope. It was a curious sight that I'd never seen before. Their mother carefully removed the rags from each girl's hair and I watched, transfixed, as deliciously shiny long ringlet curls sprang out and tumbled down over their shoulders. I wanted hair like that, not my short, square bob with a token ribbon on top. Ringlets seemed more like me.

Every day we paid sixpence for scrumptious hot school dinners and were given a third of a pint of milk for free, which was replaced, to our delight, by orange juice in summer. I suspect it wasn't so much a treat as more to do with milk going sour in the heat. As it got nearer to Christmas, we were all instructed to save our silver milk-bottle tops, and the special tops with holly leaves printed on them, all to be washed, flattened and threaded together as classroom decorations.

During the school summer holidays I'd often wander off on my own. I joined two libraries, both of which were a bike ride away. I tended to base my activities as far away from home as I could, mainly to avoid people I knew who might report what I'd got up to to Dad. One library was at the edge of our estate and the other on the neighbouring Longhill Estate. It was there that I discovered books on Greek myths, which opened a whole new world of thinking for me. I developed a voracious appetite for reading.

Then I stopped going there, for reasons that had nothing to do with books. Over the course of my frequent visits to the library I became friends with a group of girls who lived nearby. A strange situation emerged. They invited me to go with them to see an old man they visited regularly. I felt like I was viewing from the outside as I stood back and watched their scenario play itself out. They'd knock on his door, be let in, and when he was out of sight one or two of the girls would go and steal sweets and money from a suitcase he kept under his bed. It was full of bars of chocolate and bags of sweets all mixed with silver shillings and sixpence pieces. I had an unnerving feeling that he knew exactly what was happening, as the suitcase seemed always to be restocked for the girls' next visit. I have no idea how they'd even know there was such a suitcase – and in his bedroom. I only went a few times. It felt odd then, and in hindsight is rather suspicious.

And maybe my dad was aware of such things, judging by his reaction to an earlier incident. One afternoon I had an accident. I fell off my bike and was knocked out cold. I remember waking up with a man stood over me asking if I was all right. I was pretty dazed and only remember him giving me a sixpenny piece, which I was very pleased with. I said thank you, took my bike and went home. When Mum and Dad got back from work that evening I told them what had happened. Dad went mad at me for taking money from a strange man. I had no idea what the hell he meant. Maybe it was Dad's unexpected reaction to this that seeded my unease about the old man and his suitcase of sweets. But it was also due to an experience I'd had in Beverley Westwood, when me, Les, his sisters and two friends went on a ten-mile bike ride to the woods. We'd been there a few hours playing Hide and Seek and ambushing each other when suddenly Louy shouted, 'Look at that man!' Through a gap in the trees we could clearly see a man stood looking at us, then looking down at his hands, back at us, and down at his hands again. Our eyes followed his . . . down to his erect cock held in his hand on a pure white handkerchief. We were gobsmacked. Then the shout went up: 'Get him!' We grabbed the largest fallen tree branches to hit him with and set off at full pelt, hurling stones and screaming, 'You dirty bugger!' He ran out of the woods and across the field. I'm not sure he even had time to put his cock away. We talked about it all the way home and swore it seemed to be steaming in the cold air.

Our 'gang', as it was, had quite a reputation and wasn't messed with often. Louy was tough. One day, when we were playing in East Park's 'Rockies' (a faux castle-like ruin), quite a way from our housing estate but a regular haunt of ours, we came across a group of kids from the adjoining Longhill Estate. There was a rivalry between them and Bilton Grange Estate children that often involved fights, bike thefts and night-time raids to steal the wood from each other's Guy Fawkes bonfires. The group of Longhill boys were all yelling insults at us from the tops of the walls and throwing rocks down on us. Without hesitation, Louy ran up and laid into them all, one after the other. She was fearless and strong, as was her elder sister, Pat. If you came at them with any weapon, they'd swiftly toss it aside and give you a good smacking. That was all part of the pecking order of our environment, and not only on the new housing estates; a self-survival mentality extended across town, with some of the more deprived areas having the most violent and dirty fighters. Les and I were confronted by three boys from a rougher part of town when on a trip to East Hull Swimming Baths. When the head-to-head happened, Les quickly turned to me and whispered, 'Scratch, poke eyes, anything, because that's what they do.' No etiquette, just the basics of striking first, fast and furious.

The strategy worked and we got home unscathed . . . but not before making our regular visit to the sweet shop across the road. It was a typical run-down shop you'd see in any old British black-and-white film of the 1950s, and was owned by an old man who lived in the back. We were always ravenous after a swim and bought packets of Tudor Crisps and as many sweets as we had money for. One day the old man had to go out the back for something and left us alone. Big mistake. All those flying saucers, sherbet dips, liquorice and, my favourite, Fry's Five Boys bars of chocolate screamed, 'Take me! Take me!' We scooped up what we could and ran out of the shop before the old man came back.

We had no summer schools or clubs to keep us amused; just Brownies, which I'd got thrown out of when caught in the boys' toilets with some Boy Scouts. When me and Les were about eight years old we took on a project – what I regard as my very first artistic 'performance'. We decided to stage our version of *The King and I* in Les's back garden. It was a big production – for us, anyway. We even made handwritten tickets and cakes to sell afterwards. I was cast as the governess, while Les took the starring role of the king and diligently practised his dying scene. Alas, that never happened because, when all went quiet in readiness for his star moment, his sister Pat thought the play had finished and put on a Billy Fury record full-blast. Everyone lunged for the cake stall, consuming everything in sight, then proceeded to dance to the music on Les's dad's precious lawn. Les was furious, all our plans to sell cakes failed, the lawn was ruined, and there would be repercussions when his dad got home. That was an exceptional day. Ordinarily I'd either venture off on my own or with Les to a small quiet village about three miles away that had a gentle stream set back from the road. We'd go fishing with a net on a bamboo cane, paddling barefoot in the crystal-clear water under the bridge, catching tadpoles or little fish to put in our jam jars. The surrounding countryside, away from watchful eyes, was my childhood heaven.

When our parents wanted time on their own, it was common to be told to 'Go out and play – but be back for your tea.' That meant we were often gone for hours, and to wherever we felt like going, especially as our bikes allowed us to stray miles from home. Such freedom was a gift that fed my imagination and suited my inquisitive nature as we went on our explorations.

Being given free rein inevitably lead to a visit from the police after we'd had some very good times in the nearby churches. Churches were open 24/7 so, as we roamed around the area on our bikes, we'd pop into any church we came across. They were adult-free zones, places of old rituals that had an atmosphere of mystery and a point of access to another world. We got so excited when we discovered one particular church that had a microphone in the pulpit. That's no big deal today – it's a given – but we'd only seen microphones on TV. We had a great time singing our hearts out, screaming, laughing and loving the hugeness of our amplified voices echoing up to the rafters. We returned there often. Eventually we were reported to

13

the police. I remember seeing the police car draw up at Les's house down the road and my stomach lurched with fear and dread at the thought of my dad's reaction. I hung around until Les ran out of his house to tell me he'd kept my name out of it and not to worry. He knew only too well what my dad was like and I'd have been given the hiding of my life. In fact, when my dad heard about it he knew I must have been involved because me and Les were inseparable. Dad delivered his warning in his deep monotone voice: 'If I find out you had anything to do with that, I'll knock you into the middle of next week. I'll chop off all your fingers.'

I believed him. Just like I believed him when he said he was going to kill and eat my pet rabbit, Panda. He made out it was a joke, but I thought he was capable of doing it. His 'joke' made me panic because he did go shooting rabbits at weekends. I took Panda to Les's house for safekeeping and visited him when I could. In the end, I had to give him away so I knew he was out of Dad's reach. I was quite confused over the whole situation because Dad had built me the rabbit hutch and put wheels on it so that I could easily take it from the safety of the shed into the garden, for Panda to have a run around. I just couldn't understand why he'd want to kill him after doing all that. He never did mention the sudden disappearance of my rabbit, and I lost trust in him as someone I could rely on to protect me. I began to see him as an enforcer of my unhappiness. Yet I still wanted to please him, wanted him to love me (because I really didn't think he did), all in the naive hope that I could reverse his feelings towards me. Although there were some happy moments with Dad, his orders and threats dominated and overshadowed my relationship with him, and ironically made me behave worse than I would have done had he been more reasonable and affectionate.

The winter months were often too cold to play outside for very long and the nights drew in well before teatime. Winter indoors wasn't warm once you stepped out of the living room. Our new house had three bedrooms and a bathroom, living room, dining room, kitchen and hallway. Unlike the old Victorian houses that sensibly had fireplaces in each room, the only room that had a fireplace in our so-called 'better' house was the living room. The kitchen had a paraffin heater. 'The paraffin man' would come down the streets with a huge vat of highly combustible paraffin in the back of his van. He'd dispense it with a large metal funnel-shaped jug into cans we brought from the shed, and it would slosh about down his van, on to the road and over my shoes, making them sodden and stinking of fumes. We had no central heating or electric fires in the other rooms of our house, which meant we hogged the living-room fire to keep warm. Winter bedtime meant my sister and I put on our pyjamas and socks, slid our feet through the arms of our dressing gowns to keep our legs warm, and then climbed into bed. Luckily we shared a bed at that stage in our lives, so we kept each other warm.

When I wasn't gallivanting about outside and was in the house alone, I'd frequently go into my parents' bedroom to play with my mum's jewellery and dress up in her numerous dance dresses. I must have looked a sight, me so tiny and the dresses so large, but once I slipped into them I was magically transported to imagined enchanted worlds, feeling like Cinderella or a fairy queen. Mum and Dad went dancing regularly and she had so many beautiful gowns, and all with matching stoles: from an incredible azure-blue silk-and-net gown shot through with silver thread, to luscious pink satin, to ones that were splattered with sequins, and an amazing Spanish-inspired silk-and-velvet dress with stripes of black velvet edged alternately with silver, red, green and deep blue. In my exploring I ventured from the wardrobe to the dressing table, where, in pride of place, sat a marquetry musical jewellery box that Dad had bought

Mum on one of his journeys overseas. It had a main compartment on the top that was locked, and two small drawers either side. I soon discovered the key at the back of one of the drawers. This beautiful jewellery box was an inner sanctum I innocently breached time and again. It held my mum's most treasured pieces of jewellery, all nestled together and sparkling on a bed of quilted pale-blue silk.

Snooping around doesn't always bring such joy. When going through my dad's books, Les and I laid our hands on a small paperback full of black-and-white photographs. When we looked through it, none of the images made sense to us; we'd never seen anything like them before. We were shocked and silenced by what we saw. Why were all these people in their pyjamas? They looked so thin and ill. Piles of dead bodies. An air of sadness enveloped us and a sense that we had inadvertently ventured into very forbidden territory. We, as seven-year-old children, should not have been looking at these images. We returned the book to its place in the cupboard and I never took a second look. I later discovered that it was photographic documentation of the liberation of Belsen.

My chaotic and risky play activities ran counter to my rather rigid home life. Obedience was the watchword. 'Do as I say, not do as I do' was my dad's mantra whenever I dared to question his orders with 'Why can you do it and not me?' He was very strict and we had a schedule in the house. Both my parents worked full-time, my father as a fireman (later becoming fire chief) and my mother as a wages clerk for the Metal Box Company. My dad's job meant that he stored some strange things in our house and shed. All the houses on our street had a brick shed and separate brick coalhouse. Me and Les had a kind of Enid Blyton *Famous Five* set-up in his Dad's shed – it was our den headquarters and empty except for a solitary sweeping brush we used to keep it clean – whereas our shed was in constant use. It reeked of oil and was full of old cans, bikes and garden tools. Along the full length of the shed, my dad had built a big heavy-duty wooden workbench. It was filthy-dirty, chipped and worn with use, and strewn with all manner of tools for carpentry, jars of nuts and bolts, motorbike parts and whatever else he felt he needed to turn his hand to. There were two metal vices I played with constantly, even stupidly putting my fingers in them and tightening the vice until I couldn't bear it any more, like thumbscrew torture devices. I'd rummage about in the shed for hours, but only when my dad wasn't home. I was under strict instructions not to mess with his things in there – or anywhere. At any one time the hallway might have his rifle leaned against the wall for his weekend rabbit-shooting (and subsequent rabbit pie), or his oxygen bottles and aqualungs for when he went scuba diving. Sometimes he brought back sea urchins or starfish that ended up as ornaments around the house. One object I never quite understood as a child was a small grey metal container that had only a simple, odd-looking yellow pattern painted on the side. I asked my dad what it was but he just barked at me never to touch it and to mind my own business. I now know that simple pattern was the hazard symbol for 'radiation'. Such were the 1950s, when you could bring your 'work' home with you, even if it was potentially lethal.

Dad set out a list of chores for me and my sister, and in return we were paid pocket money. We started on two shillings and sixpence a week, increased as we got older to five shillings, then £1, from which we had to buy or make some of our own clothes. As we got older and more proficient at our household jobs, Dad kept adding to our long list of things to do. On returning from school we had to light the coal fire so the house could warm up for when Mum and Dad got home from work. We were both under ten and I still don't know why a fireman would even suggest such a thing. Pam would be in charge and I'd help screw up the newspaper and lay the kindling on top. Then she'd light the paper and we'd each take a corner of a large sheet of newspaper (usually the *News of the World*) and hold it over the front of the fireplace to draw the flames. That was my favourite part. I'd get so excited by the long, bright-orange flames shooting up the chimney, roaring like a rocket. Sometimes the newspaper would catch fire and we'd have to act fast and throw it in the grate. One evening I was sat in front of the fire with the poker in the red-hot coals, watching the end glow red, just like the irons the cowboys used to brand their cattle. Pam scolded me for doing such a stupid, dangerous thing and I waved the red-hot poker at her as if to say I'd put it on her arm if she didn't stop bossing me around. She sat rigid, stern-faced like a teacher, and said very dramatically, 'You wouldn't dare.' But I did dare to do it. I made as if to put the hot end on her arm, but misjudged it and actually made contact. I don't know which of us was the most shocked. We both panicked and ran to the cold tap, then slapped butter on to her arm.

All the chores we did were no doubt part and parcel of the nurturing of girls to be good, obedient housekeepers – priming us for married life. Sunday mornings, Mum and Dad had a lie-in and read the salacious stories in the *Sunday People* and the *News of the World*. We had to make them a full cooked breakfast of egg, bacon, black pudding, fried bread and mushrooms. Dad would then go to the pub until about 3 p.m., when we'd all sit down to a full Sunday roast dinner followed by one of Mum's delicious puddings. The most wondrous smells of food permeated the house, making our mouths water and stomachs rumble. Occasionally Dad would come home from the pub having won on the one-armed bandit and he'd pour bags of copper pennies on to the living-room floor for me and Pam to count out and share. Being pre-decimalisation, there were 240 pennies to the pound, so the sheer volume of coins made it seem like a fortune.

I really looked forward to when we had family or my parents' friends round for Sunday lunch and I got to play with their children, although, if I was enjoying myself too much, my dad would bellow, 'Stop showing off!' His presence and dictatorial demeanour always cast a shadow over any potential fun. Each day I'd wonder what I'd do wrong to trigger his wrath and subsequently what punitive measures he'd dream up for me. I dreaded him coming home and was thankful that he worked shifts so that I could plan my life around when he'd be away from home.

My mum conspired with me to attempt to ameliorate the effects of his behaviour and make my life as good as she could. It was a tough call for her because she and my dad absolutely adored each other. That was one of the great things I learned from their relationship. I learned a lot about openly showing affection, touching, kissing, unashamed nakedness. My dad would chase my mum up the stairs laughing, and her giggling all the way to bed for Sunday-afternoon sex. I just didn't understand (until much later) why my dad's open affection didn't extend to me and my sister. Pam never got punished because she was always good and unquestioning, scared to do anything in case it was wrong – she was all but invisible – whereas I fought to be seen and heard. I longed for some emotional rapport with my father. I realise now that his own childhood had made him incapable of that.

On Saturday afternoons my mum took me and my sister to visit my granddad (my mum's father). Dad never came, having made himself unwelcome to yet another member of the family. Mum was understandably very close to her father and I loved being with him. He was a very kind, softly spoken man, always well dressed with a pocket watch tucked neatly into his waistcoat. I'd play for hours with the broken silver watch chains he kept on the mantelpiece, pretending they were snakes slithering along the floor. What strikes me most, looking back, is just how uncluttered people's homes were. Just a few ornaments and sparse functional furniture. People were thrifty, a hangover from the war, rationing having only ended in 1954.

My dad's family visited us a lot in the early years, before he all but banned them from our house. His mother, Olive, had expected my sister to be named after her but Mum and Dad had refused. That, and the fact that Olive regarded Mum, a widow, as second-hand goods, was the final straw – harsh, considering Olive's own mother had also been widowed and remarried. Dad's sister, Beryl, was my mum's best friend for years. When I met her about ten years ago she showed me a photo she'd kept from the late 1940s of her and my mum on a day out at the coast, laughing their heads off. She told me they had been very close, that we'd played a lot at her house as children – and then my father told my mum she must never speak to Beryl again. He isolated Mum (and me) from anyone he didn't approve of. The only friends she had were those at work and the two couples she and Dad regularly socialised with: Brian and Mavis, who lived on our street, and Marion and Jim, who lived off Holderness Road. Me and Pam babysat for Marion and Jim's two children, Peter and Pamela, who were younger than us. My sister recently told me that Peter became my dad's surrogate son, and Peter's grandmother my dad's surrogate mother. Why he created a second family baffles me. It must have made Mum feel sad and inadequate. His detachment from me and Pam was enough to provoke us both separately to ask Mum if we were actually Dad's children. Pam thought she might be the daughter of my mum's first husband, Donald, and I thought I might be adopted, seeing as there were only two or three photos of me as a baby.

Before all that happened, my dad was close enough to his brother Mike for him to be our lodger and live in the third (box) bedroom.

Uncle Mike was instrumental (no pun intended) in introducing me and Les to the guitar and harmonica. Whenever Mike played them I'd sit at his feet, mesmerised. He was a different generation from my dad. He was 1950s-Elvis-Presley cool. He and his girlfriend, Val (who became his first wife), sometimes babysat for us. Val was a typical attractive 1950s fun-time girl, with bleached-blonde back-combed hair. I thought she was great and wanted to be like her when I grew up. Mike's guitar was irresistible to me and when he was at work I'd sneak into his bedroom and play it. I obviously didn't have the sense to put things back as they should be, because one day I was summoned to a 'trial' in the living room. I was found guilty of tampering with Mike's private things and my dad gave Mike permission to spank my backside. Mike still remembers it to this day. I guess being spanked was the acceptable and expected punishment for badly behaved children back then, but it's a bit weird bestowing on someone else your 'right' to inflict pain on your child.

Uncle Mike's musical talents, Mum's singing and Dad's interest in electronics, building radios etc., all fed and formed my notions of music and sound. When I was about ten years old my dad bought me and my sister a Grundig tape recorder. Everyone we knew had record players and we wanted one too – we so wanted to be like our friends and go out buying records and spinning them on our own record player at home. But the Grundig was Dad's sensible alternative. And we weren't allowed friends in the house anyway (unless Dad was on shift). My dad saw buying records as a waste of money when you could record the music off the radio for playback, and record yourself too.

The recording part was what I loved most. My sister was too shy to do it but I recorded myself a lot. Maybe my dad wanted a tape machine himself and used us as an excuse. I can remember him showing me how to do it and me singing 'Bobby's Girl' into the microphone. My dad's passion for electronics meant we had one of the first televisions in our street, which took pride of place in the living room. A neat wooden cabinet with a built-in speaker and a tiny black-and-white screen. We had to wait what seemed ages for the valves to warm up before the picture came on. My dad subscribed to *Electronics Weekly* magazine and kept piles of them stored under the sofa. He had all kinds of projects on the go. He built a speaker into the kitchen cupboard and wired it to the living-room radio so my mum could listen while she cooked our meals. One day he plugged in the microphone and said, 'The next song is for Winnie Newby.' It stopped Mum in her tracks. Those special fun moments they shared were wonderful to witness.

Dad may have had a challenging childhood, but his time in the Navy had given him a point of entry to the education that directly fed his fascination for technology. I've no doubt that my interest in and acceptance of unorthodox sounds is largely due to the influence of his electronic experiments and all those strange noises that echoed through our house while he tuned radios and worked on circuit boards.

Dad and his brothers all had motorbikes. Ken used to come round to our house to visit Mike when I was about five or six years old. I loved their bikes, and would climb on and pretend to ride them. One day they took a photo of me sat on one of their bikes. When my father saw the photo he went crazy that I was in my vest and knickers. I really couldn't understand what the fuss was about. Indecently dressed on the street? Only he was allowed to take photos? My mum and dad often went out on their motorbike wearing padded satin fur-lined jumpsuits that looked like air pilots' uniforms. We'd regularly go to the seaside at weekends. They would go on the bike together and put us on the bus under the supervision of the bus conductor, then meet us at the other end. We were saved the trauma of the lonely bus ride when Dad bought a sidecar for the motorbike. I think that's when I developed claustrophobia. My sister was put in the front seat, which was big enough for an adult, and I was squeezed into the tiny luggage space behind it. I could hardly move. Then Dad would close the Perspex top and clip it shut. It was like a coffin to me.

Despite being disciplined for my numerous misdemeanours, I don't think of myself as having been badly treated – not in comparison to some of my childhood friends, who were beaten by their parents with belts, shoes, sticks, etc. Dad had a punishment system of 'Three strikes, then I'll smack you.' I always went the whole three strikes – pushing to provoke a reaction to my actions. And I certainly got one to remember when I was about nine years old. Me, Les and his sisters went hitch-hiking and I didn't get home until around 9.30 p.m. It was still a few years before the Moors murders but my mum and dad were sick with worry. As was normal in the school summer holidays, our parents would go to work and leave us to play all day, with orders for me and Pam to go to Auntie Irene for our dinner. But instead I'd hitch-hike to the beach with friends, getting back in time for our parents returning from work. But on this particular day we couldn't get a lift back. We ended up getting on a bus and giving the bus conductor our addresses so he could collect the ticket money from our parents. It was the only way we could get the sixteen miles back to Hull. I was so scared to go home and face my dad that Les had to force me to walk down our side passageway to the back of the house. We took care not to make a noise but each footstep seemed to echo loudly off the passage walls. I stood rigid, facing the back door, not daring to make a sound that would summon the storm of my father's anger.

Les said, 'You've got to face it sometime', and rattled the back-door handle. The sound reverberated through the house, then the kitchen light went on and I knew this was it. Les ran home to face his own father.

My dad's face was like thunder. As he dragged me into the hall-way he lost control, either out of fear or relief that I was safe and not abducted or dead. He unleashed a torrent of full-hand slaps on my bare legs. The pain took my breath away. I recall gasping to get air between the strikes. They kept coming, fast and furious, as he vented his anger. I tried lifting my legs, running on the spot to avoid or at least limit the impact. My legs were burning and red-raw, and Mum was weeping at the scene being played out before her. Finally she lifted the telephone and screamed at my dad to stop or she'd call the police. It ended. He seemed to snap back to reality. I don't know whether he regretted what he'd done but I was sent to bed sobbing uncontrollably.

I was grounded – again – banished to my bedroom and forbid-den to see Les, no pocket money or comics, barred from watching TV or going out – and as a further punishment my dad made me learn the Periodic Table of the Elements by heart, testing me when he got home from work. It was a miserable month, only mitigated by Mum sneaking me comics and sweets and letting me downstairs to watch TV when Dad was on night shift. I suppose he thought knowledge of the chemical elements would help me at high school, as he was steering me towards studying the sciences – my big Christmas present that year was a microscope. I should have been disappointed but in fact I was thrilled. I loved it. It was on a par with Les getting a build-it-yourself electronics kit, and a welcome change from always getting the blue version of my sister's presents. I was colour-coded 'boy'-blue: blue bike, blue hula hoop, blue umbrella, blue yo-yo, blue Cinderella shoes, and so it went on. Even a blue Cinderella watch, which I duly took apart to see how it worked and couldn't get back together again.

A rather fearsome family called the Mathers moved in round the corner from our house. Like some of the other families on the estate, they'd come from a rough, all-but-derelict area of town as part of the rehousing programme. Their aggressive behaviour – they were a rowdy family prone to arguing with neighbours and amongst themselves – fed the anticipation of trouble and people gave them a wide berth.

I hooked up with Pat Mathers when she started at the local junior school. We both recognised the rebel in each other and I was drawn to people who had spirit (good or bad). We were about nine years old, sexually curious, and both our elder sisters had recently 'come of age'. We'd heard all the talk about periods and breast development and suspected it wouldn't be too long before we'd be entering womanhood. I suppose we were a bit impatient to get started, as we took to stuffing hankies and socks down our vests to make it look like we had big boobs, and we'd strut along the street repositioning our padding if it slipped out of place. It was the beginning of me embracing the inevitable bodily changes that I'd face.

Up until that point, I'd just enjoyed playing sexual-exploration games with boys. I knew it would stop being fun and get serious sometime soon. When periods came, I was led to understand, it was time to be very, very careful with boys so you didn't get pregnant before you were married. It all sounded a bit like laying down boundaries in an area that I'd relished as having none. They say kids grow up too quickly today but I was sexually adventurous at an early age. Messing about with boys under blankets in tents and playing the Nervous game, where boys put their hand up your skirt to see how far they could get before you shouted, 'Nervous!' Unlike the other girls, I never said 'Nervous' – and also unlike them, I reversed the roles and played the Nervous game on the boys. Some boys said 'Nervous', but I didn't always stop. I was really into boys at junior school. I got caught in the store cupboard 'messing about' with two of my classmates, Brian and John. Playing sex games with boys had become my favourite pastime, especially during the summer holidays. A friend of mine had a tent in her back garden, and about six of us, boys and girls, would all play there together and draw cards as to who went with whom under the blanket in the corner of the tent. The lucky two would snuggle together, kissing and fumbling around inside each other's clothes. It was intimately enjoyable, to say the least. But it lasted just a few summers.

I was coming to the end of my time at junior school when America and Russia came close to nuclear war. The ensuing 1962 Cuban Missile Crisis had a profound effect on me. All I knew was that nuclear bombs could destroy the world. It was a frightening, life-changing moment to be told in my junior-school assembly that we could all go home early to our families because the world might end tomorrow. As a ten-year-old, that was incomprehensible. We all set off home from school scared, yet strangely excited about what we'd all do if this really were the last day of our lives. We had carte blanche to choose anything at all. I said I'd be a boy for the day so I could have sex and see what it was like without the fear of getting pregnant. Make of that what you will. I was glad the world didn't end but felt robbed that I wouldn't get my wish.

Then, in 1963, President Kennedy was assassinated. I was totally shocked. Scenes like that had never been televised before.

~

High school was the beginning of a disconnect between me and Les. He went to Eastmount School on Longhill Estate and I went to Estcourt High School for Girls. Like everyone of our age, we had a fear of the unknown and of being separated from friends. I was lucky that my closest two girl friends came with me. I'd passed the mandatory eleven-plus exam and scored high enough marks to be given my first choice of school. I had no idea what I wanted to do after high school but I never saw myself as following the usual pattern for women upon leaving school: working, getting engaged then married and having children. I wanted to make my own decisions about the future, an attitude no doubt fostered largely in reaction to my dad's oppressive, controlling manner.

As me and Pam entered the high-school period of our education, we had to learn to play the piano. By order of Dad. It was his idea of giving us the opportunities he'd never had. He bought a dark-brown upright piano and positioned it in the dining room, where we were expected to practise each day. We were sent for piano lessons once a week after school. I hated it. I was set specific pieces to practise, but I preferred to play *with* the piano, crashing the keys and delving inside and plucking the strings like a harp to see what sounds I could get out of it. Little soundtracks to imaginary scenarios. Maybe I inadvertently adopted my dad's interest in the mechanics of things. I'm glad to say that I've forgotten most of the music theory and practice, so much so that I can't write music and feel constrained by traditional music practice.

I marked my first day at high school by getting a detention for wolf-whistling at one of the only two male teachers. What a way to start. We were assigned house teams, all named after distinguished people from Hull: Andrew Marvell, William de la Pole, Thomas Ferens and William Wilberforce. I was put into Ferens, which, in hindsight, seems very appropriate. The philanthropist Thomas Ferens not only founded and gave his name to the only art gallery in Hull but he also, among many acts of benevolence, championed women's rights and supported suffrage. I was allocated to Form 1i, my form mistress was Miss Kirton, and our classroom was new and purpose-built for art studies. I couldn't have landed under a better person's supervision if I'd planned it myself.

Our building was separated from the main school, which meant it was 'off-piste' from the headmistress's regular inspection patrols, so we could make a hell of a lot of noise. At times it was more like scenes from the *St Trinian's* films. Miss Kirton was quite unorthodox in both her dress and her approach to teaching and discipline. She'd also suffered from polio, which had noticeably affected her gait; she was slightly hunched over and her (always) bare legs were pale and very thin. She wore striking, fashionable clothes and white stiletto heels, and would tell us stories of her time at art college and life-drawing classes, including one of a man who always insisted on wearing a 'flower bag' (condom) when he posed nude. I still can't figure that one out. She encouraged me to explore beyond any imposed boundaries, seeing potential in me and tolerating my anarchic behaviour and high spirits. I gave her such a hard time, yet she never punished or reported me. She was the first person to instil in me the confidence to embrace openness and self-expression.

Considering how sexually active I'd been in junior school, my going to an all-girls high school probably saved me from getting pregnant in my early teens. There were quite a few who left prematurely for that very reason. Girls in my first-year class were already having sex. I wasn't shocked; I was fascinated. But eleven or twelve is very young to lose your virginity.

Along with a more grown-up curiosity about boys, I'd started to get interested in make-up and fashion, and me and my friends would meet up in the town centre on a Saturday afternoon, all dressed up. I remember one particular Saturday, stepping outside my front door proudly wearing my tartan mini-kilt, black Beatles-logo polo neck, Beatles stockings and red-and-black patent-leather kitten-heel shoes. I felt so trendy and grown-up. Then I saw Mick Ronson (who later became David Bowie's lead guitarist) with his blonde hair, looking tanned and gorgeous, stripped to the waist, mowing the grass verge outside my house. He stopped and looked at me and wolf-whistled. I squirmed with embarrassment and nearly tripped up as I scuttled off to catch the bus to town.

Although I'd dressed sexy (or so I thought) in my miniskirt, I didn't really know what sexy meant or fully understand the repercussions of attracting that kind of attention. My dad turned out to be right in that respect. A couple of years later I spent weeks crocheting a pink-and-blue minidress that ended up too short, simply because I ran out of wool. When I put it on to go out, Dad asked to see me for his approval, and immediately told me I couldn't go out in it. 'I know what men will think when they see you in that.'

Me and Mum went upstairs and stretched the dress – Mum taking the top and me the hem and both pulling as hard as we could. I put it back on and stood still, hoping the wool would hold its new shape long enough. Dad approved. But by the time I'd got to the bus stop it had sprung back to its original bum-cheek micro-mini length.

There was much talk at school about music, boyfriends, fashion and sexual awakenings, and I bought into that big time for a while. Then one day, as I was looking out of my bedroom window, daydreaming, I realised I wasn't that interested in entering the grown-up world sooner than I needed to. I had another option. As a smallish, skinny, underdeveloped twelve-year-old, I could just about get away with being a tomboy 'child'. I'd be an adult for the rest of my life once I took the plunge, and would never be able to get the childlike years back.

I made a decision to opt out of 'growing up'. I put on my old pre-teen clothes and took off on my bike, roaming the estates and countryside. I spent more time with Les. We'd both been introduced to chemistry at high school and decided to perform our own experiments, gradually acquiring an astonishing array of equipment, from Bunsen burners, test tubes and evaporating dishes to all the necessary apparatus to form a condenser (as used for distilling).

Like most schools back then, Estcourt High School channelled girls' education to suit various careers. Girls were steered towards academic subjects to potentially become teachers, but were mostly encouraged to do secretarial work via commercial studies. It was the age of the typing pool and the school had one of sorts, in the guise of a large annexed classroom dedicated to secretarial work and fitted out with about forty typewriters, each enclosed in a custom-built desk. The noise was phenomenal when the girls were all clanking away. Although I was intrigued by the machines and took every opportunity to play around with them, that line of work wasn't for me. I was determined to pursue my passion for art and the sciences.

By year three I was expected to focus on subjects that would equip me for my chosen career (of which I had no idea yet, despite my dad having decided for me). I excelled at art and science, and both mistresses were determined that I continue in the two subjects, and arranged for me to do so even though it was against school protocol. It felt good to know people cared enough to bend the rules, and, small as the gesture seems, it suggested there were possibilities for working outside systems. It turned out great: I knuckled down and succeeded in the art and science exams, receiving prizes for both, and with some of my artworks framed and hung on the school walls.

~

My teen era was one when we no longer felt the need to follow our parents' lead in dress, music or lifestyle. Music was the 'thing' for teenagers and provided a rite of passage. The arrival of rock and roll had laid the foundations for teenage rebellion. Elvis, 'Beatlemania' and, later, psychedelia took it to a whole other level. My parents didn't understand what they'd never experienced and saw the music and personal choices I made as unacceptable. There was a schism between those who fought in the war and the teenage children who were breaking away from the traditions their parents had defended with their lives. Like my sister, I was expected to focus on getting a good education that would lead to a decent job, then start a 'bottom drawer', collecting things in readiness for marriage. But art and music came first, both as an escapist delight and as a means of expressing myself. I'd draw or paint for hours, inspired by the new materials I had access to at high school and those I'd accumulated myself.

Like all my friends, I kept up with what was happening on the music scene via the weekly top-twenty radio chart show *Pick of the Pops*, and TV shows *Top of the Pops, Juke Box Jury*, with its panel of celebrities reviewing and judging new record releases, and my favourite, *Ready Steady Go!* with Cathy McGowan. But most of all I wanted to hear live music and see my 'idols' in the flesh. In October 1963 my sister went to the City Hall to see her favourite band, Johnny Kidd & the Pirates, complete with Johnny's famous black eyepatch. I was so excited I wanted to hear all about it, but all she told me was that Johnny Kidd was great but the other band playing were terrible, looked dirty and had long hair . . . The Rolling Stones.

I had different taste to Pam. Les and I obsessed over the Beatles but never got to see them when they played Hull in 1964, though we had 'Help!' on rotation at his house. Until I was allowed to go to concerts, I had to settle for listening to Radio Luxembourg or the pirate station Radio Caroline on my little transistor radio. It came with a small earphone, so at night I'd lie in bed, tune in and listen to music.

TV was a huge influence as I entered my teens. Not just the music shows but also programmes like *The Man from U.N.C.L.E.* and *Batman*. I was totally smitten with *The Avengers* and the female leads, Honor Blackman and Diana Rigg. They were my kind of women: self-assured, bold and more than capable of handling themselves, and I aspired to be more like them than the expected 'norm'. My dad had other plans for me, which were revealed one Sunday lunch as we were all sitting at the table eating. Something had happened, I can't recall what, but it was enough to trigger the following.

'I'll be glad when I can walk you two down the aisle,' Dad half-shouted at Pam and me.

Pam kept her head down, as usual, but I replied without hesitation. 'You're not walking *me* down the aisle because I'm not getting married. I'm going to live with someone.'

The conversation ended. Whether Dad was dumbstruck or just ignoring me, I have no idea. I wouldn't give him the satisfaction of mapping out my future in that way. I had every intention of taking charge of my own life.

15 April 1966
Went to see Mindbenders, Herman, Dave Berry, D&J,
Pinkertons . . . Eric came out. Fans got him, got thumped on the
back by bouncer.

I finally started going to see bands with my friend Elaine. Although the Monkees were the band everyone went crazy over (yeah, including me), my big teenage crush was for Eric Stewart of the Mindbenders. I was allowed to go to their matinee performance at the ABC and was among the hordes of young girls screaming Eric's name, rushing to the band coach and stage door to get a glimpse or a touch – and getting a thumping instead.

Dave Berry was on the same bill. His stage act and presence was strange in comparison to the others, and somewhat creepy to a fourteen-year-old. The stage curtains were closed, a spotlight shining where they met, and then a black-gloved hand appeared, caressing the velvet fabric as the body slowly emerged, stretching out one leg and thigh as if teasing the audience. His face peeked out and, with microphone to his lips, almost obscuring his face, he started singing his hit songs, 'The Crying Game' and 'Little Things', as he wriggled and entwined himself in the mic cable. It was an extraordinary sight, but memorable as it was, it didn't get a mention when I gave a talk at school about seeing the show.

I got the live-gig bug after that and went as often as I could, either with Elaine or my friend Jo. There was no 'theme' to the concert line-ups, so you'd get an eclectic mix of musical styles: the Rolling Stones, the Walker Brothers, Dusty Springfield, Geno Washington, the Moody Blues, the Ronettes, the Pretty Things, Heinz, Roy Orbison, the Troggs, Marianne Faithfull, and so on. That rich variety of so many different sounds was something I feasted on, indulging my shifting taste for the beautiful Heinz with the Joe Meek 'Telstar' sound, Phil Spector's 'Wall of Sound' (which would mean something totally different to me many years later), to the Motown sound and rock and roll. Me and Jo went to see the Small Faces. She was mad over Steve Marriott and cried all the way through the concert. She called round for me on the way there and I was late getting ready. Mum tutted at me for keeping Jo waiting. 'No man will ever wait for you,' she said.

'If he won't wait for me, he's not worth having,' I replied, and waltzed off with Jo.

My clandestine trips to a club in the centre of town, dancing to songs like Marvin Gaye's 'I Heard It Through the Grapevine', the Equals' 'Baby, Come Back' and 'Young Girl' by Gary Puckett (about a girl being under the legal age of consent – like I was), led to the last time my dad hit me. It was for getting home past his set 10.30 p.m. curfew and for lying to him that I'd been at my friend's house when really I'd gone somewhere without his permission.

As I came through the front door as quietly as I could, Dad appeared in the hallway, stone-faced, with Mum stood behind him looking fretful. He asked me where I'd been. I said I'd been at Bridie's house. I lied.

'Don't you ever lie to me!' He slapped me across the head and knocked me off my feet.

In a split second as I lay on the floor, I remember thinking, 'I'll rise with what dignity I can.' I pulled myself up, turned away from Dad, looked into my mum's worried eyes and said quietly, 'Goodnight, Mum', and at a measured pace made my way upstairs to my room. I hoped it would go some way towards showing him that I had no fear of him any more. I never really spoke much to him again.

I continued to disobey Dad, with invaluable and much-appreciated assistance from Mum. She's the one I thank for being who I am now. She believed in me and encouraged me by finding ways around the restrictions imposed by him, and smoothing things over whenever possible. She was in a difficult and unenviable position, in the middle of a battle of wills between two headstrong people. She was the one hurting the most in the ongoing struggle. Dad seemed to apply his experience of military discipline to parenting, barking orders with no option to question them. I must have frustrated him because his authoritarian method wasn't that effective; if anything, it made me more determined to challenge him.

By the time I was in my final year and preparing to sit my exams, things were changing fast – markedly so in my schoolwork, it seemed, as I was unexpectedly awarded the 'Most Progress' certificate that year. My friend Elaine moved far away to Leeds and my taste in music shifted quite considerably – from 'pop' to protest songs by the likes of Joan Baez and Bob Dylan. 1967 was the year of Procol Harum's 'Whiter Shade of Pale', the Doors' 'Light My Fire', Jeff Beck's 'Hi Ho Silver Lining' and the Stones' psychedelic album *Their Satanic Majesties Request*, to name but a few. I went to see Jimi Hendrix at the Skyline Ballroom, supported by Family and two other rock bands. Hendrix was resplendent in a velvet suit, performing 'Hey Joe' and 'Purple Haze'. His charismatic presence and his vocals and lyrics, combined with such unrestrained, expressive guitar-playing, gave me shivers and goosebumps. It was unlike anything I'd seen or heard before and I bought the album *Are You Experienced* as soon as it came out. It quickly became my most treasured album, alongside *Disraeli Gears* by Cream.

July 1968
Carol is a sociable girl who has shown powers of leadership as form captain and team captain. She has much ability and has been industrious, producing some very good work. She has a great deal of energy. D. Aveyard

The final words from my headmistress's rather guarded and no doubt partly generic 'To Whom It May Concern' letter for potential employers. I like that 'industrious' and 'energy' both feature. It makes me sound like a hard-working troublemaker.

Although I was distracted by boyfriend activities, I managed to get good exam grades and left school with seven certificates under my belt. I loved school and was gutted that I had to start work.

I'd pinned my hopes on going to university or art college, and my science and art teachers had encouraged me to take that path. But, true to form, Dad dismissed my ambitions. My sister hadn't gone to university so Dad's logic of fairness was: 'Your sister didn't go to university, so you can't.'

I had no choice but to leave school and get a job. I applied for work as a laboratory technician, Dad's chosen career for me, duly inscribed in ink on the first page of my school report book. First I applied to Reckitt and Colman, where I'd seen an ad for someone to work in their animal laboratories. I was so naive I didn't realise it was related to animal experiments for their product research. Asked at the interview whether I liked animals, I said I adored them. I didn't get the job. So I then applied for the position of assistant lab technician at nearby Saltshouse High School, preparing the experiments and instructing and assisting the students and teachers in the science department. Until that came through, I got a job as an office junior.

~

The local Mecca and Locarno dance halls were a bit straight and no longer to my taste. I started going to the only discotheque in town, at the rear of a shop down Whitefriargate. 'Disco', as it was known, was where the 'in-crowd' went; they played great music, had all-nighters too, and we'd all meet up first at the Black Boy pub for a drink. By now I spent most of my time with Jo and a girl I'd met called Maz. I managed for a while to fit late nights out around my dad's night shifts, but my social life became more and more compromised by his enforced curfew. I found it impossible to fit that in with the more liberal schedule my friends were granted by their parents. No amount of reasoning or pleading changed Dad's mind, so I made up one lie after another to keep him happy. It worked OK for a while.

I was always trepidatious about getting buses or taxis from the town centre station. It was where the 'Station Gang' hung out, hurling insults, jeering at people and fighting with anyone who challenged them (few did). Me and Jo constantly drew their attention and dreaded running the gauntlet of chat-up lines, whistles and lewd comments from two of the guys in particular, Adge and his sidekick Killer, so named for his fierce, fearless fighting and freaky look of peroxide-blonde hair and bushy black eyebrows. They were scary guys and known for screwing girls round the back of the station. The undercurrent of violence and edginess was palpable, but I must admit that it wasn't a total deterrent to me. Adge was very good-looking, in a long-haired-hippy kind of way, with a warm smile and engaging eyes. But his look didn't match up to a peace-loving hippy ethos. He and the other guys answered to renowned town hardman and reputed pimp Ray Harvey.

Ray's main watering hole was the Earl de Grey pub. It was infamous for prostitution and criminality, and legendary among sailors the world over. It was a place I never set foot in. For whatever reason, Ray was often in trouble with the police and spent time in jail for various offences. I saw him in Paragon train station one time, having just been released, returning to a fanfare welcome from a cluster of girls. He told us his girls always met him to take him straight out for a meal and a drink. It was quite a strange sight, this imposing, tall, wild-eyed black guy surrounded by fawning, laughing girls. How much was genuine, I have no idea; I wasn't part of that side of his life. I knew him from gigs, when I'd see him take to the dance floor with his customary wide-eyed stare into space as he launched himself into his inimitable crazy dance. He was the most tattooed person I'd met and would proudly show me whatever new work he'd had done – notably the 'Raymond' on the inside of his bottom lip. He relished telling me how painful it was.

It's odd how mundane routines can lead to small but thought-provoking encounters. When I hung out with my friend Bridie we'd go out together, but only after she'd been to church. Her parents were Catholics and insisted she went, so I'd accompany her to her local church about three streets away. It was there I saw two beautiful sisters dressed in personalised deep-red-and-black Victorian-style velvet coats. They had an aura of mystery about them that oozed individuality, confidence and class. They were art students. I'd sometimes see them with their rolled-up artworks under their arms, envious and sad that that path had been denied to me. But they motivated me to be more overtly expressive with my clothes.

This came just a few months before my time in the office job, where I met the boss's secretary: a petite, pretty, long-haired blonde with thick black false eyelashes (not unlike Jean Shrimpton) and a quirky way of dressing. Modern but with an unorthodox twist. I discovered she bought some of her clothes at a charity shop, which I sought out. I didn't have a lot of money and couldn't afford Quant or Biba like Jo, so I made the most of my own clothes with help from Mum and the use of her sewing machine. I started going to jumble sales each week, where I could buy vintage dresses and coats at a pittance. I'd modify or dye them, or adapt dress patterns to suit my ideas and use the fabrics and any trimmings. I must have made a mess with all the buckets of dye and the clothes dripping coloured puddles as they hung on the washing line. But Mum indulged me: 'I know it's just a phase you're going through.' Then, as time went on and she realised it wasn't: 'I thought it was a phase but it isn't, is it?' she said, smiling and shrugging in resignation.

With my customised clothes I felt more myself. Jo's elder sister, Jan, encouraged me. She was a hippy flower child and had gone out with Jimi Hendrix and run off for a while with Graham Nash. I admired her spirited quest to be independent, to break away from home. Seeing her battling and striving forward was like seeing my future self.

8 December 1968
What a terrible day it's been for our family. Granddad died. Mum said I'd never see him again and she was right, though I wish with all my heart for once she was wrong.

I got home from babysitting with Maz and banged merrily on the front door. Pam answered and just said, 'Granddad's died.' I was speechless, then burst into tears. I was riddled with guilt for not seeing him before he died. He'd had lung cancer for some time but I'd chosen, as selfish teenagers do, to go out with my friends despite Mum asking me to go to Granddad's with her.

He was buried three days later and me and Pam viewed his open coffin. I really needed to see him again. He looked beautiful, the same kind, soft face I'd always known. I felt I'd betrayed his kindness at the end of his life. As they lowered his coffin into the ground, I let out a loud groan of grief from deep within me; it sounded like my heart was breaking. My mum was inconsolable and my dad was amazing in comforting her. The atmosphere when you lose someone so close is suffocating. All you want is for the sadness to end, for someone to make it all 'unhappen'. On returning home from the funeral I wrote in my diary to Granddad, 'I'll always remember the way you used to say my name. It had a kind of magic in it all its own.'

I felt unequipped to deal with death and desperate to do something that would ease the heavy weight of loss. Then I remembered Bridie's church. I went one afternoon when it was empty. I lit a candle for Granddad and said a little prayer.

Life went on, we all went back to work and Grandma Rarity came to stay and spend Christmas with us. That helped Mum a lot and she told me to go out and have a good time, not to allow losing Granddad to spoil my Christmas.

24 December 1968
I nearly got bloody raped.

I resumed my nightlife at Disco, getting drunk and having fun, changing one boyfriend for another, and committing myself to none. Then Rogan, the kingpin Disco hard case, took a fancy to me. I didn't mind. Even though he had a fast turnover of girl-friends, he was also gorgeous and appealingly enigmatic. But it didn't last long. I wasn't servile enough. I stood him up a few times and refused to officially 'go out' with him (be *his*). Besides that, I was still a virgin, and with no reliable form of contraception I wasn't about to risk getting pregnant.

I'd arranged to meet Rogan on Christmas Eve but I was late get-ting to town and he went off thinking I'd stood him up again. I was with Maz and Jo and we met up with some guys we knew, piled into a van together and set off to a party. We ended up getting thrown out, but the night was still young so we made our way back to town to consider other options. One of the guys suggested we all take a taxi to his father's bingo hall. Other friends had gone before and had a great time blasting music through the big PA system. The hall had previously been a cinema so it was a vast space, but we were corralled into a smallish area where a load of booze was laid out and we all proceeded to get a bit drunk(er). The whole set-up didn't feel right and I suggested we three headed to the loo together to talk . . . about leaving. My gut instinct was correct.

As we came back out, the three guys jumped us. One, called

Steve, got me – and more than he'd bargained for. I fought and punched him so hard he put his hands up in surrender. 'All right! All right!'

I called out to Jo and Maz, and told the guys to unlock the door and let us out. We walked to town and got a taxi home.

1 January 1969
Started 1969 a virgin, hope to end it in the same way too!

I never made it.

1969 was a pivotal year in ways I couldn't have anticipated. I hadn't stayed long at my office job – I left as soon as my laboratory technician post at Saltshouse High School came through. My wages rose to £8 a week. I never told Dad: I just paid him his mandatory £2-a-week board.

The prep room where I worked was positioned between the biology and chemistry labs to provide immediate accessibility. Preparing the work for the students was often interrupted by teenage boys crawling into my room, looking up my (very mini) skirt, all the while pleading that they were just looking for their dropped pen. I was given a typewriter and access to a Banda spirit duplicating machine for putting together and printing science worksheets. In between duties I spent my time drawing and typing up poetry and Leonard Cohen lyrics, which I pinned on my bedroom wall, overlaid with coloured gels from the lab cupboards. As part of my new job I'd been enrolled on a lab technicians' day-release course and had met a different and exciting set of people – artists, writers and musicians who had formed their own band. I finally felt like I'd entered a world that I had an affinity with.

When one of the teachers at Saltshouse High School started getting a bit too 'hands-on' with me, I left that job and moved, in the same role, to my old school, Estcourt. Going back was a mistake. Most of the same teachers were there and I still felt deferential to them and uncomfortable socialising with them. I'd stay in the labs all day, even taking my tea and dinner breaks there. I was at a junction in my life. I hated work, had two very different sets of friends and ran two social lives in parallel, which at times crossed over but were ultimately incompatible. I was out six nights a week, going to gigs, parties and round people's flats, increasingly with my friends from Hull College and University.

I was closest to Snips and I sensed in him a similar restlessness to my own. We wanted more. And we both turned out to possess the necessary determination to get it. He was a musician, always singing and playing guitar in the college refectory or anywhere the mood took him. He formed his own band, Chest Fever (and later worked with Chris Spedding and Andy Fraser as lead singer in Sharks, plus Steve Marriott, Ginger Baker and more). I went to the band rehearsals in an old church hall, where Snips's friends Chas, Rick and Oddle worked on the band's oil-slide light show. The whole crowd of us would go along to the gigs, loon-dancing in front of the stage to the final number, an extended jam version of Bo Diddley's 'Mona'. The drums and rhythmic guitar were the driving force and it was a great tribal vibe – our tribe. That's where my love for the physicality of live sound and the raw power of rhythm began.

We were a mixed bunch of individuals, recognisable by our askew hip style, from Rick in a shirt and suit jacket to Tusca with his head of Afro-style ginger hair, big glasses and ankle-length coat. He looked like a cross between Woody Allen and Harpo Marx, with a stuffed parrot attached to his shoulder as he'd walk along in 'Keep on Truckin'' style (inspired by a comic strip by Robert Crumb). I considered the guys to be friends, kindred spirits, and never thought of taking it any further, even though some made advances on occasion, like when we consumed the cheap wine Merrydown (known to us as 'Get 'Em Down') or dropped 'Randy Mandies' (Mandrax).

Through connecting with Snips and the others, I went to different gigs than I'd been used to, mixed with actively creative people and heard the music that would have a significant influence on me – Captain Beefheart, Frank Zappa, Pink Floyd, Velvet Undergound and Nico. Listening to Pink Floyd transported me in sweet surrender to another place, stirring my deep-seated emotions, evoking very different feelings to the visceral sounds of the Velvets and Beefheart. Protest and folk music was a big thing too. We'd gather at someone's flat, where there was always someone singing, playing acoustic guitar, bongos or mouth organ. But hearing women like Joan Baez, Joni Mitchell, Janis Joplin, Grace Slick and Nico was a revelation. They were singing about change, about their world and their emotions. I'd found a place where I felt I could belong.

I'd meet up with everyone either at the Gondola coffee club or our usual, the Black Boy pub, where many different groups met. It was there one unsuspecting night in April 1969 that I met Steve B., my first infatuation, the first love of my life, the person with whom I turned on, tuned in and ultimately dropped out – and lost my virginity. Quite a cluster of firsts and all in a relatively short space of time.

My relationship with Steve B. proved to be the crucial turning point in my life. My world opened up in ways I'd hoped for but never thought possible. The words 'groovy', 'man', 'far out', 'plastic', 'bad scene', 'don't bring me down' and 'bad trip' entered my vocabulary. It was 1969. The hippy movement had already happened in America and the music had filtered through to the UK, bringing with it a wondrous glimpse of a collective experience of liberation from expectation and the conventional lifestyle Dad had mapped out for me. The Mamas & the Papas, the Doors and the song 'San

Francisco (Be Sure to Wear Flowers in Your Hair)' encapsulated the sentiment of the Summer of Love. I spent the next two and a half months with Steve in a love dreamworld, going to see the Who, with Pete Townshend smashing up his guitar, Free, Jethro Tull, and blagging our way into gigs whenever possible. We'd often take off in Steve's car to Tunstall on the coast, light a bonfire, smoke joints and sit on the beach for hours, babbling stoned nonsense. After we dropped off Jo and Steve's friend Ian, we'd sit in Steve's car abandoning ourselves to the most intense sensuous passions and talk into the early hours.

But the 1960s spirit of 'free love' got in the way of our deep feelings for one another. We both played the 'no ties' game. That, and Ian and Jo insensitively playing gooseberry way too often, meant our relationship was doomed to falter.

On 2 August 1969, my parents went on holiday for a week. While they were gone, I took the opportunity to sneak away with Steve, Ian, Jo and the rest of our group, including Snips, Oddle, Chas and Ez. We headed for Plumpton Festival and the four of us were then going on to Torquay for a week, where we hoped to score and sell enough dope to fund our trip. That's where I took acid (LSD) for the first time. I spent the weekend drifting around the site in a tripped-out haze, with a huge smile on my face. I remember coming across other people in the same zone as me and we'd hook up for a while in silence, smiling at one another then moving on. I stood beside one guy, our arms around each other, watching Soft Machine and Pink Floyd. The music seemed to fill the entire space from the stage to the edges of the field and up into the sky, enveloping me in blissful waves of ecstasy.

I didn't see much of Steve and Jo but I remember lying with Ez on a mattress in the band's van (a converted ambulance). We were both tripping on purple haze and patting the mattress, watching

44

coloured spirals drift into the air. Then someone came running in, screaming that the mattress was on fire. Those mesmerising spirals were the smoke from the burning mattress that had been set alight by an abandoned joint. We moved on to a tent, tripping out at the beautiful shifting markings (dirt) on the tent walls. Such is the perception of the world when senses are heightened beyond comprehension.

We then went on to Torquay to stay at Jo's sister Jan's flat. As we arrived, there were clothes strewn everywhere: Jan was busy packing to take the hippy trail to India. When we woke the next morning she'd gone. That night was the last time I slept with Steve. All four of us went to the beach, mooched around and made contact with the dealer we'd been told about. We handed over our equal share of the dope money to Steve and Ian, and me and Jo nervously waited for them to return. When they did, we looked in awe at the rich black opium-streaked cannabis in Ian's hand. It was the size of a small bread roll. We immediately rolled some joints and enjoyed our newly acquired stash, setting aside a fair-sized portion to sell later.

I never did know what happened to it or the proceeds from selling it. By that point I was feeling excluded and at best tolerated. Ian and Jo seemed to purge themselves of the hostility and resentment they'd apparently been feeling towards me and I became a target for their jokes and jibes. Steve just laughed. The weeks before we'd set off on our holiday, Steve and I had been talking of breaking up and had agreed to see how we felt when we got back. My world seemed like it was beginning to fall apart. On our long drive home, Steve's car broke down. The 'big end' had gone, and it was left for scrap. Rather like our relationship.

As we decanted all our belongings, it felt like I was removing myself from a great friendship, a sad, farewell unpacking of every awakening that vehicle had facilitated. The car in which I'd lost my virginity was now gone. For the week or so after our trip I hardly spoke to Steve, and the distance between us grew until it all came to a head one night when he dropped me home. As I stepped out of the car on to the grass verge, he flew out of the driving seat, threw me to the ground and knelt astride me, screaming in my face to say something, anything, to him.

'I have nothing to say to you! Get off me before I knee you in the balls.'

There was no official split between us. I was busy with more pressing matters.

I'd been dreading returning from Torquay. My parents had arrived home from their holiday while I was still away, to find me gone. My dad went berserk when he saw me. I'd 'flounced' off without his permission. It was the last straw: he threw me out.

Luckily the schools were still on holiday so I didn't need to go back to work for a few weeks and could use that time to try and sort something out. My dear friend Bridie helped me look for somewhere to live. We went to a strange boarding house, a lot like the house in the film *The Lavender Hill Mob*, complete with little old lady and frilly curtains everywhere. I remember being freaked out by its spookiness at the same time as thinking I could hide away here and not see anyone, just be in my own nest. It never worked out. Les came to my rescue again and I went to stay in the spare bedroom at his house, six doors down from my family home.

During the upheaval I heard less and less from Steve and Jo, only that they became a couple for a while. I spent more time with Les, Snips and the crowd. On 22 August we went to a great all-night festival at Burton Constable Hall, just outside Hull. It was the start of the three-day Humberside Pop Festival put on by Hull Arts Centre to raise money for their new building off Spring Bank. But it wasn't really what I would've called 'pop', with psychedelic light shows, bands like Third Ear Band, Pretty Things, (Mick Ronson's) Rats, Chicken Shack and the Nice, and films such as Dalí's surrealist *Un Chien Andalou*, *Wholly Communion* featuring Allen Ginsberg, and Spike Milligan's *The Running Jumping & Standing Still Film*. I can remember wandering from the cobbled courtyard and riding school to the various gigs and films. So much to see and hear, and all for the princely sum of £1.

The next afternoon we all met up to watch Snips's band Chest Fever playing at the East Park free open-air festival, along with Brave New World and Barclay James Harvest. There was a lot happening in and around Hull; it was a hive of creative activity and it felt good and energising to be among those involved. Hull Arts brought some great events to town and were involved in instigating the opening of the Phase Two club in the Bluebell Inn (where COUM would later perform). There were folk concerts with Ralph McTell, Michael Chapman and Roger McGough, but also 'extras' like Dylan's *Don't Look Back* documentary, and Ron Geesin.

~

I frequented Spring Bank, where a lot of older hippies and dealers lived, who I'd got to know during my time with Steve. I'd go to Dougie and Claire's or Bobby and Dee's. Bobby was drop-dead gorgeous in a Jim Morrison, pure-sex way. He had an ace motorbike that growled as he hit the throttle and roared off down the road, with his long blonde hair blowing freely. I'd spent many hours at his place, firstly with Steve, lying in each other's arms, stoned and listening to Love's *Forever Changes*. But it was from Dougie and Claire that we and others scored acid. I heard later that Dougie became an acid casualty, which freaked me out as I'd started having flashbacks myself.

One weekend a number of us decided to trip together. We'd kind of buddy up for trips, tending to take acid with those we trusted. There were a lot of stupid mind games that went on in the late 1960s. Some thought it proved how hip they were if they could conduct 'highbrow' debates and outwit or confuse someone else – even while tripping. I thought such one-upmanship was pretty pathetic and a waste of time. From previous acid-trip mishaps, we'd learned to ensure we were in a safe environment when we took it, usually someone's house. On this occasion, a crowd of us had gone to trip together at a friend's flat, and I secreted myself in a bedroom, away from noisy fellow trippers, with John Bentley, who had joined Snips's band and our circle of friends, Jo and a couple of others. Me and Jo were listening to the Beatles' *Abbey Road*, laid on a double bed and seemingly melting into the dark-blue velvet cover, emotionally overwhelmed by the beauty of the music and hallucinations.

John was looking through a book of Salvador Dalí paintings when suddenly he slammed it shut with a bang. 'That's it: the bird just flew off the page.'

We adopted the phrase 'Nothing ever happens' as our default reset whenever we had any mishaps or confusions during trips. That way we could dismiss them and carry on. Nothineverappens also became the name of Snips's next band, with John on bass guitar.

The first and only time I took mescaline was in Snips's flat. About four of us dropped it together and we decided to make ourselves some soup. Ha! Of course, anyone who's tripped knows that it's difficult to maintain attention on any one task for very long – especially when bubbling, red tomato soup is involved. It looked amazing and three of us were stood around the cooker, transfixed by this wonderful redness that was spreading everywhere. We followed it as it finally spilled over on to the floor, upon which our attention was immediately diverted to hallucinatory pastures new – the strange pattern of the kitchen lino. The geometric design became an optical illusion that soon had us freaking out. The black-outlined squares turned into a grid and all the other markings became something deep and sinister that lurked beneath. We were all desperately trying to get off the grid and on to solid ground – the carpet. That's when we realised we'd lost track of the soup. We were lucky someone came to our rescue and turned off the gas – and we were lucky again when someone came to our rescue some months later when we all dropped a tab of acid and headed for the Lawns Centre, Cottingham, to see Pink Floyd.

It had been snowing heavily and we were totally hypnotised by the beauty of it all as we walked across untrodden expanses of pure, glistening whiteness. Then we heard a voice shout, 'Hey! Get off the lake!'

We had no idea we'd wandered from the grass on to the frozen water. We carefully inched our way to the safety of the bank. My ankle-length purple velvet coat was sodden and I was numb with cold, but it didn't bother me much. We forged on to the Floyd gig, where I sat crossed-legged throughout, lost in the music and hallucinations, and only momentarily distracted by Nick Mason's cymbal mallet landing in pieces in my lap.

I continued to drop acid for a while and through that scene had met Steve's uncle, Graham. He was quite a few years older than me and looked like a tall, willowy Viking, but with a Geordie accent. I loved the way he said 'knickers', but can't remember in what situation he would have said it to me. Graham slept in the very large communal hallway in a flat down Spring Bank. It was bigger than the rooms that ran off it and he'd pitched an Arabian tent arrangement, using diaphanous fabric to cordon off his sleeping area. He'd also painted the ceiling like a night sky, with clusters of stars that were mirrored by painted stars on the floor, which in turn had loose paper stars scattered amongst them.

Me and Ez had gone there to drop acid together and were sitting on the bed, totally lost in the trip until I got up to go to the loo and happened to kick some of the paper stars and knock over a glass of water on to Ez. He completely lost it. He thought he'd pissed himself and that the stars were not only falling from the sky but also moving around on the floor. He shot out the door and ran off up the street.

People having bad trips was becoming a little worrisome. I'd already given up dope, having seen how everyone just got smashed and did nothing. It seemed like a waste of time. At least acid was challenging my view of things.

Early November 1969
Cosmosis he named me after seeing me just once.

I'd gone to an acid test at the Union at Hull University. I walked into the room, paid my entrance fee and received my tab of acid, but didn't stay in the room long. It was a sensory overload, but not a good one if you were on acid – well, for me, anyway. People were already tripping when I arrived: they were laid on the floor, groping one another or playing with a bathtub of coloured jelly, slopping it about to create patterns. But the last straw for me was a guy playing a saxophone, free-jazz-style. The notes were so jarring, fast and scatty, it drove me crazy. As I went to leave, I saw what I thought was a hallucination – a small, beautiful guy dressed in a black graduation gown, complete with mortarboard and a wispy, pale-lilac goatee beard.

About a week later, I was out with Rick and another friend, Wilsh. We were at a gig-cum-disco event, laughing and dancing to

'Sugar, Sugar' by the Archies, when a guy came over to me and said, 'Cosmosis, Genesis would like to see you.'

'What?'

It was explained to me that a guy called Genesis had seen me and named me Cosmosis, and wanted us to get together. I didn't know what to think of it.

'Oh. OK, then,' I said, meaning to deal with it later.

11 November 1969

There is only one boy I have seen who made me forget Steve and that was a musician called Genesis. He was so beautiful. His eyes were a clear blue, his hair dark brown and his skin a clear, golden colour. He smiled so beautifully. As I'm writing this I remember my reaction when I first met Steve, and this seems not to compare to it at all . . .

I had begun to fall for Gen. My attraction was partly influenced by my crush on Phil 'Shiva' Jones, of the band Quintessence. Gen had a similar pretty 'Indian Prince' look. But I recognised my feelings for Gen were different to, and didn't equal the intensity of, those I'd felt for Steve. I wasn't ready for another relationship but Gen had a beguiling way about him, and he seemed to care. I started seeing him but didn't commit myself.

I'd meet up with Gen at John Krivine's flat down Alexandra Road. (John later opened the BOY punk shop in London.) Gen knew John from his time at Hull University, and his other university friend John Shapeero had a room at John Krivine's flat, where Gen stayed rent-free. On one of my visits, John Krivine took a portrait of us together, me with a smile on my lips, my arms around Gen's neck, leaning adoringly on his shoulder, and Gen straight-faced, arms folded, staring down the camera. John took me to one side afterwards and with what seemed genuine concern advised me to think seriously about having a relationship with Gen. He said Gen was the most selfish person he'd met, had the biggest ego that he'd ever come across, and that I would always come second to that. I really didn't know what to think, especially when many of my friends also started voicing their concerns.

Gen knew I was in a vulnerable position and his affectionate kisses and promises of 'I'll never leave you' gave me a feeling of much-needed security. He felt like an ally in my struggle to make sense of my life. Still, after being disowned by my dad and thrown aside by Steve and Jo, the fear of further rejection made me worry about fully surrendering myself to anyone. I felt a need to protect myself, and Gen gave me the impression that he would act as my protector.

Gen went to his parents' home for Christmas and I continued to party with my friends. As Christmas drew near, Mum caught sight of me as I passed the house on my way to catch the bus and begged me to come home. She'd persuaded Dad to let me back. I said I would, but when I returned Dad told me in no uncertain terms that nothing had changed – the same rules applied. I was happy to be with Mum again, though, and she did all she could for me, and I love her so much for trying to make it work.

29 December 1969
Genesis got back tonight. Very strange because I never went with him at all, I just ran off home.

I'd been eagerly awaiting Gen's return after Christmas, more so after receiving a declaration of his love for me in the form of the most beautiful, colourful letter I'd ever seen. It was a veritable rainbow of words, interwoven and flowing into various shapes across the page. But when we met he was moody and there was no reunion kiss, which I thought odd. I left him to it and went home. He was in a better mood when I saw him the next day and we arranged to see each other on New Year's Eve.

31 December 1969
Went round to Gen's, he wasn't in. Went again an hour later, he still wasn't in. So got a taxi to Cottingham Civic. Had a really good time . . . Even got a kiss from Steve. John Bentley too . . . Didn't get in until 4.30–5.00. All in all I thank the acid test at the Union for Genesis x.

New Year's Eve with Gen wasn't to be, and I didn't intend to spend it sitting around waiting. I took off for a party with the usual crowd, dancing, singing and kissing hello to 1970.

We all met up the next day at the Gondola coffee bar, hung over, laughing and happily reliving the fun of the previous night. I needed some light relief and could always rely on my friends to lift my spirits. They knew what I was going through. My life after returning home hadn't been easy; there was a tense atmosphere.

3 January 1970
I was going to stay in but Dad was so nasty to me I went out and met up with Panch, Oddle, Chas and Dennis for a meal.

I gradually started seeing Gen more often, and my friends less. I'd never met anyone like him before. He was very well read, had dropped out of Hull University, was quite the archetypical revolutionary-cum-bohemian artist, prepared to buck systems, and appeared committed to an alternative lifestyle which seemed in keeping with my own aspirations. He'd moved into a flat down

Spring Bank where my friend Graham (Steve's uncle) also lived. Gen slept under the kitchen table, curled up in a sleeping bag inside a polythene tunnel he called his rainshell, a remnant from his time in a London commune. It was a strange and unromantic place to conduct our liaisons but it made some sense sleeping in the kitchen: it was free and always warm from the cooker.

John Krivine had leased an old fruit warehouse at 17 Wellington Street, opposite the pier from which the ferry crossed to Grimsby. He and a group of friends were remodelling it as a commune. Gen and John Shapeero had joined the project and were helping with the work in preparation for moving into a shared room together. My visits weren't the hot, lusty love affair I'd come to expect from previous relationships, and there were arguments, which were very unexpected at such an early stage of us being together. I put it down to Gen being very sensitive, and also his liberal view of relationships – that 'no ties' posturing, and reinforcing the boundaries of personal 'possession' . . . again.

> 4 January 1970
> *Genesis rang up and I went to see him at Spring Bank . . . Was*
> *very sad about Gen going to Nottingham for 2 days. We hardly*
> *spoke then suddenly he got up and took me out. Apparently*
> *the fact that I'd have nothing to do with him freaked him out*
> *completely. He said both him and John are expecting me to live*
> *with them soon. He knows I love him and knows he loves me.*
> *But I am uncertain.*

Gen mistook my quiet, contemplative demeanour for my ignoring him. I was just trying to figure out why he wasn't as bothered as I was about being apart, but also I was wary about him and John talking about my 'expected' future home being with them.

It would answer my problem of finding somewhere to live, for sure, but it all seemed to be happening too fast and decisions were being made for me – one of the overriding reasons why I'd wanted to leave home.

Our rocky start came on top of the ongoing saga at home. I didn't know whether I was coming or going with either Gen or Dad. The deciding factor was when I was officially declared unemployed on 5 January. I'd left my job and dropped out. Dad told me he wouldn't have anyone unemployed living in his house. I had a week to find the rent, get a job, or get out.

I hid my head in the sand for a while, visiting Gen or, when he was busy decorating the warehouse, going out with my friends, and using my last wages to pay rent to Dad to buy time while I sorted out somewhere to live. I knew the monetary transaction was fundamental to the relationship between father and daughter. As soon as I was unable to give him his money, I would have to leave his home. His notion of 'support' was pretty black and white. It all came to a head over the space of a week.

19 January 1970
What the fuck can I do? I've got to get a job by the end of the week or I'm thrown out. It's not that I'm thrown out it's the fact that I don't know whether to live with Genesis or not.

I still had lingering doubts about Gen. I was about to be homeless and I was broke, and yet to receive any dole money seeing as I'd made myself unemployed by leaving my job. I was in a desperate situation.

22 January 1970: FULL MOON
What an utterly terrible day. I went to S. Security, I got no

money. My ring snapped, the film theatre was full at the Union,
then we got locked out of the building and had an argument.

23 January 1970
From my unemployment file: 'Miss Newby called re vacs. States if
she doesn't get a job quickly her father is throwing her out.'

Les went with me to social security to get the rent. I explained my situation but they gave me short shrift and dismissed my claim with a brusque 'No money', and shut the hatch in my face. They'd wanted to make a home visit. I knew that was impossible. My dad wouldn't have them in the house. The shame of it. I knew from that moment that I was to be homeless. Much to Mum's distress, I was told to leave home for the second and final time.

Ironically it was the prevalent 'free love, no ties' philosophy that Gen espoused, and which had proved fatal to me and Steve, that provided a 'no commitment' cushion, allowing me to enter *a* relationship with Gen – one that I wasn't sure would last and wasn't sure where it would take me. Les helped me move my belongings. I wasn't given enough time to move them all, so while Mum and Dad were at work I broke into my bedroom by shimmying up the porch pole and unlatching the window to climb in and retrieve the rest.

It was the end of January 1970 and I was in the first home of my own, living in the commune at 17 Wellington Street, now named the Ho Ho Funhouse. But I rented my own room opposite Gen and John. I needed that separation: it gave me a feeling of my new-found independence and the choice to be with Gen or not.

2

My relationship with Gen was, to say the least, an adventure. After my experience with Dad and having to cope with the associated emotional baggage it had heaped on me, I was understandably inclined to tread cautiously and to try to maintain control of my life. This turned out to be a wise decision, as, over the coming years, and to my disappointment, I began to recognise signs of assumed positions of power in my relationship with Gen, and an expectation of deference on my part – not the best foundation for our life together.

Like others who find themselves in those circumstances, I worked out a way of managing challenging situations. I'd learned from a young age that power and control work by making disobedience and questioning a punishable sin, and deferential obedience of the 'word' a virtue. Gen introduced me to the life and works of Aleister Crowley, and his mantras became 'Do what thou wilt shall be the whole of the law' and 'Love is the law, love under will'. I bought into that; I believed we all had our own spiritual core self, that everyone should have the freedom to find and be themselves, and to live their lives accordingly. I came to realise, though, that the freedom this implied applied to Gen but not to me and other close friends – their actions to discover their True Will were more often than not 'guided' by Gen and subject to his approval and judgement. It was an unexpected twist on my father's house rule of 'Do as I say, not do as I do'.

The Ho Ho Funhouse was my first home away from home

and a far cry from Bilton Grange housing estate. It was part of Wellington House, a Victorian building designed by Hull-born architect Cuthbert Brodrick, and stood very close to the thriving fruit market on the corner of Queen Street and Wellington Street. My room, which was quite small and dark, faced on to the dank alley at the back of the building and was on the top floor, up three flights of stairs. John Shapeero (or Moses, as we often called him, due to the way he looked) and Gen's shared room was opposite mine and had a clear view of the River Humber. The other floors were occupied by Baz and his then girlfriend, Dee; the beautiful red-headed Copper and her boyfriend, Paul Frew (who, with Gen, had named the Ho Ho Funhouse); Bronwyn, whose room was the largest and opposite the communal sitting room that led off to a small galley kitchen; and Roger. The only toilet was in the basement, four flights down from my room and not quite close enough for Roger on occasions. He'd escaped prison, taking the 'Midnight Express' from Turkey, and had arrived back at the Funhouse having been severely beaten on the soles of his feet and suffering from terrible dysentery. He was often seen with a bucket as he couldn't always make it down the basement stairs in time.

At first I'd felt a little out of my depth in the Funhouse, being the youngest and the only person who hadn't gone to university, but mainly due to there being a kind of hierarchy within the hippies of Hull. I seemed to have migrated seamlessly from the lower-ranking weekend hippies with day jobs to the higher echelons as a member of the Ho Ho Funhouse commune. Gen and John were very welcoming and helped me settle in, and I got into the rhythm of a new routine, cooking and eating together – very different food from what I was used to – and getting to know the others as we all sat around chatting in the communal room.

I also got to know more about Gen. I was slightly in awe of his exceptional life. He'd done so much in such a small space of time. I learned that he'd won a poetry prize while studying English at Hull University, that he and radical student friends had started *Worm*, a student magazine that was free from editorial control but short-lived because of obscene and 'dangerous' content, and that, after he'd dropped out of university, he'd joined a multimedia artists' commune in London.

It's been said that Gen was in the Exploding Galaxy – but not according to original member Jill Drower, who has said, 'The performance artist Genesis P-Orridge . . . was never part of the original Exploding Galaxy.' The Exploding Galaxy had disbanded and their house (99 Balls Pond Road) sold by the time Gen arrived in London, but he joined the offshoot, Transmedia Explorations, headed by Fitz (Gerald Fitzgerald), a kinetic artist and one of the two leading original Galaxy members. The Exploding Galaxy was founded in 1967 by David Medalla, an incredible artist who I was to meet some years later, along with other former Galaxy members including Mark Boyle and Joan Hills. Its activities had connections to the UFO Club and the *International Times*, and it was at the centre of London's countercultural hippy scene.

Gen learned a lot from his short time with Transmedia Explorations, was particularly influenced by and enamoured of Fitz, and would talk a lot about him, and of how, at times, he found life there very difficult. But he never mentioned to me that much of what he presented as 'his' concept and the whole ethos of his new project, COUM Transmissions, came from that of the Exploding Galaxy and Transmedia Explorations: 'Life Is Art', communal creativity, everyone is an artist, costumes, rituals, play, artworks, scavenging for art materials, street theatre, rejection of conventions, and the advocation of sexual liberation. Even the idiosyncratic form of merging capital letters that Gen presented to me as his new COUM alphabet was actually devised by Fitz in 1967 and called 'quaquascript'. It features a lot in COUM writings and artworks, and I (unwittingly) based my 'Cosey' signature on Fitz's unique script – for which I now give him due credit. Influences are a given, appropriation has its place too, and a symbolic, written or verbal credit to the original source is usual, honest and expected – but Gen led me to believe the ethos on which he based COUM was original to him. Being two hundred miles from London, I wouldn't have known otherwise, nor did I have any reason not to believe him.

Me and Gen became an inseparable couple, living together as one. He'd talk about his music and described to me the birth of the COUM Transmissions project – that he'd experienced a profound out-of-body 'vision' whilst on a trip with his parents in Shrewsbury. He spoke of it as if he'd been chosen by a higher power. In his vision he saw the COUM symbol and heard the name 'COUM Transmissions' spoken to him. Full of ideas largely influenced by his time with Transmedia, he returned to Hull in late October 1969, so by the time I met him at the beginning of November, COUM was beginning to take shape with occasional collaborators John (Moses) and the mathematician Tim Poston.

Gen had met Tim at Hull University. Tim is what I can only describe as a genius and was like a mentor to Gen. He researched and co-wrote the book *Catastrophe Theory and Its Applications* (still in print), among many extraordinary projects and achievements, and is now Chief Scientist at Sankhya Sutra Labs in Bangalore. He cut a strange figure back in 1969: his look was more Greek Orthodox priest than academic hippy, with his long hair and beard, and his ankle-length black gown and tall black hat. He carried a beautiful wooden staff, the full length of which he'd carved by hand into a continuous interwoven spiral which converged at the top with the yin-yang sign, above which were small horns for his thumb to hold the staff firm.

COUM was given its own logo, designed by Gen, of a post-coital, limp, sperm-dripping penis formed from the word 'COUM', which I took great delight in drawing, and embroidered as 'penee patches' for many people. COUM performed only a few improvised acoustic musical pieces in 1969 and 1970. Auspiciously, the first-listed COUM performance had been on the night me and Gen met for the first time – November 1969's 'Clockwork Hot Spoiled Acid Test' at Hull University Union. The second, 'Thee Fabulous Mutations', involving COUM and other Hull musicians, soon followed at St Peter's, Anlaby, and came about through my connection with Snips.

Gen's health had been problematic. He told me he'd had asthma since childhood, for which he used an inhaler, and that the steroids he'd been given as a child had left him with a defunct adrenal gland. As a consequence he needed to take a daily dose of the steroid prednisone, without which, he said, he'd been told he could die. But he also said that the only time his adrenal gland worked was when he was angry, and he couldn't always control himself. I was confused as to how a defunct gland could function at selective times, but it made a kind of sense as I'd already experienced his short fuse via the arguments we'd had. His medical condition was to stand as an explanation for any untoward behaviours and in order for me to understand (and excuse) any outbursts – which I did, for instance, when he threw my shoe at me from across the room, narrowly missing my head. I'd ducked quickly, and as calmly as possible asked for the other shoe to keep them as a pair. I understood that the subtext of his information was that I should avoid upsetting him lest I trigger either an asthma attack or rage – in which case I would be to blame . . . as was the case when we had a disagreement in the kitchen one day while cooking our breakfast porridge. Within seconds he had hurled the saucepan of hot bubbling oats out of the open window. It came to a sudden thunking halt as it wedged, upright, in a narrow gap between the two brick walls. It was quite comical and made me smile. Gen wasn't amused; he added some serious drama by taking his bottle of prednisone tablets out of his pocket, holding it up in front of my face for me to see, and then tossing his 'lifeline' out the window. That had the desired effect. As he expected of me (after all, he saw the episode as my fault), I apologised and rushed off to the doctor's surgery to get replacement tablets for him.

Cooking time in the kitchen usually brought a few visitors to the window by means of the small sloping roof of the extension below. The alley at the back of the Funhouse had quite a colony of feral cats, which the fruit merchants encouraged as they were useful in keeping rats and mice away. One tortoiseshell cat in particular became a regular and we'd feed it whenever it dropped by. Then one day we found out 'it' was a 'she'. We heard a kind of muffled 'miaow' and there she was, looking at us with a tiny kitten hanging from her mouth by the scruff of its neck. She placed it on the rooftop, stepped back and stared at us. We took it that she was leaving her kitten in our care. I leaned out the window and carefully scooped it up before it could start wandering and fall off the roof, all the time watching the mother cat to see if it was OK. She looked me in the eyes, blinked, and left. She did the same thing the next day with another of her litter. We adopted the first kitten and called him Moonshine, and Baz took the other, naming her Izzy. Moonshine was a sickly cat with canker in his ears, and, being feral, was a hissing, spitting little thing. Over the next month I got him healthy and gently coaxed him round to being handled.

~

Gen and some of his friends would go on shopping trips together, returning with a holdall full of books and other items all 'liberated' from various sources. Some were kept and others sold for extra money to live on. I went shopping with Gen and a friend one day to the food hall in Hammonds, the 'Harrods of Hull'. When we paid and went to leave, store detectives moved in on us and escorted us to a side room. I was confused but assumed it was because of the way we were dressed – we certainly weren't their usual clientele. But no, they asked to search our bags. I hadn't taken anything, so handed my bag over on request without a second thought. They emptied our bags to reveal stolen food – two items were withdrawn from my bag. I was gobsmacked. My attempts to explain that the items had been dropped in there, that I hadn't known or done anything, fell on deaf ears – I was with the guys when they did it so was regarded as their accomplice and arrested for something I hadn't done.

We were all taken to the Central Police Station in Queens Gardens and charged with shoplifting, to appear in court the next day. We were asked our address but gave 'no fixed abode'. If we'd given the Ho Ho Funhouse address, the police would have gone there to search the place and we knew what they'd find: drugs in some of the rooms. As we'd declared ourselves 'homeless' we were put in the cells for the night. I was escorted off to the women's section and given a cell to myself. After about an hour I heard clanking and footsteps in the corridor, then my cell door opened and I was taken to the front desk. I saw Mum, so small and sad, her eyes red from crying. She rushed over to me and held me tight in her arms. I asked her how she knew I was there. The police had rung Dad and said, 'We have your daughter here. She's been sleeping rough with two young men.'

No wonder she was upset, and no doubt Dad was appalled. She'd begged him to drive her to the police station, which he agreed to. He didn't come inside; he sat in the car and waited for her. I assured her as best I could that I was fine, that I wasn't sleeping rough or with two men. She left feeling relatively comforted. I went back to my cell and consoled myself by singing Joni Mitchell and Joan Baez songs at the top of my voice, and finally fell asleep.

The next morning we were taken to court. I was put in a holding cell in the court basement with my fellow inmates, all very friendly prostitutes, and we had a good chat for the hour or so we were waiting for our court appearance. Me, Gen and John were stood in the dock and pronounced guilty, fined £10 each (despite pleading poverty), and set free. The air had never smelled so good.

~

Pet dogs had been a constant throughout my life and, even though I was struggling to look after myself, I was overjoyed when Gen took me to the RSPCA dogs' home to adopt a stray as a Valentine's present. My eyes fell on a tiny little dappled-grey puppy who was silent, terrified and trembling constantly. I asked what had happened. She'd been found in the street being kicked around by children. Without hesitation I said I would take her. I called her Tremble. I made her a beige leather collar and put a yellow satin tassel on it. She gradually settled down into a happy, mischievous pup, often escaping out the front door of the Funhouse and running me ragged trying to catch her.

My unemployment benefit had finally come through and I received £5 a week, which I budgeted conscientiously: £2.50 went on rent and 50p on a week's food for Tremble and Moonshine (now called Moony). The rest was used for food and paraffin to heat my little room. We had a spartan diet, made up of a carrier bag of muesli from the health shop or cracked-wheat porridge (for breakfast); Ryvita crackers and cheese (for lunch); rice, pasta and vegetables from which we made our various hot evening meals.

Just around the corner was Humber Street Fruit Market, a noisy, bustling distribution point where lorries collected their loads of pallets stacked with bags of fruit and vegetables – very redolent of the Covent Garden location for Hitchcock's *Frenzy*. It became a helpful source of free food. We'd go round after the workers had shut up for the day and collect what fruit and veg lay on the floor from split bags; sometimes we'd cut bags ourselves that had been left out ready for the early-morning load-up.

The trauma of the shoplifting arrest was eclipsed by something far worse just a few months later, when I discovered I was pregnant with Gen's child.

Gen hated and refused to wear condoms, and I foolishly went along with it. I was eighteen, with a meagre means of support, and I couldn't go back home – pregnant or not. I'd known Gen for less than six months and neither of us expected me to get pregnant, or wanted a child yet. I was thrust into a whirlwind of emotions.

After much talk and angst, the decision was made. I rang my friend Bridie, who by now was training to be a nurse. She came straight away to see me. She was concerned that I'd started bleeding off and on, and was worried I might lose the baby whether I went ahead with an abortion or not. She knew the procedure of applying for what she called a 'termination'. Yes, I thought, 'termination' sounded far less brutal than 'abortion'. I comforted myself and appeased my guilty conscience by using that word.

Girls at the Funhouse had suggested various solutions to my problem – someone they knew could 'do it', with slippery elm or maybe quinine. I knew how risky those methods could be and decided to go to my (Catholic) family doctor, who referred me to the hospital. I was given rough, insensitive treatment during my consultations with the doctor and a psychiatrist to 'qualify' for a termination: 'Why, at eighteen, do you think you couldn't cope with raising a child? Are you backward? Why did you have sex before marriage?' – implying I was a slut – and so on.

Abortion had only just become legal and was frowned upon, and there was still a stigma attached to being a single mother. I remember lying there, my first ever vaginal examination, with my legs spreadeagled as the doctor probed about inside me, commenting nonchalantly, 'Nice healthy colour.' This all took place at the maternity hospital where I'd been born, and the route to the clinic I had to attend took me past a ward where I saw mothers with their newborns, some breastfeeding and some who were fighting to keep their unborn babies, having previously had miscarriages. I burst into tears and was about to run out of the door when the doctor said dismissively, 'Oh, give her one, then.'

31 March 1970
Well I go in hospital tomorrow, I had to go and ring the hospital and see how long I'd be in. They said about 4 or 5 days because I'm . . .

The sentence should have finished '16 weeks pregnant'. I had conceived within two months of meeting Gen.

1 April 1970
Was admitted into hospital today. The people are really nice, really truthfully kind. I go down for my operation tomorrow. I was shaved today, bullets and blood sample taken. Wasn't at all bad. Gen came dead on time, then Les and Baz came to see me tonight.

2 April 1970

Can't have <u>nothing</u> to eat or drink and I've been waiting since
9 to have my Pre-Med, anyway I got it about 12.43 and went
down at 12.45. Got my anaesthetic in my hand (and a lovely
bruise) and knew no more until 4 o'clock.

After about four days I was discharged and I returned to the Funhouse with Gen. I felt fragile and weak. Gen did what he could to
console and care for me but I wasn't in a good state.

John Krivine was so wonderful. He came to see me almost every
day. He seemed to understand how I felt. Maybe it was because
his girlfriend had a young child. One day he brought me a pristine
white-and-lemon eiderdown to snuggle into. It seems such a small
thing, but it comforted me so much. It made me feel clean when I
felt dirty and empty.

John didn't actually live at the commune but he was always
about, always smiling, driving around in an old black London cab
with SMILE painted on the side in large white letters. He'd arranged
with a farmer at Burton Pidsea for friends to do paid farm work. We
all took turns, sharing the wealth, so to speak. Four at a time would
go out there in shifts, staying rent-free in the old tied cottage, which
John got for a peppercorn rent. He suggested me and Gen go there.
Gen could work and it would be a change of scenery for me.

Being in the countryside again was restorative. It was where I'd
always felt at home as a child. While Gen worked in the fields I'd
be with Tremble, sauntering down the country lanes to the local
shop or just sitting in the fields, daydreaming and cooking meals
for us. It was there at the farm that I had my first period after the
termination.

My body seemed back in sync but I was in a bereft emotional
state for months. The reality of what I'd done came crashing down

on me on one of our weekly visits to Mum for tea. We'd maintained our relationship despite Dad. She'd send me letters and we'd talk on the phone and visit – but only when he was at work. That particular visit we were sat in the living room, talking as usual, Gen eating his tube of Smarties that Mum always bought him. I picked up the Sunday newspaper. As I flicked through it I came across a double-page feature on abortion, with pictures of the foetus at various stages – sixteen weeks included. I was horrified to see little arms and legs; it was so well formed. A baby. I wanted to get out of there and the tears welled up, but I had to hold them back. As far as Mum knew, I'd had a miscarriage.

~

The Funhouse was quite a hive of activity, with some wonderful people visiting or staying for varying lengths of time. We all had alternative ways to generate much-needed extra income using our individual talents: tie-dyeing T-shirts; making hippy jewellery, accessories and clothing; and distributing countercultural ideas by selling hip magazines like *International Times*, *Frendz* and *OZ*. Some of our friends, like Sandy, 'liberated' items for resale.

Sandy was a tall, strange, rather quiet girl who drifted slowly along in a daze, and was very distinctive with her waist-length brown hair and curious, benign smile that occasionally broke out into a gentle chuckle. She stole from the biggest stores in town, looking around the departments selectively, just picking up whatever she wanted and casually walking out with it – including large rugs rolled up under her arm. She successfully evaded arrest for so long she became convinced she was invisible – until she got caught. She lived in the same house as our friend Annie Ryan, who came from Liverpool. When we visited Annie one day, we saw Sandy with one side of her long hair scrunched up to her ear in a tangled mass of coagulated paint. She'd been decorating her room and fallen asleep, not noticing all the paint that had dripped on to her hair in the process of painting the ceiling. Everyone thought she would just cut it off, but no. It took her weeks, but she painstakingly picked at each strand of hair until it was completely free of paint.

Annie was the opposite of Sandy; she was small, warm-hearted, bubbly and a true pleasure-seeker who electrified any room she entered. I loved it when she came to the Funhouse. She always wore long, flowing scarves and an amazing black velvet coat that was encrusted on the back with an explosion of hand-stitched sequins and rhinestones that looked like a galaxy of stars. She wore it as a souvenir inspired by one of her acid trips. Annie lived with her boyfriend, Mel, at that time. He was pretty-boy gorgeous in a Marc Bolan way, and also the first junkie I'd ever met. I remember him sitting in the armchair and me staring at him, fascinated by how his hair was moving – until I was told that the movement was 'just' all the head lice moving around. He was infested with them but drug-addled-oblivious to the fact. One of the last times I saw Annie was when she came to the Funhouse one day looking shaken and dishevelled. She'd taken a lift with a guy on his motorbike and her long, flowing scarf had got caught up in the back wheel and nearly choked her as the bike went over, pulling her backwards. Someone came to her rescue, cutting off her scarf, and she escaped with just cuts and bruises. At least she survived, unlike Isadora Duncan, who met her fate in a similar way.

A rather unwelcome and uninvited visitor to the Funhouse came along one evening when me, Gen and a friend were sitting together talking in the communal room, with Tremble sat contentedly at our feet. Suddenly Tremble's hackles went up and she stood, turned to the doorway and started growling, low and slow. She had a fixed stare on something none of us could see, then charged at the doorway, barking furiously at her prey and chasing it down the stairs to the front door. Then we heard a loud bang as if the door had slammed shut. We were astounded and ran to the front window to see if there was anything outside. We saw a tall, unfamiliar figure dressed head to foot in black, walking slowly away from the house towards the pier. What the hell had just happened?

~

The Funhouse was peaceful and quiet. Nearly everyone had gone away to the Isle of Wight Festival except for me, Gen and a couple of others. We were enjoying having the building to ourselves when we suddenly heard the mighty roar of motorbikes, followed swiftly by a smashing sound as the Hells Angels broke in our front door and tore through the house, spray-painting the walls and ransacking the place. For some reason they didn't make it as far as the top floor. When the noise subsided we guessed they'd calmed down and quietly made our way downstairs, to find they'd congregated in the communal room and were giving one of their 'prospects' a mouth-scrubbing with Ajax toilet cleaner.

My background meant I was more savvy at handling Hull hard cases than the others, who'd mainly had a sheltered middle-class upbringing. I was immediately confronted by one of the bikers' girlfriends, a tough blonde girl they all called Glob. She was smaller than me and was surprised at my combative response to her threats. I blanked her and entered into a dialogue with a couple of the guys. Some of them came from Longhill Estate, near my family home. That commonality was our saving grace. We ended up having a half-civil conversation with them, vocally sparring until we arrived at an amicable kind of 'understanding', and they eventually left. The next day I went into the Gondola coffee bar, where they hung out. A few of them were there, including Glob. I walked over and handed her her purse, which she'd dropped at the Funhouse. She looked confused that it hadn't been emptied.

Back at the Funhouse, the other commune members had returned. Bronwyn was particularly pissed off as the bikers had sprayed BRONWYN PULLS A TRAIN in huge letters across the full length of the wall of her room. Being a term used by the Angels for women who had sex with one man after another to gain status, it wasn't the nicest thing to come home to, nor the highest compliment.

Contrary to what others may have said, the Hells Angels never had three-day parties at the Funhouse, they just popped round now and again. But their visits did upset our fellow housemates and some of the locals. The people at the corner cafe were disgusted at our 'friends' the Hells Angels wearing Nazi helmets and swastika armbands. A few days after the Angels' rampage we went in the cafe for our occasional treat of egg and chips. As we opened the door, all eyes turned to us and we were confronted by the owner.

'Didn't you know the guy over the road was in a prisoner-of-war camp and it traumatised him to see Nazi helmets?'

'No, sorry.' I don't know why I was apologising.

'I've heard about you hippies – you have orgies on the stairs, don't you?'

'No,' I said. But he didn't believe me.

After the Hells Angels episode the atmosphere towards the top-floor dwellers changed. That, and the fact that we didn't know how long the Funhouse lease would last, made me and Gen set about the task of looking for a place of our own.

We searched all over the Old Town for possible buildings to rent. The old abandoned bonded warehouses were spacious and lent themselves to our needs. The offices of one had oak-lined walls and were strewn with old invoices, rubber stamps and relics of a once-thriving business. I imagined how I'd convert it into a living space, keeping the beautiful features and feeding off the energies of past activities that had taken place there. But we couldn't find anywhere that was up for rent – or the estate agents took one look at us and said, 'It's not available.'

Then we had a stroke of luck on one of our usual trips to the stalls of our friend Lucy and her son, Sydney, in the local Holy Trinity marketplace. She had the most extraordinary assortment of clothes and antiques and would save me things she thought I should have. We bought silver vesta matchboxes (for Gen's mum), jewellery, clothes, antique daggers (Gen had a collection) and, my favourite, a press-gang cosh used to forcibly enlist men on to ships. It was a beautiful object made from a single piece of rope that had been expertly crafted into a long 8×2-inch cylindrical shape, which narrowed to form a handle that was neatly finished off with a large, complicated knot to aid gripping. The whole cosh had been dipped in tar to make it hard and effective at knocking out the poor victims. As we were talking to Lucy a short, ragged-looking old man came over to chat to her and she introduced us. His name was Jim and he owned the old stable down Prince Street, which he rented as storage space to the market traders. He also owned a row of about four houses opposite the stable, of which two adjoining ones lay unused. Jim looked more like a tramp than a man of property. He wore a flat cap and a grimy coat. His face was dry as parchment, always with a few days' grey stubble whiskers, and his false teeth moved up and down as he talked. Lucy told us that, back in the day when he had his own teeth, he used them to make money in the market square, biting off (docking) puppies' tails. I don't know what his life story was but he lived alone with his faithful dog, which he always called 'Jack – you bastard'. He'd vacillate from laughing and whistling to cursing and shouting at all and sundry. He wasn't an easy man to get along with but he took to me more than he did to Gen, so I spent a few weeks talking with him to persuade him to rent to us.

And so 8–9 Prince Street, off Dagger Lane (now a Grade II-listed Georgian building), became the home of COUM and placed me in the Holy Trinity parish, where my maternal grandmother had spent her childhood. Prince Street is a small cobbled road that gently curves from Dagger Lane, through an archway that leads on to King Street, where stands the magnificent and imposing late-thirteenth-century Holy Trinity Church.

Our buildings sat more or less midway in a row of Georgian houses and had been partly knocked into one. They were last occupied by the sauce and pickle manufacturer Priestman, Hartley & Co. Ltd., and prior to that had seen other uses, including as a toffee-apple factory. There were seventeen rooms in total, none of which had been touched in years. The top floor was unusable and unsound because of roosting pigeons and damp from a leaking roof. The ground-floor front room was taken over by Jim's junk, so we cordoned it off and later designated it as 'the cat room'. Debris and abandoned possessions of previous tenants were scattered about.

Entering the houses for the first time fed my predilection for derelict buildings and I explored every nook and cranny. Halfway up one flight of the very rickety stairs was a sliding door. I unlatched it and, though it was stiff and creaky, I managed to open it enough to see inside and squeeze through the gap. I discovered a small windowless room with bare plaster walls. As I looked around I found, to my joy and fascination, the scribbled names of children on one of the walls and a very dusty, empty art deco chocolate box on the floor. What use the room had been put to was anyone's guess but I imagined that it might have been a nursery in the days before the house was repurposed from domestic to business use. We found so many wonderful things: a large Victorian glass spoon and fork, old glass bottles used in the making of Prince sauce, along with a stack of labels and old Priestman & Hartley stationery, which we co-opted as COUM notepaper and for collage material.

Our most useful discovery was a stash of stoneware – Pooh Bear-style honeypots that lined the floor of what had been the toffee-apple room, with more in some of the upstairs rooms. Our friend Alan Worsley ran a second-hand shop and we bartered the honeypots for an electric cooker and other essentials. Worsley was an amazing person. He'd been Bronwyn's partner but they split up and he settled down with a lovely happy girl called Kate. I remember visiting their basement flat, which was ram-packed with curios and antiques, with dividing walls made from miscellaneous empty bottles. He was researching lucid dreaming, with Kate as his subject. I always thought that was just part of his eccentric personality, but last I heard he is a lucid-dream expert and continuing his experiments. He also made penis candles and gave me a magnificent large blood-red one, which still sits resplendent in my office.

Only a handful of the seventeen rooms in the two houses were fit for use – one on the ground floor and three of the first-floor rooms, which were taken by me and Gen, then later by COUM members Spydeee (Ian Evetts) and briefly Haydn Robb, my friend Jeremy and Hells Angels Gypsy and Rick. We used the toffee-apple room as the 'drum room' and storeroom for COUM materials. It was in a dilapidated extension at the back of the house and came with a large hole in the middle of the floor, which we never repaired. We seemed to navigate around it without ever falling through, and it was useful for talking to anyone in the room below, which we made into a kitchen of sorts, primarily because it was the only source of water – a cold-water tap above an ancient stone sink. In the farthest corner of the kitchen was the only (disgusting) toilet – at least in this house it wasn't four flights down.

With no heating other than coal fires in the upper rooms, the house was so cold in winter that the kitchen floor would get covered in glistening frost and the water pipes and toilet cistern would freeze up completely. We didn't have a bathroom but visited friends or the impressive Victorian red-brick Beverley Road Baths for a hot bath. The cubicles there lined either side of a high-walled, glossy-tiled and very long, cold, stone-floored corridor. It was like a trip back in time to when many houses didn't have running hot water. The cubicles were basic, with white, cream and olive-green tiled walls, a stone floor, a big bath with a ledge for soap and cast-iron wall pegs for hanging up your clothes. The attendant was in charge of the hot water, which she controlled fastidiously from a tap on the corridor side of the cubicle wall. If you wanted a top-up you pushed a call button above the bath. She also had a key to open the door – either for safety or to oust you if you overstayed your allotted time. Although it was a no-frills service, the bath swung the deal. It was so deep and long you could lie at full stretch and submerge yourself completely.

Me and Gen transported our belongings from the Funhouse to Prince Street in an old pram we'd bought, and worked hard cleaning and decorating the more decent rooms to make them habitable, acquiring free or heavily discounted cans of paint. The walls and ceilings were in a very poor state and we covered them and any crumbling plaster with sheets of reject polythene we got free from local factories. One particular carrier-bag factory provided us with a plentiful supply of rolls of polythene of varying colours and designs, which we also used later in COUM performances. Our trusty and invaluable staple gun made decorating pretty quick, and the transformation from dirty, dusty walls to something more clean and bright didn't take too long. The house wasn't just a living space; it was also a representation of COUM, with various art objects nailed to the walls and hung from the ceiling of the hallway and beyond, and Gen's inscription of 'Poetry is a dead letter' painted on the risers of each step as you made your way upstairs.

My and Gen's room was at the front of the house and had a bay window and a beautiful large white marble fireplace. We discovered Georgian wall panel features that had been covered over with plaster, which we carefully restored; we painted the room white and the panels pale blue with gold edging. A while later we turned our attention to the outside of the building, painting a rainbow over the front door and pasting pertinent COUM signages and posters on the walls. It was a spooky place and at times I had the feeling we weren't the only residents. If I was alone at night I never went downstairs and I tried my best to ignore any banging and creaking noises. I felt a presence and a chill up my spine whenever I got to the bottom step before entering the kitchen. I'd run, in fear that something would reach out and grab me.

~

Spydeee had joined me and Gen in Prince Street around mid-1970. He was handsome and slim, with chin-length dark curly locks and a cheeky glint in his eyes whenever he smiled. We'd all got on well from the beginning. I showed him the ropes for signing on, and we all split living costs, ate together, and also shared some very pleasurable intimate moments. Unbeknownst to me at the time, I had more in common with Spydeee than I realised. Like myself, he'd been given an ultimatum by his father – conform or get out – unlike Gen, whose parents who were more indulgent than ours. We rejected limitations. To us, the possibilities were endless, and in keeping with that mindset Spydeee had responded to his father's ultimatum by leaving the family home and coming to live with us in Hull. He'd visited Gen there in the summer of 1969 as part of his hitch-hiking tour around England, and the Ho Ho Funhouse sounded like a suitable place for him to join Gen to continue their creative collaborations. By the time he got to Hull we'd left the Funhouse, but it hadn't taken him long to find us.

I wasn't told much about Spydeee before his arrival, other than that he was a very close school friend of Gen's from his days at Solihull School, and that they'd worked together on different creative projects. I later learned more from Spydeee, some of which contradicted the impressions Gen had given me. According to Spydeee, Gen was a fee-paying pupil, while Spydeee had won a scholarship, and it was Spydeee who was the main active misfit, getting into trouble and eventually getting expelled for editing and distributing the alternative school magazine *Conscience*, which he and a group of friends put together. He had even earned the disapproval of Gen's mother, Mimi, who blamed him for leading Gen astray.

Inspired by their interest in Eliphas Levi and Aleister Crowley, they made their 'mark' by chalking pentagrams and Latin graffiti on the park bandstand – reported in the local paper as BLACK MASS IN SOLIHULL PARK. Then their curiosity moved on to the Beat writers. Spydeee recently described to me his and Gen's introduction to William Burroughs: 'He wasn't introduced to the work of Burroughs by a teacher, in fact there was a key book that introduced us. It was called THE NEW WRITING IN THE USA by Donald Allen & Robert Creeley, published by Penguin Books Ltd, 1967 . . . I found it while browsing and told him.'

Music was a focal point for Gen – that's how I'd met him – and he, Spydeee and their friends had experimented with music influenced not only by the more obvious underground bands like the

Velvet Underground, the Fugs and Frank Zappa but also by some of Spydeee's unconventional record collection, in particular AMM's inspirational and obscure *AMMMusic* album from 1967, which Spydeee excitedly insisted on playing to Gen. The philosophical approach to music of Cornelius Cardew, Keith Rowe, Lawrence Sheaff, Lou Gare and Eddie Prévost proved to be very influential and reads rather like an early version of what was to become COUM's approach to music: anti-harmony, no prerequisite for anyone to be able to play a given instrument, and the sound the 'group' generated was also regarded as a contributory member of the group itself. Gen and Spydeee recorded one album together, *Early Worm*, the precursor to later COUM works. All three of us often sang the jolly ditty from the track 'The Balloon Burst', which Spydeee told me was based on him thinking he'd got his girlfriend pregnant when the condom burst. We all shared similar interests in music and were familiar with surrealism and Dada, which became significant influences on us all (Gen's penchant being for Marcel Duchamp and Salvador Dalí). We'd also all read *International Times* and *OZ* magazine, with Spydeee having a letter printed in *OZ*'s 1970 'Schoolkids' edition. All considered, it was a fortuitous convergence of three appropriately primed, like-minded people eager for adventurous experiences in our quest to find our places in the world.

~

It seemed par for the course that, as part of an alternative lifestyle, many people adopted different names to replace the boring ones given to us by our parents. We wanted names that were more reflective of who we were, as well as being a mark of rejecting social norms. The practice of renaming people is generally seen as an affectionate, personal way of affirming the bonds between each other – though some may see it, in certain cult-like circumstances, as a symbolic act of possession, a subtle way of isolating and laying claim to someone.

I'd been given a new name by Gen – Cosmosis – which Gen explained to me as meaning the exchange of energy from one person to another. A kind of well-thought-out hybrid of 'cosmos' and 'osmosis'. Still, I had no objection to my new name. I liked it – it seemed apt as I started the next phase of my life – and Cosmosis was soon shortened to Cosey. I'd only ever known and called Spydeee by his nickname, which came from his love of comics, specifically because of his empathy with the adolescent angst of Peter Parker (Spiderman). He later expanded his name, adding Gasmantell as a direct reference to the original old gas mantle on the wall of his room in Prince Street. Likewise I only knew Gen as Genesis but found out that he'd changed it from Neil Megson, despite Spydeee pointing out there was already a band called Genesis. With 'genesis' having a meaning like 'the coming into being of something', it now seems highly indicative of what was to transpire. The surname he had taken on, P-Orridge, came from people's comments on his love of porridge, and Gen embraced it by changing his name legally by deed poll in 1971.

Our self-identifiers extended to us also adopting our own 'magickal' numbers and colours based on personal reasons and our interest in the occult. I already had mine in mind, but numerology also played a part in affirming my chosen number: 4. It was the date of the day of my birth, and my full birthdate also resolved to 4. Applying the numerological method to my names – Carol, Cosmosis, Cosey – brought about the same result: 4. But the number 4 was more than that to me; it felt grounded and reliable, like the four points of the compass. My chosen colour, blue, had been forming years before I met Gen. Over time, its childhood negative 'boy' connotations had turned into a positive, simply by my seeing blue as a symbol representing what my dad expected of me and by the realisation that such pressure had instilled a sense of 'difference' in my psyche – which to me was most definitely a positive. Blue represented my free spirit, the infinity of the sky, the vast depths of the oceans in constant flux in response to the vagaries of nature. My number and colour together stood for a sense of core stability that gave me confidence as I forged ahead exploring – as well as coping with, utilising and learning from some volatile life experiences.

Spydeee and Gen had their own reasons for their magickal number and colour choices. Gen's love of the colour orange (preferably Day-Glo orange) was as much to do with psychedelia as it was to do with anything esoteric, and was also, as I later discovered, possibly influenced by his time in Transmedia Explorations. His choice of the number 3 was, like my choice, partly based on his birthday, the 22nd of the 2nd (three 2s, when added together and divided by 2, become 3). But Gen also drew on the religious and occult symbolism of the number 3. There's meaning to be found in anything, if you want it bad enough. From good to evil – the Holy Trinity (3) to the number of the beast, 666 (the sum of three 6s divided by 6 = 3). Spydeee's choices were pure and straightforward. He chose the number 7, which was both me and Gen (4 + 3) and his date of birth, with additional inspiration from the significance of the number 7 within various belief systems. And, as he said, 'Usually seven signifies creation, the beginning of things.' His colour was green, the colour of nature.

~

We were happily ensconced in our own building and Gen began putting COUM philosophy into practice. I've often been asked what COUM meant – to explain it. The definition of COUM was intentionally elusive. That allowed for total freedom of expression and interpretation (including by the 'audience'), which was a core value of COUM and created a forum for debate and sometimes brought new members. COUM was not just a 'group' but also more of a movement, a collective family of diverse people from all walks of life, each of us exploring and living out our fantasies or obsessions with the aim of achieving creative and self-awareness, and confidence as artists regardless of, and in opposition to, the conventional skill sets and criteria by which 'artists' are defined. COUM was about giving free rein to ideas, about not being limited by rules or self-doubt – which lead to some confrontational situations as we challenged and broke established rules and cultural and social conventions.

As a collective, each person was supported, ideas cross-pollinated and performed, written, played out in public or private, using whatever medium or situation was the most suitable or available at the time. The drive and force of the combined energies of everyone made COUM seem like a constantly evolving, self-perpetuating creative entity. As such, COUM was an egalitarian concept; no one person could lay claim to it or the works collectively created. That was the theory and aim.

We compiled a list of '1001 Ways to COUM' (a reference in part to the Buddhist idea of 'one million and one names of God'), one-line slogans that included serious or joke references to social, cultural or personal events, and contradictory definitions of COUM, like 'Everything About COUM is True' and, conversely, 'Everything About COUM is False'. That strategy left things wide open. COUM actions caused reactions that we assimilated into further actions, generating a stream of source material. The intangibility of COUM was a perfect ploy with which to deflect criticism, blame or responsibility – and accept any inadvertent praise along the way.

Gen was fascinated by Andy Warhol's Factory and was Warholian in the way he recruited and surrounded himself with talented, wayward characters, some on the criminal fringe, others 'eccentric' – all hugely likeable, creative and with exceptional experiences and views on life. Gen was a charismatic prankster with an intellectual bent and a great line in telling people that they needed to access and be their true selves – while not practising what he preached. I don't think he knew who he was and it took me a while to realise that. He placed himself in a guru-like position, one that was resistant to any questioning of the fact that he (as guru) wasn't true to 'himself'. If anyone questioned him on things he said or did that didn't seem to ring true to what he claimed was COUM ethos, he'd respond with a reason why it was OK for him in that instance, that you had got it wrong, or he'd recite a COUM slogan to counter the criticism – or make up a new one to add to the ever-growing '1001 Ways to COUM' list. He could never be wrong, or maybe he just couldn't see it.

Gen had heavily criticised Transmedia, saying they espoused equality whilst effectively operating more as a hierarchy, with Fitz as the 'leader' – but it was a system Gen mirrored in COUM, with himself as leader-cum-mentor, but with the addition, over time, of an expanded agenda gleaned from Aleister Crowley's occultism and a touch of Charles Manson's cultism. He promoted within COUM the notion that everyone has a 'genius factor'. Gen's 'genius factor' was not art per se but the art of manipulation, as myself and others came to believe. As COUM member Foxtrot Echo succinctly put it, 'Oh yes, he was always into the whole concept of cults and manipulating people. That was his genius.'

Inherent in the COUM core value of freedom is honesty, being true to yourself as part of self-exploration, being true to one another and being selfless – all of which I found to be lacking in Gen, along-side other values related to 'freedom': egalitarianism, self-realisation and being and expressing your 'self'. 'My Life Is My Art. My Art Is My Life' is a phrase I've adopted to define my work and life, which to a large degree derives from my time in COUM. On paper it sounds simple, but it's not.

From 1970, I was a core member of COUM. I was a photographer, I built props, contributed ideas, designed and made costumes and worked full-time jobs to help fund our activities as well as feed us. Spydeee became increasingly uncomfortable with me being the only one working and found himself a job so he could contribute. By late 1970, the core of COUM had shifted to Gen, me and Spydeee, after Tim focused more on his research and John Shapeero went his own way. Other than us three, COUM had a fluctuating line-up depending on each project – including another of Gen's Solihull friends, Pinglewad (Peter Winstanley), who stayed with us and par-ticipated in COUM a few times. The varying public-performance personnel included: me; Gen, usually on violin; Spydeee on sound generators, vocals and other gadgets; Ray Harvey on vocals, tam-bourine and drums; Les Maull on guitar; Jonji Smith on vocals; Bobo (Rob Eunson, a friend of Les's) on lead guitar; sixteen-year-old Brook (Tony Menzies) on guitar; and Haydn Nobb (Robb), a uni-versity friend of Gen's, who played bass guitar a few times.

Where was I in the public's perception of COUM? I wasn't on the well-known 'COUM Are Fab and Kinky' publicity poster of that time. It only depicted a very young Neil Megson leaning on a tuba, with small photos of six (male) COUM members at his feet, including his 'Genesis' adult self. Years later I see the poster less as a good attention-grabbing publicity ploy and more as misrepresen-tation, and find myself asking why the full-time active members like myself, Les and Ray were excluded when we preceded the three 'part-time' COUM members Gen included on the poster. Maybe it was to present a particular image of a music band, but even so it's a disingenuous representation of the reality of COUM.

I also understood COUM to be far more than just a band that played 'music': it was a concept, a democratic collective and an all-embracing lifestyle. It was the sum of its parts. I doubt I'd mis-construed what COUM was about or my role within it. According to Spydeee, 'The thing was Cosey intuitively "got it" right from the start – the whole COUM thing . . . and was completely part of it from the moment I first met her . . . the 3 of us lived there and "did" COUM stuff, we all contributed in equal ways – it was just that he [Gen] took control of as much as he could.'

~

Hippydom had its conventions, even if they didn't always make much sense. You bucked the system by dropping out, but didn't see a problem with claiming social security or unemployment benefit from the state. Poverty, hunger and a sense of respon-sibility to Tremble, Moonshine and Gen forced my hand. If I got a job, Gen was free to do his art and we'd have money for food, rent and art materials. It was a practical solution, seeing as I was quite adept at communicating with 'straights'. As Spydeee said, 'There is no doubt that you were the one who made things happen in a practical way. Without you Gen would never have survived in Hull – a statement he'd deny because he just wouldn't see it.'

Much to my mum's (and the dole office's) delight, I decided to get a job. The notes on my unemployment records make for inter-esting reading:

18 February 1970
Not very enthusiastic about work. Very modern dress – wearing long boots, old fur coat and black velvet & lace creation. Not at all suitable for office work in view of appearance . . .

6 May 1970
Usually attends employment section with boyfriend who dresses most peculiarly. Still seeking clerical work but appearance has deteriorated. Untidy and extremely mod. clothing. Not fit for submission. Would reclassify except for good G.C.E. 'O' levels and it would be a waste of a good education if this girl did factory work.

3 June 1970
Miss Newby is so changeable in appearance, can look extremely attractive or dirty and shabby. Nice girl to talk to and I think she is under the bad influence of her boyfriend who is a freelance artist. He always attends with her and they both live in a derelict house shared by several hippy type characters.

There were various strategies to ensure you stayed unsuitable for employment: not dressing the part, poor communication, showing false enthusiasm for jobs offered, changing the type of work classification, and so on. Wrong as that may seem, that was what 'dropouts' did back then. I attended some job interviews (Woolworths rejected me as overqualified), and I finally plumped for factory work at Humbrol Paints. Not the career Mum or the dole office had wanted, considering my qualifications, but needs must, and at that time factory work paid twice as much as white-collar jobs.

I started work at Humbrol on 14 September 1970. It wasn't an easy decision. Hull factory girls were feared. They were hard as nails and verbally brutal and I viewed my new job as akin to entering borstal, where pecking orders were established on entry. I braced myself and entered the factory yard, following the throng of chattering girls, and took my place in the line to clock on. One of the girls kindly showed me to the office. I was introduced to the forewoman, an imposing and very stern middle-aged woman called Nan Miller, who handed me an overall and instructed me in the work I would be doing. Turbaned up, I was all set to enter the factory floor. Nan led the way. As the double doors swung open, the smell of paint and thinners stung my nostrils. Then my ears got a pounding from the noise of the machines, girls shouting over each other and the radio blaring out the current hit songs. A multitude of eyes scanned me from head to foot, trying to get the measure of me. During the first break, and again at lunchtime, I was challenged verbally and physically. I was shoved aside and girls fronted me out, posturing to get a response. I knew if I appeared 'posh' they'd assume I thought I was a cut above them. I must have come up OK as I settled in well. I loved their bluntness – saying it as it was, no pretence.

~

I needed a break. I went to Hull University to see Snips's band, Nothineverappens, with my friend Sue and met up with some old friends I hadn't seen for a while. We split a tab of acid but, as it turned out, my half had the full dose. We caught the bus to the university and were sat chatting away, waiting for the acid to take effect – which it did for me courtesy of the bus conductor making me jump as he came up behind me and asked for my fare. A shot of adrenaline sent the acid rushing through my bloodstream and I was propelled into a dense claustrophobic cocoon of colours and shapes.

We got into the gig but the acid was strong and sent me reeling into uncharted waters of sensory overload – what I now know was a synaesthetic state. It knocked me for six and I had to sit on the floor. My senses were totally mixed up and I seemed to be dissolving and becoming part of the air around me. As Snips's band started to play, I began to see giant coloured letters slowly pulsating. The air was alive, thick with vibrant patterns, fractals, microbe-like forms and scrolling trails of indistinguishable cellular structures. I couldn't see in front of or around me. It was like looking through a microscope – and it was getting more extreme. I felt like I'd totally lose it. In desperation I thought maybe if I danced, I could raise my metabolism and speed up my system's processing of the acid. I danced until I was exhausted and started to come down to a level I could handle.

After the gig a crowd of us went back to a friend's flat, playing music, talking and laughing into the early hours of the morning. Laughing on acid was extraordinary; it felt like bubbles of light bursting and releasing happiness throughout my body, making us all laugh even more.

For the first time in ages I'd gone out and had a great time on my own with my own friends, and I was glowing with joy when I returned home, eager to tell Gen all about it. I felt so good as I walked into our room. Tremble came rushing up to me but Gen was sat up in bed looking stern and moody.

'Did you have a good time?' he asked.

'Yes,' I said, beaming back at him.

I'd hardly got the word out when he said, flatly, 'Pack your bags and get out.'

I felt like I'd been slapped in the face. My skin prickled and I almost threw up. I'd never come down from a trip so fast. I found myself in a position I thought I'd left behind. Was I still not allowed to enjoy myself or come home late? Weren't we supposed to be living an unconventional life? And why should I have to justify myself when he didn't? He knew I had nowhere to go. This was my home, my life, and I didn't want to lose it.

We talked and I was 'allowed' to stay. I'd learned a very hard and painful lesson. Despite what happened I still adored and loved Gen, but those nagging doubts I thought I'd buried were back.

~

Our house (now labelled the Alien Brain) was a busy hub for people coming and going, staying over or living with us for a short time. While I was out at work, Spydeee and Gen did a lot of networking, which resulted in gigs and the founding of COUM fan clubs in the UK and USA. Spydeee had made contact with Jo Pemberton, who was at Bradford Art College and was appointed President of Bradford Van Club (COUM fan club). She was our first introduction to the artist, poet and jazz musician Jeff Nuttall, who had affiliations with William Burroughs.

It was through Jo that we got the 'Edna and the Great Surfers' gig, where we supported Hawkwind at a benefit concert for a drug-busted commune. We presented as a rabble of characters amid a mass of drums, with Brook on guitar, Spydeee and Gen on vocals, Jonji Smith on a surfboard, surfing a bucket of water underneath a large beach umbrella, and myself as a schoolgirl throwing and batting COUM penee-inscribed ping-pong balls at the audience. We tossed polystyrene granules about like showers of snow that covered the stage and made their way into Hawkwind's effects pedals, causing them technical problems. There was a lot of heckling but we were into audience participation and encouraged interaction, sometimes pre-empting the inevitable (and usual) response by leading the audience in chanting 'Off! Off! Off!' – as we did that night in Bradford. All credit to

Hawkwind, who were very cool about us and just asked us what drugs we were on.

'None.'

That we were sober and doing what we did seemed to confuse them. We'd part-named the gig in honour of Edna, a lift attendant from Bradford whose lonely-hearts ad we'd used in mail art and had printed up as a postcard.

Greg Taylor (aka Foxtrot Echo) saw us at the Hawkwind show and was intrigued enough to introduce himself. He was at art college in Bradford studying film, TV and theatre. He asked if we'd be interested in going to the upcoming Bradford Porno Film Festival and said that he could arrange a COUM gig to coincide with our trip: 'Exorcism of Shit' at Bradford's Afro Club. Just me and Gen turned up and did a bizarre, low-key and disjointed improvisation, with Gen on drums and me being 'the presence'.

After our trip to Bradford we invited Greg to Hull, and from then on he participated in and contributed a lot to COUM. He shared our interests in music and was coincidentally already working with Cornelius Cardew of AMM when he met us. His visits were always full-on. Meeting Greg sparked off a series of events that subsequently impacted greatly on my future artistic endeavours and even more significantly on my personal life.

~

The people at Hull Arts Centre, particularly Mike Walker, were very supportive, giving us access to the telephone – we didn't have one until 1973 – and other facilities to help us with our projects. We performed one of my most memorable early COUM performances there, 'The Caves of Montalbaan'. We transformed the whole of the main room of the Arts Centre into a disorientating alien environment, even making the audience enter the space by having to crawl through a tunnel-like mass of polythene. Once inside, the floor, walls and ceiling were strewn with brightly coloured polythene and gold and silver foil, amongst which we'd placed the drum kit, old shop dummies, a watering can, buckets of offal, a beach umbrella, toy instruments and even an old kitchen sink. People would chance upon strange characters performing odd scenarios, like Gen dressed as a baby in a pale-blue Babygro, laid next to a crate of milk, kicking his legs in the air and drinking from a bottle. Other COUM members played acoustic instruments and carried out bizarre enactments. Les had prepared a soundtrack, which he played back on his reel-to-reel tape machine, except the machine had a problem that made the sound 'wow and flutter' unpredictably – which actually sounded just perfect in that bizarre setting. There was no stage or central focal point, and some of the actions were hidden behind curtains of plastic or secreted away altogether – like the black coffin of new COUM member Fizzy. He had dressed as a mad scientist and got inside a wooden coffin-type box. People suspected it was empty until he leaped out and proceeded to slam animal brains on the lid, smashing them with a hammer and splattering everyone nearby. There was no escape from the hail of dead animal debris as I batted offal across the room. People had crawled into a surreal and disquieting place. Their reaction was to start smashing the place up . . . Maybe we'd gone too far.

COUM performed when given almost any opportunity. 'Disintegration of Fact' took place in 'Granny's Parlour', a small area set aside for live jazz music in the Royal Oak pub, just round the corner from Prince Street. Local hardman Ray Harvey had started coming to COUM shows and joining in, grabbing the bongos, talking drum or tambourine, singing his bluesy vocals and sometimes smashing up the tambourine as he thrashed out a rhythm. His presence, because of his violent reputation, usually guaranteed a hassle-free event. But I never felt personally threatened by him and didn't hesitate to let him stay at Prince Street one night, even though I was on my own. He was fine and went merrily on his way the next morning.

The music scene in Hull was really thriving and we knew one of the key figures, Barry Nettleton, from when he booked bands like T. Rex and Yes, but mainly because he also booked bands for Phase Two and ran the Freedom Folk Club at the Bluebell Inn, where Ray had first performed 'Blue Suede Mud' with COUM. Barry teamed up with Rick Welton to form Hull Brick Company, booking bands in and around Hull. They'd started a new venture in a refurbished old Methodist chapel in Baker Street. It was named the Brickhouse and operated as an alternative music venue by night; by day it was a great gathering place with a Saturday market, record shop and cafe. As well as playing host to Uriah Heep, Hull Truck, Hawkwind and Haydn Robb's Outsiders charity fundraising disco, it was also where COUM performed 'Fairyland Powder Puffs' – for which we set up a living room as the stage, including our carpet and armchair. To Barry and Rick's surprise, a large audience turned up, which, to their dismay, included some of our Hells Angels friends, who became a recurring problem and part of the reason the Brickhouse had to close after just nine months.

There'd been a growing, simmering tension between Snips and Gen, and it was at the Brickhouse that it came to a head. We went along to see Nothineverappens play there; Barry had become their manager. They'd started their set and Snips was singing, when Gen walked to the front of the stage and started fawning at Snips in a faux adoring-fan fashion, stroking his legs and saying, 'Oh, Snips, you're so, so wonderful.'

It wasn't meant in fun; it was a cynical attempt to provoke Snips – and it did. Snips got pissed off at Gen interrupting the band. When Gen wouldn't stop, Snips lashed out and kicked Gen under the chin, sending him staggering backwards and inflicting a small bleeding gash (that left a scar). But Gen didn't leave it there. He got up on stage and spat at the drummer, saying to one of the band, 'What do you think of your hero now?'

Gen thought he'd proved some point. What it was I didn't know, but I knew that my alliance with Gen meant my long friendship with Snips was probably over.

We spent a quiet Christmas in Hull and visited my mum, Pam and Tim Poston and his wife, Rebecca, and friends dropped by to exchange presents. One of Gen's presents to me was a diary inscribed with 'A last special surprise pressie to Cosmosis P-Orridge from her little sad hubby. Gen xmas 1971.' I don't know why he was sad or what made him add beneath it a rather depressing verse about Christmas, friends and people. One line read, 'People crack people split most of 'em just squirt out shit.'

Gen encouraged me to draw and express myself in that book, and he expected to read it too. He sent me a letter when he was visiting Tim just two weeks later: 'How is your diary? A little sad E [his terminology for 'I'] bet and mentioning me too: Don't do the coy "no you can't read it E am too embarrassed" when E get back.' It didn't seem right, but I loved my diary and I collaged, drew and coloured my way through its pages as I recorded my life every day that year, and in every diary I kept after that.

It's difficult to lock into those times when my diaries seem to reflect the constant struggles to eat, keep warm, look after Gen and maintain our relationship as well as my resolve in pursuing COUM objectives. There wasn't much spontaneous fun and laughter.

11 January 1972
Such a bad day today, it makes me dread what might happen next. For the first time I saw dislike (I dare not write hate) in Gen's eyes when he looked at me.

Gen had a thing against vacuum cleaners, and wouldn't have one in the house. I had to clean with an old carpet sweeper and broom, usually while he was out. With so many animals it was inevitable that my attempts to control their fleas were doomed to fail. I was bitten so much that, in the end, I had to have the house fumigated. The men came with their toxic, stinking chemicals and sprayed everywhere, all over our bedding, food, pots and pans, etc. I tried to stop them but they were hell-bent on a deliberate quest to ruin all our meagre belongings. Gen went mad at me for what they'd done. I spent the rest of the day doing penance, cleaning up and visiting the social security office to put in a claim to replace everything they'd contaminated. Word must have got round about the fumigation squad because a week later I came home from visiting Mum and Pam to find the words LAZY LOUSY scrawled in purple on the front wall of the house. I cleaned them off before Gen got home. Animosity towards us was growing.

Amid the pressures felt by antagonistic outside attentions and interpersonal trials and tribulations, the main focus remained on COUM – to spread the word, expand our activities and horizons. Gen went away a lot, meeting people we'd written to, sometimes a week at a time. I stayed at home keeping everything running, either working or looking after the animals, attending to COUM business, doing my mail art, typing up and compiling more COUM slogans and making things in readiness for upcoming projects. He knew I hated being left alone and would write me letters. But he never told me the full 'whys' and 'wherefores' of his trips. The flow of information was economical.

One of his trips was to London for a four-day stay with Lindsay and Nicholas from the Gay Lib Street Theatre. It was way past midnight on the day he was supposed to return and I was worried sick. Then, at 4 a.m., he arrived with Nicholas and Lindsay in tow, hungry and cold from hitch-hiking. I made us all porridge and we sat together eating and chatting, then fell into bed. We spent three fun days together, talking about Nicholas and Lindsay's planned commune, Harmony Farm, and arranging to see them again in London. Nicholas (aka Sergei – he had a thing for Russian ballet stars) was an ex-dancer from Ballet Rambert and had started working for Madame Tussaud's, making waxwork busts and wigs. He was flamboyant, very glamorous in drag with his shoulder-length golden hair, so slim and lithe, and prone to launching himself into pirouettes and high leg-kicks at the most unexpected moments and in the most inappropriate places.

When we stayed with them in London, we all went with some of their friends from the Gay Lib Street Theatre to see the film *The Boy Friend*. As the Busby Berkeley-type dance sequences came on screen, the Gay Lib crowd all shot to the gangway and joined in. It was a glorious sight. We stayed with Nicholas and Lindsay in their flat in Colville Terrace, just round the corner from Powis Square, one of the locations used for Nicolas Roeg's film *Performance*. It was ideally situated, close to Portobello Road, Ladbroke Grove and the incredible Electric Cinema, and smack in the middle of Notting Hill, which at that time was a cheap place to live or squat and known for its heady, spirited and powerful mix of radical fringe groups: socialists, Marxists, a strong, politically active Afro-Caribbean community, poets, dancers, writers, artists, the Gay Liberation Front, the Women's Liberation Front, lesbian radical feminists and more.

Lindsay was a poet and white witch, a friend of Fitz from Transmedia and the very talented mime artist Lindsay Kemp (who was a huge inspiration to Bowie). There were so many people coming and going, an extravaganza of gay, straight and transvestite, all buzzing around. It was wild and I loved it.

Before we'd left Hull, Gen had advised me what I should wear for my first trip to London. He was worried I'd embarrass him by dressing too 'provincial'. I ignored him and took the clothes I liked. He needn't have worried because it seemed my clothes were irresistibly desirable – someone stole them.

I was back on the dole, having left both Humbrol and my subsequent job at a car-parts factory. It wasn't long before we felt the pinch from my lack of pay packet and we had to rethink our financial priorities. I relied on the meat-market stall as my source of cheap meat for us – and often free leftovers for the dogs and cats. The butcher guy there was really kind and would set aside a carrier bag of lights (lungs) and small bits of spare offal and bones for the animals. I had a large pan specially for boiling the lights. The process was pretty grotesque to see. The lights would hiss as the heat forced the air out of them and there was many a time the cats would drag the pan off the stove to get at them before they were cooked, hissing themselves because the lights were too hot to eat. It was a very bleak winter; 31 January 1972 was said to be the coldest night in seven years, with 3–4 inches of snow on the ground. The water pipes and toilet froze up and we couldn't always afford coal for the fire, plus the miners went on strike for the first time in almost fifty years. That meant coal, the main source of heating and power, was in short supply. Then a three-day week was imposed. It was pretty grim.

~

1971 and 1972 had turned out to be very busy and defining years. COUM started getting more offers and articles in the press, Gen and Spydeee mainly doing the interviews as I was usually at work when they took place. Bob Edmands, a friend of Gen's from university, wrote a piece on COUM in *Torchlight* and his connections with Radio Humberside helped spread the word and get COUM coverage on radio. Our increased letter-writing to people and groups of interest and the start of our foray into mail art lead to many contacts far and (world-) wide.

The flamboyant presence of COUM on the streets of Hull also drew a lot of attention, which in turn brought many people to our door, and COUM recruitment accelerated at quite a pace. We now had a substantially larger group of COUM members who became regular visitors to Prince Street, like Harriet Straightlace and of course Fizzy (Pete Waudby), so named after both his personality and a disastrous perm that 'fizzed' his hair; Ian Goodrich (aka Lord Biggles), who often took on the role of a very pregnant Mrs Askwith and also was 'pilot' driver for COUM; Foxtrot Echo; and art student couples Richard and Elizabeth and Sean and Sarah.

Some of the '1001 Ways to COUM', number one being 'COUM Are Fab and Kinky', were used as slogans; 'COUM Your Local Dirty Banned' was for publicity and for soliciting bookings acquired by word of mouth or through inclusion in Arts Council or other art directories like A.I.R. and Groupvine, which listed small touring theatre companies and was infiltrated by the radical fringe groups. Those points of contact made a huge difference. We received invitations to various events, both locally and across the UK, which we seized with great fervour. Invites from abroad were beyond our financial means at that time.

But what had the biggest impact on COUM was mail art, which initially led to us connecting with artists who sat on a panel of the

Arts Council of Great Britain that dealt with 'experimental theatre'. COUM was difficult to define and it was a mail art friend of ours, Michael Scott (of 11th hour artworks), who suggested we should go under the category of 'Performance Art' and apply for grants. Mail art was the catalyst that expanded our horizons and activities to a whole other level.

Mail art was in keeping with COUM's 'Anti-Art, Art is Life' fun approach. Sending art through the postal system, gifting artworks directly from one person to another, circumvented the gallery system and commerciality of art. Mail art wasn't a new concept; it can be traced as far back as 1962, to George Maciunas's Fluxus movement, which was influenced by Dadaists like Marcel Duchamp and by the futurists. Fluxus-affiliated artists included John Cage, Dick Higgins, Yoko Ono, Takako Saito, Joseph Beuys, George Brecht and La Monte Young, to name but a few. We became involved with Fluxus through our mail art activities. Maciunas collated and published Fluxus membership and mailing lists that were then published by Ken Friedman and Dick Higgins. Around 1970, Image Bank was formed – the term taken from William Burroughs' book *Nova Express*. Image Bank was an artists' network set up by Ray Johnson, Michael Morris and Vincent Trasov (aka Mr Peanut). They all hooked up with AA Bronson, Felix Partz and Jorge Zontal (aka General Idea). In April 1972, General Idea produced the first issue of *FILE* magazine (a parody of the look of *LIFE* magazine), with Mr Peanut resplendent on the front cover. But crucially they published the Image Bank artist and request list and also included the Fluxus lists. That's the point at which we came in.

We received a copy of the first *FILE* magazine and saw the list of invitations to contribute art and the artists' mailing addresses. We were already corresponding with some of them but others on the list were new and exciting. The doors were suddenly flung wide open. That issue of *FILE* magazine precipitated copious letter-writing and mail art, which led to us corresponding with and meeting people from around the world who would play significant roles in our lives. Among them: Anna Banana of the Bay Area Dada Group (Dadaland), who introduced us to Monte Cazazza, Skot Armstrong (aka Science Holiday), Ray Johnson and Al Ackerman (aka Blaster, and a friend of Philip K. Dick), one of whose letters formed the lyrics for Throbbing Gristle's 'Hamburger Lady'. Robin Crozier led us to Fluxus and 'Fluxshoe', and Gen eventually met William Burroughs, Hans Clavin of *Subvers* magazine, and, importantly (for me), Robin Klassnik, who addressed a letter to me as 'Cosey Fanni Tutti' – which I subsequently adopted.

My mail art collages and works differed depending on who I was sending them to. I used materials from miscellaneous sources – found objects, newspapers, magazines, books, everyday ephemera and rubber stamps both found and bespoke from my own designs. Rubber stamps became a big thing within the mail art movement. We were initially inspired to use them by our visits to the dole office, where the rubber stamps signified our social status as 'unemployed'. I also began to use sex magazines in my collages. Sex was a focal point of COUM. The COUM Orgeees were important to Gen and took place largely at his behest. The first 'COUM Orgeee 1' was on the evening of 14 January 1972. I recorded it the next day.

15 January 1972
Slowly but surely Gen has managed to break down one of my hangups? . . . the way is open for whatever comes next for us. Under the supervision of Gen.

After such an enjoyable 'free' time I didn't expect to receive a put-down from Gen the very next day when he came home. It seemed nothing pleased or appeased him for long.

16 January 1972
'Back to the Prison'. A very truthful quote from Gen about our life together. I know I make it that way for him, one day the crunch will come and I will go. Until then you'll have to be imprisoned Gen. What you don't realise is that I'm imprisoned too; because I could never go or tell you to go, I love you too much . . . Maybe I don't even know you that's what you mean when you get angry and upset.

I'd been 'guided' into group sex by Gen and also by my interest in Aleister Crowley and the subtext that our relationship was 'open'. Although I was initially reluctant to indulge (I was happy with Gen as my lover), my interest in Crowley and enjoyment of sex with other guys awakened a curiosity and triggered a desire to explore my sexuality. Whether Gen realised that it would have this effect on me, I don't know, but inevitably I tended to compare one lover to another. Some were, let's say, more skilled at certain things than others. A person's touch, skin and body evoke their own distinct sexual responses and enjoyment . . . or not. Consequently, when future chances were presented to me for repeat indulgences with someone I felt good with, or fancied, I didn't need Gen's persuasive tactics. But it was best all round to let him think he was in charge.

Gen's moods and sometimes violent outbursts were a feature of our relationship, and because I loved him so much at that time I accepted them as being part of who he was – alongside his intimations that I was usually to blame for his anger and sadness. When he got frustrated or annoyed he'd go crazy, and it didn't always take much to trigger him. That's how the 'Infra Red Bucket' artwork was created. I'd just come back from a tough interview at the dole office.

> 4 February 1972
> *Gen was typing to the Arts Council and I put him off. He threw the typewriter on the floor twice and smashed it up and then started throwing everything else around. Then he broke down in tears . . . I always make him do things like that.*

I blamed myself. We took the smashed-up typewriter (a gift from Les) to the Arts Centre, painted it brick-red and called it the 'Infra Red Bucket'. From then on we had to go to the Arts Centre or Alan Worsley's place to type anything.

It wasn't a good start to what was a busy day, seeing as 'Thee Alien Brain & Mass Panic' was to take place that night. Les arrived in readiness and brought with him a copy of the *Hull Times*, which had an interview with Gen under the heading 'COUM: They are here to perplex you'. It listed the current members as: 'Genesis himself plays drums, Spydee is the vocalist, Haydn's on bass, Brook is the "secret weapon" and lead guitar at 16 years old, Jonji is guitarist and singer from Bridlington, and Cosmosis is the costumier, conductor and spasmodic vocalist.' And we had another 'new' member – Eduardo Romero R., flamenco guitarist (another alter ego of Les's). Les was a consummate guitarist. The article quoted John Peel commenting on the COUM Bradford gig: 'Some might say that COUM were madmen, but constant exposure to mankind forces me to believe that we need more madmen like them.'

That cheered Gen up. We returned home from the show to find Pinglewad had arrived for what would be one of his last visits. Just before he left the next day he commented to me that 'Spydeee doesn't seem very happy' – something I'd noticed for a while but I couldn't work out why.

17 February 1972
Jim's chimney caught fire and stunk the place out. Omar called the fire brigade because he thought it was his club that was on fire. Who should turn up but my dad. I felt very sad when I saw him he looked worn out and as older people do, he had shrunk in size and his eyes looked heavy and worn out. He just looked at me and walked back to the engine. I cleared off to the pier cafe to save him any more embarrassment.

It was the first time my dad and I had seen each other in two years.

The fire crew had to inspect the adjoining houses to check if the fire had spread. Dad hadn't expected to bump into me; he didn't know and didn't even want to know where I was, and Mum wasn't allowed to talk about me, so he was taken aback to see me walk out the door. We both stood looking at each other, not knowing what to say – if anything. What was there to say? If he'd spoken to me his workmates would've known who the hippy girl from the derelict building was and asked him uncomfortable questions. I chose to let him save face – he had something to lose if I made any move to reconnect with him. I walked away. It was the last time I saw him.

My time spent at work during the day meant that I had no idea what was transpiring back at Prince Street, nor was I under the impression I even needed to be inquisitive about it. But small things had made me start to wonder: Les sent letters addressed to me 'only', Brook seemed to be spending more time with another crowd, Jeremy and Haydn had moved out, and Jonji had sent us a poem about how we misunderstood him, that we'd never noticed his X-ray vision since we met him. What? Most of all, as Pinglewad had said, Spydeee was certainly not happy. He'd become more distant and spent a lot of time in his room, only emerging to go out or cook downstairs. If we came across one another he'd avoid eye contact.

Then, quite unexpectedly, on 22 February 1972 (Gen's birthday), Spydeee moved out and left COUM. I felt I'd done something wrong but it turned out to be a number of other factors. He told me later that he was sick of being cold and hungry, and of living with Gen. 'The key reason was that Gen was hard to live with,' he explained. 'He always had to be the centre of attention. Gen just wanted followers, not people to contribute. He was very dominant, we had no fun.'

1 March 1972
We were on last and we bubbled and sang 'Teddy Bear Hot Water Bottle'.

COUM entered and performed at the National Rock/Folk Contest area finals. Sponsored by *Melody Maker* and MIPA, and recorded by Radio Humberside, the event was advertised as '18 Acts of Tomorrow's Stars to entertain you on their exciting road to fame'. It was held at the New Grange Club, Marfleet, where my dad drank sometimes and not far from my parents' home.

COUM attendance was good: me, Gen, Tim, Les, Brook, Fizzy, Harriet and Christine. We did a rendition of 'My Teddy Bear Hot Water Bottle', a song Gen had written about loving and wanting to fuck a hot-water bottle. We played last and came last. One of the judges was outraged – 'How did they have the audacity to get on the stage and play like that?' That comment seemed apt to us as we'd called our set 'This Machine Kills Music'.

I got the sense that Gen had finally outstayed his welcome with many of his upper- and middle-class peers. There was a noticeable shift away from them, most evident in their absence from our lives, save for Tim. Initially, Gen's antics and temper were accepted to some degree by my friends but overall they didn't warm to him. I thought it was maybe because he was eccentric; he thought of himself as a misunderstood artist, and so did I. My friends' opinions were more down to earth. Some found him pretentious, which made them distrust him – as Spydeee discovered after he left Prince Street. He told me, 'A lot of the people I got to know didn't like Gen – I was surprised when I started socialising with them that there was such dislike for him. He seemed to have upset a lot of people. Trying to look at it from their perspective, perhaps he came across as having a superior attitude.'

We had a high turnover of COUM personnel, with some people opting out for a while then returning, and others simply moving on for their own reasons or because of disagreements about what COUM was and arguments with Gen. Arguments were common between him and Les, who had his own view of me and Gen as a couple: 'Together you worked as a great unit, you grounded him. Separately you were still you, but Gen on his own was something else and people disliked and distrusted him.'

I was loyal to Gen – we were, as Les said, a unit. It was us against the world. I gradually became isolated from all but about three of my own friends as my life became focused on serving everything that orbited the world according to Gen, and in commitment to what I was led to understand was the COUM philosophy. My world had shrunk in some ways but expanded in others, and changed from a focus on indulgent fun and laughter to serious discussions on art, life, magick, politics and (ironically) systems of manipulation and control.

We lived on the margins of the fringe and were very much out-siders, along with a small but diverse set of people. It was tough stepping outside the norm in Hull. So much so that an organi-sation called The Outsiders was founded to provide refuge and support. Among the founders were our Funhouse friend Roger and COUM member Haydn, who'd lived with us briefly in Prince Street. But even within the different 'other' groups, there was dis-cord. The mods, Fisher Kids, skinheads and Hells Angels fought each other – and all of those groups antagonised or attacked any-one who hinted at being a peace-loving hippy . . . and we fell into that bracket. To be fair, our style of dress meant we stood out from the crowd, especially when Gen wore clothes in Day-Glo orange. But we felt it was our right to dress how we wanted, and we expected and accepted the antagonistic attention that came our way.

15 March 1972
Rub with a skinhead twice today.

The skinheads in Hull were a different beast to the Angels. They were led by a young guy called Skelly, who took his inspiration in part from the droogs in *A Clockwork Orange* – above-the-ankle white jeans, braces, highly polished cherry-red boots, a very confi-dent and threatening swagger, but with the stereotypical very short skinhead crew cut. They were adept at running up on their prey, retrieving their concealed cosh or slashing knife, delivering dam-age in one swift, practised movement, then running off. Skelly proudly gave us demonstrations of the technique. I mainly had run-ins and face-offs with the skinhead girls, who were known for using their sharpened metal combs to cut rival girls' faces . . . whether they were love rivals or just non-skinheads like me.

COUM 'Riot Control' at Gondola was so titled as a reference to the threatened riot between Hells Angels and skinheads that had been threatened when COUM played there. By inviting both sides to have a go on stage we managed to avert a violent clash – at least inside the club itself. Confrontations with the skins were fraught, especially when we took our experimental actions on to the streets of Hull town centre (hence the COUM action 'Skin Complaints').

As we got to know Skelly better, mainly through our common interest in *A Clockwork Orange*, he stayed overnight occasionally and the rest of his gang fell into line and left us alone. Gen liked Skelly and adopted a version of his dress, wearing shortened jeans with high-top cherry-red Doc Marten boots and braces. Gen hadn't come across anyone as down to earth, blunt and honest as the people of Hull, and he was fascinated by the characters he met, particularly the Angels, skins, Ray and others, who weren't averse to getting involved in crime. Their lives were a great source of ideas, for which Gen sometimes took undue credit. Both the future band name Throbbing Gristle and the TG track 'Five Knuckle Shuffle' (a wank) are directly attributable to Les, who was using those terms most expressively in his storytelling sessions as early as 1972. Foxtrot admired Les's extraordinary skill at storytelling: 'Les, that's the Reverend, was always telling the most amazing stories. He had a naturally poetic, extreme way of expressing things. And he talked about throbbing gristle; he was always talking about throbbing gristle. It was his phrase, you know . . . the male member. He was talking about somebody doing the five-knuckle shuffle with his eight inches of throbbing gristle.'

1 April 1972

I fell asleep again, though woke up to see Spydeee go and . . .

Jo Pemberton and her friend were visiting from Bradford. They'd gone to bed in Spydeee's old room. I'd woken up in the middle of the night to see Gen and Jo's friend on the rug, kissing passionately. I was shocked and asked what they were doing . . . as if it wasn't obvious. Gen muttered something – I couldn't quite hear what – and they separated and he came to bed rather disgruntled. I don't know whether he was more disappointed that I'd interrupted them or that I'd had the nerve to question their (would-be) secret session.

8 April 1972

Gen and I had a little disagreement. Anyway I went out and
didn't go home until 4 o'clock. I'd met Marilyn and her mum
and had been all round town with them. It was rather nice
actually.

Gen and Les had been looking for me all day. I'd taken Gen to task about Jo's friend – he didn't seem to care that I was upset or see anything wrong in what he'd done. To me, it went against the openness of our 'open' arrangement. But to Gen it was OK, in terms of how he felt I fitted into his life.

As our interest in Crowley (and associated book collection) had increased, so had the sex magick – sex with various friends instigated by and shared with Gen – and he'd pronounced me his 'Scarlet Woman'. But I discovered over time that his forays were not necessarily for me to share, and certainly not up for debate. If I mentioned or got upset by them, I was reminded of my important 'role' as his Scarlet Woman. It was a privilege. Very Crowley, down to a photographic portrait Gen took of me which replicated that of one of Crowley's wives, Rose Edith Kelly. But the notion of Scarlet Woman had some positives, representing a liberated woman expressing her sexual desires. That seemed applicable to me. What didn't sit comfortably was that the Scarlet Woman was replaceable – as necessary.

~

My long period of unemployment had triggered a lot of stern warnings from my dole officer and I was given the ultimatum of either getting any job or vocational training, or having no money. I chose a six-week clerical course at the College of Commerce. I got more money, and if I passed (I did) I'd get an RSA Bookkeeping Stage 1 Certificate to boot. There was me, following in my mum's footsteps and gaining a very useful skill. Throughout the course, my COUM activities continued.

19 April 1972
Been busy tonight putting the finishing touches to our props for our COUMglomeration of maniasco at Kent University.

Greg, with his friend Davy 'Giggle' Jones, had arranged a COUM gig at the University of Kent, Canterbury. By the time I got back from college, Greg, his friend John Bidell and Les were there, while Gen and Tony, our driver (my ex Steve's friend), had gone to pick up the hired van. It took us ages to load up. We didn't set off until 8 p.m., trying to no avail to collect Tim and Nicholas on the way, and finally arrived in Canterbury at 6.30 the next morning . . . only to find that we'd been banned from performing. Our reputation had preceded us.

But an alternative venue was found. A marquee had been hired. We created an environment similar to the Arts Centre but more music-focused, with local band Kong Kake playing and Les performing on guitar and playing tapes by him and Greg, who was in drag. It was a full house and was going well but because we had no power supply someone had hooked us up to a nearby lamp post, which short-circuited, causing a local power cut and plunging the marquee into darkness. There ensued a chaotic half-hour, with people wondering if that was part of the show; sawdust that had been scattered to cover the ground was thrown about and people generally went mad amongst the knee-deep debris and polythene. As we started packing everything away we noticed an unoccupied wheelchair lying on its side. We searched for the guy who should be in it but never found him, and assumed someone had taken him home. We called it a night, setting off back to Hull at quarter to midnight and arriving home at 7.45 in the morning.

22 April 1972
We took it in turns to sleep in the back and sit in the front to keep Tony awake. However, after a few miles whoever was sat in the front fell asleep as well. It got to one point where Tony was hallucinating aeroplanes landing on the M1. We stopped and had a drink and Tony had a rest.

We'd had a great time in Canterbury. Gen was nearly arrested for 'misuse of a zebra crossing' as he was filmed doing 'Dead Pedestrians', pretending to collapse in the road, with Les (as Rev. Maull) posing outside Canterbury Cathedral in full garb. We called the gig 'Copyright Breeches' (a project yet to be fully realised), which was an idea based around Duchamp's ready-made 'Bicycle Wheel' and Gen's run-in with the Fluxus people over their rights to their artworks.

I made Gen a pair of copyright breeches. Wide, long, skirt-like trousers in white calico, stencilled all over with copyright signs. Gen would walk around in them with a bunch of copyright stickers, sticking them purposely, copyrighting anything and everything he came across to the point of ridiculousness. Instances of 'Copyright Breeches', like during the later 'Fluxshoe' actions, were photographed and published in 1973 as a small book by Beau Geste Press. It was a statement on ownership . . . and a recurring theme.

Things were moving fast. We took part in the Hull Rag Day parade, with Gen in drag as 'Mellisa Pouts', did impromptu street-theatre-type actions, and all the time we seemed to be preparing for the next COUM gig. We were both feeling the strain of keeping so many balls in the air on a budget that barely covered our living costs. It got to the point where I had to take milk bottles back to get money on them and we seemed to be constantly ill and tired, having to make frequent visits to the doctor. Gen complained at one point that my early risings to go to college were knackering him, he wasn't getting enough sleep, so I took a morning off for his sake. Would that I could have lain in bed like him every day instead of getting up for work. It didn't help that on our quieter days we'd be disturbed by annoying noisy sightseers who would look through the letter box. To get our own back, we wired up speakers above the front door to blast them with weird horror noises or music in the hope that they'd just fuck off.

We needed a pick-me-up and John Peel provided that. We received a letter from him, giving us his new private home address and saying to keep in touch, that he'd be at Malcolm's Disco soon and to come along. So we did. It turned out to be a great night. We met up with some of the Angels, Brickhouse people and even a few of my old Disco friends. John was asking for company for after the gig, so I pointed out the blonde groupie who was already trying to grab his attention. He didn't think she'd fancy him.

'Oh, don't worry – she'll go with anyone,' I said.

He took it the wrong way . . . I didn't mean it to sound insulting to him. Before we left he gave us his card. It read: 'The most boring man in Britain', which was so far from the truth.

6 May 1972
We decomposed or whatever outside the Art Gallery. In protest
of any bloody thing you like. Also we signed a decency petition
for Festival of Light. Harriet, Pete (Fizzy) and Ian (Biggles) all
joined in and we got some good pictures if they COUM out.

The COUM actions were now being referred to as 'deCOUM-positions' and our attentions were directed to Ferens Art Gallery, where we set up our Bible stand and beach umbrella outside and gave speeches with different COUM members dressed as 'The Alien Brain' in a gold-tinsel-dressed gas mask and accompanied by varying characters. We'd take the pram around town, sometimes with Gen in it as a baby being pushed by pregnant Mrs Askwith (Biggles).

The pram was slowly being transformed into the sculpture 'Wagon Train', which was later exhibited at the Ferens Art Gallery Winter Show. That was all very well but the pram was my only means of transporting our bags of dirty washing to the launderette, which was a good four-mile walk from Prince Street. It was bad enough that only I ever did that trip on my own, save for the times Fizzy came to help me. I could just about get away with drawing too much attention when it looked like any old pram, but a gold pram with all kinds of odds and ends stuck to it as Gen gradually worked it into a sculpture meant that I dreaded that launderette trip more than ever. And I was also pissed off that so-called radical thinkers and supporters of 'liberation', like Gen, Greg and the others, couldn't see that they assumed my role (as woman) to be the washer, cook and cleaner, in addition to everything else I did within COUM. When it came to sharing domestic work, equality of the sexes seemed to escape them. It didn't matter whether I'd put in a full day's factory work or done a day of maths at college.

16 May 1972
Got home packed the pram and set off for the launderette. Just the same hot stuffy place, it's so tiring. I arrived home to see Pete (Fizzy) working very hard in the living room and Gen & Greg chatting merrily. No sooner had I sat down, but food was mentioned. There's no rest for the wicked. I cooked and ironed and went to bed. Do you blame me?

Fizzy had brought his macrobiotic music-teacher friend Robin Rat to visit us and Robin had invited us to his Tao House in Ladbroke Grove anytime we needed somewhere to stay in London. We took him up on the offer when we went on a combined trip to meet our USA COUM Van Club president, Charmian Ledner, and to see Greg, who was involved in an event at the Serpentine Gallery with someone called Bruce Lacey. It took us thirteen hours to hitch-hike to London.

We were woken in the morning by a frantic Robin Rat: 'You've got to get out, they're demolishing the house!'

Still a bit sleep-befuddled, we scrambled out of bed and packed our stuff as fast as we could. When we got outside we saw a demolition squad at work up the road. That wasn't the best early-morning call I've received. We headed off up the street and got breakfast in a 'greasy spoon' cafe, then tried to find a bed for the rest of our stay, ringing Nicholas's studio repeatedly but getting no answer. We called Gay Lib and they told us he'd gone to Norfolk with Lindsay. We ended up back at the Serpentine and spent the day with Bruce and Foxtrot.

Bruce took us back to his house to stay the night – at 10 Martello Street, Hackney. He lived in an annexe of an old trouser factory that SPACE Studios had converted into subsidised artists' studios. Bruce was the caretaker and he lived there with his wife, Jill, and their three children, Kevin, Tiffany and Saffron. He showed us around his amazing workshop full of his sculptures and robots, an Aladdin's cave of disparate parts awaiting assembly alongside experimental electronic machines, synthesisers, effects units and circuit boards. We had no idea at that time that future TG collaborator Chris Carter had known Bruce for some years and they used to swap circuits and notes on how to build and modify them. Bruce was a fireball of energy, all but running from one place to the next, excitedly showing us his work, bubbling over with enthusiasm for art and life. I thought Greg could talk a lot but Bruce hardly drew breath and he talked *at* you – a stream-of-consciousness of facts and ideas about himself and his work. We were shown around the factory, which, as well as the studios, had a huge communal space for everyone to use for working on large projects. We were totally blown away and inspired by the whole set-up.

We set off back to Hull the next day feeling elated and more determined than ever to expand on our work as COUM. Greg introducing us to Bruce was serendipitous. It brought about a sequence of unexpected events that set us on a path to something we could never have anticipated.

31 May 1972
We arrived back home at about midnight to lots of mail, cheque

for £100, Gen's invite to Holland and a door that was only half
locked and had 'Jacko' and 'Max' scratched on it.

When we arrived back from London, someone had broken into the house while we were away – another repair job to do. It was all becoming quite depressing. But at least we'd received our first Arts Council grant of £100. We could start looking for a second-hand van to make COUM more readily mobile.

Bruce had given us the idea of getting an old Post Office van, as they were pretty cheap, robust and large enough for all our props. It wasn't long before we got a red two-and-a-half-ton ex-GPO (General Post Office) van for £65. We managed to find a place to garage it for £1.50 a week . . . Well, it wasn't actually a garage; it was a tannery. A vast space full of tanks that stank to high heaven of rotting animal hides undergoing the various stages of processing to become leather. The skins had to be scraped free of any residual animal flesh or fat and the smell was so foul and acrid I dread to think what chemicals were being used. The men there told us it was piss and other solutions, and I could well believe them. We were given a corner to park the van, as far away from the tanks as possible, and a key to the padlocked door so we could come and go as we needed. We named the van Doris. Having her stored there meant we could paint her up and deck her out while we were waiting for the insurance and tax to come through.

12 July 1972
We went to Pam's with a cut-lipped dazed Shanti. Gen threw her
across the room for shitting and she crashed into the door. She
was shocked like Moony and I rushed to the vets with her but it
was shut. Luckily she was OK.

I think it's fair to say that Gen wasn't as fond of animals as I was and to some extent I can understand why, with his borderline cat allergy, and particularly as Moony would sometimes shit in Gen's shoes instead of using the cat-litter tray.

One day Moony did it again and Gen snapped. He grabbed Moony by the scruff of his neck and threw him out the bedroom door with such force he went flying across the landing and down the stairs. I shot after him. He'd landed on the second flight down, where he lay silent and still. I thought he was dead and gently picked him up. He stirred a little, so I grabbed my coat and put him inside against my chest to keep him warm and safe and ran off to the Blue Cross vet. Halfway there I realised he was probably in shock when I got a hot, wet feeling – he'd peed and shat on me. I didn't care; he was coming round and I hoped he'd escaped serious injury. I'd left Gen at the house, looking worried. Moony was thankfully OK. Not long after, Gen had another cat-throwing episode when we looked after my sister's kitten, Shanti.

7 July 1972
Bought 'Curious' which had Bobby on the front (he's really
pretty) unfortunately he'd had trouble with his tits and had to
have them off.

My short time at Colville Terrace in London, and the friendship with Nicholas and Lindsay, sparked a curiosity and urge to explore beyond my present sexual indulgences. I aligned myself more with Gay Liberation than Women's Liberation. It spoke to me more. Whatever other people took it to mean, I liked that Gay Lib wasn't gender-specific: we are people first and foremost and our sexuality is our individual free choice. The Gay Liberation Front (formed in 1970) blazed the trail for breaking down the social stigma attached to being gay, lesbian or bisexual. I took some of their slogans – 'Gaylib supports Womenslib' and 'There are as many sexes as there are people' – as promoting sexual liberation and inclusiveness, unlike the radical feminists of that time, who seemed more divisive and prescriptive. Freedom 'to be' was my thing. I didn't want another set of rules imposed on me by having to be 'a feminist'.

It was in Colville Terrace that I had a chance meeting with the first transsexual I'd seen, the lovely Bobby MacKenzie. Such a brief encounter, in conjunction with other factors and meeting up with Greg, turned out to be highly significant in relation to my future sex-magazine work. Greg, being a photographer, helped me out a lot with useful advice. I'd acquired a 35mm single-lens reflex camera for documenting COUM and saved up some money from my bookkeeping course for a flash unit.

As well as being into photography I was an avid filmgoer. One of our Sunday routines was to go to the local Tower and Regent cinemas, which had a double bill of A- and B-movies. The B-movies were always a source of amusement and surprise. On one trip to see Hitchcock's *Frenzy* the accompanying B-movie was a documentary on nude modelling.

4 July 1972
Went to see 'Frenzy' but the film on with it was much better. It was a documentary on nude posey girls. Quite quite interesting.

That really caught my attention and came just a few weeks before Greg visited us again with the idea of taking nude photos of me.

He'd already taken some head-portrait photos of Harriet's friend Christine and entered them into a photo competition. Then he saw an ad for a *Men Only* sexy photo competition. That joint venture was what instigated the start of my nude modelling project. This all fitted in with me using more and more sex-magazine images in my collages and diaries. As I sat cutting around the naked bodies, the idea of cutting around my own body and collaging myself as a nude model from a sex magazine struck me as having an honesty and potency that I felt could be the embodiment of a consummate artwork. I would have created the very image that I then used to create a work of art. That approach and process seemed to epitomise what I wanted from my work – 'My Life Is My Art. My Art Is My Life' – and I'd get to enter a world that intrigued me and was (at that time) shrouded in mystery.

20 July 1972
Nudie rude photos feel very nice.

Greg had arrived for the *Men Only* photo shoot. I was excited about the possibility of acquiring my first printed nude image. We discussed what kind of nude photos of me to submit and decided on something unusual – some of me naked or in stockings and a garter belt, laid across our old dentist's chair in the drum room. That was a bit different but more or less OK. But we didn't leave it at that: we added Fizzy as a clown and Elizabeth as a nurse but in a strange, doll-like face mask, then Fizzy again but this time as a mad scientist.

Needless to say, it wasn't quite what they were looking for and they returned all the slides with no covering letter. Never mind. But, having seen Bobby in *Curious* magazine, which promoted itself as a sex-education magazine with more 'open' articles on transsexuals, Beefheart and Bowie, I wrote in enquiring about posing for them. I enclosed one of Greg's photos of me naked on a bed of ribbons of gold cellophane, with glitter over my breasts. I was thrilled when I got a more encouraging letter back saying, 'The nude work is in London; contact us when you're here.'

That invitation, and later meeting Roger Shaw's nude-model girlfriend Nanny (Jacquie) Rigby when we stayed with Robin Klassnik at Martello Street, gave me a great starting point to begin my sex-modelling work. We were forming new and exciting alliances outside of Hull. Everything seemed to be pointing us towards living in London. But that would have to wait, as our plans to move there and share a flat with Nanny fell through.

~

Doris soon came into her own when me, Gen, Fizzy, Greg and Biggles went on a trip to Gorleston-on-Sea to visit Nicholas and see his exhibition of wax figures at the Rumbelow Gallery. Biggles drove Doris up and down kerbs and through red traffic lights. He was tired and not used to her hulking size; with her double-declutching gearbox and no power-assisted steering, she was unwieldy, so he wasn't best pleased at getting a caution from the police. Neither did he like me nagging him about *not* peeling an orange or rolling up a fag whilst driving. He seemed to think it proved how good a driver he was but it scared me shitless and the veering off up the kerbs was proof it wasn't a good demonstration of his ability to multitask.

When we finally arrived safe and sound at one in the morning, we were given a downstairs room for us all to sleep in but were immediately distracted by the sounds of excited voices and breathy moans of ecstasy drifting down from the bedrooms. I went upstairs, where one of the doors was open wide to reveal a bevy of naked beauties all writhing and romping in one big bed. Reclining at the head of the bed was a raven-haired, red-lipped, goddess-like woman called Luciana Martinez de la Rosa, who we were told was an Italian countess. She seemed fully in command of the whole situation, the centre of all attentions and surrounded by gay and straight men: Duggie Fields (Syd Barrett's ex-flatmate), Andrew Logan (known for his Alternative Miss World events), Stuart 'Feather Boa', and of course Nicholas. It was an unforgettable image of luxurious decadence, with a very tangible atmosphere of utter joyous sexual abandonment.

Fizzy didn't know what to make of it, tutting in mock disgust at 'all those bare arses and bits flapping about', and what he called their slithering nakedness. 'They're like snakes,' he said, and disappeared back downstairs.

Having seen and taken a fancy to the blonde long-haired, silver-jacketed Greg, a message was sent from the chamber of passions for him to join them, but he was too scared and took himself to bed. The orgiastic feast continued for some hours and was pretty full-on, with cries of triumph from one of the guys that he'd just had sex with a woman (Luciana) for the first time in his gay life and that he loved it.

The morning after the night before was a time of reflection for us all. I was feeling a little deflated that I hadn't been invited to join in the orgy but got the feeling it was Luciana's domain, so fair enough. Then it was a long drive back to Hull in Doris.

Our two-day sunny summer seaside trip to Gorleston-on-Sea had been memorable and wonderful in the most unexpected ways. I never saw Luciana again but her sensual presence and the shared happiness of that night of mutual, enjoyable group sex had made a long-lasting impression on me. Luciana later worked with Derek Jarman on his films *Sebastiane*, *Jubilee* and, interestingly, *In the Shadow of the Sun*, which years later TG recorded a soundtrack for.

~

The added cost of running Doris meant I needed to get another job. Luckily the brother-in-law of my friend Stephen had a chess factory called Griffin Studios, which was not far from Prince Street. I went for an interview and got a job finishing off resin chess sets.

During our breaks we'd head for some fresh air to give our lungs a rest from the fumes. Me, Steve and Baz and some of the other workers frequented a quaint Dickensian house just around the corner. It was dark and in a very dilapidated state, with a most distinctive odour of damp, and was run as a type of food takeaway by a stern, overbearing woman called Vera. You couldn't call it a cafe as it had no tables or dining area, no signage and the windows were shuttered. In fact, if you hadn't been told, you wouldn't know anyone even lived in it, let alone that you could buy food there. We'd have to knock for admittance, then we'd hear Vera's trusty manservant's footsteps as he scuttled to the door. Len was like Frankenstein's assistant, Igor, slightly hunched over, giving him an air of subservience and of being downtrodden, but he always had a smile for us.

'Who is it?' he'd say behind the closed door.

'It's only us, Len. We've come for our tea and toast.'

We'd hear the bolt slide over and he'd open the door and hold it till we were all in, then shut the door and slide the bolt back. We were only ever allowed in the downstairs front room, where four chairs were arranged around a roaring fire. That fire burned all year round, no matter what the weather, for the simple reason that it was used as a toaster and sometimes for boiling water. Len would take our order and scoot along the hall to Vera, who was always in a room way at the back of the house, and where I presume there was some kind of kitchen, seeing as she also did egg and bacon sandwiches. Len would bring us mugs of dark-brown tea with a stack of thick slices of white bread, and we'd grab a toasting fork each to make our own toast, sitting at the old fireplace, chatting away and comparing degrees of singed bread. Len would often stay and join in with us for a while, until he got summoned by Vera or had to answer the frequent knocks on the front door, vetting and letting people in on Vera's say-so. But no one ever came into our room and we only caught glimpses of the other people coming and going as they passed by the half-closed door or if we happened to be passing on our way in or out. Going to Vera's was a ritual we all looked forward to, all the more because it felt so very odd, rather unfriendly apart from Len, with its strange, furtive comings and goings. I had the impression we were tolerated as a necessary cover, along with the food service, such as it was, for other more financially rewarding activities that took place there. I suspected there was a lot of fencing of acquired goods going on.

25 November 1972
CID came to see us today. Les has been taken into Central. I hope he's OK.

Tiger Jack Pepper was a charismatic local antique and second-hand-goods dealer, and very distinctive in his Union Jack trousers and knee-high boots. He'd travel around selling things he'd obtained or won at auctions, like the wonderful Victorian dentist's chair we bought off him and used for the nude photos. He gave us a backstory to it, that it had belonged to a dentist who was struck off for sexually interfering with women patients while they were under knockout gas.

Jack would come round to see us quite often and Les knew him well, doing business with him occasionally. The friendship all turned a little nasty when Les got arrested for theft and Jack was investigated for possible involvement in fencing stolen goods. It was a frightening time, with accusations flying about as some people grassed each other up to keep themselves out of it all, and some diverting attention away from themselves and on to me and Gen. You certainly learn who your friends are when the shit hits the fan. There was a lot of hasty dumping of suspect items before the police searched various premises.

It all coincided with thefts from the chess factory stockroom. Someone had been nicking and selling chess sets and boards, so when the police came to search Prince Street they enquired about that as well as Les's activities with COUM and any items we may have had in connection with the thefts. All my chess sets were legit – I had permission to take rejects or could buy pieces really cheap – but the heavy-handedness and accusatory tone of the police made me feel guilty as hell. As far as the charges against Les were concerned, he ended up taking the lion's share of the blame. It wasn't looking good for him. I couldn't bear to think of lovely Les locked up in prison. The thought of what might happen to him in there scared me witless, what with all the first-hand nightmare stories of violence and rape that we'd heard.

So me, Gen and Les all decided to have tattoos done as a way of marking our bond and commitment to each other. They weren't the traditional anchors, names or heart tattoo designs, but were based on our magic numbers. We wanted them to act as a comforting reminder for Les while he was away from us. We all went together to the well-known King Arthur tattooist down Anlaby Road – 'Tattooing since 1948', it proudly boasted on his business card. Our tattoos were meant to be discreet, on the backs of our wrists and small enough to fit under a watch or bracelet. Arthur was taken aback when I walked in to have mine done. It wasn't the done thing then for women to have tattoos. My tattoo of the number 4 turned out just as I'd wanted but Gen and Les drew their designs large enough for the tattooist to see the detail. Good idea, but King Arthur tattooed literally what he saw on the paper they gave him, indelibly inking them with the designs at the scale they'd drawn them. Our tattoos were still healing when Les was charged to appear in court.

28 November 1972
We went to the solicitor with Les. It's all very frightening . . .
We did, however, manage to design the Ministry of Antisocial
Insecurity between us. After much confusion. We had stamps
made too. 'NO ART' and 'NOTHING'.

It seems bizarre that at the same time as all this we were exhibiting our mail art at the Midland Group Gallery, preparing for the 'Ministry of Antisocial Insecurity' project, and Les was playing in his band, Bullneck – the name being a cynical reference to the big tough guys built like bulls, with no definitive necks, just solid muscle.

I'd also been given the title 'Miss Gateway to Europe' by Michael Scott in readiness for the Fanfare for Europe Festival in January, and was having official photos done by a local photographer we nicknamed 'Figleaf' – that name referred to the fig leaf Adam wore to hide his hard-on, as Figleaf kept getting hard-ons while taking my 'sexy' photos. It took me two visits to get the photos anything like what I wanted, some in my COUM costumes and some half-naked, for when I got to London to start modelling. They weren't very good or suitable, really; they had too much of a family-portraits vibe about them. That was Figleaf's speciality, after all.

We carried on with COUM but all the while knowing full well the time of reckoning for Les would come and could devastate us all. I'd turned twenty-one three weeks prior to the day that Les was arrested. Twenty-one was traditionally a coming-of-age milestone celebrated by being given 'the key to the door'. That was lost on me. I'd already had the key to my own door for three years. Still, Mum gave me all the usual token presents associated with the big event and I truly appreciated it – a cake with a '21' key on it, £21, an engraved silver bracelet and all. How sad for her to want so much to enjoy that time with me and having to hide it from Dad.

~

A new year had begun – 1973 – but it wasn't a positive start, with the uncertainty of Les's future hovering over me like a dark cloud. The frenzied activities of our involvement in the Fanfare for Europe Festival were a welcome distraction and kept us busy, with setting up our work in the group show at the Arts Centre and installing in the foyer of Ferens Art Gallery all the necessary props of desk, chairs and filing cabinet that we needed for the inaugural presentation of 'The Ministry of Antisocial Insecurity'. This was our centrepiece for the Fanfare for Europe.

The MAI was more than a pun on the words 'Ministry of Social Security'. It wasn't just about commenting on a system regarded by those who used it as far from social or secure. It was fundamentally a work based on questionnaires specifically intended to provoke debate about social and cultural values and the value of art and Life as Art. MAI represented our opposition to defining people and art, and was an ironic, cynical statement in the form of a playful twist on the bureaucracy of government form-filling, filing systems and qualification criteria that we knew so well from applying for our Arts Council grant and our time signing on. The various forms which had officially stamped each of our workless days and defined us as unemployed, thereby qualifying us to receive benefit money, were reworked into mock questionnaires and application forms for artistic subsidy, artistic classification, concluding with (MAIps4), the (non-) payment slip claimants were given to sign as a receipt for 'NOTHING' – well, for those who produced 'NO ART'. If the applicant did nothing creative, 'NO ART' was rubber-stamped next to each listed creatively unproductive day, and 'NOTHING' was stamped in the subsidy payment box. To get to that stage, people had to complete the other forms, first determining their 'Artistic Status' through the (MAIsf2) form, on which they answered questions about Dada, what was art, Miss Gateway, and chose their status from many categories: Art Lover, Art Critic, Artist, Art Object, Member of the Public, Philistine, Racing Cyclist, Groupie, Connoisseur, Common Marketeer and Other (to be specified). We'd also included alongside that list (and upside down) part of the artist status section of the Arts Council application form that we'd completed to obtain the very grant that made the MAI possible. Form 1, perversely to be completed after form 2, was the 'Art Claim Form' (MAIcf1). This parodied some of the Arts Council grant questions we'd faced – but with the difference being that the MAI grant currency was specified as art itself, not money. And those whose application was deemed 'successful art' were given a choice of 'artistic' currency. Questions such as 'Why can't your art support itself?' and 'Have you tried other ways to get art money?' were references to the struggles we had in funding our work and the process involved in applying for and receiving government funding. In keeping with all institutional procedures, we provided an appeal form for anyone who wished to object to the MAI decision. Unlike the unyielding social security appeal system, MAI presented positive hope, clearly stating, 'All artistic appeals upheld'. We had a steady flow of applicants, setting the ball rolling with COUM members and Fizzy doing his best to usher people to the desk.

MAI was only part of our contribution to Fanfare for Europe. We had to work around the theme of European cultural events, so we also provided something more immediate and approachable, playing improvised music, dancing and making sculptures in the centre of Hull and encouraging people to participate. We also took inspiration from the very British 'Bonny Baby Competition', giving it a more appropriate and inclusive title of 'Baby of Europe'. Me, Gen as a baby in the pram, and Fizzy as a clown, headed for the streets of Rotterdam via North Sea Ferries from Hull. It was my first trip abroad and my first stay in a hotel.

I was dressed as a 'Dutch Girl', with my hair in pigtails decorated with long polka-dot ribbons, a colourful, short, chequered, low-cut dress and a push-up bra that found great favour with Jeff Nuttall. 'Oooh, Cosey, you're a comely lass,' he grinned from ear to ear as his eyes fixed on my boobs.

9 February 1973
Les got 18 months, I can't bear to think of him being in prison.
I hope he writes so that we can visit him soon. Lee and Baz got
borstal at Queen's discretion. Jack Pepper? . . . We bought the
'Daily Mail' with Les's case in it. Jack Pepper got 9 months. I
cried a long time tonight for Les.

Les was gone and I was devastated at losing him. He'd been with me my whole life and without him Hull felt like a stark, unfriendly place. I needed plans for me and Gen to move to London to pick up pace. It was awful seeing Les in prison; he didn't fit. But he was self-effacing, never showing any sign of feeling sorry for himself on visits or in his letters; he just asked me to make sure his mum and Baz were OK. And I did – I'd visit his Mum regularly. I knew he was struggling but he didn't want anyone to worry about him. I knew he'd attempted suicide when he was fifteen and went voluntarily, with his mother's consent, for psychiatric care into De La Pole Hospital. 'I lived out *One Flew Over the Cuckoo's Nest* in there,' he told me years later.

I continued working at the chess factory. It helped cover the cost of visiting Les and I managed to save something for our planned move to London. Gen continued with his frequent travels, visiting artist friends. With just the two of us now living in Prince Street, I felt quite isolated and lonely when he was away, and somewhat excluded, but accepted and understood that, for us to take COUM further, Gen's times away from home to hook up with people were necessary in order to make things happen. Besides, he thrived on it and the bookings and opportunities that increased as a result.

It's no stretch to say that by 1973 mail art had played a vital role in bringing together a very active and diverse network of artists dedicated to exchanging and collaborating in visual art, music, publishing and performance. There was a real cross-pollination of great talents and exceptional people, some of whom, like us, embraced the concept of Global Infantilism, which fitted nicely with our approach to art as fun, unpretentious and accessible.

Our most prolific mail art exchanges were with Robin Klassnik, who we'd met through the Groupvine register and the *FILE* artist contact list. We built up a great relationship with him and stayed at his Martello Street SPACE Studio a number of times, including prior to setting off on a Global Infantilism trip to Belgium for the Open Theatre Festival at Leuven University. It turned out to be a crazy, crazy time. Everyone was off the rails. We performed in collaboration with Robin, all of us enclosed in a box, sawing and smashing up a statue of the Virgin Mary and throwing out the pieces, then performing a cycling piece, hurtling round and round in cynical honour of the renowned Belgian cyclist Eddy Merckx.

But the craziest times were being around, and collaborating as, The Revolutionary Spirit with the insanely wonderful art performance duo the Kipper Kids, Harry and Harry Kipper – or, to give them their full names, Brian Routh, who was married to Nina Sobell at the time (and later married the artist Karen Finley), and Martin Rochus Sebastian von Haselberg (who is now married to Bette Midler). They caused absolute mayhem on the ferry as they frantically ran around in 'Harry Kipper' character and full identical costumes, complete with big clumpy boots and joke bald skullcaps. They looked like mutant versions of Desperate Dan. Being such tall, strapping and stroppy blokes, they were scary, imposing figures and freaky when they made the most raucous and weird guttural noises at other people and each other in a kind of Kipper Kid language. It was one momentous ferry ride of wet-knickers laughter.

I saw quite a lot of them after that trip. Their work was uncompromisingly crude, surreal, astounding and outstanding. They became notorious for being gross and dangerous, particularly their 'Boxing' piece, in which one of them boxed himself till he bled while the other acted as referee. It was difficult to watch at times, simply because anything could happen. Their work was at the extreme end of the spectrum of Infantilism art, and a far cry from the COUM infantile capers and the pseudo-institution 'L'Ecole de l'Art Infantile', formed by Robin, Gen and the artist and poet Opal L. Nations. The launch of L'Ecole was marked by a postcard celebrating the first winners of the 'BabyCOUMpetition' in Oxford. Opal ran Strange Faeces Press and published a magazine of poetry, fiction and art under the same name, which was our introduction to its contributors Allen Fisher, John Giorno, Jeff Nuttall, Robin Crozier, Kathy Acker and David Mayor of Beau Geste Press.

28 May 1973
Ooh my darling you came home to me and Uncle Bill loved you as I knew he would. I loved and missed you too much.

Having written to William Burroughs, Gen had received an invitation to visit him if he was in London. He'd given Burroughs (now called Uncle Bill) Robin Klassnik's phone number as his contact, and was gutted to hear that Uncle Bill had called only to be told Gen wasn't there – and had been more or less treated as some prankster posing as Burroughs. Gen made a special trip to London to visit Uncle Bill. I didn't go; I wasn't invited as it was something Gen wanted and needed to do on his own. I wasn't that interested in Burroughs and I had a more important appointment of my own – to visit Les in jail and deliver the transistor radio he desperately needed. Keeping it real, as they say. I was so happy for Gen. When he got back, he was ecstatic at finally getting to meet Uncle Bill. He told me little about it. While he was away, I'd been sorting our things out, throwing stuff away and buying old packing trunks ready for when we made the big move.

~

Before we left Hull we had our final contact with the Hells Angels. It was heartwarming and most appreciated. Me and Gen had gone to the cinema and were heckled all the way through the film by a whole row of skinheads we'd never met before. When it came time to leave we knew there'd be trouble – they'd threatened us constantly and very loudly. As we passed their row they got up to follow us outside. We were dreading the inevitable beating we'd been persistently promised and wondering if we could find a way out to escape them.

Then we heard loud voices and scuffles behind us. We turned to see about twelve Hells Angels, some across the aisle and some at each end of the row where the gang had been sat, blocking them from following us out. The Angels stood there, arms folded, bike chains wound around their fists like knuckledusters, and glowering as they warned the gang of lads to stay where they were until they were told they could leave. They were intimidating, to say the least, ready and looking for the least excuse to give any of the gang a good beating. Two of the Angels came up to us and escorted us to the foyer. 'We heard those cunts giving you shit so we thought we'd see you out safe and sound,' they said.

We were touched and extremely grateful for their protection and act of camaraderie.

~

Our time in Prince Street was coming to an end. We were at best tolerated, but spat at by the locals and market people. Jim must have hated us painting his building, on top of all the odd visitors we attracted. He wanted us out. 'I'll have you outta there!' he'd shout at us whenever we saw him or he was passing the house.

Jim spread rumours of us not paying our rent (when we always did) and it wasn't unusual to see him gathered in a group with his allies, discussing their distaste for us, raising their voices if we were nearby to make sure we heard their nasty comments. One of the group was Fred. He was a strange, tall man with white hair and wore a brown knee-length warehouseman's overall. He ran the old-fashioned corner shop, selling general goods, tobacco and his handmade sandwiches and hot egg or bacon rolls. We never shopped there, especially after Spydeee came home late one night and saw a mass of scuttling cockroaches streaming under the shop door.

The police seemed determined to rid Hull of its 'troublesome elements', which included us. Many of the people we knew were either facing various charges or were already convicted and serving time: some of the Angels; our peace-loving hippy friend Far Out John, who was in prison for possession of dope; Ray was serving another term for the petty offence of stealing a bottle of milk off someone's doorstep; Bobo had a spell in borstal and had his two front teeth punched out; and other friends had been busted for dealing and were on remand, facing substantial sentences. We were persistently harassed by the police; they'd move us on whenever we did street actions and they'd stop us in the street to update us on how they'd nicked someone we knew, or visit the house gleefully hinting that we were next on their list for prison. A vindictive female market stallholder who hated us being in Prince Street had gone as far as reporting Spydeee to the police as a possible murder suspect, simply saying that she'd seen scratches on his hands (which were actually from his cat). When Spydeee left the house one morning he was jumped on by two policemen, hustled into a squad car and aggressively questioned at the station, then released without charge. The police intimidation, loss of COUM members, and our increasing collaborations and work with people outside of Hull led us to conclude that it was time to move on. Les's (now) twenty-seven-month prison sentence had been the last straw for me. Proud as I was of being born in Hull, I no longer loved it there and Hull didn't appear to love me. It was time to go. A timely phone call from Robin gave us our way out.

25 June 1973
Oh what a lovely day! Robin rang up about a studio at Space, Martello Street. We got it! £17.60 a month. Hooray!

3

6 July 1973

There's nothing more depressing than sitting on your own in an empty house. I'm about to cry . . . I feel so lonely and lost. I wish Gen were here I really do.

7 July 1973

COUM Porridges move to London this very day. Bye Bye Hull we must leave you. Sad. Boo! Hoo! Bye everyone!

It had taken me and Gen days to pack our belongings into Doris. Gen didn't do the move with me; he'd gone to London on COUM business. It was left to me, with Biggles as my driver, to get all our worldly goods, Tremble and three cats to our new home in London.

The day before I left, I'd had a visit from the local Children of God cult, who'd taken to trying to save us. This particular visit was to inform me there was no hope for me, that I was destined to go to hell – oh, and that they'd loot the house once we'd gone. Nice people. Mum, Grandma and Pam had called, a little sad but happy for me, wishing me farewell and good luck. Fizzy didn't come round to say goodbye – he was still too upset about us leaving. I spent my last night in Hull feeling terribly lonely and forlorn.

My first impression of the Martello Street studio was mixed. It was one large room in the basement of the old trouser factory, with iron bars on the windows that looked out on to a brick wall. You could just see London Fields out of the top panes of the filthy windows. There was one cold-water tap with a small washbasin, a prepayment electric meter we had to feed with shilling coins, no form of heating, and a floor so mouldy from damp and dry rot that it gave way underfoot in places as you walked across it. We'd really downsized – from seventeen rooms to one.

Access to the studio was through the main doors, past a courtyard and down twelve steep steps that had a sharp bend halfway down, leading into a short, narrow passageway covered by a pretty useless roof made of broken plastic sheeting. Whenever it rained, the passage became a shower, with all the water from the leaking roof pouring down – mainly outside our door. The basement area had just two studios and a disused boiler room.

An Australian artist, Bill Meyer, was our very friendly and helpful neighbour. To my delight I discovered he had a darkroom and screen-printing set-up and he generously helped me by developing my black-and-white films, generating prints and screen-printing posters for us. Out of all the studios throughout the factory, we were the only 'unqualified' artists. Even the caretaker, Bruce Lacey, had graduated from the Slade. We were like sewer rats disappearing into the dark underworld while the 'real' artists worked towards gallery shows in their naturally lit, airy studios above. We only mixed with a handful of our fellow tenants, like Robin and Kathy, and Jules Baker and Rosie Antrobus.

Jules and Rosie built the most amazing huge monster inflatables from canvas and latex, including the tentacled Axon monsters for *Doctor Who*, a 170-foot-long dragon and two twelve-foot-tall wrestlers that helpers would strap to their backs and wrestle with, while Jules and Rosie acted as clown referee and trainer. Jules made Gen a shoulder bag in the shape of a large alien-like vagina, with latex labia teeth and long tentacles all around it. That bag instigated many an interesting conversation as we went shopping and got manhandled by curious admirers – so much so that it would often go to Jules for repair.

Overall we got the feeling we were looked upon as interlopers by all but a few at Martello Street. The SPACE Studio lease stipulated that no one could live in the rented space but a lot of artists did, building themselves a sleeping area disguised as best they could. We did the same. In the driest corner of the room, farthest from the door, our friend David helped Gen build a large 9×9-foot wooden box with a raised floor and padlocked door. The box bedroom was big enough for the double-mattress-sized beanbag I made for us from strong ship's canvas and filled with polystyrene granules. It was a good insulator, ideal for our new cold, damp home. We disguised our sleeping nest by putting my office desk on the side that faced the studio door and pinning up various posters and paraphernalia. The other side was hidden by three six-foot-tall glass-fronted haberdashery drawers that me and Fizzy (who was visiting) had sourced from a shop in Mare Street that was closing down.

They, and the clothes rail we snapped up, were perfect for COUM materials and our clothing. We also got hold of a number of shop dummies and wooden stools to make into Duchamp 'harps' for our next project, 'Marcel Duchamp's Next Work', with Paul Woodrow of W.O.R.K.S. That was to be a twelve-piece 'orchestra' playing bicycle wheels mounted on wooden stools, based on Duchamp's ready-made 'Bicycle Wheel'. With our new headquarters came a new slogan: 'COUM the greatest human catastrophe since Adam got a hard-on'.

In the meantime there were other priorities.

10 July 1973
Cosey hit the modelling scene with a bit of a thud yesterday.
5 bloody hours. Am I popular or am I being used? Geni, my lover,

he misses me awfully and is getting very depressed. I only think of coming home to him.

I hardly had time to catch my breath from the big move. I started my first nude modelling job within two days. Nanny had arranged it. She'd worked there before and said it would be a good introduction for me – that the modelling work would only get better from there on. In hindsight she was wrong: there would be worse to come.

For this job I was to be the 'glamour' model for hourly hire to budding amateur photographers who came into the shop, Premier Cameras in Whitechapel Road. It was run by a middle-aged, smartly dressed man called Monty, who was polite enough towards me but worked me hard. It was a weird set-up. I had to sit behind the shop counter and be on show as he offered my nude modelling services to his customers. If they took him up on the deal I'd be sent upstairs to the small dingy studio above the shop. As soon as the first photographer stepped into the room I understood what Nanny had meant in one respect: it was a good introduction as far as managing uncomfortable situations was concerned.

It was a seedy atmosphere and resembled the studio in the film *Peeping Tom*, all very 1950s with a gold-painted, wrought-iron, pink-velvet-covered bar chair and a grubby, well-used sheepskin rug for posing on. As requested, I'd taken some sexy lingerie with me to change into and there were awkward moments when the men obviously wanted me to strip off but couldn't bring themselves to ask. After a few days I amused myself by toying with their discomfort, especially if they were just there to ogle. It annoyed me that they thought I was too dumb to notice they had no film in their cameras. I could easily tell, simply because they failed to wind on after each shot or change their film. As I moved from one pose to another they'd be transfixed, staring at my boobs, pussy and bum with wide-eyed lechy looks and a sweaty brow, clearing their throats and making shifty, furtive little body twitches. I worked there a week and there wasn't much downtime other than tea and lunch breaks.

Monty invited me back any time I wanted. As if. My spell at Monty's didn't provide any documentation for my project; I approached it as research and training. It was a good start for learning how to be comfortable with being naked in front of strangers, learning to pose for the camera – what looked good and what looked bad. It's not easy being scrutinised and told you look odd or not quite right.

23 July 1973
I did a phoney lesbian polaroid session tonight. Enjoyed meeting
Maggie, don't like Christine or the set-up, very suspicious.
NEVER again.

From Monty's to a dodgy Polaroid job a week later that turned out to be yet more 'research'.

I needed real magazine work so I could secure the images I wanted for my art. I looked up where the offices of *Fiesta* magazine were and went to enquire about doing a shoot for them. No luck. I think taking Gen with me was the wrong strategy.

The journey turned out to be worth it, though. On my way back to the Tube a guy came running up to me in the street as I waited for Gen near Oxford Circus and asked if I wanted to work in his fashion showroom, modelling for his buyers. I didn't take him seriously at first. He turned out to be genuine and I started at GM Fashions, Great Portland Street, two days later. Within just two weeks he'd brought a new girl into the office to model for him, all big hair and lashings of lip gloss. He could be a nasty bastard, and when I refused to tell what he called 'a nuisance buyer' to bugger off when she rang for the umpteenth time, he sacked me. I was glad to be out of there, even though the money had been useful.

Gen had signed on the dole again, so at least the studio rent was secured, and quite by chance I managed to get some casual work through a friend who was working for a small animation company called Crunchy Frog. It wasn't far from the studio, just down Kingsland Road. I had no idea whether I had the necessary skills to do the kind of work involved but tried my luck and was taken on, trained up and set to work painting animation cells. It was intricate work, getting the paint at the right consistency to flow seamlessly and accurately, but I loved it and got a real kick from seeing my handiwork on the TV ad for Fine Fare supermarket. I was also working whatever modelling jobs came my way and had been lucky in managing to fit them around work and our increasing number of COUM bookings, sometimes doing a photo session and then rushing back home to load up and travel to a COUM gig later the same day. Art is Life was tough going.

~

Gen had had an at times antagonistic and interesting exchange of letters with Ken Friedman, and COUM were invited by David Mayor to participate in a Fluxus event. David (with the support of the founders of Fluxus, George Maciunas and Ken Friedman) coordinated 'Fluxshoe', an Arts Council-funded UK touring exhibition that ran from October 1972 to October 1973. When we met him, he lived on a farm in Devon with the Mexican artist Felipe Ehrenberg in a kind of art colony set-up, working on the Fluxus exhibition together and starting Beau Geste Press. The 'Fluxshoe' project brought artists together not only in inspiring and influencing one another but in generating unexpected collaborations, like the COUM/Paul Woodrow (W.O.R.K.S.) piece 'Marcel Duchamp's Next Work'. Being part of 'Fluxshoe', I met old-guard Fluxus artist and Yoko Ono collaborator Takako Saito, who became David's partner at that time, and through David's philanthropic spirit I was introduced to many of the other artists and their work, including Helen Chadwick, Marc Chaimowicz, Henri Chopin and Carolee Schneemann.

The second phase of COUM at 'Fluxshoe' was me and Gen as wayward funsters 'The Terribull Tasteless Twins', roaming around making small random interventions throughout the town centre dressed identically in black hot pants, pink, blue and silver cardigans and striped knee-high socks, with our hair in three pigtails.

The 'Fluxshoe' exhibition was at Blackburn Museum and Art Gallery, where we also took part in creating impromptu artworks and adding them to the exhibition. Gen drilled 4,000 holes in the Blackburn phone directory and mailed it to John Lennon, as a witty Fluxus reference to the lyrics of the Beatles song 'A Day in the Life'. We mailed out a small edition of postcards we'd painted black, as a comment on the darkness and coal-mining history of Blackburn. David and Takako were two of the most self-possessed, kind people I'd met and we spent five days living with them in a council flat they'd leased for the two-week stint of 'Fluxshoe'. After long days in the gallery or on the streets of Blackburn, our evenings were often spent on prolonged collage sessions, discussing ideas and talking into the small hours while playing games like Yahtzee and Mousie Mousie. We later used the slogan from one of the games, 'A riot of laughter and excitement', for a TG T-shirt.

'Fluxshoe' moved on to Hastings and so did we, this time performing at the Victor Musgrave Gallery with Foxtrot and our artist friends Malcolm and Peter Davey. The streets and the beach there were where the 'Orange and Blue'-themed work of transformation was implemented for the first time – me dressed all in blue and Gen in orange setting off orange smoke bombs and putting orange and blue stickers on the pebbles: landscape 'painting' the beach.

8 September 1973
Yesterday I rang 'Pussycat' mag. Turned out to be a rubber fetish mag. R-U-B-B-E-R! Went along to Ragdoll and Eugene for test shots.

I continued to solicit modelling work, and went to see Leslie B., who ran the rubber fetish magazine *Pussycat*. I had to go to his flat for an interview to see if I fitted his subscribers' profile. They preferred something they could relate to – more readers' wives style than straight glamour.

He'd insisted I went along in the evening, which I really didn't like. After about half an hour of awkward attempts at relaxing conversation, he got me to try on some outfits, having me talc my body up so I could slide more easily into the tight rubber pants. He was very polite and hospitable but I felt uneasy being alone with him in his flat, which he picked up on, suggesting I come back another time when I felt more confident with him.

Getting into strange situations like that made it all the more important that I join a model agency, to give me at least a chance of filtering out any possible weirdos. Nanny suggested her agency, Ragdolls. They interviewed me and set up a test-shot session with a photographer, to get some decent photos to start a portfolio. With a model portfolio and auditions, it was getting serious, like the real thing, though I still got messed around a lot. Photographers would offer to do test shots for me, then I'd realise they were using me to do free photos they could sell to a magazine. I didn't complain because I got some prints for my portfolio and I'd more often than not get used by them for paid work later. I was role-playing, being a 'model', to secure the work. My personal style of dress was so far from what was expected, and each time I had to transform myself into a presentable and bookable glamour girl – doing my hair and make-up and dressing the part. I didn't tell many of my friends about my nude work project, nor the modelling contacts about my art. I wanted to be treated like the other girls so I could get as close as possible to a genuine experience of what it was like to be a glamour and porn model.

10 September 1973
I was so busy today. I was all set to just see 'Pussycat' today. Then I ring Bill. He offers me a big job this Thursday. I couldn't refuse. I bombed over for 1 o'clock. Then had to go see the editor of 'Alpha'. Then rush home just to rush out again to East Putney to 'Pussycat'.

27 September 1973
Well I finally did my job for Bill. Silly bastard. He tried to get off with me four bloody times. He won't take no for an answer that bloke.

I worked for Bill quite a lot. He was shorter than me and quite skinny so I could fend him off when he started with his wandering hands and crawling on top of me. That particular day he'd used the excuse of wanting a sympathy cuddle because he had a really painful tooth abscess. Oh yeah? I ended up punching him in the jaw. Surprise surprise, there was no excruciating scream as you'd expect from an abscessed tooth.

I had no patience for opportunist groping; I was busy working towards my solo piece, 'Blue Mover', for the Reading University

Art Exchange. I had posters put up around the university, inviting people to participate by coming along dressed only in blue. The title was obviously a pun on blue movies and my colour – me being the 'blue' mover working my way into those inner porn circles. But the physical and visual objective of the work was about creating a space that moved with flowing shades of blue driven by the interaction of the blue-clothed people. I wanted to give life to (my) colour. Had I had access to the technology of today, I could have realised my idea more fully – I was thinking along the lines of form that was experienced and viewed from within and outside but could also be moved through, akin to a virtual reality. That was even more the case later, with the development of the 'Orange and Blue' piece, which I envisaged ideally as a room divided equally into orange and blue, with me as blue (positive/female) and Gen as orange (negative/male), slowly shifting and transforming as orange and blue clothes, objects, floor, walls and ceiling were transferred from one colour section to the other – from positive to negative, female to male, male to female. Somewhere in that shifting exchange process lay the perfect balance.

On a cold October night I found myself naked in a small room above Hangar Lane Tube station. I was doing a half-hour job for the Central Line Photographic Group. It was a stressless 'Cos(e)y affair', as *London Transport News* reported in their paper a few days later. Unlike Monty's place, the photographers were very polite and serious about their work. When I first arrived, I stood outside contemplating whether to go in or turn around and go home. Everyone else was going about their business and here was I about to do something I might regret. I can't believe I put myself into such risky and unpredictable set-ups. As it happened, everything was above board, and unlike at Premier Cameras I actually ended up getting published.

Nothing had come of the *Alpha* test shots I'd done or of ones me and Nanny had done for *Men Only*. So much was going on with COUM that I was happy to plod on, hoping things would work out as I'd wanted. Also it was coming up to my birthday and the first of my Martello Street parties. Having sent invites out to friends in Hull and London, I was excited that everyone was coming along. It turned out to be a wonderful, very drunken, fun night full of unexpected sexual liaisons – and a blueprint for my future birthday parties in the bowels of the old trouser factory. Such happy, carefree times helped offset the prevailing concerns of everyday life.

26 November 1973
I reckon the end of the world is nigh. Also if I reckon that, what the fuck do I bother with a diary for? Or entering Miss Office World?

The move to London was a few months after the four IRA car bombs in London; two were defused but two exploded, one at the Old Bailey and one near Scotland Yard. The trial on 14 November dominated the news. Up until this point there'd been few bombs in mainland Britain so I'd felt relatively distant from the Troubles. It was a harsh awakening, especially after the bombs at King's Cross and Euston stations. I'd been walking up to King's Cross station on my way home when the blast there happened. It was chaos, with everyone screaming in panic and running in all directions. I spotted a bus that was starting to pull away and jumped straight on it. I didn't care where it was going.

The early 1970s was a time of social, political and economic turmoil, as well as a very active period for violent militant groups like the IRA, the Angry Brigade and the Baader-Meinhof group. There were bomb warnings, some true, some hoaxes, which made everyone nervous about travelling around London.

Still, we forged on with our COUM show for the week before Christmas – three performances at the Oval House Theatre as part of Ian Hinchcliffe's Matchbox Purveyors' 'Hot Chips for Christmas' programme. Ian was a performance artist we'd met through his mentor, Jeff Nuttall. Ian's group consisted of either just himself or varying numbers of artists, poets and musicians, depending on how he felt at the time. He was incredibly talented but could be wild, dangerous and uncompromising. Our kind of person, really. The first two COUM shows were in the afternoon, which meant I couldn't be there – I was stuck at work (as a secretary at a local dress factory). Joseph L. R. Rose from the Reading crowd and John Lacey (Bruce's son, aka John Gunni Busck) had been working with us for quite a while and did the matinee shows with Gen.

The big performance was on the Friday night. I'd been practising playing the tom-tom and snare drums in preparation for our musical 'deCOUMposition' and felt pretty good about my first public drum performance. Biggles turned up and our SPACE artist friend Ted brought along and played his Farfisa organ. It was a very Christmas-party atmosphere with so many friends coming along. As was becoming the norm, we went to Gen's parents' for Christmas, taking an arduous coach journey all the way to Shrewsbury and returning in time for New Year's Eve.

I loved working with John Lacey. He was full of ideas and made every aspect of the creative process fun and enjoyable. Any hitches that cropped up were never seen as a problem. He'd just smile and say, 'We can make it happen', and set about putting things right. John was also my entry into using electronics. Before him, COUM music had been mainly acoustic but John had interests and skills that helped steer COUM in a new direction. He and his friend Chris Cobb (who worked for the BBC) were building quadrophonic speakers and amps, which we brought to use in the studio and for COUM events. John lived in a semi-detached four-bed-roomed house in Durnsford Road, North London, with his mother, Pat, his brother and four sisters. Each of the six siblings had their partners, friends and musicians coming and going and staying over, which made the house heave with chaotic creative energies.

On one of my many visits to Durnsford Road, I met John's friend Chris Carter, who was staying in John's room until he found his own place. Chris had played bass guitar in a band called the Dragsters with his friend Chris Panniotou, until they both started doing light shows for bands like Yes and Hawkwind and for the BBC. When Chris met John, he refocused on music, shifting from bass guitar to building his own synthesisers, and all three of them and other friends joined forces in various collaborative configura-tions to contribute to each other's projects. It was hard to find a place to sit in John and Chris's room; it was so full of equipment. There were near-complete and finished synthesisers, parts of gear awaiting their final purpose, boxes of electronic components, cos-tumes, papier-mâché masks and props from John's theatre works, Chris's projectors and slides, reel-to-reel tape recorders and John's Super 8mm film equipment.

Considering how close John was to Chris, how often they worked together at Bruce's Martello Street workshop at the same time as John was working with me and Gen in our studio, I don't know how we'd not managed to run into Chris sooner. He had been just a figure fleeting across the landing or passing us on the stairs of the Lacey house until our first face-to-face meeting, when we visited John to find Chris and his girlfriend, Simone, talking to John about their forthcoming wedding. I was quite surprised that such unconventional people were contemplating marriage, but even more surprised when Simone invited me and Gen to their wedding, having only just met us. I declined the invitation: 'I don't go to weddings – I don't agree with marriage,' I said rather dismissively. Chris was very quiet – in fact, I don't remember him saying anything. We didn't fully connect with him again until some time later.

John's musical and technical contribution to COUM had helped so much by enabling us to expand and transform some of our existing projects from visual to amplified audiovisual pieces, and we received an invitation to perform 'Marcel Duchamp's Next Work' as part of the 4th International Festival of Electronic Music and Mixed Media at the Stedelijk Academy in Ghent, and at the Palais des Beaux-Arts in Brussels. Both shows fell within a week of each other so we coordinated with Paul Woodrow for him to fly from Canada to the UK and travel together in Doris with me, Gen, Biggles, Joseph and our equipment. John didn't come along and Fizzy stayed at the studio to look after the animals for us – and take the opportunity to wear as his daily garb the black latex wart-covered rubber suit Jules had made for us. He liked rubber and said he was practising for when he and I went to perform as COUM in Gross-Gerau.

The Ghent trip was fraught with money issues. We got paid expenses but there were poster costs sprung on us when we got there, which reduced our food funds considerably, and we were all grumbling about it, as were our stomachs. I distracted myself by getting Godfried (the organiser) to take me to the local (and very imposing) medieval Gravensteen Castle, which he'd told me had an impressive dungeon. It didn't disappoint, but it was a disturbed place: its cruel history was palpable, which fed my morbid curiosity for horrendously gruesome torture devices. I left feeling both amazed and sickened by the ingenuity of human beings at devising methods of inflicting excruciating pain on one another.

The next day the inaugural performance of 'Marcel Duchamp's Next Work' took place, my recollection of which is overshadowed by our Brussels show a few days later. My main memory of the Ghent show was the installation, when I found myself treated to the meditative, soothing and melancholy Gavin Bryars endlessly looping 'Jesus' Blood Never Failed Me Yet'.

26 January 1974
A beautiful piece we have in Marcel Duchamp. So pleased with it. Joseph too. Herve loved it, sat, should I say lay down and looked happy watching the slides. Henriette took part, lovely Henriette. Big critic lady came and congratulated me on the superb slides. Quite embarrassed I was. What can I say? Apparently she was the art ents critic for Belgium's biggest newspaper. Didn't bother us all that much really but Herve was thrilled to bits. Herve and lovely Henriette are perfect hosts x x x x

Two days after our Ghent show, Biggles drove us on to Brussels for the second Duchamp performance. Moniek Darge, the organiser, had arranged for us to stay at the home of the director of the Palais des Beaux-Arts (and friend of Stockhausen), Hervé Thys, and his wife, Henriette.

We arrived just as it was getting dark, which probably played a part in our feeling that we'd arrived on the set of a Hammer Horror film. Their house was in the grounds of the Thys family estate, a large old chateau with huge, tall and locked metal entrance gates. Biggles had pulled up so one of us could go and get someone to let us in. We didn't set foot out of the van, nor did we need to ring any bell . . . On hearing the van pull up, four ferocious and very angry German shepherd dogs appeared in the courtyard, barking and snarling and throwing themselves at the gate in a vain attempt to attack us.

I wasn't in the best mood for the performance the next day. I'd had little sleep, not because of the dogs but because me and Paul had come down with really bad colds. Once I got into the venue and saw the amazing space we had at our disposal, though, I perked up as excitement took over. The Duchamp piece was a work of two parts and was performed by a twelve-piece ensemble arranged in a circle, each with near-identical instruments – twelve Duchamp-style bicycle wheels mounted on stools, each put through a contact mic and a quadrophonic PA system. We provided a selection of tools for playing the instrument, ranging from hearth brushes, screwdrivers, cutlery and paper to drumsticks, violin bows and pieces of metal. There were no rules about how to play, just two separate scores that provided a point of entry. Like the Ghent show, COUM members took a wheel each and we co-opted other people to play the rest, including Henriette. The score for the first part was a pack of playing cards from which each person selected at random, using the cards numerically as rhythmic time signatures or interpreting them any way they liked – with the option to not use them at all. The first half sounded quite erratic, as people felt their way tentatively until they got into their stride. I scored the second part of the work and had someone replace me at my wheel so I could work the projections. I had spent quite some time creating and photographing graphic images of varying colours from an assortment of source materials, then had the transparencies mounted into slide cases to project as the score for the players to interpret in an imaginative way. The visual score changed the mood from disparate actions and sounds to one of subtle and sensitive collaboration by having the ensemble focus together on the visual projections, responding individually but always mindful of being one element of a unified twelve-piece unit. And that unit extended to me as I used my slides in response to the sounds, lingering on one or switching slides slowly or swiftly to bring some rhythmic movement.

The reaction of the Belgian music critic was complimentary. Such praise was new for us – we were so used to being slagged off. I've always found it easier to handle criticism than praise, so much so that I can recall and deal with the bad things people have said far more readily and easily than the good. Either way, I'm not hanging on anyone else's opinion.

~

As a consequence of our ongoing and substantial lifestyle changes, the COUM approach was becoming less ad hoc and more considered, largely due to the influence of my magazine work, which shifted our public actions in a new direction – the subject of sex. Up to that point our sexual activities had been private. Through modelling, my public nakedness wasn't an issue for me.

'The COUMing of Age' at the Oval House Theatre in London was the first COUM action that involved nudity; it proved to be a huge turning point as it also caught the attention of someone who was to become one of my closest and dearest friends. While we were sitting in the Oval House cafeteria having lunch prior to performing the show, we were approached by a smartly dressed young guy who had a camera hanging around his neck and was cradling the lens in his left hand. He quietly and very politely introduced himself.

'Hello. My name is Peter Christopherson. I'm really interested in your show. Would you mind if I take some photographs tonight?'

There was something about the way he sidled up to us that was a bit creepy but also made me smile and say, 'Oooh, you're sleazy . . .' – and so 'Sleazy' became his name. It seems a rather unexceptional meeting, considering the impact we were to have on one another's lives, but it was the best thing about 'The COUMing of Age'.

The show was an odd collection of innocent, clichéd sexual

fantasies and scenarios – but with twists. We took the sugary-sweet image of a virgin-like girl on a swing revealing brief glimpses of her knickers as her skirt blew in the wind and presented me naked on a pale-pink swing hung centre stage from the theatre ceiling. That was all still pretty 'sweet' until . . . as I was pushed higher and higher to send me above the audience, I peed through the heart-shaped hole we'd cut in the seat, releasing an arc of warm wetness as I swung back and forth, slowly coming to a dribbling standstill.

One of my other 'roles' was a bit of a busman's holiday – a nude model being photographed by a lechy photographer, played very well by Foxtrot. Its purpose was to show the behind-the-scenes process of creating the finished fantasy magazine image. I was captive in an eight-foot cylindrical cage covered in blood-streaked, flesh-coloured latex tentacles (borrowed from Jules), modelling under Foxtrot's direction until released to wander the stage striking various glamour poses while a girl on a trapeze ladder performed nude acrobatics hanging by her knees, then by her ankles. There was no safety net for her, nor for Hermine Demoriane when she performed a tightrope striptease, so it was risky to say the least – art and aesthetic riding roughshod over health and safety.

We had Hermine perform in black light and changed her costume to Day-Glo colours worn over a full black leotard, so as she removed her clothes she effectively disappeared. A striptease revealing nothing. Simultaneously me and Gen were dressed as black dogs set against a backdrop of a house and tree outlined in Day-Glo paint. All you could see of us in the black light was our Day-Glo genitals as we performed doggie sex – two huge dangling balls and a fat fourteen-inch cock pumping away at my glowing lady-dog parts. We also gave a nod to the male artist painting 'the female nude', with me stood exposing only my bare torso, framed by a rectangular hole cut in a large black polythene sheet. Dressed in only an artist's smock and French beret, with palette and brush in hand, Gen proceeded to paint me.

John didn't perform in the show front-of-house; he was doing the vital job of lights and sound, playing his home-built synthesiser, but came down to take a bow and join the end-of-show throwing of polystyrene granules everywhere. It was the last time we ever did that . . . It took us hours to sweep up.

28 January 1974
Well here I am at last Cosey's first pubic appearance without any.

At last! I finally got my naked image in a magazine article: 'PROSTITUTION' in *Curious* magazine. That felt so right, having *Curious* as my first point of entry.

My pubes were just growing back after I'd shaved them for a *Health and Efficiency* magazine shoot . . . Well, I say 'I'd shaved them', but in fact it was the editor who shaved me, insisting it had to be to his particular standard. I'd said I would shave myself. I didn't like the idea of someone using a razor blade down there and poking about. But he'd have none of it, saying that he must do it as he didn't want any cuts, and explaining how difficult it would be for me to completely remove all traces of hair or get into every nook and cranny. The word 'cuts' leaped out and made me even more nervous but if I wanted the modelling job I had to let him do it. It was very disconcerting looking down at him as he set to work. The whole procedure seemed to smack as much of fetishism as the aesthetic, especially as his depilation rule didn't apply to men. He was very gentle and knew what he was doing, carefully parting my lips to get every little hair. He'd obviously done it many times before – unlike me. It was my first time and it had been a tough decision because shaving off your pubes seriously affected the number of nude modelling jobs

Top: Me and Dad, 1952
Above: Me, my sister Pam, Dad and Mum: a happy family day at the beach
Right: Me, aged fourteen to seventeen, with friends Jo, Shirley and Jean: from school to disco to dropping out

Me and Gen, 1969 (© John Krivine)

Me with Spydeee on Hull pier waste ground, 1971

Me on Prince Street with Les's Bible stand, 1971

COUM outside Ferens Art Gallery, 1971: (*from left*) Sarah, me, Foxtrot
Echo, Biggles and Fizzy

Creating this page in my diary, 25 February 1973, at Prince Street

Reunited with Les, Beck Road, 1974

Party at Martello Street, 1975: Fizzy, me and Sleazy

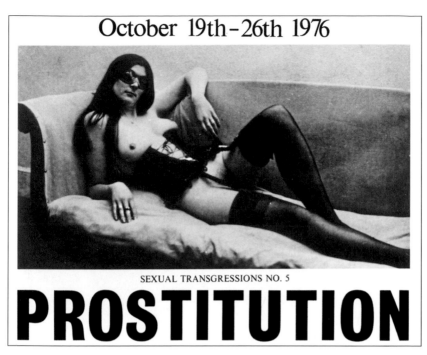

From the ICA 'Prostitution' exhibition poster

TG launch gig at the 'Prostitution' show (© Paul Buck)

Out and about in LA with (*from left*) Kitten, Eric and Skot, 1976

First official TG promo photo, 1976

What a day! We got on the road around one o'clock as planned. Arrived in Brighton about quarter to four. Went for a tea and back to the Poly. It was open. So we unloaded and had a fantastic stage. Looked great. Chris took a photo with his new camera. Got Gen a bottle of whisky. He drank the lot in the first factory music section. He was pissed, Jonji too. He did a fantastic introduction, and Sleazy didn't get it on tape! Well some shouted, a lot were smiling (felt sick) bewildered and blinded by the lights. We got unplugged. The D.J. gave them hell over his P.A. and had Gen and Jonji shouting too. Gen met his school friend Bag Hannan. He ran the bar there. Also he nearly got in shtuck with the police when he moved Doris. LUCKY ONE. Got home around two o'clock. Knackered, well and truly.

Diary entry, 26 March 1977

Left: One of the many photos taken by Szabo, July 1979 (© Laszlo Szabo)
Right: Modelling/stripping at the Ship, Brighton, for the *Evening Argus* Pub of the Year Award, 1978 (© the *Argus*)

Stripping at the Westminster Arms, London, 1979

you could get, simply because (unlike today) shaved pussies were a niche market and you'd be out of work until your pubes grew back.

Even though I'd tried to keep my art and modelling separate, there were times they merged, mainly because some of the people I met through my sex work were really interesting. Tuppy Owens was one such person and she came to see the COUM show at the Oval House. She was the top female sex publisher in England, writing and publishing her own books, writing for sex magazines, and (still) a very outspoken campaigner for sexual freedom and sexual health. Unlike now, most of the magazine sex articles and fantasy stories of the 1970s were written by men, usually under a female pseudonym or by using a sexy female as a front. The idea of women writing about sex was a turn-on: it attracted male readers but misled them into thinking what they read was a woman's perspective on sex. It gave scope for men to write about their sexual fantasies, which would appeal to their mostly male readers, but which also had the unhealthy effect of upholding male attitudes to women, male sex fantasies and notions of women's sexual likes and dislikes. Considering all that, it was great to discover Tuppy was around and I felt an affinity with and respect for her, not only because of her pioneering spirit.

I often visited Tuppy's place in South Street, Mayfair, to have dinner, to audition or just to chat. Living in Mayfair sounded very posh so on my first visit there I was curious as to why Tuppy told me to go to the back entrance of the seven-storey apartment block and ring the bell. It seemed to take a long time before she answered the door and I was beginning to think she'd gone out when she appeared with her usual smile.

'Follow me,' she said, and led me to her basement flat, taking me on a long winding walk along corridors lined with industrial-sized water pipes, past huge boilers and through narrow gangways, until we emerged into a small open area that Tuppy and her partner had acquired somehow and made into a compact but very nice and inexpensive living space. A Mayfair address was not always what it seemed.

I worked for Tuppy on two magazine jobs and as one of the decorative hostesses at the launch of her 1975 *Sex Maniac's Diary* at the Bristol Hotel in Mayfair. She put me in a Marilyn Monroe-style blonde wig and I wore my own 1930s ankle-length white-and-green dress split up the leg to the bust line. My name tag read 'I most certainly am Cosy [sic] of COUM Pornographic Pantomimes' – 'pantomime' being Tuppy's description of the Oval House show, referred to as such in her 'Porno Panto' review that was published alongside my six-page photo spread in the same issue of *Alpha* magazine. I was pretty ecstatic at the double infiltration, of appearing in both guises, as model and artist.

Things were beginning to work out at last – perseverance had paid off. Being published in *Curious, Health and Efficiency* and *Alpha* magazines spurred me on and I started to keep a record of what magazines I'd worked for and sought them out, aiming to acquire at least two copies of every one I appeared in. It wasn't easy with magazines working a month or two in advance, or if freelance photographers had sold photos of me to several different magazines. I found it exciting hunting for my artworks on the top shelves of newsagents and in Soho sex shops. The shop owners would look at me suspiciously as I flicked through magazine after magazine, and were very confused when I uttered a triumphant 'Yesss!' as I marched to the counter to buy two or more copies of the same magazine.

8 March 1974
Dusty and Billie of Rinky Dink came last nite. Should be moving into the house next Saturday.

The nearest shops for food were in Broadway Market, just a short walk across London Fields, where I walked Tremble every day and always with my hefty bunch of keys in the palm of my hand, in readiness for trouble. I held them so I could strike straight in the eyes of an attacker. I saw it as a necessary precaution in view of the run-ins I'd had with gangs of skinheads and groups of young black guys throwing stones at me and Tremble, or shouting obscenities and threatening to beat me up or rape me – or, as one very young boy who looked about ten yelled, 'Hey, pinky girl, I'll fuck you right up the arse!!'

I was shocked that he'd even think about anal sex at such a young age, but more shocking than that was that he'd referred to me as 'pinky'. The mention of race was a whole new thing to me. Hackney was very rough in the 1970s and, the young kid aside, I noticed residual elements of racism that disturbed me. And it wasn't the black gangs – I was used to gangs and threats from Hull – it was the lady park warden who proudly told us she was a former member of Mosley's Blackshirts and was very vociferous about her beliefs whenever she stopped to talk to us in the park. Then there was Bella, a small, frail-looking, grey-haired old lady who ran the time-warped grocery shop and had a black cat she called Nigger. That alone was unacceptable but she'd go down the market calling, 'Nigger! Nigger!', trying to get her cat indoors. I was gobsmacked when I heard her but no one seemed to think anything of it.

As I was walking through London Fields as usual on my way to Broadway Market, I heard a very familiar Yorkshire accent. I turned around to see two young guys. 'Nice to hear a Yorkshire accent – where you from?' I asked.

We had a great chat. They were in a band called Rinky Dink and the Crystal Set and had just secured a record deal. They'd also been living in a squat in nearby Beck Road and were about to leave.

'Do you want to take it over when we move out?' they offered. A three-bedroomed terraced house? Hell yeah!

It was in a state, with a small leak in the roof and umpteen layers of lino and sodden carpets in the upstairs rooms, mattresses nailed to the walls as soundproofing – but it was such a gift. We moved in as they moved out, making sure the council couldn't seize the house back and board it up. The whole street was earmarked for demolition and redevelopment, and all council tenants were slowly being relocated. I had big plans for Beck Road. Les was due out of prison in August and we'd talked about him living in one of the rooms. I was happy that we'd have more space for the cats and Tremble to roam, a proper bed at last and our own toilet, even though it was outside. We became Acme tenants (an artists' housing association), paying £3 a week.

The house had arrived at a good time: we were fast outgrowing the studio and it was within easy walking distance of both my job at a local clothes factory and Martello Street. The studio became a dedicated workspace and store for our growing collection of performance props and audio equipment. A corner of the rotten floor had finally caved in and we built a raised wooden platform and used it as a stage, setting up the PA and speakers with John for COUM jam sessions and working on material for music gigs.

2 April 1974
Wonderful news today. COUM to get a grant of £1500. Could it be an April Fools trick or are we really going to be able to get all our equipment?

Gen's copious letter-writing had paid off. We had some money to finance our many ideas and wasted no time putting together a COUM promotional info sheet, with a contact strip of photos from 'The COUMing of Age' on one side and on the reverse a COUM statement, CV, press quotes and a notice offering workshops and lectures. The usual address and phone contact details also included COUM Transmissions, now a registered company with directors listed as 'Cosey Fanni Tutti' and 'Genesis P-Orridge' and a technical director, John Gunni Busck. Despite this seemingly official promotion of COUM as a bona fide group enterprise, there was already a change in focus, from the music and experimental theatrical and environmental installations advertised on the poster to more art action-based work, mostly featuring just me and Gen.

COUM had been booked for six nights at the Howff Club, London, and we put a lot of work into getting a show together. Foxtrot was dressed as Martin Bormann in only an ankle-length Nazi leather coat, with a hat and sunglasses, singing 'Bormann of the Jungle'. We did a rendition of the early COUM song 'The Balloon Burst' and a new song, 'Now You Hear It, Now You Don't'. As promised, COUM didn't fail to disappoint and the next five nights were cancelled.

That experience of being more of a 'band' and repeating the same chaotic madcap COUM stuff left us feeling like we were going nowhere and, for me, contributed in part to the change in direction. What also affected that change was that, shortly after our move to London, Fizzy moved to York and Biggles to Leeds College of Art. That distance meant their presence and creative involvement was limited, leaving me and Gen at the helm to procure bookings, create opportunities and fund COUM, with the others turning up if available. Financing COUM was becoming a heavy burden, even with the grants we'd managed to get.

20 June 1974

It was just like any other drunken party. Carolee Schneemann did a 'piece'. A two minute Happy Birthday song . . . COUM went home early, or when everyone was too drunk for mediocre art performances but just enough to dance to a lousy tape of shitty music . . . a projector got stolen . . .

The shift in direction to COUM being mainly me and Gen also coincided with my leaving full-time work and connecting with other artists at the Art Meeting Place – where the drunken party took place. AMP, as it was known, was set up by John Sharkey (along with others) in one of the buildings left vacant from the relocation of the Covent Garden fruit, veg and flower market. Other buildings had also been opportunistically acquired by activists for use as community centres and alternative arts spaces. AMP was a kind of Arts Lab that provided free facilities for artists across the spectrum – musicians, poets, film-makers – and was run by the artists themselves, with open meetings every week, exhibitions and performances. Me and Gen became regulars there, using their resources and trying out ideas in the available spaces – as did Anish Kapoor, Carolee Schneemann, John Latham, David Medalla, David Toop and Susan Hiller, amongst others.

Participating in the meetings was always interesting, watching people getting antsy with each other over art or politics, or art being a political act, feminism and Marxism. Some people had great ideas and ideals to uphold but there were time-wasters whose posturing made me angry and I got the sense that they didn't fully appreciate what an amazing thing AMP was. Discovering and being with so many diverse and alternative-thinking artists, many of whom shared the same collaborative and collective approach, was refreshing to me and gave me a break from what was at times a rather incestuous feel to working as COUM. Playing the live soundtrack for someone else's performance piece, being asked to contribute my (thwarted) part in David Medalla's 'Porcelain Wedding' and just chipping in to help others with their projects was new and exciting.

Despite the 'open to all' ethos of AMP, there was still a feeling of 'them and us' and I was often irked by the sarcastic comments and air of superiority some of the artists had. Their elitism was useful, though: it was fuel for my fire, pushing me further than I might have gone had they been politely encouraging.

We took advantage of the 'free' space and performed naked as and when it felt right, which was actually quite often, as it was with 'Gainsborough's Blue Movie Boy', which alluded to Gainsborough's painting, my sex work and my previous 'Blue Mover' action – Gen as naked 'blue' movie boy. I poured thick pale-blue flour paste over Gen, covering him from head to toe, leaving him standing motionless, dripping like a melting statue.

AMP was where we first publicly used the name Throbbing Gristle, unaware of what that name would come to represent. 'Throbbing Gristle' was not just us being mischievous but was also a reference to and celebration of Les's recent release from prison. Using the name acted as both an acknowledgement of his introducing us to the term and a representation of him 'in absentia' – effectively making the very first version of Throbbing Gristle me, Gen, Les, Tim and John Lacey.

'Orange and Blue' was becoming our flagship action and I liked doing it. I might not have been so enthusiastic had I known then that the Exploding Galaxy (and Transmedia Explorations) had for years prior to us performed a piece entitled 'Orange and Blue', which was based on a very similar idea . . . I wonder if David Medalla saw us do 'Orange and Blue' at AMP, and if so what he thought.

At least when we performed at AMP there was no threat of arrest, just tuts and people walking out – unlike when we did

'Orange and Blue' in Manzoni Gardens, Birmingham. We were naive to think stripping off in a public place with families around was no big thing – but it was. It began so well, very measured and calm, until we got to the changing-clothes part, revealing our naked flesh – at which point a very angry teenage girl came at us, shouting incoherently, throwing milk in Gen's face, scattering our props and getting increasingly aggressive. We managed to contain it but not before someone had called the police. We were threatened with arrest and prosecution for 'nudity in a public place', had names and addresses taken and were told we'd be hearing from them. We never did.

15 July 1974
No job from Ragdoll, I don't expect any at all this week. I was supposed to go to Ragdoll to see Avril today but I just couldn't take it. I undercoated the pyramids ready for the gloss paint tomorrow. Gen went to ACGB to take the bulletin . . .

Each day was a juggling act, making COUM props, keeping on top of Arts Council applications, COUM booking enquiries, massive amounts of mail art and ringing round for modelling jobs. I was still with Ragdoll model agency but only sporadic work was coming in, and travelling to their West End office to check in, then being sent across London to auditions in Barking, West Hampstead, Teddington or wherever consumed so much energy, money and time. With other COUM commitments it was difficult, especially when any modelling jobs that did come my way seemed to cluster within the same week as COUM bookings.

I'd expanded my 'repertoire' to lesbian and group-sex photo shoots but wanted to make sure I was covering the different genres of sex magazines, from high-end glossy to the lower end of the market. Agencies had their client bases and Ragdoll was sending me to the same people all the time and just wasn't getting me enough work to cover the areas I needed for the project, so I joined the Jan Lawland agency as well – who weren't much better.

At least, unlike other COUM works, my modelling project was largely self-financing through the fees I got paid, which also helped no end in subsidising COUM and with the day-to-day living expenses and paying for mundane necessities like the fitting of a gas fire and cooker in Beck Road. It wasn't just the fees that cast us a lifeline; the contacts I'd made also came in useful. We rented out our Victorian dentist's chair as a prop for *Pussycat* magazine to pay for the van insurance, and one of the guys I'd worked with on a shoot was in the rag trade so I called him and asked him for some home sewing work. 'Yeah, sure,' he said. 'Come round to the factory and you can do a trial bunch of garments for me. I'll show you the ropes.'

When I turned up, he sat me at the industrial sewing machine then gave me a dozen men's boxer shorts in an incredible assortment of the most lurid patterned fabrics I've ever seen (or would want to see) worn as boxer shorts. I reckoned it was all leftover material from other ladies' blouse and dress jobs: both tiny and huge brightly coloured flowers on equally brightly coloured backgrounds. Crazy pants sewn by Cosey. I didn't expect I'd be sewing bloody boxer shorts to pay gas and electric, but at least I was resourceful. The room I'd hoped Les would live in was now my sewing room. Les never moved in. I'd gone to Hull when he was released and stayed with him for a week, talking till three in the morning, just loving being together again and so relieved he was free. All too soon I was back in London, taking Les with me. I showed him round, we jammed in the studio, ate in the local Forlini's Cafe, and he transfixed us for hours recounting tales of his time in prison with his inimitable sense of humour.

12 September 1974

We didn't realise the journey was going to take us 24 hours ... I realise now, looking up and finding it difficult to focus, just how tired I am. The German passport man asked us to open our bags on the train and if we had any hash or hemp ...

I felt regrounded after Les's visit. He'd returned to Hull and I was off to Germany. COUM were taking part in Stadtfest, Rottweil's city festival. Over a hundred artists, including Robin Klassnik, Robin Crozier, Pauline Smith and Bridget Riley, had been invited to design and supply a flag to be hung throughout the city. I'd sourced the plastic from a tarpaulin supplier and took the bus across London early one morning – with a frustrating detour as I realised I'd got the wrong bus and was going in the opposite direction. I lugged the plastic all the way back to the studio and then me and Gen cut out the three pieces that made up the design. The flag was red with the COUM sunburst symbol in fluorescent orange within a large white egg shape. I tried in vain to sew them together and asked Bruce if he had any ideas that would help us out. He came to the rescue with some special plastic glue, which I tested on a few scraps and left overnight in case any nasty melty reaction happened. The flag was completed over the next week and shipped out to Germany ahead of our arrival. We took the ferry from Harwich to Holland then travelled by train to Stuttgart, arriving at 4 a.m. and then boarding the 6 a.m. train to Rottweil, finally reaching our destination at 8.30 p.m. The journey was quite an experience.

We performed on the streets of Rottweil each of the next two days. Getting such a positive response to our actions from Bridget, Ernst Jandl and Erich Hauser seemed to validate our artistic status and reputation, which helped us considerably in our pursuit of arts funding to support our work. Also, being in the mix with people so well connected with the tangled web that was the London art scene was an unforeseen advantage and led to invitations to participate in the 9th Paris Biennale and later to represent Britain in Milan for the 'Arte Inglese Oggi 1960–76' exhibition. Our unconventional actions were straddling both the fringe and fine art.

31 October 1974
Finally got to Bridget Riley's at about 11 o'clock. Still she got both
of us a glass of scotch and brought Robert over. She said she'd
have us to dinner soon.

Me and Gen arrived late to Bridget's party, having come straight from dropping off our gear after doing 'Birth of Liquid Desires' at Goldsmiths. We walked up the steps to the front door of her large Georgian terraced house. We knew we'd got the right address when we saw a very shiny brass plate stating simply RILEY. Such perfection and class.

The party was in full swing when we got there. Bridget came straight over and gave us a glass of Scotch each and introduced us to her other guests. Some were by now pretty sloshed and I wove my way through everyone, avoiding the slurry-speeched, droopy-eyed ones as best I could, just looking around me in awe at the art on the walls and then ecstatic when Bridget showed us some of her works in progress. Small-scale sketches of future Rileys, showing a variety of colour sequences and shapes awaiting precision application to their final large format. I loved these as much as the finished works. At the unrealised stage, drawn by Bridget, they held her charge, infused with a potency that screamed out the wonder and magic of the creative process.

The cumulative effect of our diverse activities, collaborations, friends and contacts in the art, literary, theatre and sex-magazine worlds made 1974 and 1975 the years that everything started to come together as the processes of progressive transmutations began. Feeding off creative and personal experiences, aspects of the turbulent melting pot of what was my life informed and affected my perspective on life and my art. The coalescing of life and art at such intensity allowed the flow of new works and projects to seemingly form quite effortlessly. I was receptive to new challenges, whether instigated by myself or by unexpected events. I wanted to take things further, step outside my comfort zone, even if the mere thought of prospective ideas made me want to run for the hills. Breaking through barriers in my pursuit of self-discovery was a heavy burden at times – more so when Gen tried to push me. I didn't need to be pushed: it wasn't about someone else's idea of what I should or shouldn't be or do. I wasn't doing it solely for art, or for feminist ideals, or for Gen. I didn't think of my work as acts of transgression. They were a means to an end and gave me an overwhelming sense of freedom, *self*-achievement, confidence, strength and belief in my*self*.

5 January 1975
What a day! Gen had a terrible flare up. He smashed one of the dinner plates and then grabbed one of his drawings from the wall. When I tried to take it from him, he smashed it over his knee. I held him and we were both shouting. Me saying 'That's it, that's enough' and him saying 'No it isn't'. I started it by going on about him not turning off the kettle when it boiled . . .

Domestic life continued to have its regular ups and downs and I carried on shouldering the responsibility for Gen's tantrums. It was easier than having things escalate by making him face how unacceptable his behaviour was. Either way, leaving a kettle to boil dry is never a good thing and calming things down was, seeing as it was the night before we were due to model for Hipgnosis, a company Sleazy worked for that designed album covers for musicians like Pink Floyd, Peter Gabriel and Paul McCartney.

We'd been asked to model for the new UFO *Force It* album cover they were doing. Sleazy was late, a trait that we became very familiar with, eventually building in an allowance by telling him to arrive an hour before anyone else. That ensured he'd arrive more or less on time. We all took a taxi to Aubrey Powell (aka Po)'s house to wait while the set was prepared in the bathroom of a house in Fulham. The shoot didn't start until after 5 p.m., and the house was being renovated so there was no heating. Posing half-naked in a shower meant we were turning blotchy and we shivered with cold between dowsings of warm water for a faux shower effect. Sleazy loved every minute of it in his role of photographer's assistant, and I was used to modelling. But Gen wasn't familiar with being in that situation and took a while to relax and take directions. It dragged on longer than necessary, then at the end, and to everyone's amusement but mine and Gen's, we got showered with cold water. At least the £30 fee paid the phone bill.

Through David Mayor and his work in publishing we got to know a literary crowd, including the poet Allen Fisher, who visited us often and knew the editor of *Art and Artists* magazine, Colin Naylor – or Collette, as we called him. He became a great friend and we got into a routine of going to eat his fabulous tasty spaghetti at his flat in Clapham any Saturday we were free. 'Spaghetti Junction' visits led to us meeting other artists, art critics and *Studio International* guest editor and art historian Barbara Reise, who we also started regular meal meet-ups with. Barbara was full-on; she could be ultra-nice, bloody-minded and argumentative, and was often depressed, but I was quite fond of her. She'd sometimes join us at Collette's spaghetti evenings and conversations would get feisty. Collette was commissioned to do a book on contemporary artists for St James Press and asked Gen if he wanted a job helping to compile and edit all the information. It was a mammoth task that took more than a year and included 1,350 artists. Gen had never had a job and the reality of working each day at set times was a huge step for him. He decided to take it on. It was a prestigious project and paid well, giving him a regular income. But he wasn't happy about it. The first thing he typed on the office typewriter on his first day was a letter to me intimating that working was akin to death: 'In celebration of death this is my first daze work and it is 3rd February 1975 . . .'

Our routine changed. I'd wake him each morning and make him breakfast before starting my day. Him working nine till five doubled my workload, as he wasn't around to do anything. In addition to the everyday chores and sewing damn boxer shorts, I took on more of the grant and bookings correspondence and travel arrangements, phone calls and meetings, repairing and maintaining Doris, as well as organising any modelling jobs that came through. I was constantly knackered and ill but more worried about Gen getting tired and overdoing things, as he'd go to the studio in the evenings to catch up on stuff. As the letter-writing to artists for the book increased, I was called on to relieve some of the strain. I squeezed it in between everything else. I'd thought St James would do Gen good but Collette's constant cigarette-smoking in the small office space was bad for Gen's asthma, but more than that Gen resented the job taking time away from his own work. When the book was published in 1977, Gen had an entry under his own name, with a half-page photograph of me and him doing our 1976 COUM action in Milan. Neither COUM nor myself were listed in the book.

The 'Orange and Blue' had expanded to include a large dual-coloured floor made from sheets of chipboard I'd bought and painted. It also became an audiovisual piece, with our actions amplified through contact mics, creating its own soundtrack. It was the most complete the work had been – and the last time we performed it. It was put into storage and the floorboards eventually used to repair the studio floor when more of it collapsed.

Gen's job also meant I started to do COUM actions without him. Me and Fizzy went to Gross-Gerau in Germany and had a great time staying in a converted water tower with a lovely family and being treated so well. We did three days of actions in the street, the first being stopped by the police and the remaining ones moved from the main thoroughfare to a small square – and away from any children (by police order). There was too much blood and chains involved. The TV filmed our action and interviewed me, and on the final day of the festival all those involved had a last-night party. Me and Fizzy got through a bottle of Polish vodka supplied by Mishoo, a Polish artist and a bit of a Casanova.

The action in Gross-Gerau prompted a recommendation and secured COUM's participation in Kieline Spieline in Kiel, Germany, where me and Gen once again met up with Mishoo and his partner, Ewa (Zajac). This time Mishoo succeeded in seducing me when Ewa told him to escort me to my hotel room after I'd thrown up and nearly fainted from sunstroke during our action. Hardly romantic. I didn't know Ewa was his wife. (They were the parents of the little girl, Kama, who would later appear on TG's *D.o.A.* album cover.) Gen was furious with me for having sex with Mishoo. A guy gave us a print of a photo of us performing the previous day and Gen said I couldn't have it, I didn't deserve it – what I'd done was to him the end of an era between us.

Gen got drunk, I continued to throw up for the rest of the day and night and was unable to make sense of Gen's reaction, especially as just weeks before he'd told me to make myself scarce for when he brought home a married work colleague to have sex with. I felt terrible about Ewa and apologised when I saw her.

6 February 1975
Peter Christopherson came round. Very willing to take part in COUM anything. May COUM to Holland too and be a guest star. But his professional casualty thing is coming on very well. We were saying how it'd be good in shows.

Since we first met at the Oval House, Sleazy had visited us when he felt like it, gradually getting more interested in the idea of joining us in our activities. He became a member of COUM and joined us for the first time when we did a version of 'The COUMing of Age', retitled as 'The COUMing of Youth', at the Melkweg in Amsterdam. Being a sexually liberated place, Amsterdam seemed a great opportunity to indulge ourselves and we took the brakes off . . . Sleazy was a seditious influence. The three of us together made for a volatile mix, encouraging each other to indulge in our sexual interests and explorations and putting them centre stage in Amsterdam. We used some of Charles Manson's music for the show, not least because we were performing at the Melkweg – the same name as his band, Milky Way.

To start proceedings, Foxtrot walked on to the stage looking menacing in his SS leather coat and hat, his riding boots and sunglasses, wielding a blowtorch which he used to light the torches on the stage. He and I had a scene together, both dressed identically as homosexual soldiers, kissing and groping. Gen had wanted me to give Foxtrot a blow job but I refused. Biggles was on a table being massaged by Fizzy in his 'Shirley Shassey' dress, who offered Biggles the 'extra' service, turned to the audience, smiling, and proceeded to oil and massage Biggles' bits – rather too vigorously for comfort, judging by Biggles' face. Sleazy chose to perform a type of confessional. He was positioned to one side of the stage, fully dressed, seated alone on a chair, softly lit, reading aloud his public-schoolboy sexual fantasies from handwritten notes. I had a much more full-on time. I strode on stage dominatrix-style, in high heels and naked save for a strap costume that didn't cover much. I'd made it from strips of black PVC and gold buckles I'd found in a bin outside a handbag factory near Martello Street. I felt the part as I stood watching a naked Gen being chained and tied to a large wooden X-shaped cross that was placed centre stage, where he would await my treatment. I daubed him in flour paste and chicken's feet and whipped him hard. He pissed on my legs, I inserted a lit candle in my vagina, cracked the whip and left the stage. Gen had told me to whip him properly – it had to be real. I liked the idea of that, something new for me, and I'd practised and mastered cracking my bullwhip. I don't think he'd really thought about what being whipped meant in terms of pain, nor that that I'd actually do it, but I really got into it and Fizzy was itching to have a go too. I had to hold back a bit the second night because of the welts that I'd inflicted.

We'd performed to 1,500 people each night for £240 and free accommodation – of a kind. We were put up in an old, derelict, damp and filthy squat, cooking on a small camping stove. Being March, it was freezing cold. As an attempt at providing privacy for the different performing groups, areas had been sectioned off by dirty sheets of cloth strung on thin wire. With everyone coming and going at different times, no one got much sleep. It was a depressing place so we spent a lot of our downtime wandering around the red-light district and looking at the girls in their windows displaying their wares to attract business. It was relevant to our show as well as personally fascinating, and there was talk about us having our own window as an action piece, as well as other possible indulgences that

Foxtrot remembers: 'We used to walk past a beautiful mulatto girl in her window every day and Gen wanted us all to club together to pay for me to have a session with her. He mentioned it regularly. At that time I was a little wary and also had suspicions of how he might use it.' Like Gen's suggestion of my blow job with Greg, it never happened.

We'd had little sleep but felt elated at what we'd done. Fizzy was excited as he'd 'come out'. He and Sleazy had been together the whole trip. Whipping Gen crucified on the cross worked so well that we restaged it in Martello Street for a new COUM poster image. Sleazy borrowed a large-format Mamiya camera from Hipgnosis and did some photographs with Gen drunk, cuffed and chained to the cross, covered in fake vomit and feathers, and me in the foreground in my strap costume clutching my trusty whip and adopting a strident, assertive stance. Me and Sleazy loved it but Gen wasn't too keen. It was printed up as a large-format poster, a bold, powerful, black-and-white image that reflected a shift in the dynamics of my and Gen's personal and working relationship. For the first time I was portrayed in the dominant position.

6 March 1975
Today I made my very first blue movie. 'Pussy's Galore'.

The COUM shows were a hybrid of art and music, with an increasing emphasis on more extreme and obscure actions. Things were changing, including the Ragdoll agency, which had now been taken over by none other than Nanny Rigby, who called me about going in to talk over what work she could offer me. She'd always been discreet about blue movie work and I was asked if I'd be interested in doing some hard-core films with a few of the main players – John Lindsay, George Harrison Marks and a middleman called Alan Selwyn.

I told Gen. It excited him, it paid well and he was all for it. I thought some more and decided to go ahead; for me it was part of my infiltrating the sex industry. I was about to find out how tough a task it was and how much I was asking of myself.

Nanny sent me on auditions and I got a lot of work, including lesbian and group-sex shoots. It's not easy getting naked with people you've never met before, let alone having sex with them in front of a camera crew and lighting technicians, but I adjusted to it, facing each challenge that presented itself. I dealt with it by looking at it as a 'job', disengaging from emotion, focusing on the required techniques, giving head or whatever was required, while also placing myself to give the best angles for the camera, learning how to 'fluff' to help guys get up and stay up, and to hold off for the come shot. It was pretty clinical and that's how I approached it to help me cope.

I was certainly no actress – I was embarrassingly bad at that – but I performed the sex well enough. There was no pleasure, love or desire involved; it was simply job-descriptive sex – that in itself was a revelation to me. Most girls I worked with held back on something, set boundaries to retain a part of themselves as sacred, only to be shared with those they loved. The sex part was something I had to manage as I went along but what unnerved and challenged me more was the risk of the unknown. I'd already been questioned by a detective about the recent Bunny Girl murder case – did I know any photographers that had tried it on? Where would I begin? Hardcore pornography was underground in the 1970s, simply because, under the obscenity laws, it was illegal to make and distribute it in the UK. John Lindsay, who I did my first blue film for, was harassed by the police and had his shops and cinemas raided. I wondered what risks I could be exposing myself to.

When things go underground to avoid the law, the normal rules can get bent out of shape to suit the purposes at hand. There were some very tricky moments when I felt unsafe and couldn't wait to get away. No matter what I'd agreed to beforehand, there were often extras added on once I got there, some in the form of favours for friends of the photographer or magazine editor who wanted an exciting time with a naked girl and hoped for more. Those people were hard work. They didn't know how to model, for one thing, and some thought they'd get free sex. One guy was particularly bad. His flat was the location. I immediately got the impression he was expecting sex and he was persistently groping and trying to put his fingers and cock inside me. The photographer apologised but I felt set up, and the attempts to coerce me were relentless and intimidating. The male 'model' made us all coffee, asking, 'Does "that" want a cup too?' 'That' was me. I just wanted to get out of there. In the end I mentioned the magazine editor's name, saying it's not what he said I was booked for, and that I'd walk off the job if the guy didn't stop. He got aggressive and nasty, calling me a slag and more.

That session was later published with the heading 'Prick Tease Tormentor and Keith the Randy Tycoon' . . . I was presumably the 'prick teaser' indicated in the title and the accompanying text. That was the reader's fantasy delivered as per usual. The reality of providing that fantasy was my torment from the full-on sexual harassment of the 'Randy Tycoon'.

Pornography in the 1970s was a closed shop run by a small circle of people, including some dodgy chancers. I made the mistake of choosing the wrong people a couple of times before I figured out who were the safer ones to work for. By and large, the films were made using professional cameramen, lighting technicians, TV and film producers and actors, make-up artists and (rarely) a wardrobe lady. The main players all worked with a small group of trusted and reliably capable people who did hard-core work. I became part of that group. We looked after one another. We knew our boundaries and would modify requests if they involved anything that made someone uncomfortable – something as simple as one girl preferring to take the lead in a lesbian shoot. I took on the challenge of new experiences. Some I found I liked, others I didn't and I chose not to repeat them. The models I worked with didn't know the reason behind my doing modelling and porn. They did it for various reasons – some for the money, whether through necessity or in preference to lesser-paid straight jobs, some stumbled into it through friends, and some just for the sex. Those who only did it once or twice and were inhibited by shyness or nerves were difficult to work with and needed careful handling. Working with familiar faces made life much easier. We knew our job, were efficient and had some fun. A lot of the soft-core films also had a hard-core version for the export market. I did both and body-doubled for actresses who didn't want to be naked on camera.

Relinquishing control of my image and identity was an important part of the project, and that intrigued me as much as the experience of the process of co-creating those images. Whether I was 'Tessa from Sunderland', 'Slippery Milly from Piccadilly', 'Geraldine', 'Susie' or 'Cosey', I was just like the other girls, sexual fantasy material for masturbation. Anything too close to (my) reality would dispel that illusion. As a willing participant I'd placed myself in a position to be used this way, and right in the line of fire of 1970s feminism. The sexual exploitation and objectification of women by men was the feminist hot topic, very high on their agenda, and I and other sex workers were perceived as the enemy. I didn't identify with 1970s feminism: it didn't speak for me or the diverse and complex nature of women. I was a free spirit and didn't want yet more rules and guilt thrown at me about my actions. Yes, by doing my sex work I was contributing to, but not necessarily endorsing, the thing they were fighting against. But I was no 'victim' of exploitation. I was exploiting the sex industry for my own purposes, to subvert and use it to create my own art. It was my choice. I wanted to get to know the sex industry from within, to speak from first-hand experience. I wanted a purity in my work, to push against existing expectations and my own inhibitions, and to understand all the complex nuances and trials it imposed on everyone in that business, including the target market. I was transgressing rules – feminist ones included. I live my life as a 'person', seeing all options as being equally open to me and everyone else. I refuse to be defined or confined by my gender.

Most of the films I did were typical of the 1970s porn set-up: orgies, frustrated housewives, or plumber knocks on the door – 'I've come to fix your pipes, darlin' . . .' But the film I did for Lasse Braun (who was introduced to me as Alberto Ferro) was different. The basic premise was familiar: a party scene turning into an orgy. We all turned up at the location early in the morning, a large four-storey terraced house in West London. There were at least twenty of us, a real mixture for possibly every variation of sex Lasse could think of. We were gathered in the back room waiting to be assigned roles and sorting out costumes. I was given skintight pale-pink satin trousers, a matching feather boa and a pink leotard worn back to front to expose my boobs. There were three familiar faces, Tim, John and Lotus, and the rest were all new to me, including a vivacious girl called Bobby, who was dressed in a satin corset, fishnet stockings and high heels, doffing her top hat at everyone. She and her biker boyfriend were an odd combination but great fun. The other cast members were reserved in comparison to Bobby and a pretty, petite, blonde transsexual called Daisy, who was undergoing hormone therapy in preparation for her sex-change operation, and doing the film to fund it. She was a constant delight, dressed in pretty white satin lingerie, dancing and gyrating around the place, rubbing herself flirtatiously against people and singing Donna Summer's 'Aaah, love to love you, baby . . .', panting, pouting and looking alluringly at people. A young guy in very brief, tight, black PVC swimming trunks was wandering around striking poses like he was the greatest hunk in the world, giving all the girls the come-on and looking like Elvis. He and Daisy were put together for a scene. Him buggering Daisy was a sad sight, and I really felt for Daisy. Neither of them wanted to do it and Daisy was self-conscious about her small, atrophying penis, which was cruelly made the main focus, to drive home that she was transsexual. While the camera filmed them others were getting it on all around the room. It was unusual to have so much sex action going on at the same time, and with only one camera it meant that whoever was in the background had to do it all over again.

But Lasse had chosen his cast well: they were reliable guys who could deliver on demand. I and another girl, Janine, were to go with 'Big John'. He was laid on the sofa and we were told to take it in turns to climb aboard for the ride – until he proudly revealed the largest cock I've ever seen. They say 'as big as a baby's arm' – and it was, and very ugly too, all veiny and lumpy. Me and Janine recoiled. We had to reshoot. There was no way either of us was going to sit on that thing. As chance would have it, there were some who were so in awe of the massive cock that we were able to arrange an alternative plan that wouldn't involve being impaled and possibly torn. We did a lesbian scene instead.

The whole day was chaotic. With so many people, it was verging on unmanageable. The extras were dancing (badly) to disco music, with couples and threesomes groping each other and screwing in the front room, the hallway and on the stairs. The chaos went up a gear into near hysteria when the police arrived and raided the place. We hadn't been told that they were actors, so everyone panicked at first, but it got a genuine response from us. The police, looking like something from *The Sweeney*, bundled everyone into a van that drove off as if to take us to the police station. By then we were all giggling at the ridiculousness of the day. Cameras stopped rolling and we were driven back to the house to get paid.

That's when Lasse told us his briefcase with all the money in had been stolen. One guy was missing and assumed to be the culprit, but there was no way the real police could be called in to investigate. I don't know how, but it got resolved and everyone was paid, and Royston, one of the 'extra' guys, drove me home at 5.30 a.m. I was so tired I was hallucinating and slurring my speech, but had to go to another job for the *Sun*. I hadn't slept for thirty-six hours.

8 July 1975
I fell asleep and got woken by Selwyn trying to shag me. I told him no. Sat and read 'Diary of a Drug Fiend'.

My day started at 5 a.m. so I could get to Twickenham Studios on time for filming *Custer's Thirteen*. I arrived exhausted, not least because Gen had kept me awake talking till 3 a.m. Once in the dressing room, I fell fast asleep – and prey to Selwyn's unwanted attentions. He soon got off me when I told him I'd started my period.

Guys trying it on was commonplace. Because you did porn they thought you'd fuck anyone – and some girls did, as a token payment for getting more work.

I didn't do my scene until 6.30 p.m. Waiting around on set was boring and infuriating when I had so much else to do. I was Custer's 'thirteenth' girl, dressed as a gasman in a long black coat, with a hat and stuck-on moustache. I looked like Blakey from the sitcom *On the Buses*. I accosted Custer in the gas cupboard on the pretence of reading his gas meter. I had a few lines but I was rubbish at it and my Yorkshire accent was still quite strong. It just didn't work so I did it 'mute' and they got what they wanted.

When I got home, Gen wasn't there – he'd gone off to have sex with his workmate Pat again. I waited up as long as I could but I needed sleep to look half-decent for the rest of the film scenes over the coming week. I took Crowley books with me to fill the hours between calls to set, where I was doing a short dream sequence of me dancing on an office desk . . . Very *Tales of the Unexpected*. Then reshooting the gas-cupboard scene.

I was back at Twickenham Studios within a few weeks, working on a straight film in a bar-room fight scene with another girl, having beer poured over us before I smashed toffee-glass beer bottles over Graham Stark's head. It was all very *Carry On* but great fun working with Mary Millington, Tim (again), Rita Webb from *The Benny Hill Show* and, surprisingly, James Booth from the film *Zulu*.

26 April 1975
Gen had a freak out early tonight and pushed me into the water heater. I hurt my knee and he tried to kick the telly in . . . I have a couple of big bruises . . . but what worries me more is that my arm really hurts bad.

Working at St James Press was continuing to stress Gen out and I found myself on the receiving end of one of his violent outbursts. Bruises weren't a good thing, full stop, but any mark on me also meant I couldn't model. There was no Photoshop then and only the high-end magazines like *Playboy* used airbrushing.

I put off any job offers and prioritised COUM, spending hours in the library researching towns for the 'Tree of Life' tour (which never happened), working out ideas and making the main prop for the AMP action, a long, ritualistic-looking, five-foot-long wooden pole studded with five-inch sharp nails, feathers and with a black dildo at each end. The action took place with me naked but for a leather studded G-string I'd made and a black strap-on dildo, and Gen in black trousers and a black eyepatch. As the action came to an end, we picked up one end of the stick each and inserted the dildos – me into my vagina and Gen into his anus. The room was very quiet. No one seemed to want to comment, and Tom, who was supposed to document it, didn't take a single photograph. Not sure if he was put off by the mechanics of having to zoom in to focus on our intimate penetrations. Still, our friends Collette and Alan Fisher enjoyed it and someone else took some photos.

We didn't take any chances at missing out on better documenting our next action, 'Studio of Lust', at Nuffield Gallery in Southampton. We had Sleazy put his camera on a tripod and set it to automatically take photos every two minutes throughout our one-hour piece. Just me, Gen and Sleazy in separate corners of the room, each working with our objects and bodies. There was blood, cutting, urination, masturbation and oral sex as we slowly joined one another to interact in creating various forms from our entangled naked bodies. It was a challenge for Sleazy, having not been with a naked woman before, and I positioned myself carefully when I sensed his hesitation as he came to lie beside me.

Me and Sleazy would meet up quite often when Gen was at work, sorting out photos and talking through ideas together, including the COUM invitation to participate in the prestigious 9th Paris Biennale. Its own stance on championing non-standard practices in art fitted us well and we were chosen to represent Britain with the support of the British Council. We were going up in the art world and in good company with Bill Viola, Marina Abramović, Urs Lüthi, Gina Pane, Lynda Benglis, John Stezaker, Orlan, and more.

Preparations for the Biennale had been ongoing, with my making numerous trips to the British Council offices to sort out travel and other official paperwork, organising the construction of objects and arranging their shipment. Sleazy had some great contacts through Hipgnosis and put me in touch with Design Animation, who were able to make a Perspex box for our Paris action. I got the box done to spec for just £35 and had that and the other objects crated and collected for shipping.

The box worked well and stood to one side in the space we'd been given for our action. The idea was to have a large, clear Perspex cube with air holes in the top and a large closable tube on one side as an access point. Within the box would be my soiled tampons, pieces of red meat and maggots. My tampons were in varying shades of red, from heavily to hardly soiled – the bloody menstrual cycle made visible – life's blood, my period pain, my fertility, my tampons. The live maggots would feed off the meat and hatch into flies, audibly buzzing with life and flying around in the confines of the box. A living sculpture. The work, 'Jusqu'à la Balle Crystal', was as much about the cycle of life as the aesthetic, and I'd had to collect my used, bloodied tampons for a while. Tremble took to eating them if she got the chance, so I had to store them out of her reach to save her from damaging herself – and me from having to pull the string to extract them when they came out the other end. That had proved embarrassing a few times when she did her toilet in the park.

On the walls of the space we'd been allocated were small glass-fronted mouse cages containing Sleazy's black-and-white casualty photos of young men. These were slowly eaten away as the mice used them as nesting material. We fed and watered the mice each day but when we arrived the morning of our final action they'd gone, escaped – or been released into the museum somewhere.

The Perspex box and the remnants from our actions stayed as an exhibit, as documentation of our live actions.

My trip to Paris coincided with a new passport in the name of 'Cosey P-Orridge'. I'd changed my name by deed poll. Still single – Gen, if asked, would refer to me as his sister.

I'd crocheted Gen a multicoloured suit for him to wear in Paris. I wore a silver lurex Mary Quant top and matching tights and a satin miniskirt. We were wined and dined at the British Council and cocktail parties, and approached by various magazines, including *Time Life*, who came to photograph our second action. We had our own photographer, Barbara Reise, who with her friend Alan Harrison documented everything for us.

All that was pushed to one side when we met up with our artist friend Gary Glaser, who we'd met in Kiel. He lived in Paris and wanted to show us around. Gary took us to a small theatre called Raymond Duncan's Academy. Raymond had been Isadora Duncan's brother and their mutual advocacy of spirit of freedom of expression in all the arts was still very much present in the theatre and in the Greek-influenced decor. Each Saturday between 7 and 8.30 p.m. it was open house for people to take the stage and do what they wanted. The atmosphere was incredible, the smell unique; it was timeless.

On our return from Paris, David Mayor invited us for a weekend stay at his stepmother's farmhouse, which stood in so many acres of land we walked for hours. I made the most of the unusual setting and did some semi-nude photos for my first model 'Z card'. Sleazy developed and did prints for me and I took them to Walker Prints, the go-to printer for model cards. I now had a model card and a classy-looking portfolio case. I just needed to fill it. I'd been collecting some prints as I'd been going along from the more generous photographers I worked with. My ideas for the card were a little too focused on art, not enough on the glamour market. I credited the photos to COUM Transmissions. I was a bit naive to even think of using a known photographer's name to garner interest. No one knew who COUM were – not that it mattered. It was an art project, after all, and COUM Transmissions acted as 'sign'.

13 November 1975
Mary's given me her boyfriend's telephone number as he runs 'Whitehouse' and 'Park Lane'.

An obstacle me and other models had to navigate was the 'casting couch', which was very much in practice for securing some modelling and film work. I went to most auditions assuming I'd have to carefully negotiate NOT having sex to get the job – any I did have off camera with photographers was my choice.

I'd worked a lot for Michel, who was with Tabor Publications, a small but prolific mid-market sex-magazine publisher, and we built up a good friendship. He had a different vibe from the other photographers. He was French, about forty, on his third marriage and had led an interesting life as a mercenary before doing photography. Michel and I became lovers – something Gen had encouraged (much to my pleasure, not that Gen knew).

I'd meet Michel outside Notting Hill Gate Tube station, where he'd pick me up either on his Harley-Davidson motorbike or in his bright-orange, two-seater, three-wheel Reliant Bond Bug car. It roared like an aircraft. I was shit-scared it was going to take off if the wind got under it. We'd go to his flat for afternoon nooky and just to be together and talk about the deeper things in life. He'd studied magic for over twenty-two years and had an enviable collection of books on the subject and other philosophical works, and the walls of his flat were covered in his drawings and paintings. I liked him – he made me feel safe and taught me so much about sex, not least his focusing on my pleasure, placing it before his own, taking his time and giving me my first unassisted orgasm.

He gave me copies of the Tabor magazines I'd been in and some prints of my favourite shots. I did a job for him with Mary Millington, who he'd used numerous times, and she put me in contact with her boyfriend, David Sullivan, to get more work. Mary was featured throughout David's magazines and had a large following of admirers. She was a pretty blonde, perfectly formed and petite, and always happy. Michel wasn't pleased to hear our conversation as Sullivan was a competitor who ended up taking a large chunk of the market.

But I took up Mary's offer and rang David, who called back about my audition and arranged for a taxi to take me to and from his place. We got on well and talked for hours. I passed the audition and was photographed in a blonde wig two days later for *Park Lane*. David also published the soft-pornography magazines *Playbirds* and *Whitehouse*. I always thought of the latter title as a direct and ironic reference to Mary Whitehouse, the zealous anti-obscenity and anti-pornography campaigner. I admired David's spirit and ambition and I respected his honest approach to the business he was in. It was a rare thing in the sex industry at that time. More than that, he was an anti-censorship and a sexual-freedom campaigner, and as such an adversary of Mary Whitehouse. He was shrewd in using his magazines to further his campaign, placing straplines like 'Genuine Pornography' and 'Fully Uncensored Pictures', which helped boost sales. He wasn't afraid of sticking his neck out, and in one of his *Whitehouse* magazines (in which I appeared as 'Susie'), instead of the usual open-crotch centre spread he published a text on his opposition to the censorship of pornography, posing the question 'Which is the real pornography? THIS? or THIS?' – violent atrocities shown on TV to all ages or sexual images for adults. It was illustrated by a sex photo on one page and a bloody Cambodian war casualty on the other.

17 January 1976
Awakened by a sergeant wanting to deliver a summons to Gen.
He managed it and I photographed it and then he fucking took
it away again! The court appearance is for February 23rd. We are
contesting it.

Mail art had started as an exciting exchange of personal gifts of art and defiance against the preciousness of art, but as it grew that original spirit got lost. Theme-based mail art exhibitions started springing up, specifically to be shown in galleries. Mail art was a victim of its own success. The art world wanted it – it had become precious. With that shift in motivation came a decline in quality. I started getting more and more instant-printed impersonal dross in reply to my handmade collages and objects, and I eventually bowed out of the mail art scene except for a few special people. What also contributed to my parting company was Gen being prosecuted and found guilty of disseminating pornographic material through the mail, relating in part to his postcards depicting the Queen collaged with cut-ups from porn magazines. They weren't new – I'd done one in my diary back in 1973. Difference being, Gen posted his. The trial had turned into another work, 'G.P.O. v G.P-O', which was carefully documented throughout.

When the trial finally took place on 4 April there was huge support, not least from William Burroughs, Bridget Riley, mail artists, the British Council and the Arts Council – to no avail. The seriousness of the situation was driven home when Gen was told he might get a jail sentence or a large fine. He got very scared and we sought proper legal representation. How odd that my pornographic activities were taking place simultaneously to him being prosecuted for one of the main reasons I'd begun my modelling project – collaging (my own) nude images from sex magazines on to postcards – and that my fees for modelling would help towards some of the costs involved in the trial.

Ted Little, the then Director of the Institute of Contemporary Arts (ICA), offered us two shows, one on mail art and one on COUM. I'd spent three days printing photos of our actions so he could see what was available for exhibiting. They would meet costs within reason and pay a fee of £150–200 for the performance/exhibition – which evolved into 'Prostitution'. That same week we attended a British Council meeting to be told that, on the strength of the work in Paris, COUM had been selected to represent Britain in 'Arte Inglese Oggi 1960–76' in Milan. The exhibition was a mix of established and up-and-coming British artists, including Jeff Nuttall, Bridget Riley, Allen Jones, David Hockney, Peter Blake, Gilbert & George, and Mark Boyle. As many artists as possible were assembled in Trafalgar Square for a group photo for the catalogue, for which me and Sleazy also printed up the COUM photographs and me and Gen each wrote statements and a description of the work 'Towards the Crystal Bowl'.

The action took place over two days in the Galleria Vittorio Emanuele II arcade, where we had a square structure built in the form of a very large maze of scaffolding above a vast square vat surrounded by a ring of polystyrene granules. The vat was originally meant to be filled with milk for me to swim in, but there was a milk shortage and an alternative was sought – the trusty old polystyrene granules. It was a good choice as it kept me warm once submerged but it also shot up my nose if I wasn't careful when holding my breath. It was a silent balletic piece, me in matching silver lurex top and tights, and silver ballet shoes, slowly climbing down from the top of the scaffolding and striking elegant poses before descending into the bowl of granules to use its vast whiteness as a canvas on which to create abstract forms by exposing parts of my body, while

Gen photographed them from the scaffolding above. Dressed all in black, he had emerged from a shower of chains at the side of the structure to climb to the top, sometimes suspending himself by chains attached to the frame. It was a huge success: the people loved it and watched in quiet fascination, someone shouting 'Bravo!' at the end.

The next day there was a crowd waiting for us. After the official exhibition opening, various meals with the British contingent and gallery people, and another action I performed at the Galleria Borgogna, we flew back to London to a warm welcome from Sleazy, who was super-excited about just being made a partner in Hipgnosis.

~

I'd been going to Hipgnosis when Sleazy had free time and he'd shown me the basics of the developing and printing process in their darkroom – just a small sectioned-off area in the corner of their office with a blackout curtain and heavy with the smells of developer and fixer. He'd helped me set up my own darkroom at Beck Road in what was a small downstairs kitchen at the back of the house. It had the requisite water supply and sink – it was just right. He helped me get all the necessary equipment as and when I could afford it and I painted the room, made blackout curtains and sorted out wood to use as a workbench.

Having the darkroom had brought Chris (Carter) directly into my life. I'd taken photos for the multimedia Vacuum show that he and John had worked on together. John and Chris needed prints doing and came to use my new darkroom. Chris had been working at a photographic studio in Soho, so he knew the ropes already. I remember the day clearly. I was sat on the sofa in the upstairs living room close to the kitchen doorway. John and Chris walked through to the kitchen to talk to Gen about showing them the darkroom. Chris stopped short outside the doorway and right in front of me, just a foot away from my face. My eyes were on a level with his slim hips, clad in very tight denim jeans that enhanced every contour of his crotch and firm, pert buttocks. As my eyes moved up from his narrow twenty-six-inch waist to his broad shoulders, he turned to go downstairs to the darkroom. 'I'll show you,' I said, taking the chance to be in such a confined space with him.

It was the first time he'd been to Beck Road. We sat and chatted and he asked to hear our music, then invited us to his flat in Crouch End, where he lived with his (now) wife, Simone. We made frequent visits to each other's places and much talk of collaborating musically eventually turned into reality, with Chris bringing his synthesiser and other equipment to Martello Street to jam together and experiment.

~

Throbbing Gristle took some years to finally arrive, and in a workable format. The line-up and sound had gone through many guises, including, as John remembers, Gen's proposal that John's group Vacuum become 'VaCOUM' – a would-be Throbbing Gristle. As Vacuum involved Chris and he'd become an increasing part of our lives, the music was getting closer to what TG became known for. All the jam sessions and recordings we did were experiments to find something that clicked with us all. Nothing had worked before Chris arrived. Les had decided to stay in Hull, and John left with much regret. He knew, like the rest of us, how difficult it was to find like-minded people to work with, but, as he told me, 'I got out before Gen did another purge – either on me, or witness it on anyone else. I wasn't going to be bullied out by being made to cry inside.' Gen steered the COUM ship and anyone unwilling to fall in line was 'encouraged' to leave by his insidious tactics that undermined their self-esteem, making it unbearable for them to stay. As well as the music and art, John and I had enjoyed meaningful times on our own together; he'd sit with me while I wrote and drew in my diaries or talk with me in my workroom. He came around less and less, and I missed him as a collaborator and friend.

COUM continued for a while but had shifted in intent and personnel, eventually reduced to just me, Gen and sometimes Sleazy. It was no longer about fantasy costumes and frivolity, instead relating to the self and reality, with the actions getting more extreme. As far as the music was concerned, there was me, Chris, Sleazy and Gen, and we all lived in London, which made availability easier than it had been with COUM. Chris wanted nothing to do with COUM and saw TG as an entity in itself, a collective – although he hated the name Throbbing Gristle and would only call it TG or Gristle. TG was four equals, each bringing their unique life experiences, talents and abilities to the melting pot. And we were strong individuals who, once united, formed a solid and unshakeable whole – which had its setbacks.

Chris was staunchly resistant to Gen assuming the position of any kind of leader of TG. He saw TG as being the four of us in mutual collaboration, with decisions made based on a majority vote, not on the appeasement of any one individual. Because Chris was quiet and reserved, Gen made the mistake of assuming he could be easily manipulated. He misread Chris completely. Chris wasn't green, but he also wasn't the type to push himself forward or shout from the rooftops when he did anything of note. Underneath that kind, reserved exterior he was strong-minded, ingenious, very well read, familiar with Ballard, Crowley, Burroughs, Huxley, Manson, etc., and was au fait with magick and many of the references and interests that me, Gen and Sleazy shared. The difference between him, Gen and Sleazy was that (like me) he didn't subscribe to a movement or cult. He was his own person.

We'd set up a regular TG get-together for every weekend (all other commitments allowing) . . . with Sleazy not turning up as often as we all would've liked. Chris's rekindled enthusiasm for music didn't sit well with Simone, and things gradually started to get awkward. As usual, Gen began moves to have group sex. Simone wasn't interested. Chris was happy to come with us for TG sessions and to sleep over, assuming (rightly) there'd be sex. Both Gen's sex-game play and Simone's indifference to Chris backfired. Me and Chris both fancied each other: he was beautiful in body, mind and spirit, and wasn't at all shy. Our making love for the first time ignited such passion and lust between us that neither of us could go back – or wanted to accept anything less than what we felt for each other. It far exceeded anything either of us had experienced before.

We were faced with a dilemma as we were both in relationships and committed to TG. Was it love or lust? It was both, and we decided to keep TG on track and our emotions in check. Well, we tried, but Gen's partiality for watching us have sex just fed our desire for each other and our resistance waned, especially when opportunities arose, usually when Gen went to sleep with other women.

~

Investing £175 in an answerphone so my agency and photographers could contact me had worked out great . . . but I also got other messages. I'd been getting dirty phone calls from a man who called himself Jeff. I figured out that he'd probably got my number from a photographer or someone at Tuppy's launch. His calls didn't freak me out so much as fascinate me. Maybe it was his methods of persuasion to get what he wanted from his illicit wank calls. There were times his calls were inconvenient, but rather than miss out altogether on a good masturbation session he'd politely ask if he could call back when I was less busy.

'Hello, it's Jeff. Is now a good time for you?'

'Err, yeah, OK, but I haven't got long. Make it quick.'

I found it amusing for a while and at times he'd forego the sex chat and we'd have some great conversations on other subjects. I viewed it as another aspect of my sex project and taped some of his calls, until I finally brought a halt to the whole thing and told him never to call me again. I used some of the recordings for TG, along with threats from Simone.

She and Chris were going through a really rough patch and she wasn't happy about Chris being with TG, and particularly being around me. She started leaving non-messages on the answerphone to use up the tape, as well as threatening messages and warnings for me to leave Chris alone. We weren't an item at that point. I caught her call once and she screeched hysterically down the phone, 'I'm going to get you – you're a pervert, a slut, filthy, you've probably given Chris clap and fleas . . .', accusing me of luring Chris into bed and suchlike.

I said, 'Yes, mmmm, oh, hmmm . . .', took the phone away from my ear for a while – I couldn't get a word in – then when I put it back the screeching stopped. 'Hello? Have you finished yelling at me?'

Then she put her mother on, screaming down the phone. I hung up. Then Chris's mum rang me – at least she asked me for my version of the story. I just said it was between Chris and Simone. Chris was really embarrassed about the whole thing and upset because I was so angry at being the target of such venom. He consoled himself by getting immersed in recording and editing David Mayor and

Alan Fisher's cassette magazine, *Revealer*, a kind of audio *Fortean Times*: art, poetry and interviews.

After a month of continual harassment from Simone and trying to make their relationship work, they decided to separate. We and John helped Chris move his belongings into a room at John's mother's new house in Queens Avenue, Muswell Hill.

I thought the Simone troubles were over, but much later TG had gone out one evening to the Pindar of Wakefield pub near King's Cross and were enjoying the entertainment when I got pushed in the back. I turned around to see Simone stood behind me, flanked by two of her friends. Their stance was challenging and intimidating. After her phone threats to attack me, and given that she had previously slashed Chris across the stomach with a shard of broken mirror, I suspected I might have to defend myself.

'You still haven't got over it, then?' I asked.

She went to attack me. I moved swiftly to defend myself. It was her or me. I pulled her down by her long hair, brought my knee up and threw her to the ground. I wasn't going to let her get back up to retaliate. Her friends were motionless with shock. Chris and Gen came and pulled me off her and told her friends to get her out of there.

31 May 1976
Had a go on lead guitar and Chris on synthesiser. Gen played lead . . . I decided to stick with lead and a bit of bass and percussion. Chris wants to be on his synth not mixing. Sleazy may like that anyway.

Sleazy, Chris, me and Gen had all tried out different instruments and ways of generating sounds. Sleazy played Chris's synth but decided he didn't like it and wasn't that interested in TG at the very beginning. He was more into COUM, and his full-time job with Hipgnosis took up most of his time. Being made a partner meant his responsibilities lay with Hipgnosis first – and the money was so good he'd started saving up to buy a flat. His absences caused friction at times because all of us were working too, yet managing to set time aside dedicated to developing TG.

The three of us carried on working together and investing in equipment. I'd bought myself a cheap Raver lead guitar from Woolworths. The way I used it there was no need for anything expensive. I didn't know how, nor did I want to learn how, to play guitar. I never tuned it.

> 6 July 1976
> *And today we had our first ever public performance of*
> *'THROBBING GRISTLE'. It went very well . . . first number*
> *was great, VERY GOOD, then we got lost in the middle but*
> *everyone thought we were tuning up having just changed*
> *instruments.*

Chris's last performance of his audiovisual 'Waveforms' solo show was only three days prior to our very first Throbbing Gristle gig at A.I.R. Gallery in London. We adopted 'TG' pseudonyms for ourselves: Teresa Green (me), Terry Goldstein (Sleazy), Ted Glass (Gen) and Tom Gozz (Chris). Sleazy didn't take part in the first TG gig – he was away working with Hipgnosis. Loading up the gear was difficult as me and Gen had to lug everything ourselves – Chris had had an accident at the Italian furniture shop where he worked. A large glass table had fallen and shattered into pieces, one piece going straight through his shoe, severing a vein and sticking in his foot like a spear. He was rushed to hospital. Having had six stitches and lost a lot of blood, he wasn't feeling too good, especially after he'd worked late into the night at the studio – then he got an electric shock from a wrongly wired extension cable while setting up the gear, which almost threw him across the room (it wouldn't be the first time).

All considering, we had a good time and the gig was well received. Changing instruments, no vocals, not much rhythm to speak of, but loops we'd prepared in the studio, an industrial ambient vibe – and very loud.

We crashed out at Beck Road, talking about what to do next with TG, maybe songs but with an interesting, strong subject matter. The next evening was my solo art action, 'Woman's Roll', back at A.I.R. Gallery. It was very slow, quiet and graceful, focusing on the body and form. Sleazy had taught me some of his casualty make-up techniques. He'd passed the necessary exams and was a fully paid-up member of the Casualties Union in London, so was qualified to take part in the training exercises for industry, hospitals and emergency services. Watching him apply imitation open gashes and stitched wounds had fascinated me and I got him to teach me some of the basics and put together a kit of very convincing fake blood and materials for making skin.

Chris had never seen any COUM actions up to that point and was quite taken aback, telling me the next day that it had affected the way he saw and felt about me . . . which made me wonder what he'd thought before.

The next day me, Chris and Gen went to Walker Prints to collect the first TG poster. There'd been some debate as to whether Walker Prints would take on a job with an image of a Nazi death camp and the slogan 'Music from the Death Factory', but they agreed and it looked fantastic. The slogan referred to our basement Martello Street studio, which was rumoured to be on a level with plague burial pits in London Fields, just opposite to where we produced the dark, uncompromising sound of TG. It was an old factory aligned with death. The image of the death camp was a comment on the inhumanity of building an actual killing factory. The TG sound was to be evocative of the subject matter we chose and we wanted to address the full spectrum of human behaviour. We felt it important not to shy away from grim realities and were mindful of Santayana's saying, 'Those who cannot remember the past are condemned to repeat it.'

Our approach was counter to, and a reaction to, disco and pop music (although Chris loved ABBA), the culture of exclusivity, the tendency to bury past or present atrocities and 'distasteful' crimes, and the political upheaval of the time, which impacted on us daily, with strikes causing chaos, and the ever-present ambient sounds all around our studio – factories at work, saws, machinery, Tube trains, children playing in the park. We were creating the soundtrack to our reality, warts and all. There were no half measures.

7 August 1976
Chris was experimenting with sounds and had the whole of the studio shaking. Sounded frightening but he's going to do it tomorrow for us and maybe we'll do it at Winchester. Probably make the building collapse.

Sleazy had been MIA for months on Hipgnosis business, and then he got back in touch. He still wasn't fully on board with TG but started coming to Hackney again. He was surprised by how much gear we'd amassed, how the studio was changing.

While me and Gen were away visiting his family, Chris had painted the stage area matt black and had brought almost every piece of equipment he owned to the studio. We taped all our sessions on his Tandberg or AKAI reel-to-reel, or Wolfdale cassette machine.

He'd built a mixer, repaired the Norman and Sinclair amps, rebuilt an old COUM bass guitar for Gen, and we now each had an echo unit to put our sound through, me using a Sound Dimension tape echo, Gen a Simms Echo Dek. Chris put Gen's vocals through his Roland Space Echo and his synth through a WEM Copicat tape echo machine. Chris had experimented with sine waves and sub-sonics and we loved the physicality and power – we'd never felt that before with any music. It was awesome and inspiring and set in motion the direction we'd take the sound of TG.

We'd also started on the androgynous military look of TG. I'd bought a very well-worn biker jacket, army trousers and knee-high lace-up boots. Gen followed suit, as did Chris. Sleazy had recon-nected at a good time – everything was more or less in place for him to jump in – but he was uncertain what he could do as he had no gear of his own. We suggested he do the mixing and he could apply his Casualties Union skills.

By the time the Winchester gig came around, we'd each found our places – well, a point from which to start that was adaptable as and when we felt like it. We had our first 'songs', 'We Hate You' and 'Very Friendly' (about Moors murderers Myra Hindley and Ian Brady). Gen with a fake bloodied forehead, me with a large fake bloody gash on my boob applied by Sleazy, and Chris razor-ing his arm for real. Not entirely suitable for the front row of very young children, but they seemed to take it as (horror) theatre, with Gen screeching, 'We hate you!' then adding, 'Little girls', directly addressing them. David Mayor came along to help and offered to be TG roadie for future gigs. We made him a 'Death Factory Worker' T-shirt.

∼

You tell yourself you're used to doing porn, it's not that difficult – until you get bowled a curve ball. For me that was Chris. I'd coped with sex work by removing emotion as best I could, detaching myself from my body. That became impossible after Chris and I got together. My whole body was crying out only for him. I didn't want to give myself to someone else, even if it was transient, meaningless and shallow – it was a part of me that didn't belong there any more.

Once with Chris, I was back in my body, I felt whole. I stopped doing hard-core films. Then Chris asked me not to do a job with Michel and offered me the same fee NOT to go. I still went. It wasn't about the money: my response was the usual kneejerk reaction of refusing to have someone else tell me what to do, and telling myself that if he loved me he'd accept me as I am and for what I choose to do. It wasn't that simple. He wasn't trying to control me, and my being with someone else was hurting him. I'd been thinking of breaking off my affair with Michel for a while, as he'd been getting demanding and a bit possessive, talking of my being 'unfaithful' to him by going with Chris. I guess Chris was right to be worried.

I broke off the affair with Michel, which pleased Gen because, even though he had his own lovers, he had been getting increasingly antagonistic towards Michel. Me and Chris had tried to keep our feelings for one another in check, but Gen prompting group sex between the three of us so often gradually ate away at our resolve, bringing me and Chris closer and closer. Neither of us wanted to hurt Gen, yet pleasing his sexual desires fuelled our own for each other. The three of us spent so much time together: long talks on group policy, compiling 'Best of' cassette tapes of recordings of our TG work in progress . . . Chris had a tattoo done on his neck as a symbol of unity with us – a number 7 inside a crescent moon, based on alchemy and cosmology.

We were caught up in the excitement of working on the TG project but also in a ménage à trois that was leading somewhere none of us had expected it would. Chris was in the middle, which often got him down. I'd go for walks with him in Victoria Park, talking things through, cheering him up. Those walks turned into stolen opportunities to be together, to lie in the sun and pretend we didn't have a care in the world.

~

When I switched model agencies from Ragdoll to Suzannah-Jon, I was a relatively new face and body to the magazines Suzannah-Jon worked with, and my bookings escalated as the photographers smelled fresh blood. Magazines used girls up pretty quickly. Being featured over and over again was a no-no, unless you were someone who had a dedicated fanbase, like Mary Millington.

When you'd been 'used up' you could disguise yourself by wearing a wig, turn your hand at blue movies, body doubling – even private 'parties'. I was invited to go to a few such parties: one for Paul Gadd (Gary Glitter), which I declined, and one for some visiting Arabs who knew George (Harrison Marks). He rang me one day and asked, 'Do you do anal? That's all they want. They'll pay you a couple of grand. It's in their flat in Mayfair.'

That sounded decidedly dodgy to me. 'No, thanks, George,' I said.

He seemed relieved that I'd refused. I turned down all such offers and eventually wasn't asked again.

My new 'Z card' had helped a lot in getting me so much work. The photo was stereotypical of the time, in mood and pose, with me holding a silk scarf across the front of my naked body, revealing just one breast and staring directly down the lens with come-to-bed eyes and lips parted invitingly. That got me a lot of work – and the 'Z card' got a place on Chris's mum and dad's mantelpiece.

It had been taken by an American photographer called Szabo, who my agency had sent me to. He lived in a flat in Earl's Court and had a small studio set up there, with a makeshift but adequate dark-room in his bathroom. I didn't know what to make of him at first. He seemed eccentric, about forty years old, wore Andy Warhol-style glasses, had a limp and was a little weird – but not in the usual weird-photographer way. He intrigued me, not least because he had Crowley and Buddhist pictures over his mantelpiece, as well as a large black-and-white photo of him naked from the waist down, one leg on a chair, with his substantial-sized penis hanging between his legs. I'd gone to Szabo for test shots and we got on great. He'd come from New York, where he knew Allen Ginsberg and had been in with the Beat Generation, been a junkie and drunk bottles of Dr Collis Browne cough medicine, which (then) had a high enough opiate content to keep his cravings at bay.

That aside, we shared so many interests that our one-hour book-ing slots turned into entire afternoons sitting around exchanging views on art, literature, magick and sex. He often said he fancied me and would give a dirty, low laugh, but he never tried it on, even when he chained me up for one of his photo shoots. As he lay over me, securing the wrist chains, his nose touching mine, he smiled and said, 'I could do anything to you right now.'

'I know you could, but you won't,' I replied. And we both laughed.

I'd arrive at his flat and he'd usually be sitting naked, doing hatha yoga, calming himself in readiness for work. He taught me the yoga basics that the photographer Sheila Rock's classes hadn't managed to. I confided in Szabo. I took Chris to meet him, and he became my much-needed sensitive, supportive friend. Szabo was special to

195

me. I was his muse and Chris recognised and accepted that – but Gen didn't.

3 September 1976
Gen says to gain more power I am to screw each cock that I don't want but take as a sign of my power increasing.

19 September 1976
Gen told me what's been keeping us apart the past 3 days. He said he wasn't going to make love to me again, it was better to be just friends and forget about sex. It was like being thumped in the stomach. It was all because I never fucked Szabo and I'd said I would . . . it's Gen's source of energy . . .

I found Gen to be testing in many ways. The Cult/Magick task 'test' was back. I'd already screwed cocks I didn't want for hardcore films. But that didn't count, that was my (art project) choice, so Gen tested my love and commitment to him by demanding me to do things he knew I really didn't want to do. Upping the stakes (for me). His reasoning was: if I'd hurt myself for him, that would prove my love and dedication to him beyond doubt. These 'tests' were a self-serving ploy presented to me under the twisted notion that submitting to his demands was a way for me to gain strength. He never pushed himself or took risks; he always stayed within his comfort zone, seemingly feeding off my discomfort.

I'd stopped acquiescing to his suggestions for a while. He used sex as a weapon, as a means to exercise his power and control. It wasn't about love or mutual pleasure. I'd return home from working on porn jobs and have to describe the whole event for Gen's sexual gratification. Home didn't feel like home but more like work, providing another sex fantasy. Gen wanted me to screw Szabo and other models and photographers I worked with. I didn't want to. I told him I would, just to shut him up and leave me alone. He was constantly pecking at me. Where had I been, why did I want to go out again, what was I doing when I was out. It was an endless questioning and checking on my movements, like picking at a healing wound and making it bleed again.

As for Szabo, he was my friend, he was married, and I knew and got on well with his wife, Tris. Gen said he wouldn't have sex with me until I did as he asked. That hurt, but I wasn't going to be bullied. I was pretty good at sexy phone calls by now, having talked to Jeff so much, and I made up stories of my sexual adventures for Gen. I wasn't ready to lose another home and everything I'd worked so hard for, just for the sake of Gen's expected daily orgasm.

And I didn't want TG to suffer – it was too important to me. It was all working so well. I'd had 'Death Factory' T-shirts done for us all, we had John Krivine asking to manage TG, and Chris had worked hard on gear, making me an auto-wah pedal, buying himself a new Korg keyboard synth and spending hours rewiring the equipment in the studio, adding a custom slave amp and arranging it into a wall of sound. It sounded awesome. 'Wall of Sound' became one of TG's signature tracks. TG material was coming together very nicely.

4 September 1976
Off to Death Factory to play Gristle music. Did our one hour set and it went very well. On the Myra Hindley/Ian Brady number got a really good backing. I'd like to keep it. Chris thought it was the best we'd done. Wall of sound it was, bricked up to the ceiling!!!!

11 September 1976
We did a nice new tape with 'SLUG BAIT'. Was really nice. A new number for Gristle.

COUM was running in parallel to TG. Me and Gen were invited to go to the USA to perform at N.A.M.E. Gallery and the Marianne Deson Gallery in Chicago, the Los Angeles Institute of Contemporary Art and the Institute of Design Environment and Architecture (I.D.E.A.) in California, and had applied for a grant from the British Council. There was so much to organise, with the dates falling shortly after the planned ICA exhibition.

By this time I'd got a half-decent portfolio together. I thought I'd almost finished with my project and had enough material for the exhibition, but when I joined the Suzannah-Jon agency I was the busiest I'd ever been – even diversifying into being put forward as Mike Yarwood's naked card-trick assistant, going a bit upmarket and auditioning for *Playboy* (which I never did), and filming with Paul Raymond's lover, Fiona Richmond. I had to buy my first pocket diary to keep tabs on what I was doing where and when. Other than the TG get-togethers and times I was working on COUM or away with COUM, I was out with my model portfolio, doing photo shoots or films, sometimes working till the early hours of the morning.

The ICA exhibition was getting ever closer and I made a final push, writing to different magazines asking to buy three copies of each issue I'd appeared in. I didn't get many responses. But Michel and David Sullivan were really helpful and I'd collected over fifty different magazines already for the show. I extracted all the images of myself and the associated text from each one – those pages were my 'action', to be framed as my work, thereby subverting the 'male gaze'. The title of the exhibition was 'Prostitution', not only as a direct reference to my first appearance in a sex magazine, as well as my subsequent sex-magazine works, but it also represented our thoughts about the art world – talent being touted and sold for a price, the relationship between high art and money. We felt we'd come to the end of the road with Arts Council grants: the conditions were too restrictive.

The exhibition opening would be the official launch of Throbbing Gristle and a support band was needed. We thought of John Krivine. He'd started and managed a band called LSD (who became Chelsea), with Gene October as lead singer. They also had Bill Broad (Billy Idol) on guitar and Tony James playing bass, who later formed Generation X together. John had asked TG to go to see them rehearse and advise as to whether he'd selected the right people. I remember walking to the Tube, with Bill talking about the band and practising his Elvis lip-curl-cum-sneer.

There was an incident at the audition. Tony insulted Sleazy, questioning his qualifications as a judge for the band, calling him 'just a knob-twiddler' (which was true in another respect). Gen punched Tony in the face for being so insulting and disrespectful, sending his sunglasses smashing to the floor and splashing his can of Colt 45 everywhere. We didn't say a word.

Regardless of said incident, Tony made it into John's punk shop BOY band, which was later formed in 'opposition' to Malcolm McLaren's band, the Sex Pistols, and his and Vivienne Westwood's shop, SEX. The shops were just up the road from each other and each had a brand and a band to help sell it. Sleazy ended up with a foot in both camps, as window dresser for BOY and photographer for the first publicity shots of the Sex Pistols. Hipgnosis Studio, where he worked, was close to where the Sex Pistols rehearsed and he arranged with Malcolm McLaren to do some photos. They were never used – McLaren thought they were too extreme (very 'Sleazy'). When John opened BOY he had Sleazy make a window display that attracted police attention and investigation. They thought the contents were from a real crime scene. He'd created a forensic-like display of what looked like the dismembered, charred remains of someone who'd broken in. Sleazy loved that his work looked so authentic.

25 September 1976
We did some Gristle music. Seems we can do it now so no need to practise. Just looking forward to getting the Alpha Wave machines.

Sleazy arrived at the house a little late, as usual, but all excited and bursting to tell us about his train adventure on his way to his Casualties Union meeting earlier that day. He got flashed by a guy in the carriage and had oral sex. They'd just finished when the train stopped and his friends from the union got on, and the guy got off. Sleazy started chatting away as if nothing had happened. What a perfect day, he said, all smiles.

Then Tony Bassett arrived. We'd invited him for dinner after David introduced us. Tony was a small, quiet, gentle, unassuming man with amazing imagination and skills, and made special effects for TV and film. We discussed ideas with him on negative-ion generators and the possibilities of hooking ourselves up to alpha-wave machines and feeding the alpha-wave signals through the PA. That was impractical, just because of safety and noise interference, but he made us an industrial-size negative-ion generator that would clear the venue of cigarette smoke (a real problem back then) and make people feel good.

Two weeks before the ICA, Chris left his job – rather convenient in retrospect, as it meant he was around all the time to help while I went to Greece for a week on a modelling job.

16 October 1976
Gen was a little cold at first, upset me. Seems like the show has

caused trouble. He only knew yesterday that it was definitely
on still. Been in the papers . . . still the ICA have decided to go
ahead even when threatened by the ACOGB with a reduction in
their grant . . . Doesn't feel real to me. Feel in a dream. Greece
this time last night and ICA chaos now.

My arrival back at Beck Road was not the homecoming I'd expected, or wanted. Gen was pissed off with me that my sex-magazine works – or, as he put it, 'your fucking magazines' – had caused so much trouble, with the ICA coming under fire for exhibiting 'pornography', and had nearly robbed *him* of the exhibition.

Such an unwelcoming return was depressing and hypocritical, considering we'd both agreed about the show taking its title from my magazine works, which had inspired and formed the core of the show. Anyway, the invites and posters stating that were all printed. So it was too late.

The exhibition was opening on the 19th but the private view was on the 18th and, despite me, Gen, and Chris having already framed some works and done the Tampax sculpture boxes, there was still so much work to do. I really needed to sleep but Gen blamed me for the ICA chaos, made me feel so guilty that, despite having travelled back overnight, I went to the studio to work on mounting and framing the photographic documentation of the Milan and Kiel COUM actions.

I'd spent months printing the COUM photographs in readiness for the exhibition and Chris had managed to get the frames cheap through his father's glass shop. The budget from the ICA was pretty minimal and Gen suggested I be given just £50 for the framing of my magazines and could pay for the rest myself. The original quote I'd got for framing was for £500, which was crazy expensive, so the ICA framed a few for me and I paid for the others myself. In the last week of September Martello Street studio became a framing work-shop. Chris delivered all the glass and hardboard and cut it to size. All forty-one framed magazine actions and the photographic documentation of the COUM actions of Milan and Kiel were assembled ready for installation at the ICA. It was all going so well and looked amazing . . . but.

After the troubles over my magazines and the intervention of both the Crown Commissioners (the owners of the ICA's lease) and the ACOGB (Arts Council of Great Britain), it was decided that my sexually explicit magazine works could not be shown on the main gallery walls for legal – and what was described as 'diplomatic' – reasons. Not just that, but they would be housed in boxes and form part of a members-only exhibition in a separate room at the back of the main gallery – to be viewed 'on request' and only by members of the ICA. I was told that this would enable the magazines to be included in the show and avoid any of the obscenity regulations that applied to public displays in the gallery itself.

I always felt this was, intentional or not, like relegating the magazines to a place comparable to their original context – in a back room, an under-the-counter situation like a Soho sex shop. Sex shop to art gallery to back room. All it needed was a dusty velvet curtain in the doorway.

While the ICA staff concentrated on making the boxes for my framed magazines, we set to work installing everything in the main gallery – the large 'Orange and Blue' wooden pyramid, the shower of chains from Milan, the Perspex box of tampons and buzzing flies that was shown at the Paris Biennale, and the photo documentation of COUM actions and related press on the walls. Then we positioned display cases containing relics from COUM actions, assorted objects and clothing, including my bloodied tampons, which were used as raw material for many pieces – and which (unknown to us at that time) became the focus, alongside my magazine works, of the furore that descended upon us the very next day.

We'd decided that the private view for the exhibition would not be like the usual polite, wine-sipping art-crowd gathering. As the exhibition was both a farewell retrospective of COUM and the official launch of our new project, Throbbing Gristle, we would make the private view a special evening to shake things up a bit. We'd arranged for John's band, LSD (aka Chelsea), to play as support to TG, booked a stripper called Shelley through my friend Lynn's stripping agency, Gemini, and also a beautiful, tall, intimidating transvestite bodyguard called Java. Well, it was indeed a special night . . . that kicked off big time.

It turned out to be a good decision that my magazines were in the back room – especially for the private view. They needed to be out of harm's way. Having bump-started Doris the van and loaded up all the TG equipment, we arrived at the ICA around two o'clock in the afternoon. We set everything up and made sure the gear was all working. Our friends turned up to help and Ted Little was totally supportive, despite all the hassle and pressure he'd had about the show. The press were already buzzing around as we prepared for the party.

LSD and John didn't get there until 3.30 and spent two hours doing a soundcheck, then blew the monitor speakers. As the party started at 6 p.m. time was getting tight and we now had to repair the monitors. The tech people sorted it out pretty quickly and Chris took the opportunity to have a last check of our gear before we started our set. Something was amiss – someone had purposely fucked with our equipment by jamming a screwdriver into the PA amp. It would have ruined the gig. Chris removed it immediately, and the sabotage was thwarted.

When we opened the doors to the main gallery, people flooded in and the place was heaving. We were to play first as most of our equipment, being self-built by Chris, was best left set up and undisturbed once it was all working. We took up our positions. Chris on rhythms, synths and machines, me on Raver lead guitar and effects, Gen on vocals, violin and Rickenbacker bass guitar, and Sleazy using his tapes. I wore my leather biker jacket, hung open with nothing underneath. I had Sleazy apply his casualty make-up to my boob so it appeared to be gashed open and bloody, and during the performance I took my jacket off. Gen had the front of his hair shaved into an inverted 'V' (Peter Gabriel-style) and had a bottle of Sleazy's fake blood to hand, which he proceeded to pour into his mouth as he sang, spitting it out as he screamed apocalyptic lyrics into the mic.

The set began slowly, building intently into 'Very Friendly' (the Moors murderers song), 'We Hate You (Little Girls)', 'Factory', 'Slug Bait', 'Dead Ed' and finally letting rip, no holds barred, with 'Zyklon B Zombie'. Throbbing Gristle's official launch was complete and we were pleased with what we'd done. I didn't know, or care, what the audience thought.

Next up was Shelley the stripper, who enthusiastically took to the 'stage' for her striptease, playing to the audience and ending up rolling on the floor naked in the spilled fake blood left from TG's set. People loved it. LSD then took over from Shelley and thrashed out a punk set, to the cheers of their friends (including pre-Banshees Siouxsie Sioux). Their little crowd were all garbed out in their punk outfits, some undoubtedly bought from SEX or even John's shop, BOY, and as expected were rather stand-offish about the art.

There was a lot of alcohol consumed that night, including Gen, who liked a good tot of whiskey prior to performing. The bar had been very busy, the evidence of which was all over the floor of the gallery. We'd put our equipment to one side and as far away as we could from the main hub of party people, and went to join our friends. We were no strangers to violence or trouble so we thought nothing of the agitated atmosphere. I was glad to see Kipper Kid Brian – I always had such fun times with him. He was very drunk when he walked up to me and Gen accompanied by Ian Hinchcliffe, who was also drunk as a skunk.

By this time, Ian had gained a reputation for his spontaneous, aggressive verbal and physically violent outbursts, either against property, himself or others. He had issues with Gen. Ian hated pretension, and had previously squirted Gen in the eye with washing-up liquid. As he approached I could see blood on his mouth: he was in the throes of his glass-eating trick. I don't know who threw the first punch at Gen, but the language was vitriolic against Gen's 'use' and deplorable treatment of me. All hell let loose as fists, feet, bottles and glasses flew in all directions, and they all ended up in a writhing heap on the floor. People stepped back, some left, Ted Little tried to intervene and in the tangled web of fury got kicked in the balls so hard that he had to be taken to hospital.

Gen sustained a suspected broken finger and we ended the evening with a visit to Charing Cross A&E department. The doctors were immediately attentive to Gen's bloody face, fearing serious injury, only to discover the blood was fake. They became rather dismissive about his finger, which turned out not to be broken. While I was at the hospital with Gen, Chris and Sleazy stayed at the ICA to pack away the gear and load it into the van. When me and Gen returned we all drove back to Martello Street, unpacked the gear, carried it down the narrow basement steps into our studio, locked up Doris and trudged across London Fields back home to Beck Road.

We thought that the previous night's dramas would be the end of it, but we were in for a rough ride. The show opened officially the next day, Tuesday 19 October, and that's when the eruption of press 'outrage' began. Me and Sleazy were due to perform together at the ICA on Wednesday, Friday, Saturday and Sunday. We'd decided on a kind of demonstration of casualty make-up, in part to disappoint the press, who were expecting a nude sex action, and thereby remaining true to our COUM slogan, 'COUM, We Guarantee Disappointment'. When we arrived at the ICA on Wednesday for the one o'clock action, the audience, including artists and a heavy contingent of the press, were already in place. We only did the one performance.

20 October 1976
Fucking ridiculous today at the ICA. So many reporters and so aggressive. Can't do any more performances now, it's impossible, they'd all be there again. Three pics were broken today, reckon there'll be none left by next Tuesday. The reporters chased me through the gallery and nearly broke the door down. They punched Chris and called him a cunt. We had to be sneaked out of the back way, and went off to have some lunch with Paul (Buck). He's been so good to be with.

The explosive media response to the exhibition was totally unexpected but ironically fed well into our show, which was primarily based on how COUM was perceived by others and how our image was at times distorted. What a gift, what a spontaneous collaborative work, forming itself via the media day after day after day. We seized on the new material and me and Chris went to the ICA each day to collect the press cuttings, photocopy them and pin them to the wall of the gallery alongside the existing documentation. What had set out to be a retrospective exhibition had been transformed into an evolving show that was increasing in size as the press fed their own hysteria.

It was my and Chris's closeness during the harassment and intense stress of the ICA that cemented our relationship. The ICA show was pivotal in determining all our futures. It proved to be not only the end of COUM and the beginning of Throbbing Gristle but also the beginning of the end of my relationship with Gen as Chris and I fell deeply in love, and also through chance meetings that led to Gen's pernicious liaisons with a girl called Soo Catwoman. It also caused the end of my relationship with my mother and father.

24 October 1976
'Cosey Fanni's Deep In Blue Movies'. Headline from 'Sunday People'. Bet Mum sees it. Feel bad about it for her but there's little I can do.

My mum and dad read the story and believed every word – even though it said I was the daughter of a wealthy family in West Hartlepool. I spoke with Mum: she said she was absolutely shattered by what she'd read. That was the end. Mum had kept in touch regularly until the ICA. The scandal separated us forever. It was me or Dad and I completely understood her choice, even though it broke my heart that I never saw her, heard her voice or received anything from her again.

Pam and Grandma wrote to me and kept me informed, and fed her information on my well-being. I was so thankful I'd met up with Mum in London and gone for coffee and cake in Soho before all the ICA troubles.

All those Sundays Gen had routinely lain in bed reading the scandals in the *News of the World* or *Sunday People* with a cuppa tea and chocolate . . . He was now reading scandalous stories about us, the repercussions of which only affected me. The press hadn't had their fill; they pursued and continued to 'report' on us for another two weeks. The *Evening News* had found out where we lived (from Acme – how nice of them), and would bang on our front door for hours on end, then go to the studio, the neighbours, the Broadway Market shopkeepers, to muck-rake what they could. They didn't get much – everyone was very kind about us.

After interviews with the BBC and Thames Television, we withdrew ourselves completely, ignoring any press, radio or TV requests. I suppose any other band would have jumped on the back of all that and used it to promote themselves, but we weren't a 'band'. We were independent of the usual record label, PR, etc. – we had our own idea of how and when TG would be presented and promoted and had decided to set up our own record label, Industrial Records. Virgin had made noises about being interested in TG so me and Chris took a TG tape, photos and poster to Simon Draper at Virgin Records. Sleazy was against accepting any offer, and me and Chris weren't serious about it anyway. Gen was more interested in a deal, though, and when *Melody Maker* heard about the Virgin visit, Gen did a three-hour interview with them on TG – on his own and not telling us until afterwards, which didn't go down well. TG as a whole should have discussed it first and then, if agreed, done the interview.

~

The outrage surrounding my magazine works caused questions to be raised in the House of Commons and recorded in *Hansard*. Tory MP Nicholas Fairbairn's hysterical response – 'These people are the wreckers of civilisation' – appealed to our sense of humour and was adopted by us and others when writing about Throbbing Gristle and COUM. His cries about our decadence and debauchery were hypocritical, seeing as he was known for his outrageous drunken behaviour and extramarital affairs, and later accused of alleged child abuse.

It was the magazines and tampons that the press focused on. For fun we had Sotheby's value one of my soiled tampons: £80. Not bad. I didn't understand what the fuss was about and was rather blasé about the objects displayed – the five-foot-long double-ended dildo smeared with blood, syringes we'd used for injecting blood and urine, knives, my soiled bloody tampons and other relics were everyday objects to me, but were obviously shocking to other people.

And others were fascinated by us. We were invited to a dinner party by a sexologist, with the guests being psychiatrists and sexologists, opera singers, me, Chris and Gen (Sleazy opted out). It was all very polite but creepy and we felt under scrutiny, our actions and comments being carefully assessed. After some drinks and nibbles, the sexologist entered the room wearing a catsuit and bird mask and playfully swinging a whip. 'Time for fantasy games,' she announced. What?

We were all led upstairs and told to form a circle. One person stood in the centre, describing one of their sex fantasies. They then spun the knife, and whoever it pointed to when it stopped had to act out their fantasy with them or forfeit a piece of clothing. A sexologist version of Spin the Bottle. It was all a bit clinical, even the sex play. They seemed rather repressed (maybe that's why some of them were there). It felt like we were the evening's entertainment but that didn't bother me. Chris was whipped, Gen chickened out, and I ended up with a nervously sweating big man called Henry (the 'butler'), both of us stripping off as slowly as possible. He was anticipating a voyeuristic feast of my nakedness but I insisted we did it back to back. There was a freaky sex fantasy played between two opera singers – both naked, singing and biting each other all over . . . and they thought we were weird. An interesting evening.

Selwyn and a couple of other people I'd worked for kept ringing me to do jobs. They saw the ICA debacle as an opportunity; others blacklisted me, thinking I'd 'used' them. Through Selwyn, David Grant, a known porn-film-maker, approached me and Gen to do a half-hour film (called *Sensations*). He wined and dined us with his friend Peter. Chris wasn't interested – he thought they were exploiting us (he was right) – but Sleazy wanted in.

My annual birthday party never happened that year: I was preparing for our trip to the USA, and did a modelling job for Michel and worked on the David Grant film in the evening.

4 November 1976
Sleazy turned up on the film set, along with Diana Dors and her husband Alan Lake and kid Jason.

We got on like a house on fire with Alan Lake. He told us he and Diana had been brought in to make fun of us, but he really liked us, gave us their home address and said to come visit them sometime. Diana was talking about her experiences in films and how her romantic scenes had to adhere to the Hays Code: the lady keeping at least one foot on the floor during romantic embraces. That was supposed to ensure there were no sexy love scenes in bed. Things had changed a lot. I did a glamour model shoot and a simulated sex scene.

Selwyn was there and commented on how thin I'd got, and told me not to lose any more weight. I hadn't noticed – it must have been the stress of the past month.

We were filmed in conversation with Diana, Alan and an actress from *Coronation Street*, discussing our approach to life. The actress misunderstood what we meant about freedom to explore and express yourself, no boundaries. 'What, so if I feel like shooting someone I can? Just kill them?'

We looked at her as if she was mad. 'That's not the normal train of thought,' I said.

~

Although the ICA had been a farewell to COUM, the last few actions involving just me and Gen took place in America. We left the UK the day after my birthday, flying away from the shitstorm the 'Prostitution' show had caused, harassed by press photographers right up till we boarded the plane, one reporter telling other passengers that we were filthy pornographers.

The British Council had funded our trip, so the press still had some muck left to poke with a stick and throw at us, greatly exaggerating the funding we'd received. Going to America meant we could meet our mail art friends who had contacted us through our *FILE* magazine artists' ads and contact list, including Anna Banana, Bill Gaglione of Dadaland, Arethuse, Monte Cazazza, Jerry Dreva and Bobby Bonbon (aka Les Petites Bonbons), and Skot Armstrong (aka Science Holiday). Monte and Skot became the most regular and valued mail art collaborators and remain my very close friends to this day. I'd spend hours embroidering postcards to send to Skot, making collages or small handmade and interesting artworks. In reply, so did Skot, Monte, Jerry and Bobby. That mail art was personal and treasured, including Jerry's gift to me of 'Wanks for the Memories', a masturbation book, full of his boyfriend's semen.

Our first stop was Chicago, where we stayed in the studio loft of our artist friend Kit Schwartz. She was working on a piece involving large broken mirrors and we helped her assistant Dan devise ways of smashing them to get the effect she wanted. We'd arranged to meet up with another mail art friend, Arethuse, who'd travelled to Chicago and was going to do much of our US road trip with us.

Within days we'd started to regret that decision, as him dossing down in Kit's loft wasn't acceptable to her and he seemed pretty untogether, stoned a lot of the time, coming and going whenever he felt like it and disturbing our sleep. He was invaluable in some ways, though. He told us about a way to drive across America at minimal cost by delivering someone's car for them when they moved states. The only cost would be petrol money and we'd all share the driving. We had another week in Chicago yet.

Our action at the Marianne Deson Gallery went really well. Our N.A.M.E. actions were more relaxed and we managed to get them photographed and videotaped, and some dollars from door takings. It was hard saying goodbye when it came time to leave for LA. We were going to stay with Harley Lond and meet up again with Arethuse, who drove off a day before us in a drive-away car – a brand new $20,000 Cadillac to deliver to its owner.

18 November 1976
Skot rang and we talked, he's got such a quiet little boy voice.
He's moved onto Sunset Strip . . . we'll see him tomorrow . . .

We flew into LA through a yellow cloud of smog. It looked poisonous and uninviting. Harley advised us not to go out on certain days when it was really bad – he'd got an ulcerated throat that he blamed on the pollution.

Sunny California wasn't quite what I'd expected. People started calling Harley's and meet-ups were arranged. My old friend from Hull, Ann Fulam, was now living on the west coast and she picked us up and took us to her place by the beach, which was much more Californian: sitting drinking tequila on the porch, catching up on old times while watching hordes of young blonde surfers, then going to see John Waters' film *Pink Flamingos*.

Skot Armstrong and his friend Eric came over to take us to their friend Kitten's place. It felt so good to meet them face-to-face. We'd been writing to each other since 1974 and Skot had said how nervous he was about meeting me, lest I found him boring. Skot had a warm, fun and unaffected demeanour, no hard edges or underlying agendas. I felt happy and relaxed with him. He described his ongoing art project to me: 'Science Holiday is an artist collective that mimics secret societies and occult lodges, with a focus on creating modern myths and exploring the effects of context.' He had an extraordinary, and staggeringly wide, range of knowledge and an approach to art that was immensely inspired and idiosyncratic, perceptive yet whimsical, but intelligently thought-out. He's a genuine eccentric and I can well understand why he was identified at ten years old as a gifted child.

I noticed a wariness between Gen and Skot but at that time didn't know why. I've since learned that Skot and Gen had had heated letter exchanges on art, but particularly regarding Gen bragging about being like Charles Manson, being friends with bikers and having loyalty tattoos. Skot hated cults, so Gen's interest in Manson concerned him, especially after Albrecht D had written to him saying Gen was behaving like Manson, which had prompted Skot to write to me asking if everything I did for Gen was voluntary. I was surprised but Gen was incensed and had me write to Skot defending Gen's position, criticising Skot for questioning his motives.

Skot remembers: 'I was furious at Gen about whatever he had invented to tell you. There was actually a pattern to his keeping us at odds . . . At one point he and I were arguing about Charles Manson and he had you write to me to argue his position. It was written in your hand but it sounded like it was dictated by Gen. It created the illusion that you agreed with more of his ideas than you probably actually did, so that caused me to use more caution about writing to you. In fact, he may have used similar tactics with other people to keep you isolated under his "control".'

I'd played my dutiful role of protector well enough to set more alarm bells ringing for Skot. He was worried for me – he recognised signs of certain cult methods of control and wrote me letters to alert and support me. I never received them.

Regardless of Skot's disapproval of Gen's interest in Manson, he agreed to Gen's request to be taken to eat at El Coyote, where Sharon Tate reportedly had her last meal. Then we went back to his house to watch the first Dada-like Science Holiday films, *Gaucho 96* being of particular note. Gaucho 96 was one of the fake bands they formed. If any record label showed interest they'd be sent the film of the band – which was silent. I liked Skot's logic and informed sense of play, his apolitical, guerrilla, spontaneous street performances, driving around LA and recruiting strangers for their interactions, then retreating, leaving people thinking, 'Was that real?' I was in like-minded company, where laughter sat comfortably alongside serious discussions on art, magick and other subjects of mutual interest.

23 November 1976
Well about half the people walked out on the performance. First time ever, including Chris Burden. Can't be bad. I syringed my pussy, stitched my arm. We ended up all locked together lying in Gen's piss, blood and vomit . . .

The action was intense, probably the most extreme we'd done to date, and it didn't sit well with some people, especially the controversial performance artist Chris Burden, who stormed out in disgust. I don't know what they expected, but they shouldn't have assumed anything other than the unexpected. Those who stayed till the end gave a thumping round of applause – that was new. We washed ourselves down and joined everyone for a celebratory meal, Gen dry-fuck-dancing with Ann Fulam, and me sat talking intensely to Skot and Bobby. The next day we took the one-and-a-half-hour bus ride with Harley to Santa Monica to do our I.D.E.A. gallery action.

~

After an emotional farewell to Harley we landed in San Francisco and made our way to the Greyhound coach station to meet Monte Cazazza. We tried calling him but the lines were busy. It was scary hanging around in the station getting hustled the whole time; creepy people were circling us. Then we got through to Monte and he turned up, using his last few dollars to rescue us – 'before you were murdered by the pimps, perverts and prostitutes there', as he put it.

We dropped our luggage off at Art Silva's place and went to Monte's. He lived in a huge old municipal building, with two rooms the size of church halls, big enough for him to rollerskate round, with small rooms running off all over the place, and a spooky basement with laundry and shower facilities. Monte was part of the Bay Area Dada Group, alongside his friends Tim Mancusi and Bill Gaglione. Bill and Anna Banana, who we'd been corresponding with, also published *VILE* magazine as a parody of AA Bronson's own parodic *FILE* magazine. But *VILE* concentrated on art and material that was bizarre and offensive. Front covers included a hanging corpse with an erection and Monte stripped to the waist, sneering and looking like he'd torn out his heart, holding it up to the camera. Monte had a reputation for unpredictable, outrageous behaviour, once turning up to a dinner party with a briefcase. He placed it on the table,

215

opened it to reveal a decomposing cat he'd found, set the cat on fire and then left the party. His art project for college was pouring cement in the main entrance door and staircase, a statement that I'd say pretty much summed up his opinion on the 'teaching' of art.

Monte didn't have much trust in people and kept us to himself – I didn't mind at all. Bill Gaglione had rung when we were asleep, asking us to go round. Monte told him to come to us.

'Are you trying to keep them to yourself?' Bill asked.

'Yes, I am!' was the reply. Bill never came over to see us.

Monte wasn't what we expected from his letters and reputation. He was caring and offered for us to sleep at his place our first night, and we ended up staying with him for the whole of our stay in San Francisco. It was a fantastically happy time, non-stop talking, him showing us his slides, books and artworks, throwing ideas around and just enjoying being together. It felt right – it felt like home for the first time since we'd been away.

27 November 1976
His bedroom is like a cell. Just one single bed and black cover and pillows with a nazi flag laid in the middle.

The irony of the flag wasn't lost on us. Monte was as confrontational with his art as we were, and we decided to do some 'Nazi Love' photos, amongst others. Me naked and Monte stripped to the waist, blowing smoke into each other's faces through very long glass tubes, juxtaposing them as we went along, some of me naked, bent over with the sharp blade of a shiny dagger held delicately but precariously just inside the lips of my pussy, and Monte holding a sawn-off shotgun as if he'd fucked me with it then shot me, fake blood smeared all around my crotch. I didn't get to bed until almost 5 a.m. and was woken by the sound of Gen photographing

Monte in bed and Monte raging at him for being out of line. It was 7 a.m. I went back to sleep.

We'd spent the afternoon in book shops. Monte bought us a book on San Francisco murderers, and we bought fresh fruit for our trip and danced in the street. We got back to Monte's to hear the news that murderer Gary Gilmore had got his wish to be executed. The case had been big news since we got to the USA, and Gilmore's attitude was unprecedented and intrigued us.

We decided to do a set of photos and form 'The Gary Gilmore Memorial Society' in recognition of his asserting control by refusing the stays of execution made on his behalf and instead demanding the death sentence be carried out by firing squad, to ensure it was quick. We found a large wooden chair in the building that could pass as an executioner's chair. We each dressed in a black shirt, army trousers and boots, and one by one sat in the chair, got tied in by our wrists and ankles, blindfolded, and with one of us pointing Monte's gun at a target sticker positioned over our hearts. It was a freaky feeling going through the ritual. The photos were made into a postcard when we got back to the UK, which was in turn made into a T-shirt and sold at John Krivine's BOY shop on the King's Road.

Al Ackerman (Blaster) was coming at 7 a.m. the next day to drive us to his home in Portland, Oregon. None of us wanted to say goodbye. Monte was sad and I was sad; he sat staring and smiling at me over breakfast. I wanted to hold him and take him with us but Monte was contrary and fierce in his determination to only do what he decided to do – which was fine by me. Monte couldn't be coerced (unless it suited him) and that had showed the previous day, when Gen had tried to set me and him up together during the 'Nazi Love' photo session on Monte's Nazi-flagged bed. There was a lot of eye contact and body language between us, signalling a refusal to be manipulated. Monte could and still can be a pain in the neck,

217

but deep down he's good-hearted, very sensitive, and I love him for everything he is.

Blaster turned up as arranged. He looked like Orson Welles and was very warm and friendly. Caes Francke, a Dutch artist and mutual correspondent, was with him, as well as his wife, Patty, and young daughter, Stephanie. That meant we had to fit five adults and a child into Blaster's small two-door VW Beetle. Being claustrophobic, I almost panicked when it came to getting into the back with Gen and the very quiet Caes. It was such a squeeze I decided to try and sleep as much as possible to take my mind off it. It took fourteen hours to get to Blaster's house. We had soup in a local hippy cafe, bought books, wrote postcards to all our family and friends and sat and talked till the early hours about Blaster's work as a nurse and his time in Vietnam. Heart-rending stories of bravery, suffering and death. He later wrote us a long letter describing his feelings about one of his burn patients, who he and the nurses called 'The Hamburger Lady'. It became a classic TG song and was included on the *D.o.A.* album. Arethuse turned up at long last, and wasn't too sociable. I think he was itching to get driving back to Chicago.

~

Chris met us at Heathrow, bursting to show us everything he'd done in the house and the studio. He'd bought some high-frequency, high-powered piezo tweeters and fitted them into the speaker cabinets, serviced the mixer, and was making another mixer for Sleazy. The PA had needed a good overhaul and upgrade, as far as he was concerned. Me and Sleazy had previously gone to see about buying a second-hand PA but it was pretty battered and had belonged to the band Hot Chocolate – not quite the musical lineage befitting TG.

Chris's expertise and dedication to TG was uncompromising and invaluable. He built two huge bass bins in the studio that were big enough for Gen to get inside. Along with the piezo tweeters they increased our frequency range and brought substantive power to the sound and joy and inspiration when we played together. TG changed up a few gears. But neither Chris nor we had thought about the struggle we'd have later on when we had to get the bass bins out of the studio and up the narrow steps to load into Doris for gigs. They had to be lifted over the railings and caused Sleazy to go almost purple in the face with the effort . . . which made us all laugh and him get arsey as we saw him lose his cool for the first time. He wasn't used to physical labour, and from then on often seemed to be missing when it came to loading and unloading the van.

13 January 1977
I feel like I'm lined with shit and oozing out love that is spiked with death. I'm going to the studio to see Gen.

All was not well in the TG camp. There'd been a bust-up between Sleazy, Chris and Gen. There'd been something simmering for a while, an unsettled feeling, but I couldn't figure out what. I'd noticed that Gen had sensed that me and Chris meant more to each other than he'd anticipated we would, but there was something else making him miserable and argumentative. It couldn't have been him being made redundant from his job at St James Press, because that came with a fat £1,000 cheque.

That day, Sleazy took photos of Gen with his new short haircut and they had a disagreement. I was at the studio with Chris, who was all excited having spent the last three days building a new effects unit he called a 'Gristleizer'. We were trying it out, putting my guitar through it, totally thrilled at the sounds we were making. We trudged through snow and slush back to Beck Road, excited about telling Gen and Sleazy about the new unit. When they came back, Gen looked straight past me to Chris and said bluntly, 'What are you doing here?'

Chris was taken aback, then furious. A huge argument broke out. The three of them went their separate ways. Gen stormed off to Martello Street, Sleazy and Chris went to their homes, and I was left on my own in the house, thinking it was somehow my fault that TG, the very thing that connected us all and that we all loved, was possibly over.

Up to that point everything had been going well. Sleazy had registered Industrial Records as a present to Gen, with me and Sleazy as named directors (Gen was on the dole again). We'd never been so close, especially as Sleazy had started sleeping over more often and surprised me, Chris and himself by having fun exploring my lady bits. I remember the cheeky look on his face when I peeped under the duvet. 'It's my first time,' he said, grinning.

The three of us laughed and joked around so much, wrestling with each other in the big TG bed. We had a lot in common when it came to our sexual interests and indulgences, and often talked about our fantasies.

I wanted to make it right again. I talked things through with Gen and I rang Sleazy, who agreed to come over. The next day I noticed Chris had been to the studio and Beck Road while I was out doing a photo shoot for *Fiesta* magazine – he'd left some food shopping for me and had gone back home. I rang him. He'd been ready to 'Fuck everything, fuck everyone' and to end TG, especially when he saw that Gen had taken a load of his stuff down in the studio and moved it to one side. I persuaded him to come and see us. A TG split was thwarted, or so we thought.

Sleazy's job with Hipgnosis understandably took a lot of his time but he'd also started working and hanging around with Sheila Rock and a guy called John, who had a band, which further reduced Sleazy's availability for TG work. That annoyed Gen, but not as much as when Sleazy seemed to be passing on TG ideas to John, and then sold Krivine a design for BOY – it was to look like a 'Death Factory', including black knobbly rubber suits like the one we'd used in COUM. Chris was kicking off about it all too, saying he was worried Sleazy might steal the idea of his mirrored panels and the digital jewellery he'd made for us all.

We had a meeting. Gen wanted to throw Sleazy out of TG and get a keyboard player, relegating Chris to just do 'twiddly bits and mixing with a few tapes'. I was bewildered as to what Gen really thought TG was about, and what Chris's contribution and role in it were. Chris had just spent his whole tax rebate on building gear for TG and was understandably insulted. Gen sulked at Chris being hurt. Sleazy was confronted about his TG betrayal and blamed John, promising to be more involved. In the end, Chris rang him up and arranged to see him for a serious talk. Sleazy took him for a meal and to a Todd Rundgren gig; they left early, as did the Sex Pistols. Chris brought Sleazy back into the fold and we all met at the studio, did a full one-hour Gristle set and recorded it for reference.

In a fit of whimsy, we met with the Maniacs' manager, Des Pierce. He wanted to represent TG and he put an ad in *Sounds* with the headline 'Genesis P-Orridge and the Throbbing Gristle'. That pissed off Sleazy and Chris. Des didn't appear to understand how TG worked and our association ended after a gig he got us at the Nags Head, High Wycombe. The gig was, as Chris put it, 'just one big shambles. All that could have gone wrong did go wrong . . . We need to sort Sleazy out.'

Sleazy didn't turn up to load the van and got to the gig at 8 p.m. Gen did a solo 'Very Friendly' as none of the gear was working, then it all kicked in but my guitar cut out after twenty minutes and I walked off to sit with a bunch of punk kids, who Gen then took on stage with him. Sleazy kept coming to Chris every five minutes to tell him something was wrong and David Mayor had tried to help but was useless on the mixer. After forty minutes, Chris left a screeching high note on his synth and walked off.

Chris was all for calling it a day. With no one but him knowing how to set the gear up, he felt all the responsibility was on him, plus the monitor speakers and amp had been blown by Sleazy having randomly pulled out plugs left, right and centre. Gen was telling people TG was *his* newest project, Sleazy was prioritising Hipgnosis and Gen was telling Chris that I wasn't into TG but was going into film work instead. The only non-sex films I'd done were for the experimental film-maker and co-founder of the London Film-Makers' Co-Op, Steve Dwoskin, who Paul Buck had introduced me to. It was certainly a departure for me, but I'd never said I was intending to ditch TG to concentrate on filming.

I needed to keep TG going – I couldn't let it fall apart. If I lost TG, I'd lose Chris. It was our affair that kept TG going. If I'd left Gen at that time or Chris had left, TG would have ended before it had really begun. We all had our extracurricular activities going on, some shared, some private. TG was dysfunctional and always on the brink of collapse, simply because of its component parts: much like the equipment, it teetered on the edge of breaking down from being pushed to the limit. But apart from the strains of personal relationships, I loved TG. It was the first time that working with sound had excited and inspired me. It was exhilarating to explore new ways of creating a different kind of 'music'. I felt on the brink of discovery: there was so much potential yet to be realised.

4 February 1977

Got some five new Gristleizers now. Chris has worked hard this
week . . . Did a really good version of 'Zyklon B Zombie' and
went through the whole set.

The arguments, Gen's moodiness and the Gen-focused press articles depressed Chris but didn't faze him for long. He was on a roll
with his TG research and development. He built himself a mini-
synth he called 'Tescosynth', which was small enough to strap to
his wrist, and Sleazy a telephone dial with jack sockets that, when
connected to an audio signal and plugged into an amp, produced
strange effects when dialling. All he needed was for Sleazy to turn
up. Chris completed five Gristleizer analogue special-effects units
to mangle the sound, one for each of us and one to put Gen's
vocals through with the new Shure mic Sleazy had bought him.
The iconic sound of TG was being born. The Gristleizer became,
and remains, synonymous with the sound of TG. I was in my element putting my guitar through my Gristleizer and pedals – such
raw power at my fingertips.

However, the chaos continued unabated. I was used to it, and
to working on multiple projects simultaneously, and accepted the
disruption caused by TG being 'on' then 'off' as part of my life. I
sometimes felt my role was as much about sorting out the squab-
bles and sulks as it was about being a collaborator. Whether it was
a male/female thing, I don't know, but I felt like 'Mother'. Sleazy
even called me 'Mum' at times – the boys got to play while I was Ms
Domestic Goddess, food shopping, cooking, laundering and making friends when they argued, bringing them and TG back together
to prevent it from imploding. Keeping our TG family happy and
united also meant I got to do my thing. Shit, I hate saying that,
but that's how it was. And of course, when I wasn't 'Mother' I was

223

there for sex, Gen's Scarlet Woman – although that role was under review, not only because I was in love (and having sex) with Chris but also because my getting to know Chris really opened my eyes to my situation. He didn't say anything directly; it was more his actions and attitude to life and people, his disbelief at some of the things that went on in my relationship with Gen, and Gen's treatment of me (and others) being regarded as subordinate to Gen and facilitators for his needs. That, and my needs always coming second to Gen's, shocked Chris. He couldn't reconcile Gen's declarations of being unconventional, 'enlightened' and into magick with his sexist, cruel behaviour and dogmatic insistence on maintaining domestic routines like specific meals on certain days and watching *New Faces*, *Coronation Street* and *Doctor Who*. How did all that sit with how TG were promoting themselves?

Chris was the first true egalitarian I'd met. Meeting him was like an epiphany. For the first time in many years I felt someone really cared about how I felt, accepted me for who I was, and encouraged me to follow my instincts for my own purposes, gratification and experience. There was no game-playing, no 'strings', no coercion, just a deep respect for me as a person in my own right. Being in a relationship pervaded by manipulation and deceit teaches you things like resilience and coping mechanisms, like holding back a part of yourself, earning your own money just to try to maintain a sense of self-worth and control. That's what I did. But one of the many downsides was ensuring a measure of emotional distance to offset being hurt. Not allowing myself to give too much or get too close also made me forget there are good-hearted people who can bring joy and positivity to your life, instead of darkness from constantly battling against surrendering to their control.

The barrier I'd put in place to protect me from Gen fell away when I was with Chris. He made my heart sing, he set my mind at ease, and his touch sent my whole body into uncontrolled shivers of lust of such intensity that I discovered another level of consciousness. He awakened in me desires I didn't know existed. This wasn't 'sex', it was fusion: when we made love we were as one, merging through every cell in our bodies, sublime feelings and senses so heightened that we were oblivious to everything around us as we immersed ourselves in the sensuous joy of velvet-soft skin, the tenderest of touches and pinnacles of delight like shooting stars and an underlying surge of pure energy. Our love was total, a oneness that rendered words superfluous in expressing the feelings that welled inside us. I was only happy when he was around.

My world was Chris – all my focus was now on him. I knew my life could only be with him but I was locked into what had become a hideous, mismatched, failing relationship with Gen, and I felt the only way out was to let time bring things to their natural conclusion – Gen and I separating – leaving me and Chris free to be together. It was torturous over the coming years, and it felt like it would be impossible for me to leave Gen, but his actions eventually created a situation that made my exit inevitable.

21 February 1977
Went to The Roxy tonight . . . Mark P was with Gen all night and Tony Parsons. Never again. SHIT.

We had done an interview and photos with Sheila Rock and met up with her again for dinner at John Krivine's new flat, along with Leee Childers and Mark Perry, who had a punk fanzine called *Sniffing Glue*. Mark and Gen went out a lot together. I joined them on a night at the Roxy. It was a pit. I hated it. Gen had been there before without me, and to my surprise – and contrary to the low opinion of punks he expressed to me – seemed to like their company and going to their gigs with Mark and his then girlfriend (and soon to be Gen's), Soo Catwoman.

It wasn't long before the friendship between Mark and Gen led to TG appearing in *Sniffing Glue,* and Mark started coming to the studio to rehearse with his Alternative TV (ATV) bandmate and guitarist, Alex Fergusson. Gen would play with them and really get into it. That punk style influenced his playing in TG but wasn't the direction me, Chris or Sleazy had in mind. There was yet another serious group meeting. If TG was going in a punk direction, Chris, me and Sleazy didn't want to know. We all agreed to refocus away from anything punk or rock and roll.

The rhythms Chris had done previously using tape loops were quite loose, allowing for more experimental, ambient tracks. We wanted to tighten things up. I loaned Chris £40 to part-exchange his Korg synth for a Roland sequencer. He put rhythms together mostly at his flat, recording straight to tape using drum machines, synths, his new sequencer and tape samples. The Roland sequencer created the unrelenting rhythm that drove and anchored the TG sound. 'Zyklon B Zombie' took on a new life and we opened with it at our next gig.

26 March 1977

Got Gen a bottle of Whiskey. He drank the lot in the first factory music section. He was pissed, John too . . . some shouted, a lot were smiling/felt sick/bewildered and blinded by the lights. We got unplugged. The DJ gave them hell over his PA and had Gen and John shouting too.

Roger Ely had arranged a TG gig at Brighton Polytechnic for £60, and David and even our old COUM cohort John Smith turned up. 50 Beck Road was a full house that weekend. The day was like a trip to the seaside, having cups of tea and chips in the cafe. An audience of three hundred awaited our attention. After the initial assault with 'Zyklon B', we played ten-minute jam sections, but at the fiftieth minute someone unplugged us, then one of the PA stacks was knocked over and the gig ended. But we'd had a great time and got a decent tape of the gig, good enough to use as part of our planned first TG album.

The timing of Gen leaving full-time work seemed perfect. It fell just at the point when we were all well into TG; our regular jam sessions and the TG ideas were flowing freely. At last he'd have more free time to indulge himself and be happier. But the distraction of his job was replaced by something destructive.

~

Mark Perry and Gen went out together with Soo in tow. Gen told me about her, that she hung around with a lot of the punk bands: the Sex Pistols, the Damned, even Thin Lizzy. I think I was supposed to be impressed. Gen started hanging around with her, going to gigs by the Doctors of Madness and the Clash, and she took him to see the Stranglers' agent, to Stiff Records and the Sex Pistols' manager, John Miller. It all seemed at odds with my life with Gen, and especially with TG.

Gen had a talent for, and enjoyed, schmoozing people – from the music press to Tony Robinson of the *Daily Mirror*, the *Guardian*, fanzines and anyone of possible use. I let him get on with it and thought Soo was just another one of his flings, and I took advantage of the time he spent with her to be with Chris. I didn't think that anything deeper was developing between Gen and Soo (or so Gen thought). He became more distant, discontent and more aggressive than usual towards me. He'd always kept a firm grip on how much of himself he'd expose, but now he was closed off. I felt locked out. It was only when he brought Soo to the house and studio, and then out with the rest of TG, that I got the full picture. She made lots of phone calls to the house and studio to speak to Gen, demanding his time and attention, which impacted on our TG get-togethers. I only knew what Gen had told me about her, but what I surmised from the few occasions she was around, and what she told me on the phone, was that she loved Gen and wanted to live with him.

I was annoyed at the banality of the situation and her blatant clichéd seduction of Gen – even marking him with huge love bites. It was crass and Gen had fallen for it. With Gen seeing so much of Soo, being accepting of the disruption it brought to our lives and adopting such an awful attitude towards me, I got the impression he was trying to instigate my leaving him. Maybe I was the target of the next Gen purge. I thought he would be open to discussing us adjusting our relationship, and I told him I wanted my independence and the freedom to also have sex with whoever I wanted. He said I was being selfish. I said he was. It didn't get me far. He was happier having me at his beck and call, keeping TG and everything we had together intact as well as Soo as his lover. It appeared that he was slowly manoeuvring to integrate her into our inner family.

Things between me and Gen got worse but he carried on pub-licly as if everything was hunky-dory. Gen went to Soo's for what ended up being three days. When he returned he brought Soo with him, walking hand-in-hand into the studio, where me, Chris and Sleazy were in the middle of working on Gristle music. None of us were pleased about the intrusion. I wanted him to have the guts to admit we were finished so we could get on with TG and have our separate lives.

Gen invited Soo to join us on our trip to the Mind and Body Show at Olympia, walking in front of me holding her hand and kissing. They didn't stay long. Me and Chris went round the show, picking up information on dowsing, ley lines and a leaflet on a lecture by Wilhelm Reich's daughter the following week. I don't know what Soo had been told about the reality of my relationship with Gen, but when I got home she was there, moaning about pains in her groin and wanting to sleep in our bed. I was being worked by them both and felt insulted that they thought I didn't notice. I was with Gen under sufferance and loyalty to TG. Soo's 'let me stay' act was dragged out for so long that she missed the last Tube, leaving me little choice in the matter. I told her she could stay if she kept her hands off him. She agreed. But I knew what would happen and so did they. Three in a bed. I crawled into the wall to get as far from them as I could.

The next morning I confronted Gen, saying I was upset, that we needed to talk. There was no response so I went out. When I got back he didn't come to me to talk, so I went to the studio and collected all my official documents and my passport and returned to the house. He was still in bed with Soo, who was casually smoking a cigarette. (Beck Road was a strict no-smoking zone because of Gen's asthma.) He had his arm around her and smiled at me as if this was normal behaviour. I asked him to get up so we could talk. An hour later he joined me. I told him if he wanted Soo, I was happy to leave (I could finally be with Chris). I showed Gen the documents I'd got: I was serious. He just laughed at me. That made me more determined than ever to leave him – but not until I was ready.

~

For months Sleazy had nagged me and Chris to do some S&M photos with him. We three shared a taste for bizarre and fetishistic sex. Sleazy fancied Chris but knew he was with me and that the only way he could get Chris to 'play' for his camera was to have me involved. The outline plot was lean and very 'Sleazy'. Chris would be an abductee who was humiliated by me, ending with my cutting off his penis. We enjoyed practising together – bar the amputation. We were co-conspirators and Chris a willing participant, playing the unwilling victim. As luck would have it, Chris's dad had offered him a 16mm Bolex film camera, so the photo session turned into a film, *After Cease to Exist*. As it also happened, our neighbour had moved out from next door and we'd squatted it for Phil Parker, who we'd met at the ICA. He let us use the downstairs front room as our kidnapper's torture room. We'd decided on a castration scene rather than penis amputation. Sleazy cast Chris's testicles and made a realistic faux pair, complete with the sperm-transporting (vas deferens) tubes.

Gen wasn't there while we did the filming – he'd gone off, uninterested. The floor of the room was to be dusty, as if derelict, and bare except for a small wooden table on which Chris was laid on his back, with his knees bent, legs hanging over the edge, and his ankles tied to the table legs. He was secured across his body so he couldn't move, then gagged. Sleazy was a little lost as to what to do – he wasn't used to heterosexual sex – so I took over. Chris got terrible cramp in his back and we had to help him up really slowly – he was in tears from the pain. The objective was to depict a kind of home-made, dark snuff movie, with me as dominatrix fondling Chris, then castrating him as the final scene. It looked pretty realistic: good enough to have people squirm, look away and even faint when they watched it when it was first screened later.

The film had started out being me, Chris and Sleazy, then Gen wanted to do a section – to film Soo as his prisoner tied to a bed, but shot like a police evidence scene. Gen didn't want me to be in the scene but I was assigned the task of tying her up, supplying a black wig and her outfit and dressing the room. Then Chris added another section: the TG gig at the Nuffield Theatre, Southampton, filmed by David Mayor using Chris's Bolex camera.

22 May 1977
A fantastic GRISTLE GIG! No other word for it . . . Gen was on form. Pissed and hurling himself into the audience.

TG had got an invitation from Brian 'Rat' Davis to do a gig at the Rat Club at the Pindar of Wakefield pub in King's Cross. We went down to meet Brian and see what the place was like. It was run as an alternative music hall in a small room at the back of the pub. We'd gone to a few of the club nights, which featured sword-swallowers, fire-eaters, comedians, poets, strange magicians and musicians. One of the evenings we went to featured a middle-aged stripper who claimed to have a fifty-six-inch bust. She would swing her huge breasts around and slap people in the face with them – one of those people was Sleazy. The look of fear on his face as she approached and then swatted him with her massive fleshy boob was one of the funniest sights we'd ever seen. Of all the people she could have chosen, Sleazy got her special treatment – and his worst nightmare.

Having seen the kind of acts that were on, we felt TG would fit in nicely.

The day before the Rat Club gig had been full-on. Me and Gen had been up since 6.30 a.m. to go to Heathrow to meet Monte off his flight from San Francisco. He was a no-show. After a nap, we ran through some TG material, packed the gear into the van, and then me, Chris and Sleazy shot the castration scene late into the evening.

The whole gig day was relaxed. Sleazy did some filming of me and Chris walking around King's Cross for the film and then we had coffee with another act on the bill, Andy 'Thunderclap' Newman. The TG show was great, with Gen on particularly good form.

25 May 1977
I told Gen it had upset me etc. and it ended up in him punching me like a punch bag. I thought I had a black eye but I never. Don't think I deserved that.

After Monte had failed to turn up, Gen got his ticket amended and he was now arriving on the 25th. I'd spent days decorating my old workroom for him to stay in. Gen wouldn't tell us the new flight details and said he was going on his own this time, or so we all thought. In fact, he'd taken Soo with him. I was really upset and when he and Monte got back I took Gen to task about being so sneaky as to arrange it without telling or taking me. After all, it was me who was Monte's friend. I was punched for questioning Gen's actions and had to cancel my modelling appointments. As usual, he hit me when no one else was present and never said sorry, just, 'Look what you made me do', leaving me the one in the wrong who should apologise, and him the victim. Monte was sleeping in his room downstairs, unaware of what happened. The trouble with violence is that you have to want to hurt someone, to have lost at least some control – *I* didn't want to hurt Gen and *I* hadn't lost control.

Gen's defence of Soo was soon to be brought into question. As had become routine, he was going off to Soo's house, but she'd taken a real shine to Monte. We had all been out together and were going our separate ways at Tottenham Court Road Tube. While Gen waited alone for Soo on the platform to take the Tube to her place, she was kissing Monte passionately on the platform opposite. It was a bizarre scene. The train pulled in, she pulled away from Monte, and then she went off with Gen. Me and Monte went home to Hackney. Then Soo and Gen came to Beck Road the next afternoon and she took Monte home with her. Within three days of Monte arriving, Gen's eight-week 'love' affair appeared to be history. The whole seduction routine went into replay, love bites included. I was disappointed that two intelligent people who I'd thought were beyond such shallow games had succumbed so readily to flattery and the power of pussy.

While the Soo, Monte and Gen saga continued, I was working with Szabo on a collaborative project and photos of my future striptease outfits, and Chris and Sleazy were editing *After Cease to Exist* at Four Corners film suite. It was an independent, hip place where they enjoyed the company of Viv Stanshall, who was hanging out, singing and drawing funny pictures. They didn't get back until 3 a.m. We all returned to finish the final edit the next day and laid down the soundtrack at the studio. *After Cease to Exist* had come into existence and had its debut screening at the Rat Club on 10 July.

Monte lived with us for months, causing havoc at times, but he was a great, positive presence to have around, with his inimitable attitude to life and art. He was a rogue, a free spirit with a generous, warm vibe and a dynamism about him that drew you close and made collaborating with him so enjoyable and productive. Monte was having fun, Monte-style: maintaining his friendship with us in spite of the conflict caused by his relationship with Soo, which had hit Gen hard. Being dumped in that way is tough to deal with.

As far as I was concerned, what me and Gen once had was gone: he'd lost me too. I'd moved on from him but he wanted to backtrack to how we were. That was impossible. I'd become used to Gen going off to indulge himself in his various sexploits and networking, as he did. He'd go off without any consideration of how I felt about it. But when it came to me having my own interests, that wasn't tolerated. He couldn't see why I'd want to be away from him or why he couldn't come with me wherever I went. Although he was happy to make use of my sex work and all that it contributed financially to COUM, TG and his own sexual appetite, he was resentful of the time I spent away from him, no matter what the reason. I didn't realise just how much until I went to write in my diary, only to find that he'd left me a message written in brown ink. Numerous entries of: 'Not with Gen – no reason given', 'Not with Gen with Michelle & Cathy', 'It all seems a bit pointless doesn't it?' I brought my diary entries to an end. Why would I keep a diary of my own feelings, only for someone to use them in judgement against me and leave his mark of disapproval?

24 July 1977
Bloody funny day today. Everyone in funny moods. Gen kicked me in the chin. Chris went out for a walk and didn't come back till about half four.

I needed to get away for a while, to try to make sense of my life with Gen and my love for Chris. I went to visit my sister on the Isle of Wight. Chris had been working for the London office of the ABC News bureau, refitting their outside broadcast studio, and he took the weekend off to come with me. We spent a wonderful night in Southampton before getting the ferry. We were at it for hours, orgasm after orgasm after orgasm. I fell asleep exhausted, with Chris still ready for more. I got home after the most amazing weekend, and with a recording of my niece and nephew at play, which I used for my solo track, 'Hometime', on TG's second album, *D.o.A.*

Monte stayed long enough to do some recording for his forth-coming releases on IR. It was hard work getting him to knuckle down and record. We had great fun but he'd get moody and unsure of what to do. I worked with him on 'Mary Bell', singing the chorus and playing a small child's piano, taking the track in the direction of an innocent nursery rhyme. He went back to the USA having done a lot of work with us, including coming up with the photo of him shooting up into his gashed wrist. It was made into a TG promo postcard with 'Can you fix us up with a gig?' written across it. It got a reaction – not always positive, but it was a great image and we thought it funny. But it didn't amuse the manager of the Hope and Anchor pub, who read it at his breakfast table when his kids were there. He was disgusted by it, thought it in poor taste and left a message on our answerphone to say NO, he would not fix us up with a gig at his downstairs punk venue.

Gen came back on board full-time with TG and we even did another two COUM actions together. There were still times when he'd go berserk and smash things up, but overall it seemed to work OK and I was happy with my work outside of TG, which was going so well. I'd exhibited abroad, started stripping (which I'll come to later), had an underground film I'd worked on with Anna Ambrose shown at the NFT, and my filming with Steve Dwoskin was ongo-ing, as was my work with Szabo. I relished the new and unique challenges all that brought to my life and art.

With life and art bleeding into one another at an ever-accelerating rate, there seemed no time for me to sit and work out specific strat-egies or consider my options (other than the very personal) – I reacted intuitively, working on instinct and not overthinking situa-tions. There would be time for reflecting on my actions later. I didn't base my approach to life or art on Burroughs, Manson or Crowley. Interesting as they were, their methods seemed more about them and tailored to suit their (*male*) lifestyles. My interest in Manson was about how unchallenged manipulation and control within an isolated group could lead to extreme and dangerous actions and damaging behaviour. Crowley and the occult interested me a great deal but some of our peers regarded it as a prerequisite for being 'industrial', alongside owning a collection of macabre books and objects and using the kudos and mystery they provided to shock.

I wasn't into following someone else's 'formula'. Knowing oneself was a meaningful, positive goal in life that made total sense to me, and living my life through intuitive experience was my way towards that end. I was hungry for the experience itself. It provided material for further works and challenged my personal boundaries, which in turn made me more open to taking things further – all in pursuit of finding and becoming 'me'. Belief in the power of my*self* increased. I was conquering my fears, dismissive of others' expectations, and growing in strength of will – and consequently I considered myself an independent entity, no longer willing to be tied to or submissive to others' whims and folly.

~

The IR/TG branding exercise began with a slogan, 'Industrial Music for Industrial People' (devised in collaboration with Monte), and also a symbol to provide immediate recognition: the TG flash. Chris had seen the power flash on a nearby railway danger-warning sign. We chose the colours of anarchy – red and black – and put the 'power' flash in white in the centre. We had two-inch stickers made of the flash, which had a small 'TG' on it, and a black-and-white sticker of the slogan, and started putting them up everywhere we went – on Tube trains, walls, buses and shops. I'd embroidered a red-and-black eagle on my army trousers and we discussed having an embroidered TG flash patch. I made a prototype and stitched it on to my leather jacket, and also made one for Gen. Chris embroidered one of his own and drew up a graphic artwork for button badges – a thousand of them for £55 – and then later we had TG embroidered patches made up. Chris stencilled a huge version of it across the chimney breast at Beck Road and Gen painted it in, then a four-foot-wide circular wooden version was made and hung at the back of the stage in the studio. TG and its logo flash were everywhere: on our clothing, stencilled on to the equipment and graffitied on to walls around Hackney.

Even though our extracurricular activities took up so much time, TG was the main focus for each of us. The diverse and perverse activities of our personal lives fed the sound of TG, as did the cultural and political climate of the time. It could be dark and nihilistic, brutally honest in subject matter and presentation, unapologetic, irreverent and uncool – especially the name. The thought of someone going into a record store and asking for the latest Throbbing Gristle album brought wry grins to our faces.

We drew from both our own experiences and sensitive subjects people were uneasy about addressing, such as in 'Very Friendly' and 'Zyklon B Zombie'. Gen would also say, 'What shall I sing about?' One day I said, 'Persuasion' – based on the photographers' methods of persuasion I'd been subjected to. Gen's lyrics reflected that and other persuasive tactics, segueing into talking about a murderer's stash of panties in a little biscuit tin. We'd match the mood of the sound to the lyrics, and vice versa.

We were creating a forum for discussion, breaking down preconceived ideas of what was 'music' by ripping away the foundations and leaving the listener to discover their own point of entry. We didn't want followers; we wanted people to think for themselves, to follow their instincts, be creative, be industrious in their approach.

That's what 'industrial' meant; it was about adopting a work and life ethic – to be independent, active, productive, thorough and committed. We worked outside the mainstream, accessing and using existing systems to subvert or hopefully instigate change, responding to and commenting on social and cultural events through our music, art, film and writing, refusing to let the personal be silenced. Industrial Records and the 'industrial' music of TG stood for all of that, and of course related to the studio 'factory' where we carried out our work: production, systems of quality and control – but of a different kind. We were constantly researching and acquiring books and information on propaganda and control techniques, business practices, cult movements and government strategies, deviant sexual practices, genetics, the criminal mind, pathology, psychology, weapons (especially the use of sound), medical research and anything unorthodox that hit our radar and piqued our interest. We utilised selected techniques, subverting and repurposing them to suit our needs and our ironic sense of humour, including how the music business worked and how they sold their 'product'. It had started with MAI in Hull, then my model-card format used for COUM art promotion, then TG music promotion. We decided it would be the ultimate ironic statement to release an album of TG 'music': our progress report. We called it *The Second Annual Report of Throbbing Gristle*. It could sit on our shelves as a souvenir and in years to come we could show our grandchildren that we'd actually made a record.

~

Our cheques had come from John Krivine: Sleazy's for the shop design he and his friend John did, and my and Gen's for the Gary Gilmore T-shirts. We had funds to enable us to press up our very first album and we sourced a pressing plant, Orlake in Dagenham.

Sleazy paid the whole bill as promised and we set about designing the cover. We had no money for colour printing. The cheapest way forward proved to be the most suitable: a plain white cover – in actual fact just a bog-standard unprinted white album sleeve. We wanted something simple that reflected 'industrial' and we adopted the style of a company annual report – an Industrial Records business report of Throbbing Gristle's sound research in the form of an LP, with recordings from various gigs, jam sessions and the soundtrack from *After Cease to Exist*.

All of us sat in the living room of Beck Road drinking cups of tea and putting the black-and-white printed stickers on by hand: a small one on the front simply stating the title, the dates the recordings were made and the label name, Industrial Records Ltd; on the back we placed a black-and-white sticker that gave details presented as a business report, plus the label logo and small photo of TG. We included a probing questionnaire to research our market, asking their opinions on film, commercial music, the record itself, political and sexual preferences and asking them to feed back to us their own questions. Also inside was a small slip of paper disclaiming the sound quality, and two stickers: 'Nothing Short of a Total War' (to make our motives clear) and a red-and-black circular TG flash sticker for people to keep or stick in public places to promote TG.

Reviews followed, the first by Alex Fergusson's friend Sandy Robertson for *Sounds*, then more in *Melody Maker*, *NME* and even the *Hackney Gazette*. The response took us by surprise. It was helped a lot by John Peel playing tracks from the album on his show. The Rough Trade shop took stock off us; Chris and Gen did the deliveries and Chris made a window display for them of the TG flash logo on circular wooden discs left over from speaker cabinets he'd made. To our amazement, the album sold out – all 785 copies.

We didn't re-press; we let Fetish Records, run by Rod Pearce, do that to get the label off the ground. Fetish Records' presentation was different in colour, with the striking TG flash forming the front cover. We never knew that our first TG album would prove to be so influential or that industrial music would become an established new genre.

I was in awe at our ability to keep TG together, and at the fact that it even gained strength and focus under such crazy circumstances. It seemed to have a momentum all of its own despite the turmoil that existed around and within it. We each poured ourselves fully into TG, feeding off each other's ideas, creating something greater than the four of us. We pooled our combined resources on all levels, using individual talent for specific tasks but surrendering our individual psyches to the process of creating sound together – united as a 'third mind'.

TG as one was powerful and all-consuming, but the anchor was Chris. The whole being greater than the sum of its parts was never more true than in the case of Throbbing Gristle and industrial music as a genre. Neither would have existed without Chris. He was the determining catalyst. Up until him joining, there was no sign of anything near the TG sound. Gen couldn't do it, I couldn't and neither could Sleazy. The simple fact is that, prior to Chris entering our world, we were effectively three parts of TG – me, Gen and Sleazy – and we hadn't come up with anything that resembled the sound that TG would later become known for. It certainly wasn't Chris alone, but his discipline, focus, ingenuity, knowledge, technical skills and experimental ideas were the crucial elements that brought Throbbing Gristle into existence. For years prior to Chris joining us, we hadn't found a sound that gave voice to our deeper feelings and more radical ideas.

As TG we wanted a sound that hit people between the eyes and swirled in grinding, growling mayhem between their ears. A sound that caused an involuntary physical response in the body that would make people feel and think rather than just listen, dance and get drunk. In the studio, we experimented with extreme frequencies; one of us stood at the 'kill switch' to cut the power if the effects became too much. We experienced tunnel vision, our stomachs going into spasm and our trouser legs flapping. When we played live, we added an additional layer to the aural assault on the senses: we interjected with strobes, halogen floodlights shining at the audience, large mirrored panels behind us, and the industrial-strength (of course) negative-ion generator Tony Bassett had made for us, with a super-strong fan that would arc randomly if anyone got too close, sending out flashes and sparks into the audience.

We weren't messing around: there was nothing comfortable about a TG gig, for us or anyone else. We were thought to be confrontational but our intention was far from that. We wanted to connect, interact in a way that counteracted the mindless indulgences and spoon-feeding prevalent in the music business. From a limp, post-coital COUM penis to a fully erect Throbbing Gristle, up and ready for action. That kind of summed up both our change in attitude and all four of us as individuals. Being such strong characters and having our interrelationship conflicts was what made TG. When we were as one we were an uncompromising force to be reckoned with, an unstoppable, highly charged ball of throbbing energy.

TG operated as a democracy, something that COUM had failed to be. And that caused lots of arguments when Gen didn't get his way, mainly between him and Chris, who was no sycophant. Chris's work ethic was a big influence on me. He was diligent and resolute, and worked through the night if needed. He understood how necessary it was to experiment beyond the good parts, break things down and build them up again to see where they could lead to. Me and Sleazy loved doing that and would want to carry on with Chris, excited about the whole process of exploring crazy ideas, going off on tangents just to see what happened. That took time and patience but Gen's limited attention span was a problem for us all. We'd just be getting somewhere when Gen would think that was enough and want to leave and go to the Wimpy or home for hot chocolate. That angered and frustrated Chris in particular, but also me, because Gen expected me to go with him and not choose being with Sleazy and Chris over being with him – and to make his hot chocolate. It disrupted the flow of creativity and sound experiments, imposed an unwanted and unwarranted limit on our time in the studio, when freedom to explore was at the centre of our practice.

What transpired was a compensation strategy. To dispense with the annoyance and frustration, Chris worked on sounds, ideas, tracks and rhythms in his flat and then brought them to the studio – ready-made backing tracks – thereby cutting out all the time that the process usually took during the jam sessions, in the hope that TG could maximise the time Gen was willing to hang around. It turned out to be a great thing but also led to Chris's massive number of hours of work being taken for granted, unseen and at times miscredited.

Whatever Gen lacked in staying power at jam sessions, he made up for as a live performer. Assigned to vocals, he could really grandstand, be the centre of attention, something the rest of us weren't interested in. He was a fantastic frontman.

Chris and Sleazy became very close, drawn together in frenzied enthusiasm for technology that could bring a new approach to and ways of making sound. They were always ringing each other up and meeting at the Hipgnosis offices, going to music shops in Charing Cross Road and Denmark Street to look at what was new and useable or modifiable for TG purposes. With Chris also seeking out components to make circuit boards to install into his synthesisers, he was accumulating a substantial array of weird and noisy self-built gadgets.

At first Sleazy had been happy to work out front, doing his tapes and mixing us through the PA – he wouldn't come on the stage. But we turned that around, persuading him that his function as a member of TG was generating the sound, not mixing it. My answer-phone provided some inspiration for a sound machine for Sleazy. Some of the interesting and threatening phone messages left on it were used in TG tracks, but the machine also used endless-loop cassette tapes, which was quite rare and gave Chris the idea to build a TG 'sampler'. He built himself and Sleazy one each, using old cassette machines connected to a one-octave keyboard. Sleazy added to his with Sony Stowaway cassette players (which became the Sony Walkman), which he'd bought while on a Hipgnosis trip to New York. Sleazy was over the moon and he added further to his gear by buying one of the first Apple II computers with a sampling card.

As for me, I'd started playing the cornet that Sleazy had bought himself but couldn't get a sound out of. He tried but never mastered the required blowing technique and was perturbed but impressed that I got a sound on my first blow. My Raver guitar was a bit of an odd shape for the way I used it, so me and Chris went and bought another cheap guitar, a Satellite, and worked together on customising it. Chris cut it down so it was more cricket-bat-shaped, making it easier for me to access the strings with my screwdriver, bottleneck, drumsticks or other objects I wanted to use to make sounds on it. We painted it black.

I put the guitar through the small distortion box and a wah-wah pedal Chris had built for me, and the Gristleizer, which was all great but I wanted more noise-making boxes. I took my guitar to Macari's to try out some FX foot pedals. The other guitarists were all doing renditions of 'Stairway to Heaven' and there was me saying to the assistant, 'No, I don't need to tune my guitar first – I'll just plug in. I kind of know what sound I'm looking for.'

I tried out different pedals, smashing and hitting the guitar, adjusting the controls to see what extreme sounds I could get out of them, all dials set to max. Then I heard the sound I wanted and could work with. 'Yeah, that's the one – that'll do the job,' I said. It was a Boss DS-1 distortion pedal, my first off-the-shelf FX unit (which I still have). After that, I got Boss-pedal fever and later bought phaser, flanger and analogue-delay pedals. Chris ordered a bulldog flight case and installed all my pedals, connected together in a row: a neat, transportable (if heavy) case that opened in two, the pedals in one half and my guitar tucked safely in foam in the other.

The TG affair with Roland equipment had started with Chris's synth and sequencers, then my Boss effects pedals, then we got a Roland Jazz Chorus combo amp each and thought what fun it would be to infiltrate the music-business practice of sponsorship deals. We approached Roland, sending them a photo of us posing with all our Roland gear. They didn't bite. But we added Eventide Harmonizers to our arsenal of effects, one each and one for vocals, and downsized our equipment, installing the necessary units into portable flight cases to make TG sound-generating gear more portable for gigs.

4

Despite my efforts, including being amenable to Gen going to Poland for two weeks to stay with another girl 'friend', he still seemed miserable most of the time. I was constantly having to second-guess his mood swings, and to try and head them off by coming home with a box of Maltesers or an Aero chocolate bar. Nothing I did for him was enough. He showed no empathy towards me – it was always about him. If I had an early start for a photo or film shoot he'd keep me up late, talking about himself, saying he was depressed and needing reassurance about his art, stroking his ego. He fed off me like a parasite, draining me psychically, physically and emotionally. My love for Chris was so intense and I knew my life with Gen couldn't continue. I just had to be careful about the timing of my leaving him. In the end, it was determined largely by someone else.

Chris's job for ABC News came to an end. He'd finished their new studio and was part of the team that covered the outside broadcast of the Silver Jubilee for America. Not long afterwards, Bill Blakemore, the London anchorman for ABC News, got in touch and asked Chris to refit their Rome studio. It would be a full-time job and he'd have to go and live in Italy. It was a huge decision as he'd have to leave me behind. He chose to stay with me. That was the point at which we committed to each other and I looked for somewhere to live so I could move out of Beck Road.

I approached Acme for one of their houses but they let me down – I didn't fit their 'artist' criteria. That floored me. I'd got them their first house down Beck Road (ours), then squatted and handed over so many houses to them that within a few years of our living there Acme artists occupied a large part of the street. I was left thinking that maybe you needed an art degree to be one of their tenants. Gen didn't have one; Phil, a motorcycle courier next door, didn't; so why was I unsuitable? It seemed I was only good for supplying properties and performing COUM actions in their new Acme Gallery. I looked elsewhere, but it was difficult finding somewhere that allowed dogs. I couldn't leave Tremble behind. I eventually found a small bedsit above a shop in Tottenham.

On 1 August 1978, as we lay in bed, I told Gen I thought that we should separate. I knew, once I uttered those words, I would be inviting Armageddon. And sure as hell, it arrived.

First there were tears, from us both. I held him close. I hated making and seeing him so sad. When he realised he couldn't talk me round, that I wasn't just saying it to get attention and bring our relationship back on track, the reality hit home and shook him to the core. 'But you're my battery – I feed off you,' he said.

No mention of love, just the vampiric nature of his need for me. 'That's why I have to leave,' I said. 'I feel like I'm being eaten away.'

He leaped on top of me, grabbed me by the throat and started strangling me. 'If I can't have you, nobody can!' Such a cliché, but true.

I was strong enough to get him off me and hold him down until his temper subsided a bit. He looked wild-eyed and crazy and I suspected that, as soon as I let go of him, he'd flip again. I jumped up, ran through to the front bedroom and dressed as quickly as I could, and grabbed my bag of essentials that I'd thankfully packed ages ago after the Soo saga. I heard Gen get out of bed and turned as he came running at me, threatening to hurt Tremble as she stood there, tail between her legs and ears back, trembling and wondering what the hell was going on. Then he attacked me. He was so fast. 'All because of THAT!' he screamed at me as he kicked me so hard in my crotch that it almost lifted me off the ground. I was doubled over in pain, holding myself. I couldn't move. Then he unleashed a torrent of punches and kicks and delivered a verbal blow that hurt me more: 'I'd never have let you kill my baby if I'd known you'd leave me.'

I was stunned. 'My' baby? Not 'our'? How savagely cruel to use the child I'd mourned against me. Why would he think that keeping the baby would have ensured his hold on me? So many thoughts flashed through my mind. Much as I was capable of defending myself, I couldn't bring myself to hit him back, hurt him more than he was hurting already. I put his exceptional reaction down to him not knowing how to handle rejection.

I started moving my things out two weeks later, on 15 August. I got Fizzy to stay with Gen to keep an eye on him as I was worried about him. As I went to put Tremble in my Mini with my final load of belongings, Gen demanded to come with me. I said no, and the drama began. He started kicking and thumping the car and scream-ing at me. He was like a madman. I put the car into drive (it was automatic), frantically trying to get away – then he jumped in front of it and lay down on the road to stop me driving away. I leaped out to get him out of the way, not thinking the car was still in drive . . . It rolled on to him. I quickly pushed the gearstick into neutral and pulled Gen out of the way.

'You'd even drive over me to get away!' he said.

'No. No, it was an accident,' I explained. 'The car is automatic and I'd left it in drive.'

He didn't believe me. 'Right!' he shouted, and rushed into the house.

Fizzy was stood in the doorway with tears in his eyes. 'Go quick,' he said. 'Good luck.'

All I could say was, 'Sorry, I have to do this. I have to go.'

Then Fizzy was pushed aside as Gen came flying through the door wielding a nine-inch knife with 'KILL' burned into the wooden handle, blazing, staring eyes, screaming and heading for me. Fizzy grabbed hold of him, took the knife and dropped it on the floor of the car so Gen couldn't snatch it back. 'Go! Go!' he shouted.

I drove off at breakneck speed down Beck Road, turning on to Mare Street so fast I lost two hubcaps as I scraped the kerb. I wasn't going to stop.

I didn't contact anyone for three weeks after I left. I needed to let my emotions surge and resettle as I came to terms with the realisation of what I had relinquished to Gen, other than a house and home, a studio and all my worldly possessions, except the few I took with me. I'd given up so much for a life with Chris and had possibly split up TG. I knew in my heart that it was the right thing to do. I'd have lived in a tent on a hillside if that was the only way me and Chris could be together. He didn't try to influence me in any way and would have accepted my going back to Gen if that's what made me happy. He gave my head and heart space to breathe.

I felt guilty for making Gen so unhappy. He knew that I'd be feeling bad. I did still care for him but knew the only way I could leave him was to remove myself and then wait for him to be the one to decide we'd part for good. We carried on with TG – him hoping I'd go back. It was a terrible time. He sent me mix tapes of my favourite albums. How nice, I thought – until the songs were interrupted by Gen's voice, depressed, saying how he needed me to come home, declaring his love for me. Even though I'd left, he was invading the much-needed space I'd managed to put between us. I knew he was having women over to Beck Road so I couldn't take his declarations of love and pleas for my return seriously, and besides, how could I go back after what happened when I left and all the years before that? Nothing had changed; his gestures – buying me flowers for the first time ever and cleaning the house – were out of character and way too late. The fact that he asked me not to tell anyone about my leaving him spoke volumes. He didn't want to lose face and thought I would weaken and go back.

~

The TG gig at the Crypt was going to be a great night. Our friends Cabaret Voltaire, Robert Rental and Daniel Miller were to play too. All TG gigs were memorable but this one more so than others. We'd hired bouncers for the first time, supplied by a guy known as 'Terry the Pill', who also controlled a lot of the fly-posting in London. Sleazy had introduced us to him so that he could put up TG promo posters for us.

The Crypt club gig was in the basement of Trinity Church in Paddington and, on a mid-November night, freezing cold. Gen seemed OK – as usual he'd supped his whiskey – but as we started to play his behaviour changed. He climbed on to the PA speakers, which started to list precariously, and he tried to push them over, but someone was wisely pushing them back. The place was totally jam-packed and a speaker would have cracked someone's head open if it fell. Sleazy looked over at me and raised his eyebrows with concern, then frowned as if to say, 'What's up with him?' I shrugged my shoulders in reply. We both looked over at Chris and he shrugged too. By then Gen had returned to the mic and we all assumed it was just another stage act. After the gig ended we packed up the gear and all went home.

Later I was woken by the phone. It was Helen Chadwick. She lived across from us in Beck Road and we'd become friends. 'Hi,

Cosey. Gen's taken a load of pills. He's OK but I think you need to come and see him.'

There was stunned silence. 'What pills? Is he unconscious?' I asked.

'Sleeping pills and his steroids. He's conscious – he rang me up to tell me he'd taken them. I'm taking him to the hospital.' I told her I'd be straight over but she was calm, even casual. 'There's no need. He's fine. Go to the hospital tomorrow.'

The next morning I went to see him. Gen was all right. The doctors explained to me that the pills he'd taken wouldn't have killed him. They'd kept him in overnight but weren't very sympathetic. His mum and dad came to see him and took me to one side to ask what the hell was going on and to say we had to stop tearing each other apart. I couldn't begin to explain the circumstances.

I saw Gen – he was very quiet. I didn't know what to say or what I was supposed to do. Should I fall apart and say I'd come back? I said I'd drive him home, and we got in my Mini and set off. I was pulling away from the traffic lights when he opened the passenger door and went as if to throw himself out into the road. I was screaming at him, one hand on the steering wheel and the other dragging him back into his seat. I pulled over, fastened him in with the seat belt and shut the door. Deep conversations about how we'd continue followed for a few weeks and I visited him a lot, trying to ease the pain of our separation as best I could.

Our second TG album, *D.o.A.*, was released just a month later. The signs of the interpersonal turmoil fracturing TG were clear to see and hear. We all did solo tracks. Gen's track, 'Weeping', directly referred to my leaving him, while my track, 'Hometime', was from a recording I'd done at my sister's while trying to decide whether to leave him. The photo of the little girl on the front was taken by Gen on a two-week holiday liaison with her mother, Ewa.

The TG sound was also changing. Chris's 'AB/7A' track signalled a shift to more sequence-based melodic music, which was a move on from our 'United' single. It was then developed further when we recorded our third TG album, *20 Jazz Funk Greats*.

Where possible we kept everything 'in-house'. Through Sleazy's contacts at Hipgnosis we were able to rent multitrack recording gear, mixing desks from Pink Floyd's Britannia Row facility and then from Paul McCartney, so the gear was high-end. The lightness of some of the tracks on *20 Jazz Funk Greats* was a huge departure from the previous darkness of TG sound. When it came to recording the album, me and Sleazy recorded some vocals, me on 'Hot on the Heels of Love', him on the title track, '20 Jazz Funk Greats', and together on 'Still Walking'. It was great fun deconstructing disco and Martin Denny 's lounge music.

By the time we got to the single 'Adrenalin/Distant Dreams', which suggested similar vocals (if any) to 'Hot on the Heels of Love', we all sensed Gen felt his lead-singer territory was being threatened. We disagreed about 'Adrenalin': me, Chris and Sleazy wanted it to be an instrumental; Gen wanted vocals and wasn't open to anyone else trying anything or joint vocals as a compromise. His discontent may have been down to him not doing anything else on the track or on 'Distant Dreams'. The two tracks signalled the direction me and Chris would take as Chris & Cosey after TG split.

The confrontational and unorthodox presentation of TG gigs, not to mention the sound, meant we expected and nearly always encountered trouble when we played live. For our Architectural Association gig, we decided to place TG in a makeshift cage on a scaffolding platform covered by a large tarpaulin in the central courtyard, purposely separating TG from the audience and creating a funnel of sound within the surrounding buildings. The audience would either have to hang out of the windows to hear us (but not be able to see us) or watch (but not hear) us on the TV monitors that we set up around the building. It caused utter confusion, frustration and then anger, we had beer glasses and bottles thrown at our 'cage', and fights broke out as people tried to get to us. Much the same thing happened at the London Film-Makers' Co-Op gig, which we'd agreed to play for free to raise funds. For the first half we played the *After Cease to Exist* soundtrack, hidden behind the mirrored panels to keep the focus on the music. The seated audience could only see themselves beyond the glare of the halogen lights directed at them. When we emerged to continue the set, there was a growing hostile restlessness. Some of the girls from the punk bands the Slits and the Raincoats were there and drunk, and came to the front swinging Robert Rental's four-year-old son around. One of them hit Glen, our young TG fan and roadie. Then Fred or Judy Vermorel (who we were potentially going to be doing a film soundtrack for) threw a chair across the room and pandemonium broke out. The girls started to attack the stage, trying to unplug the equipment, throwing glasses and bottles at us, one hitting Sleazy. Chris jumped off the stage, grabbed one of the girls by her shoulders and pushed her away, while Gen went further and whacked another girl with his bass guitar – for which we received a threatening phone message. Me and Sleazy set about trying to safely unplug the gear and pack everything away while the room was in chaos, with chairs scattered everywhere and people either arguing or trying to calm things down. One of the Slits came over to me, trying to provoke me, saying she thought I was cool but now thought I was shit, then trying to talk friendly. I didn't give a toss what she thought of me – at that moment she was far from 'cool' in my eyes and I wasn't interested in having a conversation with a drunk.

~

I was stripping weekday lunchtimes and then going to Beck Road to do IR mail order or TG in the evenings and on weekends, unless I was doing my own art projects. Working with Szabo was both fun and intense. We'd formulate an idea for a set of photos, I'd use my own clothes, then he'd ruminate on the overall look, mood, colours, my make-up, hair and props. When I'd arrive at his flat to work he'd always point me to the mantelpiece, where the make-up and accessories had been carefully laid out. It was like an altar awaiting my presence, the point from which our creative collaborations began. As I applied my make-up he'd direct me, commenting on the position of colours. We were engaged in an intimate, ritualistic collaboration, working together to realise the aesthetic we jointly envisaged. He had an incredible eye for form and I trusted him to direct me for body shape and position.

I'd been selected to contribute to the *Hayward Annual* at the Hayward Gallery and used one of Szabo's photos as the poster for my solo three-day art action. He also loaned me some transparencies he'd taken of me, which I had projected alongside images of my striptease work on a wall of the action space. These images were supplemented over the next three days by those taken by Sleazy of my three actions, creating a slide show juxtaposing my private and public 'body' of works projected as part of the live action taking place.

From this amalgamation of my separate activities evolved a new work, 'Life Forms' – modelling, striptease and art actions echoing one another in form but unrelated in context and framed in relationship to my art and life. I first exhibited 'Life Forms' in the group exhibition 'Masculine & Feminine' in Graz, Austria, two months later.

~

Me and Gen living apart didn't seem to adversely affect TG; we were on fire with new ideas. We put together *Industrial News*, a small-format booklet containing updates on our progress, disseminating the information we'd accumulated, TG lyrics, collages and a contact page so people could get in touch with one another to potentially collaborate. TG and IR were about connection and communication and had soon built up a large mailing list through the album questionnaire and the newsletters, and had started receiving cassette tapes from people and requests to collaborate. The TG entourage had expanded to include Stan Bingo, Geordie Vals and Glenn Wallis, and also Kim Norris, who Gen had befriended at the local unemployment exchange. They helped out at gigs and with the increasing mail order workload, which had become difficult to cope with.

TG took a two-week trip to visit Monte, who was now living in Oakland in the San Francisco Bay Area with his girlfriend, Tana. Monte loved having us stay. We all slept on the floor of his living room, which was difficult as Gen kept wanting to sleep with me. The weather was sunny and hot and I took the opportunity to get an all-over tan for when I got home. I hated bikini marks – they didn't look good when I was stripping. The back garden was a suntrap and Tana and me would sit there together, reading.

I was on my own in the garden one day, lying on my front on a blanket in only a red G-string, all oiled up, feeling the sun on my body and half-asleep. Suddenly there was a great thud at my side. I sprang up to see that a large cement breeze block had landed about six inches from my head. I looked behind me to see where it had come from. Gen had thrown it from Monte's balcony and was stood there staring down at me in silence.

I was momentarily speechless. He could have killed me. I shouted at him and Monte came out to see what was going on. He was horrified and took Gen inside. The incident wasn't addressed. Gen carried on like nothing had happened. In hindsight, it's unbelievable that Gen wasn't brought to account. Maybe Monte made Gen realise what a narrow escape he (and I) had had. That put a halt to any more sunbathing for me when Gen was around.

Our label, Industrial Records, had diversified, sub-licensing a single through Jean-Pierre Turmel and Yves Von Bontee's French label, Sordide Sentimental, and also releasing material by other artists on IR – cassette albums by Cabaret Voltaire, Richard H. Kirk and Clock DVA, singles by Leather Nun and Monte, and our first non-TG album, *The Bridge* by Robert Rental and Thomas Leer. We really liked what they'd been doing together and offered for them to release an album on IR. They thought they'd record in the TG studio, using our gear, but we insisted they use their own equipment – bar renting them an eight-track tape recorder and Chris building Robert a Gristleizer. The whole point of their music was that it had its own idiosyncratic sound and we didn't want that to be lost by using our gear. We took them out for a meal in Soho and had them sign a contract. It was formal compared to Monte's, which was painstakingly written line by line and signed in his own blood. He'd cut his arm to get the blood flowing and had to cut it repeatedly as it clotted.

Monte had flown back to the UK, paid for by IR, and lived at Gen's for about four months. He contributed to TG and IR projects, filming what would be the last studio recording by TG, *Heathen Earth* – but a studio recording of a very particular kind. To keep things unpredictable and 'live', we set up a gig in our Martello Street studio, inviting a small group of friends, TG associates and fans. Monte filmed the whole gig using one camera, with Stan Bingo on the mixer. Before we started, people were advised to go to the toilet as there would be no break in the proceedings. We then locked the studio door and started the digital clock we always had on stage to keep us to a strict one-hour set, and everything was filmed and recorded. The album had taken just one hour, with a short break in the middle of the set while Chris put a fresh reel of tape on the recorder. One young fan who attended had written to TG for some time and got talking to Sleazy. His name was Geff Rushton (aka John Balance), who later formed the band Coil together with Sleazy. They became lovers and lifelong companions and collaborators.

TG was now at the centre of my relationship with Gen. TG and IR seemed unstoppable and at times unwieldy. We'd been selling our live gigs on C60 cassette tapes and then as a twenty-four-cassette box set in an attaché case, *24 Hours of Throbbing Gristle*. We'd bought two tape-duplicating machines and were spending hours every day copying tapes.

More vinyl releases came out, one after the other: singles by SPK, Dorothy (from Rema-Rema) and Alex Fergusson, Elisabeth Welch (from Derek Jarman's film *The Tempest*), an EP by Monte, and of course TG's 'Subhuman' and 'Distant Dreams' 7" singles. The live recording of *Heathen Earth* saw the light of day with our first gatefold cover featuring individual portraits, and the first thousand copies were pressed in blue vinyl. Nine live performances contributed to the frenzy of activities, playing alongside Clock DVA, Cabaret Voltaire and Monte. We put on an Industrial Records event at the Scala cinema in London, with IR-associated bands performing throughout the night – TG, Monte, Leather Nun – and screenings of films by Burroughs and Kenneth Anger. We kept ourselves awake with Pro Plus tablets and paid the price with terrible stomach cramps the next day.

Our gig at Oundle was special. It was at a seventeenth-century private boarding school of the same name in the middle of leafy Northamptonshire, very *Tom Brown's School Days*. One of the pupils had written to us and got his music teacher to agree to booking TG, saying we were avant-garde, a bit like John Cage. It was an earlier-than-usual start because we'd arranged as part of the booking that we got to eat lunch with the boarders in the old wood-panelled refectory and go on a tour of the school. Sleazy was in his element – it was so redolent of his school days. We videoed everything, including the dormitories and showers and, of course, the gig. The hall was packed with schoolboys, with the teachers sitting on the balcony opposite the stage looking decidedly worried. Monte played first and made the mistake of throwing back a toilet roll that one boy had hurled at him. That brought a hail of assorted projectiles. TG was next up and the sight of a woman (me) on stage seemed to calm the boys' aggression a little, but it did increase their testosterone levels and shouts of 'Show us your legs, show us your tits' were directed my way. I smiled sweetly . . . then we absolutely blasted them with sound, drowning out their protests until, towards the end, we noticed singing . . . They were all singing the hymn 'Jerusalem' at the tops of their voices. It was a bizarre but beautiful moment. The performance ended on some Martin Denny lounge music and the very hyper boys were ordered to their dorms for the night. One boy came over to me and gave me his rugby shirt. I could hardly hold Sleazy back from grabbing it out of my hands and he nagged me for days to give it to him. I kept it.

The stress of working every day and then spending evenings stripping, while holding TG together and still not being at a point where Gen would accept me and Chris being a couple, was really getting to me. I knew it was taking its toll because my body was out of sync and I'd lost a lot of weight. I booked a holiday to a naturist resort in what was then still Yugoslavia and escaped for some sun, sea and a change of scenery. Kim came with me for company. It was so liberating to walk around naked to the bank and supermarket.

Everyone was naked, including teenage boys and girls playing volleyball together, pregnant women and older people with surgery scars, people of all shapes and sizes and not a single voyeur.

When we got back to the UK, Chris and Gen met us at St Pancras. My eyes lighted straight away on Chris, although he was stood behind Gen, who seemed to be just a shadow in the foreground. All I wanted to do was run to Chris but I couldn't as I was expected to go to Gen. Nothing had changed for him and things picked up where they had left off, with me going regularly to Beck Road and taking Gen's new puppy, Tanith, to training classes. She was a Doberman–Alsatian cross-breed and needed careful handling. Tanith was an amazing dog and responded so well to me that the trainer said, 'She could go far – she's very quick to learn. She'd jump through a ring of fire for you.' I told Gen but he said he didn't have the time, couldn't be bothered; it was up to me if I wanted to take her training further. I'd taken him to one of the classes but the trainer suggested he not come again, saying that Gen's handling methods conflicted with the gentle training approach and my close relationship with Tanith. She obeyed all the commands I taught her and whenever I drove up she'd jump straight into my car, ready to go to class, sometimes through the open window.

Industrial Records paid for Sleazy and Gen to go to New York and Kansas to work on the William Burroughs album *Nothing Here Now but the Recordings*. Gen wrote me many letters chronicling their progress and how homesick he felt, and bored and lonely as Sleazy went cruising whenever chances presented themselves – or 'slinking off into Queendom', as Gen put it.

That album turned out to be the last release on Industrial Records. I had no inkling that the end was so close; we'd been forging ahead with TG sound and video ideas, as well as the TG style. The TG military look had moved on from army surplus and the camouflage flak jackets and trousers I'd made to our very own bespoke TG uniforms, designed and made by fashion designer Lawrence Dupré, a friend of Jean-Pierre Turmel's. The fabric was tough grey canvas with a silk-screened, unique TG camouflage print, and Lawrence had made each uniform to suit our personal specifications. I had culottes instead of trousers, the hood of my jacket was detachable and the jacket could be rolled up and folded inside itself into a pouch in the lining. They were beautiful pieces and made with such care.

Lawrence came to visit and we took a group photo of us wearing them outside Beck Road. She stayed with Gen and was crying one day when I went round there. Gen had told her to leave. She wasn't due to go home for another day but he wanted her gone immediately. Gen stormed out with Tanith and I tried to console Lawrence. She couldn't understand why he was behaving that way towards her – it was obvious there'd been something going on between them. But Gen had a new girlfriend called Paula, who was now the focus of all his affections, and Lawrence was feeling hurt. There was a knock on the front door – I answered it and there was Paula. What a strange position for me to be in, comforting one of Gen's lovers and answering the door to another. Stranger still was when, four weeks later, I received a tenth-'anniversary' bouquet of flowers from Gen to mark the day I'd agreed to move into the Funhouse. It all seemed a bit odd, seeing as Paula was more or less a fixture by then and Gen knew about me and Chris living together.

My 1980 birthday celebration was a firework party at Beck Road with some old and new friends, including Paula. It was good to see Gen happy and more light-hearted. I liked Paula – we got on well and we've stayed friends. Two days later, TG were in Germany for two gigs at the SO36 Club in Berlin and another in Frankfurt. Thankfully we took our new custom compact flight cases to make setting up quicker, seeing as we had to wait until the room was cleared from a circumcision ceremony that had taken place prior to our show – the spilling of newborn penis blood prior to a TG gig seemed somehow fitting, even if I wholeheartedly disapproved and thought it barbaric. At that gig we created a new TG song inspired by Chris's incredible industrial mechanical rhythm. Gen asked us what to sing about. 'Discipline,' me and Sleazy said. That was the birth of one of the most iconic TG songs.

Being in Berlin, I couldn't not visit Checkpoint Charlie to see the sad and brutal history of the division of Germany. The Berlin Wall was still up then and TG posed for photos standing in both East and West Berlin, with one foot either side of the border. We were being closely monitored by the armed East German guards in their watchtowers, who became impatient at us not obeying their barked orders to move back into the West. When they then aimed their guns and shouted a final warning at us to move away from the borderline, we weren't going to argue and so moved on to our next, less risky, photo location, the Reichstag building. The photos came out so well and, seeing as 'Discipline' was created live in Berlin, we used one of the images for the cover of the 'Discipline' 12" single that was later released on Fetish Records. It hadn't been a convivial trip but some good had come of it.

Discipline and a bit of common sense is what Gen could have done with when he cut a girl's arm at the TG Rafters gig in Manchester a month later. I don't know why he did it – there were mutterings of it possibly being a mark of her commitment to or trust in him. Who knows, but she bled so profusely that me and Sleazy had to give her first aid to stem the bleeding, while Gen looked on, worried that his cutting her had gone horribly wrong.

∼

We'd been working with Derek Jarman and had done a soundtrack for his film *In the Shadow of the Sun*. The recording of it was an odd experience. The studio was in a freezing cold disused mortuary. It had green lights, which gave it an eerie feel, and the ambience was dominated by the residual presence of the dead bodies that had passed through, as well as all the post-mortem procedures that had taken place there. It was a strange environment for recording music and the engineer's austere demeanour didn't help. We arrived with our compact set-up. We all watched Derek's film closely as we played along, improvising to the visuals. It was like playing a gig to a fourteen-inch black-and-white monitor hooked up to a 'piano keys' VHS machine. Then me and Sleazy did some choir-type vocals that Chris sampled into his Eventide Harmonizer. We recorded the session on to an eight-track and took it to Martello Street for the final mixing. The soundtrack had gone from one death factory to another, and premiered at the Berlin Film Festival.

After that, Derek wanted to film a TG gig, so, when we were due to play at Heaven in London, he came along with his camera. It was two days before Christmas, my busiest and most lucrative time for stripping, and I arrived at Heaven having already done three bookings. Heaven was a predominantly gay venue at the time, with a loaded atmosphere from the fetishistic activities that took place there. I spent most of my time being looked after by a young and very handsome gay guy. We'd got on so well, talking and laughing together. The gig went well and after the show, as we were stacking the gear ready to load the van, the guy asked me out on a date. I was flummoxed. 'I thought you were gay?' I said to him.

'I am, but I really fancy you.'

'But, but, I . . .' was all I could stammer. I didn't know what to do or say. He was genuine about it, fanciable, such fun and so kind, but I was with Chris and wasn't interested in getting into anything with anyone else. I said no, it couldn't happen, and we parted with a hug and a gentle kiss.

The Lyceum show in London was a Fetish Records night with Clock DVA, Z'EV, Cabaret Voltaire and TG. We played first on the bill as we'd requested, to an audience of about three thousand, mainly made up of people looking 'industrial' in an assortment of army fatigues. We'd noticed a TG 'uniform' emerging at previous shows so we decided to wear white and test their mettle with a very long rendition of 'Discipline'. The night was more of an endurance than a pleasure for me. I had really bad flu and was dosing myself with cold remedies just to get through the show.

Rod from Fetish Records hung out with us quite a lot. He'd asked me to play cornet for a Bongos album and often called me to chat and chat me up, one time even proposing a partner swap – me with him and Chris with his girlfriend. No, thanks. He came with TG to some of the meetings at the Institute of Ecotechnics in London. The institute was in a large old building where they ran workshops, research and education programmes on the harmonising of ecology and technology, as well as inviting artists and holding talks by William Burroughs and Brion Gysin. That's where I met Brion and I took on the task of transcribing tapes for him. I spent hours at Beck Road typing pages and pages of dialogue, very appreciative of the vari-speed feature on Chris's cassette machine so I could slow the tape down to understand what Brion was saying.

~

By the beginning of 1981, my life had taken some significant turns. I was in a good place despite the troubles within TG. I'd been regularly attending a photographic course to improve my skills and continued to take Tanith to classes on Monday evenings. And with the help of Chris's dad, me and Chris were looking for a cheap property to buy together. I'd been ensconced in Chris's family for some time, going skiing with them and being invited to family celebrations. They'd welcomed me with open arms and we visited them every week. The love and laughter of his close-knit London family was a revelation, not having had a family of my own for so long . . . and very different from Yorkshire family life.

Chris's parents, Rose and Albert, looked after Tremble for us when we went to Rome with TG. I'd been approached to make a sound work for RAI, Italian national radio, based on the theme of 'A Journey Through the Body'. Robert Wyatt was taking part and had asked for me to be involved in the project. Robert and I had been writing to one another for quite some time (and have remained close). I thought it would be an interesting opportunity for TG. We all went to Rome to record at RAI's studios for a week. The studio technicians were a joke – they were stoned or drunk and unhelpful most of the time – so we took over the recording sessions and recorded with their grand piano, synthesisers and other assorted instruments. When we came to leave, RAI refused to give us a copy of the recording. All we got was a cassette tape of it. It was unofficially released in 1982 on a label of unknown origin with unfamiliar titles, and one track appended with '(for Paula)', with a photo of her on the inner sleeve. I doubt Paula was fully aware of the history of the recording. Nevertheless, Gen was, and I didn't appreciate what was initially my project being appropriated and work attributed to someone else. That misrepresentation of the work was eventually rectified when it was officially released some years later by Mute Records.

24 March 1981

It's totally impossible for me to trust anyone now. I wonder what stories have gone to how many people in my name, by Gen's hand . . . We are all drifting far apart now, I can almost touch this awful block between us . . .

There were arguments about money. IR was a registered limited company so we needed and had got an accountant, Peter Edney. As directors, me and Sleazy signed cheques and withdrew money to use as petty cash for mail and admin expenses. Money was going astray and my queries as to where the money had gone didn't go down well with Gen, who then told me the accountant had asked for Sleazy to have his own IR chequebook so he could sign cheques without my signature. That didn't sound right to me. I checked with the accountant. He'd said no such thing to Sleazy but he had noticed some financial matters that needed addressing and recommended that we restore parity regarding the allocation of IR money, through me, Sleazy and Chris being paid an amount equal to what Gen had 'received'.

Apart from money, there was something else weird going on. Chris came across a letter to a TG fan among the pile of post waiting to be sent off. It was typed on my 'Cosey' letter-headed paper. Thinking I'd written it, Chris asked if I wanted to put it in an envelope to be posted. I didn't recall writing a letter so I read it. Gen had written it as if he were me slagging him off, and signing it with my special signature. I was speechless, trying to get my head around what he'd done, and why anyone could even come up with the idea of doing that. I wondered how many other people Gen may have vindictively sent letters to before Chris discovered this one. I was so upset I confronted Gen. He just shrugged his shoulders with an air of indifference.

I'd been stripping for some time (more about that later). The *Sunday Times* magazine was doing a feature on 'everything' you can hire and wanted to include a stripper. They contacted my agency, Gemini, who asked me to do the photo session knowing I'd done modelling before. I went to the photographer's studio straight from a lunchtime booking. When I walked in, there was an odd atmosphere, as if they didn't know what to expect but had in mind some archetype of a stripper. I didn't want to hang around long as I had another booking that evening, so I got my costumes out and selected a tiny silver G-string with matching bra, long gloves and a silver tinsel boa, and started posing as they clicked away. It was over and done within half an hour and I went on my way.

The feature came out on Sunday, 30 November 1980. Me and Chris happened to be driving home via Fleet Street at about 2 a.m. and saw the Sunday papers being loaded up for delivery. We stopped and bought a copy and were surprised to see that I'd ended up on the front cover of the *Sunday Times* magazine, with the strapline 'Stripper for hire: £115 per hour', next to a policewoman at £7.43 per hour. I bought half a dozen copies 'hot off the press'. But I wasn't so pleased when the exposure triggered an enquiry by the Inland Revenue, who demanded an interview with me regarding my earnings. I contacted Peter, our IR accountant, and asked if he'd take me on as a client. He accompanied me to a face-to-face meeting at the tax office. The taxman was convinced by the *Sunday Times* article that I was earning £115 an hour and I was lying about my income. I wasn't and showed him figures and my living expenses. He didn't believe I could live on so little, but I was adept at that from my frugal hippy days. It went as far as nitpicking about the cost of washing powder for my washing machine. I didn't own one – I used the launderette at 25p a scoop of Persil. There was lots of indignation on my part, with Peter kicking my leg under the table to stop me being so argumentative. Everything was shown to be above board eventually, I had no worries, and I paid my estimated tax bill.

The *Sunday Times* appearance got me a lot of bookings outside of the usual pub circuit and stag nights – one being at Guy's Hospital for a doctors' party. The room was large and packed with people, including the hospital rugby club. I was introduced and entered to foul-mouthed catcalls from a girlfriend of one of the rugby team. I left the stage and refused to go on unless she was removed. She left and the show went down very well, ending with them presenting me with a framed enlargement of the *Sunday Times* cover. I was very touched. It still hangs in my office.

~

TG was due to play its first gigs in the USA, in Los Angeles and San Francisco, arranged by Michael Sheppard. They were also to be the last. As me and Chris were together and Gen had told me he was falling in love with Paula, I suggested that she come with TG to America. He was over the moon.

TG was still operating but had split into two camps – me and Chris, and Gen with Sleazy. Chris had had enough of the acrimony towards him and me. As all four of us were sat around in the living room at Beck Road talking about the forthcoming American trip, Chris announced that he was leaving TG and that the US shows would be his last TG gigs. Gen went ballistic, grabbed a small chair and put it in the centre of the room, shouting at Chris, 'Sit there!', ordering him to take up position for interrogation, to explain himself to the rest of us. Chris stayed put and just reiterated that he was leaving and that's all he had to say. I suspected Gen's anger was down to Chris's announcement pre-empting Gen throwing Chris out of TG, but Gen changed the subject and switched to my leaving him and being with Chris – telling Chris that fate dictated that Gen's and my destiny were linked. I couldn't make sense of why he'd still be expecting me to return, when he was with Paula. Of course, if Chris left TG, I would too. That made the already high level of tension between the four of us worse, with me and Chris feeling we were deliberately excluded from interviews and other TG matters, and that Gen and Sleazy were planning another venture together. All TG-related opportunities from interested parties went to either Beck Road or Martello Street, so me and Chris never knew exactly what was going on. We felt like we were being edged out. The commitment between the four of us, and to TG, had gone.

I knew the USA trip would be difficult but was determined to get some enjoyment out of it. Me and Chris had been trying for a child and my period was two months late. The first thing I did when I got to LA was a pregnancy test. It was positive. We were ecstatic and rang his family straight away. His mum, Rose, was thrilled for us. His sister, Vicki, in the background and clearly unaware of our situation, asked, 'Whose is it?' That was a little upsetting. Then she said, 'I'm pregnant too' (with her second child).

We went and told everyone. We were so happy . . . but Gen wasn't. Being pregnant confirmed that I wasn't going back to him. He said we were no longer welcome at Beck Road unless we made an appointment to see him and that he expected me to give him half of my savings. What? We weren't married, this wasn't an alimony situation, and the only savings I had were what I'd put away from my stripping earnings after I left him.

A few days later he married Paula in Tijuana, Mexico. We weren't invited. It didn't matter. We'd decided to indulge our liking for the ambience of cemeteries and took a long walk to the Hollywood

Forever Cemetery to see Rudolph Valentino's interred ashes. It was a tranquil place, perfect for a picnic and far away from all the negativity back at the TG motel. Our friend Jerry Dreva, who'd taken the black-and-white photo for the *20 Jazz Funk Greats* album on our last LA visit, came to the Travelodge and gave us a chocolate replica of the album.

Friends didn't know what to make of the atmosphere and felt torn between the two camps – especially Skot, who later told me that, 'Gen had issued a sort of ultimatum that it was you OR Gen. I picked you. As Gen became more of a rock star I had become less close to Gen and less trustful of Gen's motives. During the early TG days, I'd often read chunks of my letters to Gen spouted in interviews as Gen's ideas warped like a funhouse mirror to suit his purposes: ASSUME POWER FOCUS. The origin of that phrase was never offered to the public by Gen.' The phrase was used by TG.

Skot picked me and Chris up the next day to drive us to the Griffith Observatory to see the amazing Tesla coil and its giant arcing sparks. We spent hours there, sitting in the planetarium, looking through the huge telescopes and the simple but magical camera obscura. We hit the second-hand record stores, the wax museum and Sunset Boulevard.

The Veterans' Hall was the penultimate TG gig and billed as a 'Modern Music Concert'. That was pretty accurate. Don Bolles' band played first, then TG headlined. The place was full of adulating TG fans asking for autographs – not something I was used to or sure about. What had TG come to when what we did was liked and our confounding expectation neutralised by acceptance?

The LA show was a nightmare. It was as if Gen had turned into Ted Nugent. He was behaving like a rock star guitarist and lead singer. Then Paula wandered nonchalantly on stage during the set, which totally disrupted the flow. I ushered her off. Me and Chris seemed an irrelevance to Gen. This was not TG. I was disgusted and walked off mid-set into the dressing room. I'd have stayed there until the gig came to a grinding, shambolic halt if it hadn't been for two couples fucking up against the lockers. I walked out and went back on stage.

Afterwards I tackled Gen about what had happened and said I wouldn't do the San Francisco gig unless he got back in line, that we all pull together as one and play as TG. Everyone agreed and TG moved on to San Francisco. Monte was now on board and we visited Rough Trade Inc. to say hello and thank them for distributing TG over the years.

Arriving at Kezar Pavilion for the very last TG gig, I was taken aback by how vast the space was and the massive PA stacked up, awaiting our arrival and instructions. A stage had been installed at one end and we talked with Flipper, who were our support band, about where we could set up all our combined equipment. Ted, their lead guitarist and vocalist, was a Vietnam veteran and wasn't having a good day. He was freaked out and frantically trying to get some cigarettes. No one seemed to want to help. If all it took to make him feel better was a packet of fags, it was an easy fix. I went and got him some.

San Francisco turned out to be my favourite TG gig. The energies that had originally brought us together and the raw wounds of what had torn us apart clashed head-on, suffusing TG with tremendous power – so charged that I felt like I was having an out-of-body experience, as if I was hovering above the stage, a feeling probably helped by the sprung floor and people jumping up and down in unison to the TG rhythms. It was a fitting end.

Before we left for the UK we all went to Bobby Bonbon's. His house was a large, luxurious place just across from George Lucas's in the hills of Marin County. He cooked us all a meal. The mood was a bit sombre, all sitting around a long table eating our last meal together with Monte and everyone. It felt like the Last Supper. I don't recall ever seeing any money from those two TG gigs. But I didn't care. I was the happiest I'd ever been and couldn't wait to return home to start our life free from the burden of what TG had become. I wasn't sad TG had ended. It had run its course.

5

A scorching summer in 1981 befitted the mood me and Chris were in as we started our life together. Free at last, everything seemed brighter than bright – blazing sunshine, laughter and positivity. First stop after our return from America was to visit Pam and Les to tell them about the baby. We went to the seaside at Scarborough. A carefree break prior to tackling the TG fallout and our future plans.

There was so much to do. For one thing, I couldn't continue stripping once my baby bump began to show. That came sooner than I expected. The landlord at the Old Red Lion commented on my boobs looking great 'that size'. He thought I'd had breast implants. Although I was only fourteen weeks pregnant, I told my agency I was leaving. I fulfilled one last job, performing a striptease to Bowie's 'Fashion' for a new format, the LaserDisc. It ended up coming out on video, with me being introduced by the actor Keith Allen.

With our new era came the task of dealing with residual TG matters. We all agreed to complete any outstanding projects and announced the official end of TG with a funeral card that simply stated 'The Mission Is Terminated', dated 23 June 1981. Me and Chris visited Beck Road at appointed times. Gen insisted I take everything that he deemed to be my belongings, as Paula was moving in: all my ICA framed magazines, my darkroom equipment – Gen didn't want it, he didn't know how to use it, and in any case he had Sleazy to do all that for him. I also took some of my negatives and asked

Gen for copies of photos of our time together. He put some in an envelope and gave it to me. I thought that was amiable of him. But when I got home and opened it, he'd cut himself out of every one of the photos. It struck me as strange and childish to go to the trouble of making a symbolic gesture of cutting himself out of my life. I took that and his reaction to my pregnancy as a sign writ large that he was ready to let go at last. It was a relief.

There was more purging to follow. I was told by Gen that Paula was allergic to cats, so they had to go too. I couldn't let them be sent away to strangers or be put to sleep so I said I'd take them. However, I was only allowed to take Hermes and Razart; Gen wouldn't let me have Moonshine. Paula's allergy aside, he regarded Moonshine as his cat. By the beginning of July, the era of me and Gen was over. The saddest final part was dear Tremble passing away on 5 July. She was buried in Chris's parents' garden, her grave marked by the twelve red roses I'd been given on my final stripping booking just two days earlier.

~

Before the TG split, Geoff Travis of Rough Trade had asked Chris to play him some of his solo tapes and offered him a solo album deal. Me and Chris went for a meeting with him at their Blenheim Crescent offices in Notting Hill after the TG USA trip. It was an incredibly hot and sunny day. Everything seemed to be in slow motion as we walked hand-in-hand down the street lined with cherry blossom trees, being gently showered by the falling pale-pink blossoms and treading softly through the drifts of flowers that had collected underfoot.

The meeting was just as uplifting. Rough Trade were very supportive and offered to front the cost of manufacturing and handle distribution, and Geoff also extended Chris's solo album offer to include the release of the first Chris & Cosey album. We'd started compiling ideas and sounds while in LA and soon after we got back we began recording in the small studio Chris had set up in one of our old bedsit rooms after we'd moved into a larger flat downstairs. We used a TEAC four-track, then took the tape to Meridian Studios, under the Southern Music offices down Denmark Street (just next door to Hipgnosis). Mick Garoghan was the resident engineer and worked with us over the two weeks, with Alex (Fergusson) helping out on guitar and vocals. It was a fun few weeks working with them both. Alex was amazing to work with, always happy and game for trying out ideas. We were cutting the album with Steve Angel at Utopia by the end of August, then completed the artwork and delivered everything to Rough Trade on 7 September.

The album as a whole was peppered with references to the huge transitional period in our lives. Not just the music, which was a crossover between TG and what was to come, but also the artwork. The front cover was an image of the first scan of our child, the title, *Heartbeat*, a reference to our new 'life'. We recorded the baby's heartbeat and used it on the title track and dedicated the album to Tremble.

During the recording of *Heartbeat* me and Chris had resumed our search for a cheap property to buy. I asked a local estate agent if they had any run-down properties and they showed us one that they'd just taken on, a very cheap 'doer-upper', a three-bedroom terraced house in Tottenham, North London. The last owner was a Mrs D'Eath, which didn't sit well until Chris's mum dismissed it outright: 'Oh, there were a lot of people with that name when I was young.'

That intense Inland Revenue meeting had paid off, as the self-employed accounts I'd had to supply also qualified me for a mortgage. The house needed a lot doing to it to make it habitable, and we continued living in a rented flat in Crouch End while it was renovated. We were overseeing the builders while also working on and promoting the new album, and meanwhile I was learning to cope with the increasing size of my baby bump. Claude Bessy, who we met in Los Angeles when he worked for *Slash* music magazine, was now living in the UK and working as press officer for Rough Trade, so we saw a lot of him and his wife, Philomena (Pinglewad's sister), during the run-up to (and beyond) the release of *Heartbeat*.

In October we were asked to support Grace Jones on her 'One Man Show' tour but had to decline as I was seven months pregnant and airline restrictions didn't allow flying at that stage. I think we had enough on our plate already anyway, as TG business was still being wound down. Fetish were releasing a five-album TG box set, with Neville Brody on board doing design. The box included a badge, booklet, liner notes by Jon Savage, the four official TG albums and the very last TG gig in San Francisco, entitled *Mission of Dead Souls*. Rough Trade were also releasing TG live in Heaven on cassette, under the title *Beyond Jazz Funk*, and Chris supervised the mastering for them. He'd also had an offer from Southern Publishing to do an album of incidental music for their BBC library series. So much was happening, and so quickly.

30 December 1981
'Heartbeat' was released and sold the first 5000 in a week. Re-pressing another 2000 now. Cassettes selling well too . . . We sorted out Industrial Records and shared out the equipment.

We'd spent a fantastic, boisterous family Christmas at Chris's parents', fourteen of us and the boxing promoter Frank Warren and his wife Sue, close friends of the family, all tucking into a festive feast while being entertained by crazy mad stories of past pranks and near misses. I laughed so much I thought I was going to go into labour.

Heartbeat had sold well, was licensed to France and Italy, and Rough Trade suggested we do another album and a single for the following year. That was a great counterbalance to the sombre task of the dispersing of TG and IR assets. We shared out TG equipment – well, I say share: there didn't seem much left in the studio when me and Chris got there. We weren't interested in the fight over the TG/IR spoils. For one thing, it was New Year's Eve when Gen told us to collect everything, and I was due to give birth in just two weeks' time, so I wasn't best pleased about the timing of it all. We left a lot behind.

~

At 3.30 p.m. on 12 January 1982, TG gathered at the offices of Peer Music on Denmark Street to sign off from our contracts with them. It was the end of TG and the beginning of a new life for me and Chris.

I thought I had the usual backache, but I'd actually gone into labour during the meeting. By the time we got home to Crouch End at about six thirty, I was under no illusion that this was labour for sure – the pains were coming every four minutes. I had to abandon my cake and cup of tea and we set off in my blue Mini to the Royal Free Hospital in Hampstead. The sudden panic of imminent birth had Chris driving in the wrong direction at first, like some comedy sketch. We were laughing, which only made the pains worse.

Just before 11 p.m. that evening, and on my mother's birthday, our son, Nick, was born after a short but intensely painful four-hour labour. I'd requested no epidural or pain relief. I had the natural birth I wanted.

I wrote a letter to Monte about the intensity of the pain, how I seemed to transcend my body when it reached a critical level. I was euphoric, if exhausted. I'd had one of the most momentous experiences of my life but didn't talk about it at postnatal classes. I was silenced by my respect for the other women's pain. Everyone else in the class had tales of postnatal depression, unsupportive partners, agonising births, and one woman had walked across the ward leaving a trail of blood as she went. I was also lucky with my postnatal hormonal plunge into 'baby blues'. It was brief and shared with a woman in the next bed to me during my week-long stay in hospital. We'd both been given strong painkillers and were a bit out of it for a couple of days, laughing and clowning around as best we could with stitches and the agony of humongous boobs as our milk came in.

Giving birth and the physical aftermath it wreaks on women's bodies doesn't tally with the idyllic picture of motherhood. A week before me, Chris's sister Vicki had her son, Peter, who was renamed Nicholas after our Nick was born. Two babies born within a week of each other in the same family meant that there was a lot of love and support. I couldn't have managed half as well without Rose and her sister, Pat. Nick was adorable and adored by the family and fitted into our lives seamlessly. I settled into motherhood without any angst or hang-ups. Nick was my child, he was dependent on me and Chris, and like most new parents we revelled in the marvel of the precious new life we'd created.

~

Just six days before Nick arrived, we'd mastered our second album, *Trance*, an instrumental in a more minimal style, still under the name Chris & Cosey but adding 'The Creative Technology Institute' (CTI), which stood for both our own label and the collective name for any forthcoming collaborations and Chris & Cosey side projects that also went under the moniker of Conspiracy International. Although we released our work on Rough Trade, we continued the independent DIY approach we'd practised as IR and TG with our own CTI label, including distributing newsletters and operating a mail-order service to our own mailing list. Such a short time after the demise of TG we were fully up and running with unprecedented fervour, a sense of freedom and an expanding fanbase.

Recording *Trance* had been a new experience. There was no lingering trace of TG, and the tracks came together so easily and quickly that we thought of it as more of a stopgap between C&C albums and proposed that it be sold at a budget price. It was to wholesalers, but generally shops sold it on at full price. That was a lesson learned. *Trance* marked a distinct shift in our musical style as we were now using a Roland TR-808 drum machine and TB-303 bassline. We had no idea it would gain status years later as one of our most successful and influential albums.

The cover artwork was as easy-going as the music. As part of my postnatal fitness plan, we took regular walks with Nick through Crouch End and up Highgate Hill to Highgate Cemetery, where we'd walk around, then have tea and cake at a cafe. On one of our walks we set up my Nikon and took the photos for the cover of *Trance* in front of the entrance gates to a tomb not far from the Karl Marx monument, with Nick in his pram just out of shot next to the camera tripod. Back then the cemetery was quite run-down and access to the catacombs wasn't difficult. Many a horror film was shot there.

As news got round that me and Chris were no longer involved with Gen, a lot of friends reconnected with us. John Lacey had kept in touch and called round to our flat late one night to tell us that he'd bought a house and was now living in Todmorden, West York-shire. After we'd moved to Tottenham, we called John and invited him to stay. That visit rekindled our creative working relationship. Me and Chris had started recording music for *Elemental 7* and John joined us in collaboration. We decided to make a video of the whole album.

I'd been invited to give a lecture on my work at Leeds College of Art. I put together some slides to base my talk around and we drove up there, with baby and all the video and lighting equipment we'd need to do some filming. We were making use of the trip to visit Hull, then go on to John's place in Todmorden for more filming for *Elemental 7*. The Leeds lecture went very well, with me feeding Nick in a small room just before, leaving Chris to rock him to sleep. The talk was taped and transcribed to form the basis of 'Time to Tell', a special edition of Ian Dobson's fanzine, *Flowmotion*. The issue cov-ered the past ten years of my work as a musician, artist, model and striptease dancer, and included a cassette of a solo music recording I'd made in our small studio in Crouch End.

John's house in Todmorden stood on a hill in a row of stone Victorian terraced houses. Just up the road was Robinwood Mill, a huge disused Victorian cotton mill. We did a recce of the place as a potential site for filming. The main part of the mill was five storeys high and we used the old rickety goods lift that was just about operational as we explored each of the floors. Emptied of their machinery they looked vast. The dusty, worn, wooden floorboards were solid underfoot and light streamed in from the windows that lined the walls. There was an underlying feeling of some lurking presence, giving it a creepy atmosphere that was magnified tenfold when we returned to film there in the evening.

There wasn't much lighting and we needed torches and the video lights to help us find our way. The lift had iron concertina doors that had to be latched into place for the thing to operate. They didn't always latch properly or would spring open with the jolts and jerks – and the lift would sometimes stop between floors, stranding us until we got the thing going again. That and unexpected and unaccountable moving shadows and noises amplified by the echoing vastness gave us a feeling that we were not alone, intruders at the mercy of the building and whatever lingering forces were at play. But we were determined to get some video footage. As we played the album track off a cassette machine, Chris filmed me and John as we danced, leaped and ran across the wooden floor. When we finished, the atmosphere had changed. It felt as if our actions had disturbed the equilibrium of whatever energies were present – that we were not welcome. Behind the lights was a blanket of blackness that none of us wanted to look into. The hairs stood up on the backs of our necks and it was fast approaching midnight. We didn't care how irrational our reactions seemed as we scrambled to pack the equipment up and get out as fast as we could, praying the lift didn't come to a grinding halt and leave us stuck in the mill overnight. We were delivered to the ground floor, slung the lift gate aside and rushed out the main entrance and up the road to the safety of John's house. We called the track 'Dancing Ghosts'.

~

I returned to stripping when Nick was five months old. I've barely touched on my stripping yet so I'll start at the beginning, even though by now my involvement was nearing its end.

My first introduction to stripping was while modelling for magazines. I worked with two girls, Janet and Lynn, who were also striptease artistes. Despite their encouragement, I didn't start until late 1977. My stripping work ran parallel to my music and art activities and any modelling jobs that cropped up. There were still a few photographers who hadn't blacklisted me after the ICA exhibition.

I was lucky that both my model and dancing agencies knew and understood that I had other priorities, so I could fit their bookings in around TG and other projects. But it was physically exhausting dancing up to four hours a day, going to our Martello Street studio at night and weekends, doing TG gigs, recordings and art projects. When I look back at my diaries, I'm amazed that I also had such a full-on social life, considering how much else was happening. But stripping did have some unexpected advantages at times. I acquired some steel surgical instruments from a pub, including a rib-spreader and a speculum. I have no idea what they were doing there, discarded in an old cardboard box in the storeroom that doubled as my dressing room. But they were most welcome and fitted in very readily with our other interesting activities of the time.

I auditioned for the Gemini stripping agency at the infamous Chelsea Drugstore in the King's Road. It had been an old haunt of Chris's and he'd also worked there on the set of *A Clockwork Orange*. Those connections made me feel more at home. But I was nervous as I knew that it was a one-dance chance and I had no idea if I'd fit the bill. I go-go danced in my silver sequinned bikini, behind the bar on a small ledge they called a stage, and I could see my potential agent, Bob, and his wife stood across the room watching intently as they assessed me. When my music finished Bob beckoned me over . . . I got the job. I was surprised but elated.

Leading up to the audition I'd spent months doing research, mainly going to the Arabian Arms in Cambridge Heath Road, Hackney, which was not far from where I lived in Beck Road. I'd watch the different dancers, noting how they moved, what music they used, their costumes and how the customers responded. As I came to understand how it all worked and how it could work for me, I decided I'd use the name 'Scarlet', with all its connotations of the 'Scarlet Woman'. It suited both stripping and my interest in magick. I made my costumes and compiled my music.

Selecting the right music was one of the most difficult tasks. Back then, in the 1970s, everything was on vinyl, and singles were either 7" or 12", so it was important to keep them to a minimum if only to limit the weight of your dance-kit bag. Also there was no room for duplication: the dancers had to use music the DJs didn't play and also select different songs to one another. The choices were limited but inevitably some great songs lent themselves so readily to stripping – in mood, rhythm and lyrics – that girls duplicated, but usually never when they worked together.

Money and ego were the two sources of competition between the girls. The issue of who was better than who often raised its ugly head. We all cultivated a 'look' and persona, and our costumes reflected that, so it was irritating when these got copied. It was also unacceptable to have two girls dance with the same outfit – it made for unwelcome comparisons. I made my own costumes so I was lucky that none of the girls could copy them, but there were arguments about who danced to any one particular record. Fortunately it only happened to me once, at a pub in the King's Road. It had a large wooden dance floor and good sound system, so whenever I was sent there I took the opportunity to really dance away to Candi Staton's 'Nights on Broadway'. The girl I was with was up next and used the same song, saying, as she passed me, 'That's my track.' She was reprimanded by the DJ.

Stag (bachelor) parties were different from pub work because there were no single dances, only stripteases, and these were performed to two or three tracks, so girls compiled the music for their stag acts on to cassette tape. One tape for each act, so the tape could be quickly rewound – but not on a machine. We couldn't cart that around with us as well as make-up, vinyl, up to ten costumes and everything else, so we had to rewind manually: pencil or Biro through the sprocket hole and spin. It was a common sight in dressing rooms to see girls sat talking while nonchalantly rewinding their cassette tapes in readiness for their next show.

It quickly became apparent to me that the striptease scene was a world apart from my art, music and modelling. Up to this point, everything had connected well, each informing the other in the most rewarding ways. But this new venture was uncompromisingly social in context, with me as the focal point to ensure that the few hours I was there were exciting, fun and erotic. This was entertainment and, unlike modelling, I had the lion's share of control. After all that time since my teens, I got to dance, dress up and more or less have a party every day. Of course, that's a simplistic view and paints a far better picture than the realities I faced, but nevertheless I recognised the opportunity it gave me to express myself within an unfamiliar environment.

Working in live and volatile situations twice a day called for a quite different means of coping, and I faced a steep learning curve. What I'd experienced in the world of pornography had been tough in other ways. I was never followed home from modelling jobs, whereas leaving pubs on my own either in the afternoon or evening left me vulnerable to being stalked and possibly attacked. That's when my faithful 'fans' helped, as they'd often see me safely to my car.

But they weren't around when I worked in Dagenham one day. It was a good money-spinner, with all the Ford workers drinking there at lunchtimes. When I left I noticed a guy in a car following me. I thought nothing of it at first but no matter which way I turned to test him out, he followed me and continued on my tail all the way to Bethnal Green. I could see the guy's face in my rear-view mirror and I began to panic. As I stopped at the traffic lights at the junction of Cambridge Heath Road, a motorcycle cop pulled up alongside me. I quickly wound my window down and shouted, 'What do I do about a guy who's been following me from Dagenham?'

'Any reason why he should be following you?' he asked.

'No, I don't know him.'

The cop looked behind at the car I'd pointed out and said, 'When the lights change to green, drive off and I'll keep him here.' He positioned his bike in front of the stalker's car and I drove off. I thought I'd shaken him but as I reached Crouch End I saw him again. I drove past our flat and straight to the nearby police station and parked, and he pulled up a short distance away. I pointed to the neon POLICE STATION sign and shouted at him, 'I'm going in there to report you and give them your registration number. I suggest you FUCK OFF!', and I walked into the station. I stood in the lobby for a few minutes, then peeked tentatively through the window – he'd gone.

When I first started with Gemini in 1977, the scene was still quite tame and focused on go-go dancing. It was changing fast, though, and topless dancing was no longer enough. But the landlords wouldn't pay the girls extra for stripping, so in answer to the customers' demands, and with the permission of the landlords and my agency, a few of the girls began to collect money from the customers by taking a pint glass around. The tamer girls didn't want to reveal all and gradually disappeared from the circuit. The costumes reflected the more dance-orientated girls, all tassels, sequins and rhinestones. It was only when stripping took over as the expected norm that the costumes and music changed. Striptease required a very different style of 'dance' movement, pace and mood. I had to deliver a fantasy for the customers. Just dancing to your favourite records didn't work. The package was all-important.

I did break out now and again and dance to personal favourites. I danced to ATV's 'Love Lies Limp', firstly just as an ironic comment I felt I needed to make. But, quite unexpectedly, it was rather popular, so I'd dig it out now and again. Captain Beefheart's 'Hard Workin' Man' was a keeper. It was raunchy and gave a no-nonsense thumping message as I entered the stage for the first part of one of my strip routines. My choice of music was diverse, driven in the main by the need for the audience to relate in some way, especially at Christmas time when all the party bookings came in.

I was always on the lookout for new costumes. When TG had played in LA in 1981, I'd visited the Frederick's of Hollywood lingerie store on Sunset Boulevard and picked up a stunning gold basque with matching gold garters complete with Christmas bells and a tiny gold whistle. Alongside diamante accessories, that became my Christmas stripping outfit for the classier stag nights and office parties.

If I wanted to exorcise some restless energies, I'd dance my heart out to Patti Smith's 'Because the Night'. I didn't give a shit at moments like that. For that one dance it was about me. I worked at so many pubs around London, Brighton and the South-East, and wherever my agency sent me. One of my regular London pubs was the Wellington at Shepherd's Bush. When David Thomas was in town with Pere Ubu, he and Gen came along with me one Friday afternoon. I'd been using Pere Ubu's 'Heaven' in my strip routine. It had all the elements I needed: a great melody, so danceable, and the lyrics were suggestive enough for me to use for such an erotically charged setting. When I finished, I joined David and Gen at the side of the dance floor. I got the sense that David didn't quite approve of my using his song. Someone suggested it might be because he was a Jehovah's Witness.

I'd be booked for the 'liquid lunch hour' break, from 1 till 3 p.m., Monday to Friday, and then in the evenings from 8 till 11 p.m., and be paid only as a dancer. The job was more than just throwing on some sexy underwear, then taking it off to music. There was a standard to maintain or you got sacked. Gemini kept a check on us to see if we'd put on weight and whether our costumes and dancing were up to scratch. If for any reason the agency had doubts, we were suspended until we hit the benchmark again. Over time I gained a certain popularity, which meant I got requests for regular spots. One was the Queen Anne pub at Vauxhall. It was a small pub but its location amid many white-collar office blocks meant the customers had well-paid jobs, so the jug money was very, very good.

Gemini acted as a safety net and filter to fend off any seedy or risky bookings and made sure, as much as possible, that us girls were not put in bad situations. But the business being what it is, you can't always predict what happens. When you're booked, the situation can turn out to be something quite different from what was arranged and agreed. Or, in other instances, the charged atmosphere mixed with alcohol-fuelled bravado could spark off terrible verbal and sometimes physical abuse for the girls. One of my friends had her nipple half bitten off by a guy who leaped on the stage as she lay on the floor during her act. Such places were put on a blacklist, but I don't recall the police ever getting involved. One of the girls had sussed out how to keep safe. She took her two huge German shepherd dogs with her to every booking and had them sit on guard at each side of the stage. If anyone came near her, you'd hear them growl, waiting for her command to attack. That was enough to deter any trouble on the stage or when she left to go to her car in the dark.

Like all the girls at the agency, I had my favourite pubs to work in and my faithful 'fans' too. So when I checked in for my next week's bookings, I always tried to secure some I knew would be easy and lucrative. More often than not I had to settle for some rough with the smooth. And there were some very rough pubs frequented by some equally rough customers.

One time I took an evening job at a club above a shop in Tottenham, not far from where I was living. As soon as I stepped off the street I felt uneasy. When I walked into the club it was clear by the comments made to me that I was the only white person in there. But I asked where the dressing room was and who to speak to about my music and time slot. I'd been booked along with a black girl from another agency, who I didn't know, and who made it crystal-clear that she didn't like me. She took to the stage first and immediately proceeded to fuck herself with a beer bottle offered to her by a guy in the audience. That wasn't a good start to the evening. Usually the first act from each girl was delivered clean. After that, depending on negotiations, it hotted up. I had to follow a full-on bottle-fucking floor show with my straight topless dance. It didn't go down well. In situations like that, I went even straighter than normal, as if to hammer home the point that I wasn't on offer. The atmosphere was so charged I kept my bag packed and ready to go if I needed to make a run for it. As I sat at the side of the dance area, the room erupted into laughter and the sound of backslapping. A calm-looking white guy was led to one of the front tables. I could feel him glaring at me. I didn't make eye contact. I was asked, or rather ordered, to join him. His name was Angel and he'd just come out of prison. I was told 'Be nice to him' by the club manager. The situation was getting really edgy and dark and I wanted to leave, but it also became obvious that I'd need to work my way out of there. I was at the farthest part of the club from the entrance, and one floor up behind two locked doors. I sat at Angel's table as instructed. He looked angelic, so I could see where his name came from, but assumed it was ironic, judging by his time inside for GBH and his obvious high status among his peers. He was a gentleman in the way 'connected' villains are, but had a shadow of sadness about him. We had a polite to-and-fro conversation, a preamble to the inevitable request for sex, which he'd clearly been told to expect. I'd been brought in for him under the pretext of 'dancer' as a gift to celebrate his release. White girl for white man. I knew I had to read this guy fast, try and figure out where his sadness lay. Lucky for me, I was somewhat familiar with guys like him, as well as precarious situations. I steered the conversation round to relationships and he expressed the importance of loyalty. Phew! That was my in to get out. No hesitation, I told him I didn't sell sex, that I had a long-term partner I was faithful to, and that we had a young son. Oddly, but thankfully for me, his body language changed, he became relaxed, his face softened and he said quietly how wonderful that was to hear. We talked a little more, nothing heavy, and I kind of liked him. Then he leaned over, gave me £50 and said he would see me to the door and safely off the premises – before it got really heavy.

Stag parties were always a bit risky. They varied from social-club strip nights disguised as stag parties to a group of guys in a flat above a shop (very dodgy). It was at such a 'party' that I first met Brigitte. There were four of us girls, me, Joanne, Jane and Brigitte. As soon as we got there the men were pushing us all to do sex for money. Joanne and Jane were happy to oblige and as soon as I told them I wouldn't they badgered Brigitte to join them. Brigitte was visibly stressed over the pressure to oblige. She sat on the edge of the bed, wringing her hands and shaking her head. I bent down in front of her, took her hands in mine and said to her that the answer is simple and short: 'No.' She didn't do it. From that night we became friends and allies and often worked together.

One Friday night in 1982 (the year Nick was born), Brigitte and I worked together on a typical stag night. It all started with the usual bookings process. I rang the agency: 'Hello. Is Bob there?'

Mandy had answered the phone. She wasn't the ideal person to deal with. She'd been a stripper herself and enjoyed doing the girls no favours at all. Her privileged position gave her a vantage point she revelled in.

'Is that Scarlet?' (She always called me by my stage name.)

'Yeah.'

'You'll have to call back,' she said dismissively.

That ritual happened with irritating regularity every Friday afternoon. Getting in quick for bookings meant you could get the best-paid pubs and stag nights and not be stuck with the nasty left-overs. To some extent I could call on my expertise and popularity to secure half-decent dates, as long as I could get Bob in a good mood. It worked more times than not, mainly because I'd entered Bob's world as someone different to the usual 'dogs' he took on (his endearing terminology). He regarded me as intelligent: I knew where I was going and striptease to me wasn't just about an easy-money game. He liked that, even though we fought for the upper hand now and again.

I had a love–hate relationship with stripping. I loved the danc-ing, the exhibitionism, the wanting looks, knowing they couldn't have me. A kind of power trip that made me feel good at times and helped me get through the down times. But sometimes it made me feel bad and I'd hate everyone and everything the situation stood for – putting myself in the position of a target for drunken lechery and insults, and having to be constantly on guard against possible trouble and unwelcome propositions for sex.

To fill in the time before calling Bob back, I rummaged through my bag of tricks in readiness. A treasure trove for every sexual fantasy. I selected the red-satin and silver outfit and the powerful, dominant, black ciré costume with zips. I never used accessories like whips (at least not for stripping) – they were too passé. Certain sex toys were for my pleasure and had to remain untainted. Besides all that, some of the rougher guys had been known to use the whips on the girls. Ugly scenes would develop if the DJ didn't keep the guys in check. It was always a fine line between teasing for pleasure and teasing to belittle and insult the guys. Some girls got off on that – those who had been totally fucked up about sex for one of a hundred reasons and used striptease as a way of exorcising some of the pain. For some it worked, to a degree. There was a lot of self-hate, come to think of it. That saddened me.

As I was getting ready to go to my stag booking, Chris took our baby son for his evening bath. I put my bag down and went through to the bathroom to join them. This was my world and the time of day I set aside for myself and my dearests. Nick was splashing happily, making those baby sounds everyone goes gooey over, and Chris's face was lit up with a smile of devotion. Nick was cocooned in love. The warm feelings of self overwhelmed me and I left Scarlet behind.

But not for long – the phone rang. Bob had called back, mainly because he wanted me to do one of his special jobs. Favour time, so he was extra-nice. I did most of his more respectable bookings. Since I had made the cover of the *Sunday Times* colour supplement as a desirable, presentable stripper for hire, a lot of work had come my way, which Bob had benefited from. People asked for me, 'Scarlet', specifically. I got to jump out of cakes and lie across cars, which made a welcome change from the smoky, dank pubs that were my regular haunts. Seeing as Bob wanted a favour, I took advantage and in fair exchange got some good bookings for the following week. Plus he'd obviously been for a drink at lunchtime and was in a happy, cheeky-geezer mood. He wouldn't have been out of place selling second-hand cars. Bob treated the girls like cheap bargains at times and he'd bad-mouth them to me. That and his attitude sat unhappily with me, not only because I had to work alongside these girls but also because I liked them and so did the guys.

I took the necessary details for the stag from Bob, quickly rang Brigitte to check she was on board, and returned to the bathroom. Chris had scooped Nick out of the bath and wrapped him in a huge, soft, warm towel. His hair was all wet and little drops of water tickled him as they trickled down his cheeks. His laughter was infectious and his face a picture of sublime happiness. Chris passed him to me and I hugged him close, nuzzling his neck and breathing in that amazing baby smell. I took him upstairs to put him to bed, lay him in his cot and gently stroked behind his ear to soothe him to sleep. I crept downstairs so as not to wake him, grabbed a quick snack, kissed my darling Chris, picked up my bag and left my boys at home.

It was already pitch-black when I set off. The roads were wet and shiny and that wonderful damp smell rose up to make everything feel very close. I was lost in thoughts when I suddenly realised I must be very near Brigitte's flat. Sometimes I got really pissed off when I had to act as a taxi service. But Brigitte was an exception – we just clicked. There was something about her that set her apart from the other girls. She'd worked in the Middle East and her passion was writing and playing her own music. A lot of the girls didn't like her, but she was just different. It seemed to me that she hadn't been successful in masking herself and that's what made the girls and men nervous of her. She did an act using lit candles, which she would squat over and then produce a knife that glittered in the stage lights. It was all a bit too ritualistic and symbolic, and, for the ordinary working man, 'fucking weird' – and too much.

I pulled up outside Brigitte's, left the car running and ran to the front door. I had to give three rings of her doorbell, wait, then ring twice more. Brigitte's little safety code. She shouted down from her first-floor window, 'Hello! I'll be right down, Scarlet.'

I waited in the car and unlocked the passenger door to her little taps on the window. She kissed my cheek. 'Hello, my darling.'

'We're at a restaurant in the West End – God knows where I'll park. Some office Christmas party. Jackie and Marianne are with us, so we'll have to pair off.'

Brigitte laughed and her eyes glinted with mischief. 'I'll make mad, passionate love to you and I'll scream as I have my orgasm.'

That's what I loved about her: she could laugh at the odd situations we got tangled up in. The lesbian act we'd perfected was a sham, but the guys never knew. They were so locked into the moment. We held genuine affection for each other as women surviving in a very real world, both playing roles within roles.

We reached the restaurant. There was always a feeling of trepidation walking into a place, with thoughts scattered in every direction, mentally marking the exits, making sure the dressing room (or what passed for one) had a functional lock on it, how to be approachable, sussing out the guys as you go, making sure they kept a safe distance. Many of the girls sold sex at the end of the shows. I'd never done that. Sometimes, out of safety for myself and the other girl, I'd step in if a girl was having a hard time getting a guy to come. I hated doing that – the guy would always insist I tried it. No way – they had to be content with my physical presence in the room. Sex was, in part, a profession to me, but I'd managed to keep all this side of it from crossing over and intruding into my own sex life. Sex with Chris was precious.

All four of us girls were chatting away when there was a knock on the door. 'Girls, can I come in?' a pathetic voice pleaded.

'Who is it?' Marianne shouted.

'It's me, Tom.' He was the organiser for the evening. He was allowed into the inner sanctum of the ladies' loo (our luxurious dressing room). He had a large plastic carrier bag in his hand and a sweaty face.

'What's in your bag, Tom?' Marianne asked with irritated sarcasm.

He was obviously embarrassed and in difficulty. 'Well, erm, you see, well, we thought . . . Would you girls mind, err, using some of these in your act. I mean, if you don't mind.'

Ever so business-like, Marianne tipped the contents unceremoniously on to the small table. As if we all hadn't guessed already. Dildos, vibrators, a whip and a very nice school cane. I quickly snatched up the cane to take home.

'You'll have to pay us extra, and Scarlet doesn't do blue, by the way,' Marianne proclaimed.

'Oh, we, err, were, err, hoping all four of you would, err, do something,' Tom stammered.

They always tried to persuade me. A little extra money. They really didn't get it. I never wavered.

I sat quietly while the girls sorted out their extracurricular fees, then announced to Tom that Brigitte and I would be happy to do a lesbian act, and that we wouldn't be needing the dildos or vibrator, but the whip would do nicely. Brigitte liked whips.

Tom's eyes went from disappointment to boyish anticipation.

'Come on, Brigitte, let's eat each other, with a little discipline for the men. And don't go mad this time!' I said with a grin as I took Brigitte's hand and we both walked out into the restaurant to the sounds of the Troggs' 'Wild Thing'. Brigitte took one side of the room and me the other.

I targeted a small, quiet man who wasn't drunk but faking disinterest. This was quite common and always a challenge to me. I walked around the back of his chair and firmly nudged the side of his face with my hips. My red satin miniskirt parted down the side and I let it slide down his cheek on to his lap. A smile crept across his face and his hands twitched restlessly. As expected, he was reluctant to show interest or make contact. I had no intention of allowing him to. I bent forward, my tiny half-cup bra bursting with my peachy breasts. They were an inch from his nose. My G-string teasingly covered everything he and the rest wanted to see as I leaned forward, moving my hips in time with the music. I whispered in his ear that he must be good and not move. I sat astride his knees, my back arched and arms wrapped around his neck, all the while my hips still moving with the music, sensuously, rhythmically. He was safe. His face was flushed with pleasure, not embarrassment, and I left his lap knowing he was hard.

Brigitte had been stern with some of the men. She strode over to me, whip in hand, traced the curves of my body with it, stroked my breasts, unfastened my bra and dropped it to the floor. She cracked the whip and clawed at her clothes, rubbing herself against me, pleading for me to be naked too. Flesh on flesh. We rolled on the floor, caressing, kissing. My tongue savoured its way down Brigitte's neck, around her small, hard nipples and over her firm stomach. We were lost in each other, Brigitte writhing and uttering sounds of ecstasy. A strange, wet silence hung over the whole scene. The music had ended; the men were mesmerised. Brigitte winked at me. We exchanged a knowing look of triumph. Applause and cheers accompanied us to the dressing room.

I dropped Brigitte off and got home around 1 a.m. I slipped into bed next to Chris, only too aware, as usual, that my hair stank of cigarettes. I hated that and knew Chris did too, but he never mentioned it, just always asked if I was OK. Always so thoughtful and caring. He knew some nights it was difficult for me and talking about it helped me make sense of the whole evening. My head spun, my body buzzed, but I was home, safe in Chris's arms. I fell into a deep sleep.

Not all the girls got on with each other and there was a lot of competition between us. Some could earn good money and others very little. But there was some camaraderie amongst us. When there was any trouble, we'd stick together and protect one another as we all recognised that it was a case of 'us against them'. That's not to say I didn't like the men I came across, just that it would be fair to say the nice and good men were outnumbered by some real arseholes. The agency had a variety of girls rated in terms of how they looked, what they'd do, how they performed and their personalities. But all of them had one necessary trait: they were all strong women, and I defend and respect them and their choice to do what they wanted with their bodies. Inevitably, like it or not, the girls fell into categories depending on the jobs that came in and their suitability. It was the same for me. I didn't always fit the job. I suspect the competition between the girls was fed as much by the agency, to keep them on their toes, as it was by the girls themselves. The 'blue' girls, who offered sex extras, earned the most and between them they competed to be the top earner, as much a mark of their sexual expertise as their desire to make as much money as they could.

A lot of the pubs I worked at have either closed down or been turned into shops, or, like the Arabian Arms and Browns, become 'gentlemen's clubs'. I've not been inside a strip club for over thirty years. I think my eight-year stint is enough for a lifetime. I don't know how 'gentlemanly' these clubs are, but in the early 1980s I did work a few times at one gentlemen's club near the Mall. It was tucked away and frequented by suited gents on their extended lunch breaks. The layout was very different from the pub circuit. Tables with crisp, white linen cloths were arranged around a catwalk. Backstage we had a proper theatre-like dressing room and would be notified politely when we were requested on stage. We were only booked to do a couple of strips each and were instructed to keep them 'respectable'. It was like going back in time to the 1960s, and brought to mind Christine Keeler or Mandy Rice-Davies. A thoroughly enjoyable timewarp, and a welcome relief from the smelly, noisy pubs.

Dancing and stripping meant I had to keep in shape. The dancing itself more or less did that for me, but the body being the focal point also meant you had to keep free of bruises and unappealing marks. I woke up one morning and went to scratch my head. 'My head feels weird,' I said to Chris.

He turned and looked at me with horror. 'Bloody hell!'

'What?'

He jumped out of bed. 'You need to look in the mirror.'

My head, eyes and mouth were swollen – I looked like I'd done ten rounds with Mike Tyson. Then I looked down and all of my torso was covered in huge, red, swollen, itchy blotches. I rang my agency straight away and cancelled my bookings. I said I'd get back to them after seeing my doctor. But it was more serious than I thought. I'd had a severe allergic reaction to aspirin and was put on steroids straight away. It was a strange feeling, watching as the swelling shifted from one area to another, all the time hoping that my throat didn't close up as the doctor had mentioned it could had I not gone to her so soon. I couldn't dance for a week. I'd been lucky it hadn't happened during my work for Steve Dwoskin on his *Shadows from Light* documentary film on Bill Brandt.

But a week off did give me time to focus on an art action I was going to do at an arts venue near St Paul's Cathedral. I had Chris video me as I worked and send the live feed to a monitor placed in front of me, giving me immediate visual feedback that I used to create a loop of action and response. The space was small but full of people, and as I was clearing away afterwards Stevo from Some Bizarre Records came up and started excitedly shouting at me and Chris about how he wanted to sign us to his label. It wasn't the best time to approach us and we told him we weren't the least bit interested, but thanks anyway. As the place emptied we got talking to a guy called Dooby who worked at London Video Arts (LVA), an organisation that provided support and free access to facilities for video artists. He invited us to their place in Soho to see if we'd like to use it.

The use of LVA's resources came at just the right time, not only for my art video works but because we'd just finished filming *Elemental 7* and needed affordable access for editing and post-production. We booked time in LVA's editing suite and mastered both *Elemental 7* and, later, *European Rendezvous*. There were fractious moments as everything was done in real time with no back-ups. With the video completed and put to one side, we prepared to do our first gigs since TG – as CTI. Rough Trade bookings organised the shows for us and we, along with John, went on a European tour.

Although we'd released our first album as Chris & Cosey, our work since then had mainly been collaborative and under the banner of CTI. The months leading up to our first gigs had been taken up with recording with different people. Glenn Wallis, one of the first TG fans and roadie, formed a band called Konstruktivits and we worked together on a CTI 12" single.

While recording the tracks, me and Chris had been taking regular morning and afternoon trips to the Muswell Hill day nursery to drop off and pick up Nick. We'd pass 23 Cranley Gardens every day and didn't give it a second thought until news broke of the arrest of a serial killer and necrophiliac who'd lived there and carried out multiple murders in the house. His name was Dennis Nilsen. He was put on trial and convicted of murdering gay and homeless young men in his flat, hiding the corpses under floorboards or dismembering them and stuffing body parts down the drains of the property. Passing the house on the way to the nursery was never the same again. We took a photo of it and used it for the front cover of the 12" and called the title track 'Hammer House' – the house of horror.

Our 12" single 'Thy Gift of Tongues', made with Brian Williams (aka Lustmord), had a similar dark theme, but based on myth: Asmodeus, Prince of Hell, the demon of wrath and lust. For Brian I suspect it was about the power of wrath, and for me, the power of primal lust. Brian had first got in touch through writing to TG, and then met us at a record-store signing. He'd started doing his own music and I suggested he contact SPK (Surgical Penis Klinik), who were among many musicians and artists squatting in one of the houses in Bonnington Square, Vauxhall. We knew SPK through the musician Graeme Revell, who had written to TG; back in 1980, Industrial Records had released the first SPK record, the single 'Slogun'. Graeme was intense and ambitious and would often ring or call round, blatantly asking Chris to give him the inside information on how we did things on certain tracks, to use in his own music. We never collaborated with him – it was too much of a one-way street. Brian ended up joining SPK and would stay with them off and on during his trips from his home in Wales. We became close friends, visiting him and his partner, Tracey, after they moved to London into a squat overlooking the Oval cricket ground. Tracey worked for a video-editing and duplication company in Soho and helped us out with mastering and duping our gig videos.

~

Nick's few hours a day at the local nursery gave us the opportunity to record. Chris had put together some sequences using our new

Roland MC-8 sequencer and tentative rhythms for a track, and asked me to try out some vocals to it. I lay on our bed as he spoke to me through my headphones. 'Just try anything,' he said.

He felt so close, and his voice so soft and sensual, that it put me in mind of when we'd phone each other during the tough times while we were apart. I started talking to him about our struggle as lovers, being impeded by other commitments, how he made me feel and the joy of being together. I started with when we initiated our love affair – on the Charing Cross Tube escalator on our way to the ICA in 1976. 'You took my hand on the stair. You said we could be lovers – I just had to say the word.' I hadn't meant it to be the actual lyrics; I just wanted to tell him what he meant to me. He came into the room. 'What?' I asked.

'I love it. Let's take the song in that direction and sing a chorus and a melody.'

The track was completed that afternoon, other than tweaking and the final mix. 'October (Love Song)' came from such an intimately personal few minutes and became a signature Chris & Cosey track. It was a total departure for us, unlike anything we'd recorded before – romantic but so uplifting. It was fun running with the love-song theme and making an accompanying kitsch video using LVA's facilities, with the assistance of David Dawson, and photographer Steve Pyke taking stills from the video and promo photographs – one of which we used for the cover of our next 12" single collaboration project, 'Sweet Surprise' with the Eurythmics.

~

It hadn't taken long for TG bootleg albums to start appearing. There'd been a few while TG were still together but it accelerated to a ridiculous level after we split. We weren't informed or consulted about such releases and were referred to in a letter from Gen to Geff Rushton, dated 1 March 1982, as 'Thee Negatives (Chris & Cosey)', with Gen giving his (and Sleazy's) permission for Geff to release TG work: 'E hereby give mine & Sleazy's blessing to your TG best of boxed set project, ASSUME POWER FOCUS . . . DON'T tell Thee Negs . . . They are best ignored on these kind of projects . . .'

When we discovered *Assume Power Focus* was by Geff, we rang Sleazy, who apologised and sent us a cheque for a couple of hundred pounds. By that time, he and Geff were working together as Coil, having distanced themselves from Gen. Over the years, as more bootlegs of live TG recordings appeared, I was sent information by concerned fans (the quality was bad). The main source was revealed with proof supplied to me by different labels and people involved, including licence agreements signed by 'Genesis P-Orridge'. Despite the paper trail of evidence, there was no offer of apology or account-ability: our approaches were just met with indifference. I'd get irate phone calls from Geff on our and Sleazy's behalf, urging me to bring Gen to book. I managed to retrospectively get some of the bootlegs converted into legitimate releases and the label to pay me, Chris and Sleazy our due royalties. It was tough, as the label had already paid a large up-front payment to the seller of the tapes.

Keeping track of unofficial TG releases that were subsequently licensed on to more labels over the years wasn't something I wanted to waste precious energy on. IR and TG signed a licence agreement with Mute Records in May 1983 but that only covered the main cat-alogue and the Fetish Records releases. And Fetish turned out to be a bad experience, considering TG's generosity towards the label. Rod Pearce (who owned Fetish) insisted on 50 per cent of TG's advance and royalties from the Mute deal. I felt like we were being well and truly shafted from every direction.

Daniel (Miller) and Mute were the only ones who held true to the original spirit of the ethos of independent music, and I felt the official TG legacy was respected and safe in their hands. We'd known Daniel since the mid-1970s, when he'd released 'TVOD' and 'Warm Leatherette' through Rough Trade when he started Mute Records. We had mutual interests and principles, and he and Chris shared a passion for electronics, conferring and meeting up to exchange information on new sound technology. I looked upon the TG/Mute relationship as 'family'.

I was shocked and sad to hear that Rod met with an untimely and brutal end after he'd finished Fetish Records and moved to Mexico. In 1997 his body was found on a beach, almost decapitated, reportedly hacked to death with a machete.

28 May 1984
For many years I dreamt of a life in the country with land and hope of all hopes an old school or church as my home. We have it!!!!

Living in London had become difficult, both financially and in terms of our lifestyle. I felt like I was running to stand still to pay bills, and every time I stepped outside our front door I was sucked into a vortex of uncompromising negativity and subjected to a pace of life that was not conducive to my creative sensibilities. We spotted a church for sale in East Heckington, Lincolnshire, and made an appointment to view it. The place was easily convertible but too small and isolated for Nick's needs.

We drove home via King's Lynn and picked up the local paper. When we got home we looked through it and saw a small village school was up for auction on the following Tuesday . . . in just three days' time. Chris called his dad, Albert, who had experience with

300

buying property, and asked if he'd come with us to view the school. We arranged to collect the key the next day and Albert came with us. He gave the building the thumbs-up. 'It's rock-solid,' he said. A beautiful, red-brick Victorian primary school within reach of all amenities. It had two large classrooms, cloakrooms and a kitchen annexe with a row of outside red-brick toilets. It was just the right size and stood on a third-of-an-acre plot that was paved over as the school playground, with a jetty on the riverbank for fishing. Me and Chris were so excited – it already felt like ours but we didn't dare let ourselves think that yet. We travelled back to Norfolk for the auction on the Tuesday. The bidding started, and there were only three people interested in it. Our bid got the school for an affordable price. It felt like a dream. We'd just bought our new home. We sold our house in London in a matter of days and moved in as soon as the major structural works were complete.

I continued to do some striptease work, travelling to London for just two days a week and staying at Chris's mum and dad's Totteridge house to earn enough money to have the playground dug up to make us a garden. Settling into the house was the first real break we'd had in years and we relished every moment of it. Life was suddenly so simple. Working with nature, planting apple and pear trees and flowers, watching Nick running round playing in the sun, and the cats tasting true freedom for the first time in their lives.

We lived in the house as the final work was completed, making special allowances for Phil the plasterer. He was the best for the job but also a cokehead, and would disappear on benders when he got paid. One of the builders would go in search to local pubs to pick him up while he was still under the influence, because once on the job he'd do fantastic plastering at breakneck speed. Other than the dramas surrounding Phil's availability, it all seemed very idyllic, until a month later, when there was a full-on shotgun shootout between feuding Essex and Norfolk travellers who lived on their own land at the end of the village. Country life was not quite the quiet idyll we'd imagined it to be.

We'd entered a very close-knit community, many of whom had been born in the village, grown up together and gone to the (our) school . . . including two of the builders. Eighty-nine-year-old Joe who lived next door had worked on the local farm all his life and had never left the village. 'He had no need to,' his daughter told us.

At the same time as we moved into the village, a family called Newby moved out. I found out later that the Newbys had owned and farmed land in and around the village, and that our neighbour had worked for them – and the local churchyard had Newbys and Carters buried there. It was uncanny when I found out that Les's family had originally hailed from King's Lynn, then moved to Hull. How had I unwittingly ended up in a place with so many connections to my family and closest friend?

I took Nick to the small toddler group in the village hall so he could make friends. I didn't have a lot in common with the other mothers and felt a bit guilty that I'd bought the school their children would have gone to (had there been more of them to keep it viable). I was there for Nick, who was happily playing with the other children. We wanted to establish a secure, happy base for him and ourselves. I gave up striptease work, which meant there was no regular income except for £18 a month child allowance. It was a struggle financially, living off credit cards and an overdraft, waiting for royalty cheques to come through so we could pay off enough to stop the bank coming down on us. It was the poorest period of our lives, and yet the happiest and most complete we'd felt. Away from the studio or gigs we found joy in the simple things, like family get-togethers, days out with Nick and his friends, and Nick's large birthday parties.

We didn't do any gigs the year we moved. We concentrated on finishing as much of the house as possible, getting the studio up and running first, keeping the school blackboard that ran the length of one wall to use for studio notes. The old school kitchen had a huge porcelain basin, ideal for developing and printing, and it became our new darkroom. The walls of the two cloakrooms were in a bad way so we covered them in old TG *Heathen Earth* posters. We had a ritual burning of some of the TG vinyl we had left over from our share of IR stock – including rare blue-vinyl copies of *Heathen Earth*. They represented the crap we'd left behind and it felt good watching it all go up in flames.

Our music had moved on to what would become known as the distinctive sound of Chris & Cosey – such tracks as 'Driving Blind', 'Love Cuts' and 'Walking Through Heaven' on the *Songs of Love and Lust* album we'd recorded in our studio in 1983, well before we left London. The front cover was a painting by Skot of a couple embracing, inspired by the James Bond film *You Only Live Twice*. The album was released on Rough Trade in January 1984. That, and the releases of *Elemental 7* and the 12" singles, gave us some breathing space to make the school a home.

Once the builders had gone, we continued recording *Techno Primitiv*. I'd take Nick out to the park, the beach or to Thetford Forest to give Chris a good few hours of peace and quiet to finish mastering. *Techno Primitiv* and Chris's solo album, *Mondo Beat*, were our final albums released on Rough Trade. Geoff didn't feel an affinity with our sound or image any more and we weren't going to change, but the parting of ways was amicable.

Alongside our music, I was still engaging with my art actions. Paul Buck invited me to perform as part of his five-day event, 'Violent Silence Festival – Acts of Transgression', a celebration of Georges Bataille. He and Roger Ely were coordinating the festival, which would take place at the Bloomsbury Theatre, London. It would include the staging of Georges Bataille's *My Mother*, the first full production in English, adapted by Pierre Bourgeade and translated by Paul. The programme included works inspired by and in homage to Bataille – music by Marc Almond and Last Few Days, dance, films by Derek Jarman, Paul Buck, John Maybury, Cerith Wyn Evans, Steve Dwoskin, performances by myself ('Such Is Life') and readings by Roger Ely, Paul and Terence Sellers. My previous work with Steve Dwoskin derived from Bataille's *My Mother* was my (and Steve's) direct connection to the festival.

It was only a month after we'd moved. Me and Chris worked on music specifically written for the piece, but he stayed in Norfolk with Nick. I travelled to London and met up with John Lacey, who worked with me projecting slides we'd prepared especially for the piece. I was dressed in white and the slides were projected on to my body, following my every movement and simultaneously appearing on pieces of diaphanous white muslin I used in my ritual action. The performance was quiet and peaceful, the audience attentive and appreciative – including, to my surprise, two of my striptease fans.

Preparing for the performance had been interesting. Me and John arrived at the theatre to begin setting up and getting a feel for the place. We were escorted to the dressing rooms behind the stage, making our way from the back of the auditorium as quietly as possible as there was a woman with a head full of hair curlers stood soundchecking at the microphone. 'That's Terence Sellers,' I was told. I knew of her but hadn't met her before. She was acquainted with Gen so I wasn't sure whether to say anything as I'd been reliably informed that my name was banned from being spoken in his presence. As I got to the stage, I said hello to her. She looked over to me and blanked me. OK, I thought, I know where I stand.

Part of my contribution included the screening of the COUM film *After Cease to Exist* – which nearly didn't happen. During setting up in the afternoon, I was informed by one of the theatre hands that the senior theatre technician refused to show the film. She objected to the castration scene.

'On what grounds?' I asked.

'You'll have to speak to her yourself. She's up there', and he pointed to the upper circle seats near the projection booth, where a rather stern-faced, tough-looking, androgynous woman sat with her feet up on the seats in front.

I made my way to her, introduced myself and asked what her objections were. She explained that she didn't think it appropriate to show a film of a man being castrated. I suggested that I explain the film to her and we could then have an informed discussion about it. We spent about an hour together, analysing and debating the film, sexuality and more besides, and she agreed to it being shown.

'Ritual Awakening' at the Zap club in Brighton was my penultimate live art action. It was part of the Taboo Festival of Eroticism run by Roger Ely. Nick was at his gran's, and me, Chris, Brian and Tracey travelled to Brighton together and stayed in a quaint bed and breakfast that owed a lot to *Fawlty Towers*. The venue was a small club in King's Road Arches, and full. My action was on the stage at the back of the room. Chris, Brian and Tracey helped me set things up, Chris did a live mix of the audio I'd prepared and we recorded the whole thing on to video. My art film, *Pussy Got the Cream*, was shown separately at the festival.

A year later I performed an extended version at the Bar Europa Festival in Amsterdam. 'Ritual Awakening Part 2' was my final live art action. I met up with Michael Moynihan (aka Coup de Grâce), who was also presenting his own performance involving cutting himself. It was intense and personal. I felt some affinity with him

305

and his work . . . but we lost touch after he joined Boyd Rice's band, NON, and became a member of the Church of Satan. After Michael, Johanna Went was on stage, just before me. Her performance was loud (screaming) and chaotic, with the stage cluttered with large props that she hurled about and then she threw liquid around the stage. I didn't 'get it' – much like some people probably didn't get early COUM. The stage was a mess and me and the theatre crew had to clean up before I could begin my piece. It was also quite late and the bar had been busy. I was made aware that my controversial history had preceded me. The audience were rowdy and drunk and making it clear that they wanted nudity, cutting and more. They got none of that. My last action was a ritual exorcism of everything that represented the spectacle people had come to expect from me. A disconnect from the tainted past. I couldn't have had better reinforcement of my decision to make this the last art action than that entire trip to Amsterdam.

~

It's never good when you get a call at 7.30 in the morning. It was ten days after I'd got back from Amsterdam. Chris answered and I could tell by the tone of his voice it was bad news.

'Who is it, Mum or Dad?' I asked him.

'Your mum,' he said.

My whole body went numb, then came a shockwave of rage. 'Why couldn't it be him? It's not fair!'

Les had made the call on behalf of Pam, who'd been told not to tell me until after Mum's funeral. I was stunned – I couldn't quite process what I'd just heard. After all this time, I was even kept from saying a final goodbye to Mum. I didn't blame Pam – she was in a difficult position and Dad was still very much a part of her and her children's lives. Chris received a long letter from Pam explaining everything and hoping that I'd forgive her for not letting me know in time for the funeral. Mum had had a stroke and been admitted to hospital. She'd asked Pam not to tell me in case I visited her. She was worried it could stress out Dad and give him a heart attack, as he was due to undergo heart surgery. So I wasn't told Mum was ill. Days later she had another stroke and a heart attack, and died. She was only sixty-six years old. All my hopes of being reunited with her were gone forever. She'd never see her grandson, Nick, or meet Chris, we'd never hold each other or laugh together again – my thoughts were all about the many associated losses signalled by her dying before Dad. I blamed him for them all. The only consolation I had was that he would be miserable without Mum.

Me, Chris and Nick went to Hull and Pam took me to the cemetery to show me Mum's plaque and her name listed on a page in the book of remembrance. It wasn't enough. I couldn't relate these markers of her life to what Mum meant to me. Pam and I laid flowers together and wept. I saw all three of us as having each suffered in our own way, all to suit the needs of my domineering dad. I made a visit to the *Hull Daily Mail* offices to place a dedication to Mum. The day after we returned home I got a phone call. A man's voice said, 'Excuse me for disturbing you. I'm from the *Hull Daily Mail*. We've been asked by a Mr Dennis Newby not to print your dedication to your mother.' Silence. He continued, 'I don't know why someone would make such a request, but as far as I'm concerned, if you say to me now that you still want me to print it, I would be very, very happy to do so for you.' He was so kind and outraged on my behalf.

'Yes, please print it for me,' I said.

~

Lost in our world of music and video, we were fully focused on releasing our work on our own label, CTI. It hadn't occurred to us to do it any other way. Then we were approached by the Nettwerk Productions record label in Canada, and shortly afterwards Kenny Gates of Play It Again Sam Records got in touch. After many talks regarding us retaining the artistic freedom we'd always had, we signed to both labels . . . and also later to Wax Trax! Records in Chicago. That gave us worldwide distribution and sparked what became the beginning of C&C's world-touring electronica success.

Having done gigs in Holland with our friends Hay School-meesters and Brecht from NL Centrum, we had them book and tour-manage us for Europe. We all got on so well, Hay with his wide smile, and tall, slim, leather-clad Brecht looking like Emma Peel, both speaking with the most wonderful strong Dutch accents. They were kindred spirits and unorthodox as far as booking agents or tour managers were concerned. They ran their own alternative art and music events and shared our DIY ethos. Sometimes Hay's cousin Frank came along. He drove like a lunatic, always too fast and way too close to the vehicle in front. Me and Chris would close our eyes as we sat in the back of the car, pretending we weren't there, our fingers crossed for a safe arrival to our next destination as we drove from gig to gig.

Hay had a dry wit. As we entered one strange venue he said, with a lopsided smile, 'I think this is a beatnik club', which I used later for lyrics. But neither he nor Brecht suffered fools gladly. A promoter didn't pay up after one of the shows. As we set off to the next gig the following morning, Hay took a detour to the promoter's flat, telling us to wait in the car while he and Frank paid the guy a visit. They came rushing back to the car ten minutes later with our money, saying we had to make a dash across the border because the guy was calling the police . . . and

Hay and Frank were supposedly on a 'suspects' list due to their past anarchist activities.

As NL Centrum expanded, a lovely guy called John Jacobs took over most of our European tour-managing and we always took along 'Jan the video beamer man'. Our touring was like being away with 'family'. Everyone was so kind, relaxed and happy in each other's company.

We hardly ever played in the UK – there wasn't the demand. Our main audience was in Europe and America but we made an exception for UK Electronica, which was a small festival with some live performances, talks and stands to sell records and related ephemera. Manning our stand led to some good new contacts and we met and talked to a lot of fans, including our good friend Joe Ahmed.

During our performance we projected one of our gig videos, which was full of cut-up images, including clips from blue films. Someone brought their ten-year-old son to see us play even though it was an over-eighteens show, and made an official complaint about the video content. Three days later we got a visit from the local police. Two squad cars pulled up in the drive with three uniformed officers and two detectives presenting us with a warrant to search our property. A friend had phoned to say that our names and address had been given to the police by one of the festival organisers, but we never expected to be the subjects of an investigation. We were kept in our living room while the police went around the house, searching everywhere and pulling out 'evidence' to take away with them.

'What exactly are you looking for?' I asked.

'Anything that shows you naked,' was the reply.

'Come with me,' I said, and gave them a pile of photos of myself semi- and fully nude, dancing, on holiday, etc. They thought (or had been informed) that we were making and selling pornographic videos. After hours of delving and questioning, they realised the accusation was possibly bogus, but still took boxes of videos, photos and paperwork away with them to look through, saying they'd be in touch. Three months later, on my birthday, me and Chris were walking around town when we saw one of the detectives. He nodded, smiled, then came over to us to say that we could collect our belongings whenever we wanted. They were satisfied that there was no charge to answer.

Nettwerk, then PIAS, released the C&C 'taster' 12" EP, *Take Five*, and we embarked on our first C&C tour of the USA. Steve Montgomery, the manager at the Rough Trade Notting Hill shop, organised the bookings and tour-managed us. The tour was a great success; we were excited about future possibilities from all the contacts we'd made and it gave us enough money to fix our leaking roof and invest in some new equipment – an AKAI S900 sampler, an MC-500 MIDI sequencer, a Roland Octapad and a Fostex sixteen-track tape recorder.

The injection of new gear changed our sound and the way we worked. We sampled like crazy, anything and everything, and started recording our next album, *Exotika*. We recorded the title track as our homage to Martin Denny, which was released as a single and was a big hit in clubs on the West Coast of America and in Goa, India, at the trance dance parties.

When so much is happening, and so fast, you just go with the flow, not realising until much later just how monumental those events turned out to be. 1987 was like that for us. Our output was prolific. We'd released the single 'Obsession' and began a Conspiracy International collaboration album called *Core* with our friends Monte Cazazza, Brian Williams, Boyd Rice, Robert Wyatt, John Duncan, Joe Potts and Coil.

I was in touch with Geff regularly. He'd call me, more often than not when he was three sheets to the wind, talking about the nuances of sex, putting the world to rights between us, him saying how, since me and Chris had been doing electronica for years, we could make a fortune now that it had taken off. We weren't interested in the mainstream or banging out music just to make money. That attitude probably contributed to our money struggles. What excited us was collaborating on an album track with everyone. It was the first time we'd worked with Sleazy since TG split and I always think of *Core* as having brought us back together. Having him in our lives again felt right: even though we'd travelled very different paths in the interim, that deep connection between us was still there.

And the album itself was a work involving people we felt a special connection to. John Duncan and Joe, along with Rick Potts, Tom Recchion and the artist Paul McCarthy, were part of a radical art/music collective called LAFMS (Los Angeles Free Music Society). I'd hung out with them in LA during TG's last gigs and John had celebrated Nick's birth by releasing a 7" single called 'NICKI'. The common factor among us all was that our work and lives were unorthodox in our own unique ways, and bringing us together would make for some very potent music.

Brian was the only one who recorded with us at our studio. All the other tracks were done by exchanging tapes through the mail – we had no email then. Working on the track 'Unmasked' with Robert (Wyatt) was very special. We held an unspoken trust in each other that made possible the effortless close melding of our sensitive music and sense of self. We exchanged tapes of his musical and vocal ideas and he sent me wonderful letters full of lyrics for me to select from. I compiled what I felt was the essence of an underlying storyline and we recorded them alongside a melody made from samples of his voice. Even though he wasn't there physically, his calls and letters were so charged with his creative energy, making it an incredibly intimate collaborative experience. He loved the track and did his own cover version some years later.

The mid-morning mail arrived. A package from Wax Trax! Records in Chicago containing animal rights literature with graphic descriptions and photographs of animal cruelty, including the horrific suffering of animals in slaughterhouses. I read it once and never looked at it again – it was too distressing. Wax Trax! were releasing an album, *Animal Liberation*, which Dan Mathews of PETA (People for the Ethical Treatment of Animals) was putting together. Jim at Wax Trax! had assumed me and Chris were vegetarian and asked us to contribute a track. We weren't vegetarian until that envelope arrived, but we have been ever since.

I sat and wrote the lyrics and we recorded the song 'Silent Cry' in about four hours. It had been sparked off by a chance meeting with Dan the previous year at our friend Lene Lovich's house. Now the album was being released, Dan was in the UK to promote it and we met up again to discuss a live performance of our song at an animal rights party he'd organised at the Limelight in London. Lene and Nina Hagen had also done a track together for the album and we were all backstage. I felt decidedly underdressed and rather demure next to them both, with their big hair and outrageous, eccentric theatrical clothes and make-up. Performing our gentle, sad song was quite emotional but I held it together. Lene and Nina blasted out their song with full-on energy and gusto and we all decamped to a local Indian restaurant. The owner looked at Lene and Nina with incredulity and was trying desperately to usher us all out. But Nina was an unstoppable force, talking ten to the dozen at him about astrology and the meaning of life, turning his shock into fascination until he smiled and seated us all with his blessing.

I took that memorable demonstration of Nina in action as inspiration for when I had to play her in the PETA promo video.

Nina wasn't available so I was enlisted to play her part, donning a wig that resembled her hair, with clothes to match and high heels. The location was a fenced-off rubbish tip near Lene's, the nearest we could get to what looked like the entrance to a securely locked animal-experimentation facility. We feigned breaking the locks and climbing over the fence to free the animals – me in my patent stiletto heels and a very short skirt scaling the fence, determined to complete my mission. I think it was pretty convincing.

Unbeknownst to us, Daniel Miller was interested in signing us to Mute Records, but Kenny Gates of Play It Again Sam had got to us first. Being officially signed to record labels in Europe and Canada, we encountered our first taste of standard record-business practice. *Exotika* was released and we were asked to go on tour to promote it. Naive as it may sound, we'd never thought of our live work as promotion before. Performing was just part of what we did: we presented our music and video work to people, shared that special time together, and hopefully made some money to enable us to carry on making music and art. There hadn't been a calculated commercial agenda attached to playing live – until now. The notion of recording an album, then performing it live on tour to 'sell' it, was a new thing for us.

And so was going on tour with a support band . . . SPK. Their line-up was now Graeme, his wife, Sinan, and Karina Hayes on additional vocals and dance. They had more gear than us, what with all their props and an angle grinder, which caused no end of hold-ups and problems at the airports. Equipment Carnets (a temporary export–import document) were mandatory when touring abroad and they were a nightmare. Every item of equipment had to be listed and accounted for as you passed through customs – every lead, jack plug, power supply. If something went missing, you could face a very hefty fine. It loaded extra stress on to our tight

313

airport connections, without the added dramas created by Graeme's unusual luggage.

The first thing that triggered an underlying discontentment in Graeme was when we went through US Immigration and he, Sinan and Karina got stopped and taken for questioning. They weren't going to be allowed in until me and Chris offered to vouch for them as our legitimate support act. That worked, but also publicly showed Graeme as subordinate to us, and that wasn't taken well, especially when the immigration officer smiled at me and Chris and said, 'I've got tickets to your show tonight – I love your music.' We gave him some C&C badges, chatted a little, then went on our way. Graeme's sense of being treated as secondary to us grew as we headlined the shows, and the number of radio and press interviews was much higher for us than him. Who played in the so-called headline spot was irrelevant and meant little to me but more to Graeme. Things started getting very strained and his persistent moaning and harassment of Dan put a real dampener on things. Dan took the brunt of it all, but no matter what he tried to do to appease Graeme, it wasn't enough. He kept the tour on track by clearing up any complaints and monetary settlements for damage SPK caused during their performances thanks to Graeme's metal chain swinging above the audience's head, his twirling and breaking of some of the house microphones and the sparking from the angle grinder as he used it on available objects and pillars at the venues. A girl in the audience at one show had her head cut open by a forceful swing from the heavy chain and she threatened to sue, but Dan managed to talk her out of it.

Fraught with Graeme's discontent, things came to a head mid-tour. As we were walking along the street after yet another confrontational episode with Graeme, Dan suddenly stopped dead in his tracks and hurled his tour briefcase down the street, screaming, 'I've had ENOUGH! I'm leaving!'

Nick was scared, and we didn't know what would happen with the tour. I went and retrieved the case and between me and Chris we managed to persuade Dan to stay on until we could get someone to replace him. He stayed away from Graeme, then we had an emotional farewell with him when he left and Steve (Montgomery) joined us to take over tour manager duties and to try and keep things on an even keel with Graeme. As soon as we hit the West Coast, me and Chris took Nick to visit friends. It was good to get away from the tense atmosphere.

The SPK damage costs had mounted as the tour progressed and by the end had eaten substantially into the tour income. Payment was to be settled at the airport when Steve took us all to catch our flights home. When Graeme was told about the money situation he went crazy. 'I've got a wife and two kids to support and a mortgage to pay!' he yelled.

Chris tried to calm things down and reason with him but, contrary to what his contract with Steve supposedly said, Graeme demanded money. That money would have to come out of our and Steve's earnings. Steve went to the men's room and Graeme followed him. When they emerged, Steve looked decidedly shaken and Graeme rushed off without saying a word to us. I was sat with Nick, trying to keep him from noticing anything bad was going on. 'What happened?' I asked Steve.

'He blindsided me. I didn't expect him to switch from verbal to physical.'

Apparently some guy had witnessed the altercation and called the LAPD, who appeared and told Steve that, as the booking agent, he was responsible for Graeme's welfare and safe return to Australia and that Steve had to pay Graeme or we'd all be taken to the precinct. Steve lost his commission and we were left with just a few hundred dollars from our own tour. We felt robbed. I heard that

SPK disbanded after that, and Graeme moved to LA and went on to do film work for Hollywood movies.

25 June 1989
Chris took me to the hospital at about 7 o'clock and I was put on a drip . . . my emotions are in turmoil.

A visit to my GP confirmed that I was pregnant. It was a shock as I had had a coil fitted. I was worried whether the pregnancy could be viable with a coil in place or if it would damage the baby. I was sent to the local hospital, where a doctor gave me an internal examination, which even I knew wasn't the preferred procedure at such an early stage in a pregnancy. I remember him looking me straight in the eyes as he stuck his fingers inside me. It was such a creepy feeling. He was brutal and I yelped as he probed about. I looked to the nurse for help, for her to say something to this guy, that what he was doing was all wrong. She was visibly shocked and concerned about what she'd witnessed. Nothing was said but I knew he had assaulted me and I'd be lucky to keep the baby. I was sent home feeling violated and in pain.

The next day we went to a village fete and I started cramping and bleeding heavily. By the time we got home, I knew I was miscarrying. Chris rang the hospital and was advised to collect whatever came out into a jar to take to the hospital, for them to confirm that I'd miscarried successfully. To see that tiny little foetus, the potential life we'd lost, was too much for me. Just eight weeks old and the size of a fifty-pence piece. How brutal and cruel the procedure was. Our child was reduced to 'evidence' of loss in a jar.

I was admitted to hospital to have the coil removed and a D&C to remove any remaining parts of the baby. I was taken to theatre and given an anaesthetic. The last thing I remember as I went under was a huge crushing sensation on my chest, like the ceiling had fallen on top of me. Then, from far away, I heard a woman's anxious voice say, 'Her blood pressure's dropped . . . Christine! Christine!'

I slowly realised they were calling me by my first christened name, not Cosey. I opened my eyes. They checked me over, then took me to the ward to recover.

Just three weeks later we embarked on an eight-date European tour, immediately followed by a fifteen-date C&C tour of the USA to promote our new album, *Trust*. That wasn't the best thing for me to have done. My health was never the same again.

~

1991 was an odd year. It seemed like business as usual but there were big changes taking place that we weren't fully aware of at the time. On a personal level, me and Chris were as one, unified in love and in our creative pursuits. That is as true today as it was then – the vital force that drives us forward and maintains the continuum of our togetherness. We were an idyllically happy family with Nick, taking regular trips to relatives, them visiting us, raucous fun parties and Christmas gatherings. Before (and after) Mum died, the only absentees from the happy group get-togethers were my mum and dad. I'd felt sad for Mum and Nick but I couldn't have done anything about it. I'd thought of just turning up and knocking on their door with Nick and Chris, but decided against subjecting them to what I anticipated would be a cold-hearted response from Dad. I was resigned to not having them in my life and I was so happy being a part of Chris's family.

Being signed to three record labels proved to be good for everyone. Our back catalogue got a new airing as each label re-released the early C&C albums and compilations. We were fortunate to work with such good people and have their enthusiastic support. Visiting Wax Trax! in Chicago to see the owners, Jim and Dannie, was always a treat, just in terms of them being such great, fun people. Just as we were riding high and for the first time feeling a hint of financial security, some labels started running into trouble. First Rough Trade Distribution folded, then the whole of the Rough Trade Group went into voluntary liquidation in 1991, owing us money (which was settled years later). Some of our publishing was with Rough Trade and after their collapse had been put in the hands of another publishing company. Things got more complicated when Wax Trax! went under, but PIAS were stable and Kenny and Michel kept our spirits up.

The demise of Wax Trax! had scuppered the release of my solo project, *Time to Tell*. Chris Connelly first proposed its release to me. We'd met him years earlier when he visited Beck Road as a very young TG fan. After his band, Finitribe, split, he'd moved to Chicago and joined Revolting Cocks and Ministry, who were also signed to Wax Trax! – that's where we met up again. He was coordinating the *Time to Tell* release with me and thoughtfully arranged for the artworks to be returned. It's never good when a label collapses – there's so much fallout and recrimination, but I never felt any malice to Jim and Dannie. I co-opted the help of Joe Banks to work on the artwork for a special version of *Time to Tell* on CD, in a deluxe package dedicated to Szabo, who had died in November 1982. The audio was extended and remastered, and the booklet updated and revised with additional material and twenty-six black-and-white cards of related art and modelling images. There was a hitch, though: the factory that packaged the inserts refused the job on religious and moral grounds . . . My nude image on the cards being the reason. A replacement and more amenable factory was found and production went ahead with no more trouble. I'd also produced a very limited signed edition, which included one of my original encaustic paintings in a handmade box.

At this point, Sleazy, me and Chris weren't on speaking terms with Gen, who was now living in the USA. Mute had the TG catalogue and acted as mediators. We'd all re-signed to them for a Mute Grey Area release with the addition of live tracks, *TG LIVE*. Me, Chris and Sleazy had gone to Mute meetings together but Sleazy didn't want anything to do with the TG artworks, editing or mastering, and, as far as any of us knew, Gen didn't either. That job fell to me and Chris, with the assistance of Brian and Joe Banks. Brian waded through the TG live tapes, selecting the best for quality and possible bonus tracks. That was a job neither me nor Chris could face at the time. It was enough that Chris then had to master them all. Joe was a graphic designer who'd worked with Brian and he did the artworks for us, and I designed and drew the camouflage box set sleeve based on our TG uniforms.

Mute had been a positive constant in our lives and we had good friends there, like John McGrath, John McRobbie and Daniel. Our working relationship with Mute expanded to include Chris's solo album, *The Space Between*, and an Erasure remix, with Daniel having done the first ever remix of any of our music, for our C&C 12" single 'Synaesthesia'.

Me and Chris were nearing the end of our contract with PIAS and recording *Musik Fantastique!* The samples were stored for playback on SyQuest hard disk cartridges. We thought we were being cutting-edge: we could store the whole album on one big disk. Three months into the album, the SyQuest drives started failing and corrupting the samples. The majority of the album was lost. What saved us was that we'd recorded the vocals, guitar and cornet on to tape, so at least we had that. After a week moping around depressed,

319

we swapped back to slow but reliable floppy disks and re-recorded the album. It probably came out the better for the 'disaster'.

After that we went over to a super-reliable optical drive and disks as soon as they became available. *Musik Fantastique!* was our last album on PIAS. We moved back to releasing material on our own CTI label through World Serpent. Sleazy had recommended them to us and introduced us to the owners, Alison, Gibby and Alan. We were completely independent again and marked the return with the 7" single 'Passion', cut at Porky's studio in London, which I etched with auspicious runic symbols.

The oddest of situations can bring inspiration. Driving seems to be when me and Chris have time free from other distractions to talk through and brainstorm ideas, usually on long journeys. But the 'Library of Sound' series of albums came about during a twenty-minute drive to do the weekly shop. We wanted to do more introspective, instrumental, ambient music, to venture into different territory and away from the Chris & Cosey sound. It suited my health situation and where my head was at too. My dance groove was temporarily suspended. *Metaphysical* and *Chronomanic* came together quickly, followed by *In Continuum*.

The now-huge music and multimedia arts festival Sonar started in 1994 and we were asked to play. Thrilled as we were, we had to refuse due to my health, so we made a video, 'Select Reflections 2', to be screened as our contribution. We were asked to perform again the following year but I was no better and the accompanying video to *Chronomanic* was shown instead.

Just as we were having a break from Chris & Cosey, JD Twitch (aka Keith McIvor, who went on to run Optimo club in Glasgow with JG Wilkes) appeared on our horizon. We knew his friend, the effervescent Jill Mingo, who had done some promo for us. Keith had been following and DJing TG and C&C music, and proposed a remix album of C&C tracks for his T&B label. Me and Chris, being in our 'bubble', had no idea just what an impact our music had once we relinquished it to the world. We never expected a 'return', simply being pleased that we were able to get our work out there and hoping others shared in the pleasure we got from making it. We didn't know then but Keith's release *Twist*, an album of C&C remixes by Carl Craig, Mike Paradinas, Mark Gage, Fred Giannelli, Coil and Cosmic Connection, was a key factor in the resurgence of interest in our C&C music and he brought us into contact with some great people.

The remix by Coil (Sleazy and Drew McDowall) kept an ongoing connection with Sleazy. But our lifestyles were poles apart, me trying to keep as calm as possible and Sleazy trying to get as high and 'up' as possible. He was heavily into his recreational drug phase . . . as Chris witnessed at a KAI Power Tools visual software seminar in London. As the announcement of a specific tool within the programme was announced to the seated attentive audience, a very loud 'YESSSSS! WHOOOOOP!' broke the silence. Everyone turned round to see someone stood with their arms in the air in triumphant appreciation of a new weapon for video effects – it was Sleazy. He was dressed in a thick, black puffa jacket, sweating, eyes popping, but with a massive grin on his face. He'd obviously been waiting for technology to catch up with whatever ideas he had in mind.

~

The start of my heart problem seemed to stem from the operation after my miscarriage. I began having trouble breathing, then palpitations, almost blacking out. I could see my heart thumping in my chest as it kicked in again after missed beats. The episodes could last for hours at a time and were unpredictable, exhausting and frightening. My (male) GP put it down to me being a neurotic, pre-menopausal woman.

I struggled on until I finally asked to see another doctor, who was more enlightened and concerned. He sent me for a 24-hour heart monitor test. I dropped the ECG recording off as instructed, and two hours later I got a phone call from the hospital to be told that the recording revealed a possible serious abnormality, that I mustn't do anything strenuous, and that I had to go back to the hospital first thing the next day. My relief at the proof that my palpitations existed turned to dread as I began to think the worse.

When I reported to the cardiac department I was given a tread-mill test – I lasted less than a minute before they stopped it and lay me down. My heart rate had soared to over 260 b.p.m. The young cardiologist was shocked – he'd never seen that before. He admitted me for further tests. Chris was in as much shock as I was and rang and faxed everyone to let them know. I received a flurry of beautiful bouquets from Mute, PIAS, family and friends to cheer me in my hospital bed. That took me by surprise. Was I that ill? I was in denial about my heart problem. Because it was sporadic, I took to think-ing that, when it worked normally, it had righted itself and I was OK. I was put on beta-blockers, then another cardiac drug to slow me down. It did just that. I'd gone from a five-day-a-week gym-and-swim routine, with bike rides with Nick, to sitting inert and zombified by the medication to try and control my heart arrhyth-mia. When I was told to avoid stress and excitable situations the first thing I asked was, 'What about orgasms?' I was more worried about being denied that physical pleasure than 'work'. I had my priorities.

Live music performances ended. I concentrated on working in the studio. That was the only way I could safely work around my physical limitations. I was keeping a log of the palpitations, chest pains and breathlessness, and sleeping at least two hours during the day. Feeling so restricted was depressing. As I sat in the garden resting, I wondered how many more summers I'd see, what a burden I must be to Chris, how I was holding him back and what Nick was losing out on because of my inability to join in the fun things in life. Sometimes the exhaustion was so acute it was an effort to even laugh. All I could think about was getting horizontal, lying down. I tried my best to do as much as possible, to try and make things as near as possible to normal. I couldn't find it in me to totally surrender to the condition. Chris was amazing at coping with the worry and helping me continue to be 'me', making sure the studio sessions were always available at the time slots my heart allowed me to work.

Then he gave me a huge boost of confidence. We were watching a documentary programme that turned out to be part of an Open University course. 'You should do that,' he said.

Doing an academic degree at that time in my life worked out to be better for me. I had the advantage of having acquired my own skills and understanding of the art world through personal experience and was interested to discover that I shared views with some great minds.

~

Other than the *Time to Tell* release and my OU studies, I was happy to concentrate on my work with Chris. I've always thought of my work as art, whether it manifests as music, visuals or actions, but had no interest in direct contact with the art world. I'd mainly been focusing on sound and video presented as audiovisual gig-style performances and sometimes as screenings and installations. Our video work for the Cabinet Gallery group show 'Popocultural' at the South London Gallery was a case in point. Our inclusion alongside Chris Ofili, Jeremy Deller, Paul McCarthy and others came about from an invitation by Andrew Wheatley and Martin McGeown of Cabinet Gallery, who knew of my work and about TG. We were introduced by Simon Ford when he was writing his book *Wreckers of Civilisation* about COUM and TG.

The introduction to Andrew and Martin was one of the best things that came out of the book. I met two incredible people, both committed, generous and driven by an uncompromising love and respect for the creative spirit and powerful art. I'd never encountered anyone like them before.

21 September 1997
Spoke to Sleazy tonight about Simon's book and how to redress the balance and correct Gen's fantasies and inaccuracies. He said to get together next week.

Simon's book actually started as a thesis on COUM and Throbbing Gristle and he visited me to go through and borrow archive material (most of which was never returned), with me reading through drafts as he progressed. It seemed an impossible task to me and I was happy for Simon to take it on, never expecting that it would turn into a book. My friend Grae Watson had started a similar book back in 1983, but rang me one day to tell me he'd abandoned it after allegedly having a tough time with Gen, who was insisting on controlling the content to the point that the book would have been an unbalanced, inaccurate account. *Wreckers* suffered from a similar problem but was tempered to a degree. It has its inaccuracies but stands as a good entry point for reference and analysis, and even before the book was published it brought about some significant introductions in the art world.

20 January 1997

Sleazy rang, nice to hear from him. Talked about COUM at
M.O.C.A., he said to be careful Gen doesn't just put himself
& text. Maybe I'm still naive. Weird compiling all the COUM
stuff, history, my past, the beginnings of me and Chris . . . It
seems Art history surfaces and I am an official part of it.

The resurgence of interest in my past artwork continued and Paul
Schimmel from the Museum of Contemporary Art in Los Angeles
contacted me about discussing the inclusion of COUM in a group
show on performance art. Me and Chris travelled to London for
a meeting at his hotel. We were shown into the drawing room to
wait for him. We waited and waited but he never appeared. We
left feeling really angry at being stood up and the waste of what
little money we had on the train fares. But Paul was feeling equally
annoyed. Through a series of phone calls, the ridiculous reason for
the saga was revealed. The receptionist never called his room to
tell him we had arrived. So we were downstairs, he was upstairs,
waiting for the call that never came. He even went to the reception
desk to ask after us, only to be told 'No' by the relief receptionist
while we sat just feet away.

After that fiasco, I thought it would all come to nothing but
Paul really wanted COUM represented in the exhibition, and by
definitive performance photos. I could provide that for him and
sent him a display book of works but suggested he also speak to
Gen about any other material. The exhibition instigated my max-
ing out our credit card to buy an A3 printer and scanner (it cost
less than outsourcing the work). I reconnected with my magazine
actions from a very different viewpoint. My memory has always
served me well but I'd already consulted my diaries for Simon's
book just to verify or correct Gen's version of events. It was strange

revisiting my past. But at least, after twenty years, some of my magazine works were finally going to be shown on a gallery wall for the very first time, and in the company of works including those by Yoko Ono, Joseph Beuys, Gilbert & George, Marina Abramović, John Cage and my friend John Duncan.

More interest in my past activities surfaced. Out of the blue, Tuppy Owens got in touch. How she got my phone number, I'll never know, but it was good to hear from her after so long. She was organising a festival called Smut Fest and I was invited to take part in a discussion at the Confessions Gallery in Islington, London, on the resurgence of political pornography. Others on the panel were Del LaGrace (photographer), Lindsey Frew from *Hustler*, Tuppy, Bill Owens from *Suck*, Hugh Scandell of *Skin Two* and an old friend, Ted Polhemus. It was an odd context for discussing my work in pornography. Most of the others were still very much a part of that lifestyle, and porn as 'business', and I couldn't relate on their level. The thing that stood out most was them complaining about the laws that restricted their freedom to produce and distribute porn. That irritated me as I'd faced worse conditions and tighter controls but managed to work around and against them to achieve the freedom to express myself (sexually or otherwise). The only thing I had in common with them was that I'd once been part of the porn business. Where was the discussion of the 'political' aspect of porn? I was up for that. But the evening overall hadn't been a pleasant reconnection with the sex industry, especially when one hard-core porn-video producer took to the floor with vivid descriptions of his seedy working practices. I was glad to leave.

3 April 1997
I am wondering how we will survive in the future. Is there a market left for our music? I am poor but in love and happy. I

love Chris and Nick. I love life. That's good, money makes life easier but love makes it happy and hard times bearable.

How you can be in such demand yet be on the breadline continues to baffle me and probably others in the same position. We were selling equipment to upgrade and just keep our heads above water, to maintain our creative lifestyle and meet the needs of teenage Nick and six cats. My illness meant I couldn't do a day job even if I wanted to, but we were fortunate that Chris's expertise and knowledge of equipment brought him paid commissioned articles and reviews for *Sound on Sound* magazine. As well as the review gear being useful in our studio, the fees kept us going for years, as did TG royalties from Mute. Chris's dad had offered for him to join and take over the family business, Carter's Glass in Crouch End, but Chris turned it down. It would have meant we'd have had a good steady income but we'd have had to give up music and move back to London. It was sad to have to refuse his dad's generosity.

After our Rough Trade and Wax Trax! experiences, we hadn't expected World Serpent to run into trouble. We were told that Tower Records hadn't paid them for our CDs. We were thousands of pounds down but luckily we still got paid by some of their other retailers. It didn't bode well. On top of that we received a package from Allan at Peer Music. Two more TG bootlegs had surfaced, then another, and Peer did their best to track down who was responsible. However, we all suspected we knew who it was.

Knowing someone was taking money from us when we had so little could have cast a dark shadow of resentment, but it didn't. My life was so full of positive things and good people that I put the rip-offs to one side and dealt with them as best I could, with the help of some great friends. Geff's calls cheered me up. He rang one day, all happy and affectionate, to tell me him and Sleazy would be coming to record with us in the summer. Then he told me all about Kenneth Anger having stayed with them for five days and how he'd slept for stretches of twenty-four hours, making them worried if he was OK. He'd emerge with press clippings of pirates, then go back to bed. Geff usually called when Sleazy was away filming music videos and ads. That work made it possible for them to eventually move out of London. Sleazy thought it may help Geff's alcohol addiction, having already tried different treatments. Even the implants that triggered a severe reaction if he drank alcohol didn't work. Nor did the twelve-step programme, or checking into clinics. Sleazy put his Chiswick house on the market and started the search for a new home for him and Geff. My financial struggles paled into insignificance compared to the havoc and pain caused by Geff's addiction.

24 April 1998
Everyone really pulled together for us on this Industrial mess.
Monte's pissed off and thinks it's a prank, we're not sure . . . Sleazy
had got on the case too which is highly unusual but welcome.

We connected to the World Wide Web in 1998, which massively improved communication and brought an end to our hard-copy CTI bulletins and the cost of printing and mailing. But it also speeded everything up, which was both a good and a bad thing. We'd always written personal replies to all our fans, at one time incurring the wrath of the mother of one of them who read one of my replies and called me 'the devil's filth witch' . . . which appealed to my perverse sense of humour. Me and Chris used it as my nickname over the years. The pace of the postal system afforded us some respite, but emails were a near-instant-response form of communication. Chris designed our websites and put together an online mail-order service. That was a lifeline.

Then one day we got a flurry of emails informing us about Industrial Records being relaunched by someone in San Francisco, and claiming that Gen was behind it all. Daniel, Sleazy and Monte responded straight away. Things went crazy as everyone tried to get to the bottom of it all. It wasn't a prank but was stopped after interventions by a number of concerned and pissed-off people. The internet has its upsides.

With emails making contact so much easier, past friends like Tim Poston, Foxtrot and Ann Fulam got in touch, and I also started to receive enquiries about my art, with requests to do lectures and interviews for academic publications.

23 Sept 1998
SO SO SO HAPPY!!!! the doctor at Papworth said he's sure he can cure my Tachycardia. I'm ecstatic and so is Chris, Nick, Rose and all. Now I can feel motivation returning. I can see the reason behind 'doing' again . . . Four scenarios: 1. I die (please NO), 2. It doesn't work (NO), 3. I need two ops, 4. IT WORKS. I have to be positive but I'm very frightened . . . Will I regret this assertive step? I hope not, I hope I will get my life back again.

Since 1993 I'd been under the care of an eminent cardiologist and whenever I went for check-ups I told him of the exhaustion affecting my quality of life and ability to work. I had an energy window of about three hours a day and struggled especially with anything that involved using the upper body, stupid mundane actions like hanging out washing or grating cheese. Also, that energy window meant me having to sleep in the car on some journeys or after our leisurely walks in the Sandringham woods. I explained all this and was told to 'be a lady of leisure'. I was furious at his condescending, dismissive attitude. He held my future in his hands and any opportunity for me to live a nearer-normal life, but he didn't see why I would want to do anything other than laze about and be waited on. I thank whatever forces that he was on holiday for my annual scheduled appointment with him in July 1998, when instead I saw a young cardiologist who referred me to an expert on electrical heart conditions at Papworth Hospital. I was given a diagnosis. It was an electrical rhythm problem! Now, isn't that irony for you. I was informed by the doctor that he'd only come across two people with the same rare condition as me, the other being a trumpet player . . . More irony. I didn't want to have a 'special' heart condition – I wanted a bog-standard one that was treatable, with proven surgical success. Then the news came that there was the option for treatment and he felt that it would be successful. I opted in. I wanted to be fixed.

10 February 1999
Daniel rang. Chris talked to him for ages and told him about our TG24 hours idea. He was ecstatic about it.

Me and Chris had thought that an official, updated, limited-edition release of all the live TG gigs based on the original TG 24-hour cassette box could offer a sensible solution to the ongoing problem of the bad TG bootlegs, and we asked Daniel if he'd be interested in putting it out on Mute Records. Daniel was very keen so we emailed Sleazy about it. He rang to say he was up for the idea, especially as Simon's book seemed to have rekindled interest in TG . . . even though we were all yet to receive a copy. It was strange how much interest there was in our work from so long ago.

I'd prepared a slide show of images from the 'Prostitution' show for an event at the ICA to publicise Simon's book. I was fine with that but Nick and his mate Greg had come along with us and I didn't know how Nick would handle seeing his mum in all her naked glory – or how to explain a film in which I castrated his dad. I needn't have worried. He took it in his stride and I gave him the nod when the sensitive images were to be shown so he could choose to avert his gaze.

By the time a feature in *Bizarre* magazine came out featuring similar images to illustrate an article on artists who push the boundaries of art and society by using their bodies, Nick was as comfortable as he could be about my magazine and art actions. His friends at college bought *Bizarre* magazine regularly – as I found out one day while at the checkout in Sainsbury's. I saw Nick and two of his mates, who were grinning and looking at me and Chris. We nodded at them and said, 'Hi.'

They came over carrying a copy of the magazine. 'Did you really do all that in the *Bizarre* article?' one of them asked.

'Yes,' I said.

'Cool' was his reply, and all three smiled and toddled off, waving to us as they went on their way.

20 March 1999
I'm determined to get a book out that puts the record straight.

Well, you're reading that book now.

Simon's *Wreckers* book prompted the diary entry, and the desire to put the record straight was further reinforced by press interviews with Gen and the book reviews, which seemed largely centred around him being the innovator and leader of TG. That misconception of TG and bias towards Gen, who was portrayed as a betrayed victim, angered me, Chris and Sleazy. We'd expected more from Simon – at least impartiality, having given him so much information to work with. Foxtrot had expected more too; he wasn't best pleased at not being mentioned much in the COUM section, commenting on Gen in an interview, 'He likes to have this mythic status, you see. He's definitely got his own view of how it should be perceived. I mean, he is a great manipulator and he likes to retrospectively re-write history. I mean, I wasn't mentioned much in the book, not that I'm an egomaniac but . . .'

Me, Chris and Sleazy didn't attend the official book launch. Two days later, Simon emailed me an apology. I can't recall whether it was for the book or the meagre twenty-five copies each we were to receive as 'payment' – and to be charged the postage.

25 April 1999
I'm fed up with being fed up now. It's got my heart doing its palpitations again. If only I had the energy to scream and run round I'm sure I'd feel better. Exorcise the frustration a bit. I feel so sorry for Chris, he's had to put up with so much because of my heart and now something else. It's potentially so depressing but I mustn't let it be. I'll treat it as another chapter in my life, a project to fulfil and put behind me in my archive of life experiences.

My heart problem affected the dynamics of my relationship with Chris. He missed what he called my 'mad half hours' and my sing-ing around the house. I didn't feel myself either. I was used to rushing around everywhere, being so physically active and full of energy, and I worried that Chris wouldn't love the slow, lifeless Cosey I'd become.

On top of that I'd been recalled after a routine mammogram to investigate a suspicious 'mass'. By the time I went to the hospital one of the lumps was the size of an egg. They turned out to be cysts. 'We'll aspirate them for you,' the consultant said. It all sounded so routine and harmless but turned out to involve inserting a long needle into the breast to withdraw fluid from the cysts. I felt like asking if they had a piece of wood for me to bite down on to.

I was relieved when it was all over but I was back at the clinic three months later, having found another lump the size of my thumb. Thinking it was just another cyst, I went into the consulting room on my own while Chris waited outside. I was taken from there to have an ultrasound scan. It wasn't a cyst and they carried out a biopsy, telling me to return next week for the results. I couldn't contemplate surgery after my last experience of a general anaesthetic. The stress set off my palpitations.

I had a close female support network, especially with Chris's mum, Rose, his aunt Pat, my sister, Pam, and a wonderful group of caring friends who all talked me into thinking positively. Foxtrot being Foxtrot sent me a large Perspex VITAL PROGRESS hospital sign. I saw the consultant and got the biopsy result – the lump was fibrous and benign. I felt like I had permission to live again.

~

Chris had done some solo shows for Paul Smith's 'Disobey' tour and Paul offered us C&C gigs for the summer, but I couldn't do them. As everything seemed to be propelling us forward, I felt my health was holding us back. I called Papworth to try and get an idea of when my operation was so we could plan ahead. I was given a date, 19 May. Now I had something we could schedule offers and projects around.

20 May 1999
Oh what a traumatic day yesterday. All so unexpected and even now as I lay here at home I feel traumatised still.

Expectations were high that the cardiac ablation procedure would work and that I'd be free of medication and back to full health with energy to spare. Yeah! Chris stayed at a local hotel, as did his mum and aunt Pat to support me and Chris. They brought love and some light relief to the whole situation, and even a lovely curry for me from a nearby restaurant. I decided on a local anaesthetic, which enabled me to watch the procedure on the monitor above the operating table. The catheters were fed through an artery in my groin and into my heart, then different drugs were injected to try and induce the arrhythmia . . . to no avail. I was in theatre for over two hours and the ablation was abandoned, catheters removed and the nurse pressed down hard on the incision.

I was taken back to my hospital bed, where the incision opened up, spilling blood on the bed as I shuffled across from the trolley – more painful pressing down. I was exhausted, so even though I was by now laid in a pool of blood I was happy to comply with the order to lie flat for an hour, then two hours to be safe. I eventually slowly sat up but felt faint, then very weird. 'Get the nurse,' I said to Chris . . .

I don't remember anything of the following ten minutes but it's burned in Chris's memory. He hit the panic button, alarms sounded, and the crash team were there in seconds. Apparently I'd gone deathly white, then red, then white, my eyes rolled back, then I had two convulsions and my heart stopped. Chris was stood on the chair in the corner of the room looking down and watching as the team worked on me to restart my heart. I woke up with an oxygen mask on, a drip in my arm and hooked up to a heart monitor, with Chris holding my hand. 'What happened?'

He just said, 'You fainted, that's all.'

I was told that a number of factors could have been the cause of the crash – post-operative shock, or an adverse reaction to iodine, calcium, adrenaline or temazepam. Whatever it was, the doctors and nurses were fantastic. But my poor body had been through a lot. I felt like I'd been in an accident. The bruising on my groin extended down my thigh and I had bad chest pains, which freaked me out until Chris told me about the electric shocks to my heart. Then it made sense. He was emotionally drained. He'd thought I was dying when I had my collapse. I suppose I was dead for the minutes it took them to bring me back.

I'd considered myself to be a spiritual person and the whole incident changed my thinking, especially on reincarnation – I wasn't going on to another life, I'd just gone. Not that I expected to, but I didn't see any of those tunnels of white light or have any kind of out-of-body experience. I find it difficult to describe the finality of your own life force other than likening it to turning off a power switch. In some ways, it's comforting to know it just ends – I felt nothing.

We'd had no reason to think there'd be any problem with the procedure – the family were excited that I'd be cured and it was just an overnight stay, so we told Nick he needn't come along. We thought we'd save him the worry and he went to stay with his girlfriend. He was really upset when we told him what had happened, and I regret excluding him. Like he said, 'What if you'd never come back?'

I did get some good news from the hospital. My heart muscle was healthy – it's just those damned electrical impulses that were misfiring. I was off medication and told to adopt a sensible approach to avoiding getting stressed or overtired. That's a tough balancing act at times, especially for gigs, and ours was now just eleven days after the operation. Les thought it was too soon but I'd checked with my doctor that it would be OK and we'd accepted Paul Smith's offer to perform as part of Labradford's Festival of Drifting, curated by Carter Burwell at the Union Chapel in London. Consequently my recovery period was a mix of keeping abreast of the gig preps, resting, and appreciating the kindness and affection of the many flowers and 'Get Well' cards.

Chris had so much to do: he was writing another *Sound on Sound* review as well as fielding calls and emails, looking after me and sorting everything for the gig. I did what I could, going through and selecting video footage. We'd reconfigured our set-up for a new approach to playing live and took a lot more gear than before, including our two AKAI samplers and running the sequencers and rhythms off our laptops. Nick and his friend Greg were our roadies and John Lacey came along with his four projectors to do slides again for us to augment our video.

The walls of the chapel were transformed by our visual projections and the space felt 'ours'. It was an all-encompassing, all-consuming C&C audiovisual experience. We hadn't played live for seven years and the festival gave us the opportunity to return to performing as what we thought of as a more incidental part of the evening. We were taken aback by the response to our show. It was a full house, with people coming from America and Europe, so many friends, family and familiar faces. Even Fizzy and Foxtrot turned up. Fizzy was now a psychiatric nurse, built and looking like a berserker, with no front teeth and dressed up for the occasion in a leopardskin Lycra jumpsuit. His appearance was at odds with his gentle, sweet, fun self, but perfectly reflected his eccentric style. With John there as well, doing a performance piece that he got Fizzy to join in with, it was like a COUM reunion.

Backstage was crammed and buzzing with so many people, big love and beaming smiles. I was hugging and kissing my close friend Andria, who I'd met through John McRobbie and her work at Mute. I showed her my beautiful bruise from the operation, which was like a painting in constant flux, all shades of blue, purple and yellow, extending across my groin and down almost to my knee. We were in the ladies' toilet, where we'd retreated for privacy and to count the merchandise takings, having been harassed by a very persistent guy from the Union Chapel production team, who wanted their cut, and was insisting on watching me count the money. I wasn't having any of that. Maybe he'd been ripped off before, but I'd just finished performing and was knackered as well as annoyed at him following me around. He waited outside the toilets the whole time we were in there, like a sentry on guard duty. As soon as I came out I handed over his cut and went back to join everyone.

Daniel Miller came over to chat and asked me and Chris about the possibility of TG re-forming. That took us by surprise. We didn't ever expect TG to re-form. Why would anyone? Then he told us that the *TG24* release couldn't happen yet as production costs were too high.

We walked out of the venue to a wonderful sight: an all-laughing, dancing sea of 'Prostitution' T-shirts. All those that had bought one at the gig had put them on over their clothes and were heading off into the night for more fun. When we went to load up the car it was covered in notes thanking us for a wonderful show. What an amazing night.

Then the adrenaline high was gone and I slumped in the car for the drive back to Norfolk, exhausted and feeling very ill by the time we got home at 4 a.m.

I'd overdone it and didn't feel good for months leading up to my post-op consultation. I thought I'd be put back on heart drugs but I was told to continue without medication and see how I got on. But the palpitations came back with a vengeance and I ended up back at Papworth. My case was apparently 'astonishing'. It was bloody annoying to me but I appreciated the interest in my extraordinary condition. I was told that the options for surgical intervention were limited and not yet developed enough to guarantee a positive outcome. I opted to continue taking medication. I'd previously spent a week in hospital trying different drugs with varying efficacy, but I was put on a different one that I'd never tried before. Those little white tablets transformed my life. My energy window expanded – as long as I respected my limitations.

2 September 2000
So as from today I am represented by Cabinet Gallery. Whoopee!

I approached the year 2000 with renewed vigour and an improved sense of well-being that held me in good stead for the emerging shifts in focus, both personal and creative. I'd worked with Andrew and Martin for four years before we made our working relationship 'official'. It all took place over lunch in a pub in London, with the details of the arrangement restated and confirmed as we crossed the busy road together on my way back to catch the train home with Chris. I hadn't been represented by anyone before so was reluctant to commit myself, but they had belief in me and my work. I trusted Andrew and Martin as friends, and admired their unique approach to art and how they operated very much on their own terms within the art world. Working with them and under their guidance has been key to my reinvigorated enthusiasm for and approach to art.

During visits to discuss works for exhibit I was rather amused (but pleased) to see my work being handled with white cotton gloves. I hadn't been afforded such respect before. It made me smile. Things were falling into place at a good time for me, having sat my last OU exam. I could return to being Cosey again full-time, with space for self-indulgence and reading non-academic material.

Studies and personal problems aside, interest in my art stepped up and I was taking part in panel discussions and doing talks, including at the Courtauld Institute with my artist friend André Stitt, at the Royal College of Art, and at other colleges and institutions. Music and art were overlapping with my and Chris's ambient albums, *E.A.R. One* and *E.A.R. Two*, both being included in the 'Volume' exhibition at PS1 in New York.

Then the music took a backseat as I concentrated on my artwork, which was included in group exhibitions at galleries and museums around the world. It was refreshing to meet a whole set of new and interesting people, especially my fellow Cabinet artists Lucy McKenzie and Mark Leckey. I'd returned to the art world at the right moment. My work had had time to find its place and was now recognised as important in the historical timeline of 1970s radical influential art.

The long gap between being trashed by press, Parliament and some fellow artists and the establishment embracing my art had also given me the chance to re-view my past work. I was in a different place now and could look at it from another perspective. I was outside looking in, with the advantage of time having allowed the assimilation of the residual 'aftertastes' and intimacies involved, as well as the dreadful experience and familial damage resulting from the 'Prostitution' furore. Back in the early 1980s I'd wanted to burn all my magazine works but Chris was horrified at the thought, saying how important they were and he wouldn't let me do it. It's not that I was ashamed of them, I just didn't see a good reason for keeping them. They were taken out of their frames, put into storage and tucked away for years. Retrieving my COUM and magazine works from the boxes in the archive room was like delving into a past that I'd been very happy to leave behind. Considering what it represented, revisiting wasn't traumatic so much as intriguing. Seeing my magazine works like that, me as I was from the position of who I had become, was an awakening for me. I still recognised and connected with my past self in the photographs and remembered everything – the smells of aftershave and the locations, the feel of the bed sheets, the reasons behind a certain positioning of my body or the look in my eyes, and the happy, heavy or unfriendly atmospheres. Sometimes I'd smile, sometimes I'd cringe.

Flicking through the pages of the magazines triggered a myriad of emotions and memories, and seeing my model friends again brought back the events hidden behind the procuring of that final printed image. But the shock wasn't that, nor the graphic detail of crotch shots, but just how much these magazines were a rich visual time capsule of the blatant 1970s sexism that I'd lived through, coped with, and which now looked ridiculous, sometimes shocking and crass. When you're living in that world you cope, steer your way through, challenging and countering when and wherever you can. Those works have since been presented within a 'feminist' context and I can now appreciate why, but for me at the time (and always) it was about my freedom to be me, not about 'feminism' per se.

9 November 2000
It all seems to be happening this year. New Millennium (if you go by our calendar) and great shifts in our lives.

Skot had forwarded me an email from Gen (at Gen's request), informing me that Gen's mum had had a triple bypass at eighty-three. I didn't know why he was emailing me after so many years. I'd also been told the week before that Gen wasn't well, with talk of him allegedly having had a breakdown after taking ketamine and ending up in hospital. If that was true, maybe it had something to do with Gen's change in attitude towards me, as well as the request from a guy who did his website asking to link it to ours as a gesture towards maybe 'building bridges'.

Then a letter arrived from Gen, with two Polaroids of his dog, Tanith, in her grave. The letter was so nice and 'normal'; the sentiment seemed sincere and friendly, wishing me health and happiness. But I couldn't believe in his words and that was sad. I burst into tears at the sight of Tanith lying dead. The letter was significantly dated 4 November, my birthday – it was a loaded missive.

We were in distant touch with Gen again about Cherry Red releasing a TG DVD. The decision to accept the offer was delayed as Sleazy's father had died, but when Sleazy got back in touch he refused the deal outright, saying we could get a better deal somewhere else.

He later called me one evening sounding fed up, which wasn't like him. He'd just got back from a Coil gig at Sonar: Geff had started drinking again and he'd had a nightmare journey back home with him. I had some understanding of the problems he faced with Geff from when they played as part of Julian Cope's two-day festival at the Royal Festival Hall. The gig had technical problems and Geff was drunk, so we decided not to go backstage after the show. Sleazy had enough on his plate. His video promo work had dried up. 'The music industry has completely collapsed,' he said, and announced that he was going into fine art, starting with a show at Whitechapel Gallery that Paul Smith was involved with. I gave him Matthew Higgs' contact details, who I'd met when I was in his and Paul Noble's 'Protest and Survive' Whitechapel show, as Matthew had shown interest in Sleazy's Sex Pistols photographs.

I was busy forming ideas for a new art action series on the theme of identity, entitled '*Self* lessness' . . . as in the lack of a sense of self. Jack Sargeant introduced me to a guy from the Arts Council, and Andrew and Paul Buck were helpfully encouraging in my applying for funding from them. I'd been there before and didn't want to be answerable to them after my past experience with arts funding in the 1970s. I found the process of application complicated, too restrictive. How could I describe an action that had yet to take place or evaluate (and justify) how it would be of benefit to the community? Also, the actions and the elements within them could easily cause offence and rejection. I wasn't going to compromise or inhibit my work to fit funding criteria, so I funded myself.

But first I had to prepare and install a solo show of my work at Galerie Station in Frankfurt, Germany. I scanned, outputted and framed one entire magazine action as well as three Ao diptychs from another, and compiled a video entitled *Fall Out*. The installation took me and Chris two days to complete, and it looked great. When we got home, I got a call from Alex Fergusson (who was by then living in Germany) to say he'd seen the exhibition and loved it, and would be coming to see us. He stayed for a few days and came with us to recce Ely before my degree graduation ceremony there. We checked out a restaurant by the river and had a meal together before roaming around the antique shops. He was still the same Alex: fun, talking ten to the dozen and squeezing my bum when Chris wasn't looking.

~

For the previous six years, and in between the many other activities, I had studied hard, written many assignments, sat nerve-racking exams, and now I was finally being awarded a first-class honours degree. I was stunned and felt like it wasn't really me that had done it all. Even the graduation ceremony at Ely Cathedral seemed otherworldly. The building dates back to the eleventh century and is an incredibly spectacular and evocative space. That day it was filled with graduates and guests as Bach organ music accompanied the gowned procession of dignitaries making their way to take

342

20 Jazz Funk Greats recording session, Martello Street,
1979 (bottom photo © Chris Carter)

Recording 'A Journey Through the Body' at RAI Studios, Rome
(© Chris Carter)

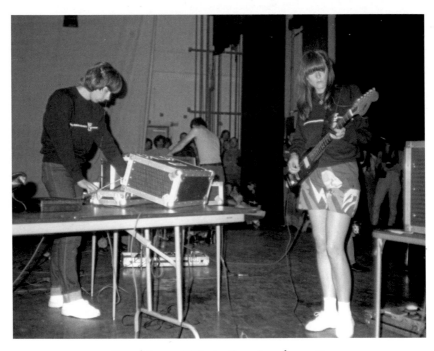

Penultimate TG gig, Los Angeles, 1981

With Skot at the TG motel, Los Angeles,
1981 (© Chris Carter)

TG promo shoot with Jon Savage, Victoria Park, London, 1981
(© Industrial Records)

Chris and Nick, 1982

Me and Nick: family holiday in Spain, 1983

CTI, 1984: Chris, me and John (© CTI)

Left: Chris & Cosey USA tour, 1989
Right: 'Studio of Lust' art action, Nuffield Gallery, Southampton, 1975

'Ritual Awakening Part 2' art action, Bar Europa Festival, Amsterdam, 1987

Left: Me and Monte, Los Angeles, 2002
Right: Me and Sleazy, Berlin, New Year's Eve 2006

TG regrouping session at Mute Records Studio, Harrow Road, London, 2009

Chris, Nick and me, Rough Trade East, London, 2011

The last 'Carter Tutti plays Chris & Cosey' gig at Heaven, London, 2016
(© Gavin Toomey)

their places for the conferment procedure. I was all dressed up in a graduation gown and mortarboard, with everyone staring at me. The one thing that made it seem more real for me was John Peel receiving his honorary degree at the same ceremony. For a brief time all the worries of debt and TG matters had been forgotten.

7 July 2001
All this TG bootleg business has really escalated. Gen is quite excited by us all 'talking' again . . . it's business. It's rather taken over all my time.

27 September 2001
We went to our 24hr TG meeting at Mute. If I hadn't got the bootleg sorted and made contact with Gen again none of this would have happened. Chris and I have totally been instrumental in all this falling into place.

One of the consequences of the first bootlegging of TG material was that the unofficial licences were then re-licensed for more bootlegging. I once again took on the task of tracking some down and started negotiating more contracts to make the bootlegs retrospectively 'official', securing our copyright and royalties. It hadn't been easy and it was extremely time-consuming, but it also reconnected us all with Gen, which in turn led to us discussing the *TG24* project.

After many emails and phone calls about *TG24*, me, Chris and Sleazy went for a meeting at Mute (Gen was unavailable). It was the first time I'd seen Sleazy in years and he looked very different. Gone was the lithe, youthful body and much of his hair – except for a little goatee beard – and he had an assertive business air about him. An open office environment where you could be easily overheard wasn't the best place to meet up again after so long, and Sleazy was a little guarded until we moved to somewhere more private. His mood had a lot to do with him recently retiring from doing promotional videos. He was very jaded about the music business and ranted about how ruthless it was, having recently been on the receiving end of some bad experiences.

The deal was done for the TG box set, and Mute were liaising with Gen. Daniel was excited and fired up about the release, talking about setting up interviews to promote it and then (again) asking if we thought TG would be up for playing live together.

'When hell freezes over!' Sleazy replied, adding scathing comments about Gen.

I just said, 'No', and Chris remained silent.

We'd worked together and Sleazy had even asked Chris to join Coil on tour as their 'analogue synth man'. Chris assessed the reality of the offer – when, where, rehearsals in Weston-super-Mare, Geff's three-day drunken comas. He'd also just sold his ailing analogue modular system to buy a Mac G4 and laptop. He said no to the Coil offer.

Me, Chris and Sleazy working together was no problem – working as TG was a whole other thing. It was the third time we'd been asked to re-form TG. A year or so earlier, a multinational corporation got in touch to ask if TG would play a one-off concert for a birthday party for one of their directors, who apparently was a huge TG fan. As we had no interest in playing live together we told them the fee would be a million dollars, knowing it would cut the offer off at the knees. It did.

After the Mute meeting we walked to the Tube together. It was a warm, sunny day and we laughed and talked about old times, in between times, and the present-day grim realities of Sleazy's ongoing difficulties with Geff's alcoholism. He painted a dark picture of his day-to-day struggle of coping with Geff and the recent trip to A&E

when Geff had a suspected heart attack while trying to 'dry out'. We lightened the mood before we went our separate ways – us to Norfolk and him back to Weston.

20 October 2001
Now we'll have to go and bring baby home. It's more upsetting than I thought it would be. Where do I put her/him? It's all very formal and I'm scared of how I'll feel when we actually hold it in our hands.

A few months after the Alder Hey Children's Hospital babies' organ scandal, I happened to pick up the local paper, which had a front-page story on a woman whose miscarried foetus had been stored in a jar at the local hospital without her knowledge. Then I saw the date of the woman's miscarriage was the same year as mine.

I called the hospital helpline and later received a letter informing me that they would investigate and get back to me. My mind went into overdrive – what would I do if they had our foetus? I'd have to bring it home. I couldn't leave it there. So many thoughts, trying to work out how to face and deal with the loss all over again.

Then the phone rang. It was Pam, calling to tell me Dad's Parkinson's was so bad he was now in a wheelchair and his short-term memory had gone. He was being put in a respite home for six weeks. I felt for her. She'd been looking after him for so long and he'd not treated her well. I just thought him being in a respite home would give her a rest.

A week after my call to the hospital, I received a letter from them telling me that they had our foetus in the form of a wax block and slides. I got a call from the hospital chaplain, who told me of the formal procedure that I had to go through. It was his job to consult with us on what would happen next. He was such a kind man but

I was angry that after all this time the hospital still dictated what we could do with our foetus. And it had to be done through the church. I'm an atheist. Having to find a way of getting my hands on what was a part of me and Chris was a miserable situation to be in. In the end the chaplain 'released' our foetus to us, and with great sensitivity placed it in a small wooden casket that he'd bought himself. We took baby home. Both of us felt that was the right thing to do.

~

The month before our meeting with the chaplain I'd fallen over in the garden and broken my ankle, so I had a plaster cast on for my fiftieth birthday. Celebrations lasted for five days, with various parties, fireworks and visits. It was a fantastic happiness boost after an often tough year. Chris bought me a beautiful 'koru' pendant, a symbol of new life and purity.

I had no clue what news was waiting in the wings to bring me back down to earth. Pam rang on the morning of 6 December to tell me Dad had died early that day. She broke down, and it upset me so much to hear her cry that I started to cry too. As is the way with grief, the tears are irrepressible, then logic kicks in. She spoke quite remotely, giving me an account of how Dad had died. It was a horrible death, suffice to say: he'd had a fatal heart attack following complications from acute peritonitis. Pam organised everything with some help from my dad's partner, Marian. She wouldn't hear of me going there – she had her children, Debbie and Danny, with her. I knew she was finding it hard enough to cope without me, the outcast daughter, turning up and causing upset on upset.

My uncle Mike called me in the evening to ask how I felt. I said I really didn't know. 'Likewise,' he said. He was confused because he'd just lost his brother and didn't feel sad. So many feelings came surging over me – anger, regret for what could have been had Dad not been such a stubborn, hurtful bastard, sadness for Pam and even more so for Mum.

Les rang and was predictably caustic about Dad after he'd tested how I felt. He really let rip, saying Dad was evil, never a father at all, and more of the same. But Pam surprised me by her revelations about her feelings towards Dad – how I was his and she was Mum's . . . Dad had said so, and she knew she could never be the daughter he wanted. She'd felt in my shadow all the time, unloved. That upset me. Apparently Marian had been on at Dad to reconcile his differences with me, but he wouldn't have any of it. He'd lose face. What a price to pay for pride.

I told Nick his grandfather had died. He was shocked and said he'd hoped and fully intended to see him at least once. I said maybe it was better he hadn't, in case he got a rejection full in the face. That was odds-on.

It's perverse that I had input into Dad's funeral and would attend when I was excluded from Mum's, who I loved so dearly. Pam talked through the choice of wreaths with me – one from the grandchildren, Debbie, Danny and Nick. It meant a lot to me that Nick was included. The funeral was a week later. Me, Chris and Nick drove to Hull. When Pam answered her door and our eyes met, we wept in each other's arms. It was too much.

My auntie Irene came to the funeral. I was glad she was there. I discovered she'd gone to school with Dad and they'd got their first jobs together in a shoe factory. After fifty years I finally understood why Mum and Dad chose her as our latchkey carer, and why she was our loving auntie.

We got ready to set off to Dad and Marian's house to be picked up by the funeral hearse. It was weird being in Dad's house. There weren't any pictures of him anywhere, just a photo of Marian and her kids. Marian was nervous to see me, but welcoming. I sat in the only empty armchair. The room went quiet. Everyone looked at me. I thought it was because I was the estranged black sheep returning for the funeral, but it wasn't that at all. Completely by chance I'd sat in 'Dad's chair'. That seemed just right to me.

6

1 January 2002

*It's all rained down on me at once. I feel like I'm stuck on one
of those knife thrower's boards and someone's throwing knives at
me. I can't dodge, I've got to accept and assimilate.*

The events of 2001 had a huge effect on me: endings, beginnings
and reconnections, as well as facing the dreaded menopause and
everything that big hormonal change presented me with. I threw
myself into my art, preparing 'The Kiss' photographic work for a
show at the Marc Foxx Gallery in LA, and was over the moon to be
told I'd made my first sale with Cabinet. The thrill was short-lived:
the buyer died from a heart attack and the work was returned –
sold then unsold. I shrugged it off with some relief. Selling my
work was a new thing I wasn't totally happy about. My work was
so much a part of me that I was reluctant to let go of it.

Simon's *Wreckers* book had made COUM and TG visible again.
My friend André Stitt also had a new book out and I was asked if
I'd do an 'in conversation' with him for the launch at the Courtauld
Institute. The event wasn't quite what I'd anticipated. I thought I'd
mainly talk to André about his work but I ended up being asked
to talk about my own. Sarah Wilson, a professor at the Courtauld,
gave an introduction in which she presented André's book, then
delivered a long, detailed and interesting description of my solo and
COUM work, mentioning Simon Ford's book in glowing terms.

It was largely through Skot and his friend Russell, who worked at Disneyland on sound design, that my art action there was made possible. Skot knew the place so well, having done his own guerrilla puppet shows there when he was fourteen. Russell had got us in for free and we arrived early in the morning to avoid the crowds. To our utter amazement it was all but deserted. We were expecting to operate around hordes of tourists and noisy, excited children but I only saw about six people and the park was eerily quiet and calm. How perfect for me. I was very aware of security and surveillance cameras and had made sure that the action was something that fell within the context of 'usual behaviour'. Nothing that would draw unwarranted attention and get me thrown out. I wasted no time and executed my action next to the twelve-foot 'C' of 'California Adventure', Chris and Skot filming and taking photographs.

I was instilling my*self* into the fabric of the site. I'd made a homeopathic solution from pure, distilled water and the burned tampon ashes of my last-ever period, decanted into a water bottle. I poured the solution on to the ground in the shape of my '4' tattoo. As the solution ran away, soaking into the dry, sloping pavement, it mutated, rather appropriately, into the anarchy symbol. It was all over so quickly and we moved on as regular tourists to go on the rides. To document the piece, and as an added essential element, I purchased a commemorative hexagon paver inscribed with my name and the date of '*Self*lessness One'. That paver now sits among many others on the entrance concourse to Disney California Adventure Park.

Back from our LA adventure, we returned to working on the *TG24* box set. Chris had already completed the transfer of all the cassettes and mastered them for CD. The four of us working together again had quickly descended into a disappointing experience. It was a vexing process at times, with limited communication from Gen. Many of our emails to him about the box set went unanswered. Sleazy was better but, considering we were on a release schedule with Mute, he wasn't as prompt or helpful as we'd have liked. It seemed that only me and Chris were willing to prioritise TG above our own work, removing other projects from the timeline to facilitate TG matters.

Maybe we were wrong to do that, but I don't think so. It was important to do it right or not at all – which would have happened had me and Chris not been so bloody-minded and driven about preserving the TG legacy. It seemed that, for whatever reason, Sleazy and Gen elevated their own projects over and above TG. That was their prerogative. But with that attitude came an underlying subtext that TG, which included each of them working with me and Chris, was inferior to them and their other work. It was an odd denial of the past (and present) that I had trouble understanding. I was happy to acknowledge that TG had a cultural importance that was different to, and in some ways greater than, Chris & Cosey or CTI. Me and Chris were aching to record our own material but were realistic that TG offered a solution to our struggling finances, and to Sleazy's, as he'd started doing Coil gigs to help fund his and Geff's indulgent lifestyle. When he wasn't giving all his attention to Coil, he got on board with us and worked on patch and badge designs and sorted through his TG 35mm negatives for photos to use. Sleazy's work practice was very much based on only working on the project most immediately at hand. Consequently we'd done most of the work by the time he'd joined in. But Sleazy being 'sleazy', he had the knack for ingratiating himself back into your good books.

12 April 2002

This is my first foray back into that phase of my life and I'm still
uncovering things I'd put well into the back of my mind. I don't
know what to think about how I feel. It's so long ago and I've
come so far since then.

I'd started *Confessions*, a new work based on one of my 1970s
magazine actions. It proved to be an intense period and writing a
postscript text for the edition was uncovering all kinds of buried
feelings. I was hit by the double whammy of revisiting TG as well
as my sex-magazine experiences. As I read my diaries and looked
at myself in the magazines, I'd veer from being curiously interested
to being drawn back into my feelings from that time, and the vivid
memories of the turmoil in my life back then.

This all coincided with a Richard Kern exhibition at the ICA and
my being invited to a panel discussion with him and Lucy McKenzie,
who had done nude modelling for him in his book, *Model Release*.
Our individual perspective on the nude model experience was an
interesting topic for debate and the difference between how each of
us had approached, performed and realised our work had potential
for a good talk. Richard and Lucy had both worked as artists in the
art world to produce their photographic works, whereas I'd operated
outside to procure mine and bring them into the gallery. We each
had our own perspective and opinion on the roles we played: Richard as artist and photographer, Lucy as an artist taking on the role of
artist's model, and me as an artist adopting the identity of a regular
nude model within the sex industry. I found Richard beguiling and
disarming and I could understand why girls surrendered to his creative requests. The techniques of negotiating and persuading played
a big part in the sensitive and sexually charged collaborative process
between nude model and photographer, whether it be for art or in

the sex industry. The persistent manipulation was endemic in the sex industry and the techniques blatant and unsophisticated, which (for me) often directly accounted for some tense, creepy experiences that all that time ago had instigated my suggesting the topic of 'persuasion' for what was now an infamous TG song.

The discussion centred on the usual: how, back in 1976, 'Prostitution' had nearly closed the ICA, with me replying 'Yes' to a question on whether the title (a jibe at the art world) was as relevant today as it was then. That received nods of agreement and critical mumblings from other corners of the room.

I met Diana, the editor of Taschen's erotica publications, a very nice, exuberant woman who had worked on *Oui* magazine in the USA in the 1970s, who told me the editor had been over the moon when he'd received photos of me for an issue, saying how the Americans didn't realise who they had in the mag. Apparently he'd added, 'It's Cosey Fanni Tutti – she's an icon in the UK. You have no idea how important she is.' I was embarrassed and had no reply to that, so I showed her my dummy copy of *Confessions*, which was the main reason for our introduction as she was working on a book on 1970s porn. She loved it and was going to follow up with Cabinet.

The next day I went to Cabinet and we decided on what form *Confessions* would take: a limited deluxe-edition, white, hardback facsimile (printed by me) in a black slipcase with a black-and-white signed photograph of an outtake from the original 'Confessions' magazine photo shoot – plus that postscript text which had reawakened deep-seated memories and emotions.

I was being thrown into my past and facing head-on the reality that my work had influenced and inspired some people – especially as that weekend was also the opening of Cosey Club, a new London venture named after me and run by Richard Clouston, Sara Burn, Caoimhe McQueen and Jon Butterworth. What a tribute.

Chris was going through discomfort of his own. Having the house reverberating with the sound of twenty-four hours of TG for months on end took its toll on him. He was getting regular migraines and sleepless nights, with the grating sounds whirling round and filling his thoughts.

He'd been ill with backache for months, then he was finally diagnosed with kidney stones and underwent unpleasant and very painful lithotripsy ultrasound shock-wave treatment. He was engaging with sonics on a whole other agonising 'wavelength'. I was so worried for him – he was in theatre far longer than any of the other day patients – and when he came out he looked white and strained. 'I'm glad that's over. It was like being relentlessly fist-punched in the kidney,' he said when I drove him home.

He recovered well and we decided to keep to our plans for my next action, '*Self*lessness Two', at Beachy Head, Eastbourne. Fizzy lived nearby, was still working as a psychiatric nurse, and had lost a few patients who had killed themselves at Beachy Head. Back in 1999, me and Geff had talked about going there to do a ritual blessing for those who had committed suicide – what he called an 'exorcism'. I realised after three years of talking that he was never going to be together enough for it to happen as a joint work. Besides, I had my own personal reasons for using the site, beyond its reference as the front cover of TG's *20 Jazz Funk Greats* album. Beachy Head is a notorious suicide spot, a site where people choose to end their lives, a heavily loaded, deeply personal place that encapsulates a sense of self.

Although so vastly different from Disneyland (the first '*Self*lessness' site), it has one incongruous thing in common: it's a tourist attraction. When me and Chris arrived mid-morning to do my

354

action, there were coachloads of tourists making their way to the famous suicide site. We turned round and drove back to the hotel, rescheduling for dawn the next day. At 4 a.m. we made our way back to the cliff. As I walked along, I gathered symbolic flowers and plants to bind with those I'd brought from my garden. It was a misty morning, the place was deserted, and there was a profound sense of peace. Even if I couldn't understand suicide, I could understand why people came there. It was beautiful and the white cliffs breathtaking and strangely enticing. I traced the outline of a prone figure on the ground, overlaying it with the flowers and plants, then began the ritual. The gestures and handmade objects, which included a part of me, represented many cultures and symbolised male and female as one, life, death, immortality, blood, remembrance, paradise, sorrow, truth, protection and the sleep of death.

The ritual complete and documented, we left the site. When we returned later that afternoon the packs of tourists were back. Groups of people were stood looking at my ritual site, which resembled a cross between a crime scene and a memorial tribute. They were respectfully walking around the action relics. Everything was intact – no one had disturbed a thing.

25 August 2002
We've lived and breathed 'TG24' for months now. Also many
emails back and forth . . . it's gone far better than we expected.
Sleazy seems to have relished collaborating with us and invited
us to stay at his place to work on the TG installation . . .

After numerous Cabinet and Mute meetings, it was decided that Cabinet Gallery would host the *TG24* launch and curate a related exhibition and installation. The visit to Sleazy's never happened. He'd been hard to get hold of, having had to sort out what he called 'distractions of late'. Geff had announced that he and Sleazy had split up for good. I spoke with Sleazy and he apologised for not being in touch and seemed cheery and resigned to the split. Coil were to continue and he took on gig bookings. That situation brought his work on TG to a halt.

> 4 September 2002
> *It's funny to think that if we ever meet up again (all 4) that it may be Gen and Sleazy that find it more difficult than me and Gen. The thought of doing a gig together got put to me yesterday (rumours of TG reunion). When I thought about it I realised that would mean getting together quite a few times prior to the show etc.*

> 13 November 2002
> *Gen has been very kind. If he continues like this then working together shouldn't be too bad. He wrote to say he was nervous about playing together again for a number of reasons, he's not the same angry Gen and doesn't want to 'act' out as someone he isn't. That's fine.*

The thought of a TG reunion held different reservations for all four of us. At the same time as holding back 'that thought', we were talking about performing and recording together, and Chris and Sleazy were working on a TG website. It was as if TG regrouping was inevitable.

Yet our own ongoing projects were what each of us were most connected with. Me and Chris had started DJing and were loving it – and seriously thinking about dropping Chris & Cosey and moving over to the moniker of Carter Tutti. Our new music had changed and was a far cry from the classic C&C sound. Chris wasn't keen on doing any gigs at all, seeing as we were already overloaded, but what with my health and OU degree studies I'd been on an enforced lockdown from creative activities for so long that I wanted to take opportunities while I felt OK-ish.

We'd turned down a lot of gig offers but accepted one for 23 November at Luchtbal in Antwerp, Belgium, and designated it as our last gig playing C&C material. We spent a month putting together a special video and C&C set. Nick took a break from art college to come with us as our roadie and ended up designing the cover of the ensuing live CD. Dropping C&C felt like a positive step forward, freeing ourselves from our earlier music. Which is odd (or not) considering we were revisiting the past work of TG.

The C&C gig was largely uneventful, another episode in the timeline of our ongoing body of work. Three days after our return from Antwerp we were in London installing the *TG24* exhibition at Cabinet Gallery. Sleazy was still distracted but back in touch, and all four of us were about to meet again in just a few days' time.

2 December 2002
3pm and we had just unpacked and were putting the kettle on
for a cup of tea when there was a knock on the door.

We'd just arrived at the Express Holiday Inn in Old Street, London. Chris answered a knock on the door. He was gobsmacked to see Gen stood there, smiling from ear to ear. At first he'd thought it was an Asian chambermaid.

Gen looked so different: well dressed, slim, with a dark shade of foundation and gold-and-silver eyeshadow. We knew he was transgender – he'd 'come out' some months earlier – but my eyes were constantly drawn to his face, trying to figure out what had happened. Then I remembered he'd had cosmetic surgery. He was quite hyper too. His hands and feet constantly danced, pitter-patter, and he fanned his long, red, false fingernails as he talked. We were all cheerily saying 'hellos' as a kneejerk response to the weirdness of the whole situation.

'This is weird, isn't it?' Gen said.

'Yes, it is,' me and Chris replied in unison.

He was edgy but full of smiles and very nice. We hadn't expected such excitement from Gen but coming face to face with each other after over twenty years, given our troublesome history, was always going to be a bit tricky for us all. Better to be cheery than solemn. The first face-to-face introduction had been brief and Gen went back to his room. We'd all agreed to get together privately when Sleazy arrived in an hour or so, for a coffee to 'break the ice'.

Reception called to say they had a delivery for me: a beautiful bouquet of flowers from Mute, along with a 'Hello' letter from Gen that he'd left at reception for us (and one for Sleazy) earlier in the day. Sleazy arrived from Weston and dropped by our room to have a few words before the group meet with Gen. He'd also had a visit from Gen. As well as the letters to us three, that was a nice gesture.

Gen's new wife, Jackie, had come over with him and we all met up at the Real Greek restaurant just behind the hotel. We sat around a table and ordered coffee. Before anyone else could say anything, Sleazy bristled and began to lay down the law, saying that before we went any further he would like to make some things clear. At this point, Gen's hands started shaking and Jackie put her arm around him. Sleazy continued, directing his words at Gen and saying that it was important that we must not start up together as TG without acknowledging that Gen had said and done some horrendous things to us, and we mustn't act like nothing had happened or that we were all best friends again.

Me and Chris were quite shocked at Sleazy's outburst. I tried to calm things a little by quietly suggesting that, bearing in mind our past, we should *all* be honest with each other – to say so if anything irritated us, not to let it fester but instead to accept any criticism as something positive for the good of TG. Gen nodded but then said that we all have our own perspective and memories of what happened. Sleazy's eyebrow went up at that, then into a frown, but he said nothing.

Gen's response was a veiled refusal to acknowledge his past bad deeds. Sleazy's request had effectively been denied. We moved on to the big question that had been floating round for over a year. Would TG regroup and play live again? All four of us had been discussing the possibility for a few months and decided that, in principle, we could do it. I hadn't wanted to regroup and had held out as long as I could, but TG being a democracy I was outvoted three to one.

The initial meeting came to an end and I passed Jackie my camera and asked her to take a photo of us all on this historic occasion. We all left the restaurant. Chris, Sleazy and Gen were in front as I walked along behind them with Jackie. She suggested that 'we girls' go shopping and let the guys get on with all the group business. It was nice of her to be so friendly but I realised that she didn't appreciate what TG was actually about or my role in both it and the *TG24* exhibition. I didn't know what Gen had (or had not) told her. I politely said no as I had TG interviews, meetings and a photo session to do. We were facing a busy week ahead.

Me and Chris spent the next day relaxing and resting before a group meal that evening. It was a business meal about Mute and TG releases and we'd said Jackie was welcome to come along. We wandered over to the Real Greek restaurant to meet everyone. Sleazy, Paul Taylor from Mute and Paul Smith were at the bar. We were led to the small private room reserved for us and were subsequently joined by Gen and Jackie, who placed her video camera on the table and pressed 'Record'. It was inappropriate and insensitive not to ask if any of us minded. Gen noticed us all looking at the little red 'Record' light and assured us that it would be turned off when we got to any serious discussions. That wasn't the point, and him making assumptions and decisions on our behalf didn't go down well. The serious discussions didn't really get far because of the disruptive antics of Gen and Jackie.

Daniel was late . . . Someone said he was with Cherie Blair at 10 Downing Street, talking about the future of the Roundhouse. But no sooner had Daniel sat down at the table than Jackie took hold of the video camera and put it about six inches from his face and started 'interviewing' him: 'Who are you? Where have you been?' It was a performance for the room and made for a very awkward moment. Daniel was polite but everyone else (except Gen) was getting pissed off.

Food was ordered and delivered to the table, at which point Jackie stood up with her camera and shouted at everyone to look up and smile. I was simmering inside, ready to boil over. I could just see her from the corner of my eye, hand on hip and huffing at me for not doing as I was told. She shouted at me again. I told her to fuck off and carried on eating. She sat down, put the camera away and began fawning all over Gen . . . then the waiter, and then Paul Taylor. It was embarrassing. Gen saw nothing wrong with what was going on. They both seemed to be in their own world.

The meeting was far from constructive – a lost opportunity on many levels. Outside the restaurant, me, Chris, Sleazy and the two Pauls were laughing and joking together, imagining the scenario of TG being put in a house like on *Big Brother* and what the consequences would be. If anything, Gen's performance that night had put us on high alert.

I never take pleasure in being right when it's about something bad. I wish I could have bonded with Jackie, as it would have made life easier in the TG camp. Gen acted up when she was around, showing off as if he were commander-in-chief of TG. We didn't see her again until the exhibition opening.

Mute had lined up a whole day of interviews in a small conference room at the hotel. Chris was quiet and happy for Sleazy to do most of the talking, and I piped up to balance things out a bit. I think Sleazy's strategy was to keep a check on Gen's input, just in case he started wrongly claiming to have invented acid house, or some such nonsense. Paul Smith came along at noon to whisk us off to Kingsland Road for a Vietnamese meal and to discuss TG gig offers from Tate Britain as well as an offer to curate at an ATP festival at Camber Sands. Gen told us all that, by the time we played Camber Sands, he'd probably be a woman and it would be Chris and Sleazy at the side of the stage, with 'us two girls in the middle'.

We all agreed that Mute would handle the merchandising and finances. Gen had wanted Jackie to do it all. We three wanted it to be as simple and stress-free as possible – wishful thinking.

⁓

After the last interview, we all prepared for the *TG24* box set launch, which was in conjunction with the *TG24* exhibition at Cabinet Gallery. I'd worked hard with Andrew and Martin selecting, collating and installing the show. We'd all loaned from our TG archives to bring together the first comprehensive display of TG and IR material relative to the release, and had a listening room set up that played the full twenty-fours hours' audio six hours a day for four days.

Me and Chris were the last ones to arrive at the private view. As I walked into the foyer the first person I saw was Kim Norris, who was now very outgoing and looking good. We hadn't seen or spoken to each other in years. 'Hello!' she screeched, as if she'd seen her best friend. 'You don't remember me, do you?'

'Yes, I do,' I said, and walked straight past her.

The place was absolutely packed with Cabinet artists, people from Mute and Rough Trade; the list of familiar (and unfamiliar) faces was endless and the excitement was tangible. I didn't see much of Gen all night. He held court in the listening room with his invited entourage. I think he might have been uneasy about the number of people in the other gallery room that he'd pissed off over the years. Jackie had been drifting around, videoing and photographing everyone and fawning. But worst of all, she and Gen had been talking to people about the proposed TG gigs when we'd all agreed to keep it under wraps. Alex Fergusson came up and told me Gen had asked him to do some work with him for when we all played the following year! I couldn't find Gen to tell him to keep his mouth shut – he'd left shortly after a fracas when a drunk guy had apparently tried to lift Jackie's dress. She'd pushed him away, which sent wine up the wall of the TG listening room and all over the floor, just missing the display. To finish off the evening, we were greeted by the sight of more red wine having been thrown up the entrance-hall walls and all over the door. Not nice for Cabinet's first show in their new gallery space but at least it was authentic in being a typical TG event.

Another heavy morning of interviews till noon, then we went to Tate Britain to talk about TG playing in the Duveen space as part of a Mute series. Sleazy said no, that we would have to be invited to do something at the Tate as 'artists'. We all walked round the Turner Prize show. We went from there to Cabinet for an interview for *Muzik* magazine with Andrew Weatherall. It was the best interview of them all: he delved into all kinds of subjects and we were happy to sit there for two hours just chatting. Then the *Muzik* mag

photographer shot off three rolls of film of us. Sleazy was so funny –
he suddenly just stood there, arms folded, looking down.

'What are you doing?' Then it clicked. 'Oh, you're posing,' I said.

'Yes,' he said. How utterly endearing he could be, and he'd probably hate me for saying that. I could have squeezed him to bits.

Our official TG promo photo shoot was with Brian Griffin at
Holborn Studios. It turned out that Sleazy knew him from his
Hipgnosis days. While Brian was setting up, we sat and signed
some *TG24* box set certificates. Gen was in a good mood and said
he thought it had all gone very well and how we'd all slotted back
into TG rather easily. I said I wasn't surprised, because our basic
characters hadn't changed that much, that friends had told me he
had, but I didn't think he had at all. His face fell. He seemed to
take it as an insult. Sleazy took over and we ended up with him at
the front, looking like Daddy Sleazy with his three kids. I was past
caring, really, and I couldn't be bothered confronting Gen about
his attitude and behaviour over the last few days. It seemed that,
after the niceties of that first face-to-face meeting, he was looking more like the Gen of yesteryear. For all his wanting to build
bridges and work together, he wasn't interested in actually being
together. In such a short time he'd annexed himself from us three,
not joining us for breakfast or hanging out. I wasn't sure how,
under those conditions, the proposed TG gigs or recording new
material could be feasible.

That looked even less likely when, back at the hotel, Sleazy came
banging on our door and charged in all red-faced and in a furious
frenzy. He stood at the end of our bed, gesticulating as he told us
how he'd had a phone call from a friend who was writing a book
on Coil and had spoken to Gen just two weeks earlier. Apparently
Gen had reiterated a lot of awful things about Sleazy and dissed
TG – Sleazy waved a press cutting at us as proof. 'What you went

through when you left Gen was nothing compared to what me and Geff went through,' he said to us.

I wasn't sure he knew everything we went through but it was obviously by the few things he mentioned that his experience must have been very nasty and hurtful to have such a lasting effect on him. Then he added, 'Right, this is what we must do: treat Gen like a Prague rent boy – make him earn his money and don't trust him an inch.' He hadn't finished . . . He said he was going to tell Gen that if he got up to any tricks he'd pull out of the TG gigs. It was beginning to look like TG the second time around could be a replay of the first.

Despite all that had gone on, Sleazy saw the potential for a TG regrouping and was excited about gig possibilities. He'd already started sourcing material and going through ideas for ATP. As curators of the weekend we were to play as TG, as our individual groups and select other acts. All under the title RE-TG. The regrouping of TG had been set in motion.

Gen returned to New York, Sleazy holidayed in Thailand and we went back to Norfolk. *TG24* was officially released on 23 December and as a special TG Christmas gift was broadcast in its entirety on Resonance FM on Christmas Day, along with a group 'Happy Christmas' message from us all.

10 April 2003
Camber Sands was a very pleasant weekend. We got to meet the organisers and see all the facilities and possibilities of the site.

The date of the TG-curated ATP had been changed. Paul Smith, me and Chris all went to check out Camber Sands for RE-TG and see Coil play there. It seemed well organised and we met up with Sleazy backstage after his soundcheck . . . which never materialised because the Magic Band seemed to think a soundcheck was as long as they felt like playing for. Geff was nowhere in sight and Sleazy was grateful for that small mercy. He said he wasn't even sure Geff would turn up to go on stage and it could be the last Coil gig. He'd had enough, saying that nothing could compensate him for the grief he had to go through with Geff. He'd lightened up by the time we left him.

Coil did an introspective and dark set, which was to be expected, interrupted at one point by Geff's interesting audience banter. Someone accused him of being drunk. 'I have no alcohol in my blood at all,' he said.

'LIAR!' someone else shouted back.

'No, I'm not lying. Well, yes, I am a liar, but I'm not lying about this. I have a horse tranquilliser for later . . .'

Meanwhile Sleazy and the other three band members played on. We went backstage afterwards and Sleazy's face lit up when he saw us. With Geff on one side of the dressing room and Sleazy on the other, I didn't know which way to go. Chris went to Sleazy and they had a big hug, and I went to Geff, then we both sat with Sleazy for his post-show wind-down.

I'd taken lots of photos of the site to email to Gen. Just as I sent it, an email came in from him asking if we'd been to Camber Sands yet because he needed to let his friend at *Art Monthly* magazine know what was happening with RE-TG. I had to quickly fire off an email saying, 'Don't say anything because NOTHING is finalised yet.'

4 June 2003
Paul Smith called yesterday to say we were all meeting on Friday at the Columbia Hotel. Chris asked Paul if he wanted him to bring anything. Paul sighed and seriously said, 'Yes there is, I could really do with you bringing a sense of humour.'

In light of the success of the *TG24* exhibition and the Tate's interest in TG, we had discussions about the TG archive. The sensible thing to do was to view it as one and not four separate archives, pooling them together to ensure the complete TG/IR source material could be safely stored in an institution and be accessible to all. Me, Chris and Sleazy agreed, and Gen had been amenable to the idea but had since begun the process of cataloguing the items he had in his possession.

A meeting was arranged to talk about it further, as well as Mute business and the live shows. We tied it in with my being in London for the opening of a group show I was in at the South London Gallery and Gen coming over at the same time. We all made our way to Gen's hotel, the Columbia, and were waiting for him in the lounge. Then I saw him go to reception in his denim miniskirt and bright yellow tights. He waved, came over to us and said, 'Hi! What are you all doing here?'

What?! He said he didn't know anything about the meeting and it was purely by chance that he and Jackie had been waiting for 'Wheatley' (Andrew) and even saw us, and anyway he and Jackie were off for breakfast now. He left us sitting there.

He was back half an hour later, a little breathless and puffing on his inhaler. By then the two Pauls had arrived, Paul Smith explaining to Gen that he had actually spoken to him three times since Sunday. 'I don't remember,' was Gen's answer.

The meeting about many TG matters commenced.

Paul Smith began by stating that he was acting on behalf of TG and not us as individuals, and he needed assurances that no one was going to walk out before the ATP or Tate events next year. Gen said he had no intention of pulling out. And neither had we three. As the finer details were discussed, Gen seemed bored. I got the impression that he couldn't be bothered with anything other than performing on stage and the money – that we three could do all the work. Maybe the intervening years of being a lead singer in a rock and roll band had instilled in him a new approach to working that was far from what was involved when working in TG. He was jibing Paul Smith again, and tapping his feet and hands constantly as if irritated, which in turn irritated Sleazy, who had trouble containing himself.

But finally we got the Mute business done and dusted. There was to be a 'Best of' TG album and, to accompany *TG24*, a *TG+* box set of the remaining historic live TG tapes, complete with metal cut-out cards that would form a TG flash. Chris faced lots more remastering and Sleazy more artworks. To avoid delays, Gen agreed to be contacted for his input at the latter stages of production, the same working practice as for *TG24*.

All that remained was the sticky subject of pooling the TG archive. I asked Gen what his intentions were. He announced that he would be selling what TG- and IR-related materials he had as part of HIS life archive, that to take it out and pool it with ours would mean his life's work would be incomplete. Which begged the questions: What about *our* life stories inherent in the jointly created items he was selling? What about the protection and retaining of the complete legacy of TG we'd all spoken of at the beginning of our regrouping?

We three were appalled and angry that he felt he could disrespect us and TG and still expect us all to continue this renewed 'relation-ship'. But there was no way out, having signed to Mute, and we felt a huge obligation to TG fans and everything TG had come to rep-resent. There was little we could do about how Gen chose to behave towards us other than adopt a philosophical approach and rise above the personal negative band dynamics (as so many bands do) with a determination to enjoy the opportunity of the regrouping and to deliver the best we could as TG . . . After all, the first incarnation had been turbulent. Gen, intentionally or not, had provided that undercurrent of tension second time around too.

25 June 2003
The contracts for Camber are being processed now. So at some point things will get more hectic. I'll make the most of the relative calm till then.

Whether or not ATP was actually going to happen, new TG material had to be created for a new TG studio album. I'd booked myself into a weekend's healing voice workshop in London, primarily to learn the technique of Mongolian overtone chanting for my music and art projects. So Chris said he may as well tie in my being away with him going to Sleazy's for a week to work on TG material. He packed his laptop and the bits and pieces he needed for the first Chris and Sleazy RE-TG sound workshop and we both set off, me for London and Chris to Weston-super-Mare. He dropped me off at the train station and began the long drive to Sleazy's.

While I was intermittently in New Age workshop hell, Chris and Sleazy had had a great time together. That made me happy. Chris had worked on RE-TG sounds and rhythms for a few weeks before he went to Sleazy's. Lucky he did, because Sleazy admitted that he didn't know where to start. It worked out better than they could have expected. They got the beginnings of about ten tracks down.

Me and Chris had missed each other so much and got straight back into recording some of my overtone chanting and overlaying it with the ambient audio recordings from my Beachy Head action piece. Everything had worked out so well and just in time to be broadcast on Resonance FM one year to the day after the original action took place.

28 September 2003

We just want the gigs to be over with – to take a deep breath and suck in the sweetnesses of life again.

After months of work putting together a new set, me and Chris played our first two sold-out shows as Carter Tutti at the Royal Festival Hall, London, and in Barcelona, Spain. Much as they were a great success, they were overshadowed by the death of Chris's uncle, Big Ernie – better known outside the family as Ernie Fossey, the legendary boxing matchmaker. The whole family was bereft. Nick was inconsolable. Ernie had been such a huge personality, the mainstay of our very close-knit family, and the thought of never seeing him again was unbearable. He and his wife, Pat, had taken Chris to their hearts and been a part of his life from the day he was born. Ernie was like Chris's second father. I clung to the memory of him as the lively, laughing Ernie I knew, who always called me 'darlin'' and greeted me with a 'Come 'ere, you' as he gave me a Big Ernie hug and kiss. Pat and Ernie were inseparable, like me and Chris, and I felt her pain so acutely.

Tributes and obituaries were in the press and television, with reports that Frank Bruno had taken Ernie's death badly (they were close friends). Ernie was as loved in the boxing world as he was in his family. Sky Sports dedicated the light-welterweight title fight in Manchester to Ernie, with the reigning champion, Ricky Hatton, saying how Ernie had been instrumental in his success: 'Please give a minute's silence for my dear friend Ernie Fossey.' Then a picture of Ernie filled the TV screen and the hall went silent.

The private funeral was torturously sad. As we stood by all the flowers, I remembered the previous funerals for Chris's nan and grandfather, when me and Ernie had stood together and he'd nudged me, saying, 'Look: everyone's thinking who will be next.' Neither he nor anyone else ever expected it would be him.

A memorial service was organised by Frank Warren, so all the boxers and boxing-world fraternity could pay their respects and celebrate all the fun, light and love Ernie had brought to us all. Frank and Ernie were very close and Frank, his wife, Sue, and their children were part of our extended family. Ernie had worked with Frank, matchmaking and more, for twenty years. The service was held at York Hall in Bethnal Green. We got there early to prepare ourselves. When me, Rose, Pat and Debbie walked into the hall, we were floored. It was like a shrine to Ernie. The walls were lined with large photos of him as boxer, trainer, cuts man and manager, and hung above the boxing ring was a huge photo of him smiling down on us. It was heartwarming to see so many who loved Ernie come up and give Pat their condolences. Me and Chris returned home feeling emotionally drained.

1 December 2003
What a month . . . again I moan but bloody hell. The RE~TG gig looks set to be called off again.

Getting back into work was difficult; with so much happening we were thankful for the positive events but reluctant to drag ourselves into anything negative. We needed to be lifted out of our sombre mood and what better way to do that than by plunging ourselves into DJing at Cosey Club. We DJ'd until 2.30 a.m., when Andrew Weatherall took over.

Returning home tired but decidedly more cheery, we were brought back to reality by emails from Paul, Sleazy and Gen. The RE~TG-curated weekend at ATP for 14–16 May was under review again. For whatever reason, Gen blamed the problems on Mute/

EMI and Paul Smith not doing enough and said that, because me and Chris were in the UK, we should make ourselves available 24/7 for TG.

I was livid. For one thing, Sleazy also lived in the UK, and Gen didn't seem to have any idea just how much we'd already done for TG in the past two years – and continued to do, with Chris presently mastering *TG+*.

Gen wanted in for RE-TG, saying he needed the money. Our *Mutant TG* remix album was going down extremely well and we were beginning to feel the press pressure, delaying all but urgent interviews until all of TG were together. Regardless of the ongoing stop-start-stop RE-TG business, we carried on with the TG plans we'd made and hoped ATP could be worked out.

Sleazy returned from holidaying in Thailand and me and Chris drove to his place to do the final tweaks to the TG gig material, ready for rehearsing with Gen. Sleazy had lost weight and was looking good but not feeling happy about being in the UK, describing it as being back in 'grey England'. I had imagined his house to be an isolated Victorian building on a hill, akin to the *Psycho* house, but it was in a street of similar houses, with a large front garden and snaking drive, and a small, grim, walled rear yard that backed on to woods. Being an old boys' school, there were about thirty rooms in all, a basement, two separate staircases and an elevator, as well as two self-contained flats, one used for 'adventures' and the other for archive/art storage.

Sleazy had made up a room for us and put a vase of fresh flowers in there. It was nice to be with him and his two basenji dogs, Pan and Moon. Poor Pan was fucked up, had started snapping and biting people for no apparent reason and wouldn't go up the stairs. Sleazy put it down to Geff's drunken binges while he was away. It had got really bad at times, with Geff having fallen down the stairs more than once – the worst being when their housekeeper had found him at the bottom of the stairs. He'd been lying there for days with the dogs by his side, unfed. She'd cleaned up Geff and put the dogs in kennels until Sleazy got back.

We set up all our gear in Sleazy's studio. It was dusty, especially the harmonium in the corner, and strewn with packaging from recent acquisitions and cables in tangled heaps. I made a space for my set-up close by the bay window, which had an amazing view of the sea. We worked all day and into the night on rhythms and sounds for the live performance, giving them the acid test by all jamming along. They felt good so we put them and the old TG tracks aside until we met up with Gen, to see how he felt about them all. Mute had given us a deadline for the new TG album of 23 April and we were booked into their studio in a week's time to start recording it, hoping to complete it in two weeks and hand over the master when we left the studio.

Maybe that was ambitious but we cracked on with sorting out the rest of the new material, going for anything that excited and ignited a spark in us. We shared the cooking of meals and in the evenings we'd watch TV in Sleazy's massive high-ceilinged living room, often falling asleep together on the big sofa. Sleazy had little time for the basics – he always had 'someone who does' to do those things for him. He just got on with life. He ignored bills and correspondence too. There was a carpet of unopened mail in the front porch that lay where it had fallen through the letter box. He'd just kick it to one side as he came through the door. It was intense working all day, but we got so much done that would otherwise have eaten into our time at Mute Studios. We composed nine new TG tracks to work with for the new album.

28 February 2004
Let's hope we can get some order into things or we won't have the album and gig material finished.

After twenty years, the four of us were about to go into the studio together to record a new TG album, and people were getting excited. Working at Mute was a far cry from our Martello Street studio (or our own C&C and Coil studios), where we had all our gear to hand and all the time in the world. It was important to use both the studio time and our being together efficiently.

Me, Chris and Sleazy arrived at about 11 a.m. and set up our gear. We'd brought what equipment we needed to London and rented an extra effects unit to mangle Gen's vocals. Gen arrived late with Paul Smith. He'd brought his violin from New York but not his bass guitar, offering to pay to hire one. One was bought for him, to be delivered to the studio the next day. We played the tracks to Gen before jamming together, which was our usual TG way of working. Gen sat and listened to us but didn't join in. He said he had jet lag and wasn't feeling good. We three carried on trying out ideas for a while, then stopped to talk to Gen about the material and which tracks he'd like to focus on first. He decided to leave early and went back to his hotel in a cab, with us saying that we hoped he felt better tomorrow.

Day two in the studio, and we were going through tracks when Paul Smith called us to say Gen would be along later. We continued working on our own until Gen and his bass guitar arrived. The guitar was quite heavy – he dropped it twice and couldn't get his effects pedals to work. Dave, the studio engineer, went home and brought his own Boss pedal for Gen to use, and we finally got to do our first jam session together.

It was sounding good – very TG but crucially and deliberately a step forward from the old TG material. I had no interest in regrouping if we weren't going to explore and create new work together. We had a strategy in place to help us avoid making music that sounded like our past or present individual music projects: we were using new equipment specifically for the TG regrouping. Mute had facilitated this by advancing each of us the money to buy new gear. Me, Chris and Sleazy had each bought a new laptop, music software (including Ableton Live) and an audio interface, and I bought myself a Roland multi-effects unit and a new Hohner headless lead guitar. We'd stuck to the plan but it seemed Gen wasn't quite on board. He kept mentioning how he hated 'laptop bands' – whatever they were supposed to be. We pointed out that TG had always been into new technology and innovative ways of working, that Sleazy had in fact used a computer back in TG in the 1970s, so using a laptop now wasn't new or alien to TG – it was just a computer in a more portable form, another instrument for generating sounds.

Despite my earlier reservations and the many 'issues', I was excited about TG. Once that collective energy and raw power kicked in, it was impossible to resist, like hitting a reflex. I was on a roll, exploring new ways of producing sounds, buying new gear to experiment and throw into the TG mix. Chris and Sleazy were the same. Sleazy was perplexed by why and how making music just 'worked' so readily with us but not with anyone else. I knew what he meant. We just had that deep connection, ability and willingness to open ourselves up to collectively surrender to the 'third mind'.

By the fifth day we were making slow progress, with Gen mostly absent. It was frustrating but we managed to get some work done and were all sat having a coffee in the studio lounge. Vince and Andy from Erasure were next door in studio two, working on their new album. Andy came into the kitchen and asked if he could take a photo of us all together. Gen blurted at him, 'And who are you?' as if he were some random souvenir-hunter. It was embarrassing.

'He's Andy Bell from Erasure,' I said.

When Andy had gone, I told Gen how rude he'd been. He apologised to Andy. We needed some time out. We left for the day and took the next day off – then back in the studio, hoping we could pull everything together in time. Gen's repeated lateness made us feel that he wasn't that interested in or committed to working with us, especially when, after my working on lyrics with him, he said he wanted the next day off to get the words together and insisted on us giving him a CD of the raw tracks to take with him. None of us were happy about new TG material leaving the studio and we'd already reluctantly given him a CD a few days earlier. Sleazy told Gen that on no account must he play it to anyone. Gen agreed.

We three worked on our own the next day, sorting out the gig and album tracks and putting the new recordings, 'Almost Like This' and 'Splitting Sky', to one side and preparing 'How Do You Deal?' ready for Gen's return to do vocals.

We finally got the vocals recorded for 'How Do You Deal?', sorted out the gig's running order and jammed the first four numbers to see how they felt. It went well and we made plans to mix the vocal tracks over the next two days, then run through a full set twice the following day. Gen mentioned that he had two art projects starting in the two weeks before the TG gig at ATP so he wouldn't be available to do anything for TG.

Paul Smith entered the studio to discuss the TG Artist Development Meeting that had taken place over at Mute. It was so weird to think of people talking about us like that. While at Mute we'd done group interviews for the *Guardian* and some magazines, Sleazy and Gen had done a phone interview, and me and Chris were interviewed by Paul Morley at the BBC. We'd been busy but rumours were circulating that we weren't actually working together and that

ATP might not happen, so we shot a thirty-second video of us all in the studio to put on the Mute and TG websites to prove we were together.

Me, Chris and Sleazy spent the last day in the studio working until 7.30 p.m. on mixes for the album, while Gen went shopping, leaving us all disgruntled, particularly Sleazy. 'I presume the publishing will be twenty-five per cent each again, despite the fact he's done fuck all?'

After a full day's studio work, we got a taxi straight to the Royal Festival Hall restaurant for a meal with Paul Smith, Barry Hogan (of ATP) and Cerith Wyn Evans to discuss the TG gig. Gen turned up dressed to the nines in a leather skirt, stilettos and full make-up, and proceeded to behave as disruptively as he had at the Real Greek meal. He sat next to Cerith, which wasn't a good idea. They both got blind drunk. We tried to discuss as much as possible but it wasn't happening. By the time dessert was served I was tired and ready to call it a night – but then, just to put the finishing touches to a trying day and evening meal, as I looked up from putting ice cream in my mouth I was greeted with the sight of Gen with one of his breasts out and Cerith feeling his nipple. Sleazy sighed in resignation at the situation, visibly flagging under the effects of a bad cold. Me and Chris left at 11 p.m.

As we rose to leave, Gen asked, 'Oh, are you going?'

'Yes, it's late,' Chris said.

'You call eleven late?' Gen laughed.

I felt the anger rise in me. 'It is when you've been working in the studio all fucking day!'

Gen went into scolded-dog mode and politely asked what time he had to be at Mute the next day. Chris said 11 a.m.

'What time are we meeting, then?' said Gen.

We gave up. He was too drunk to understand.

The Cabinet Gallery official launch of my limited-edition book, *Confessions*, brought some respite from the preceding few weeks. It was refreshing to be out meeting new and interesting people, discussing and being invited to contribute to their academic and art projects. We'd coordinated the book launch with our DJ set at Nag Nag Nag. The club was run by Jonny Slut and had been described as the new Blitz, except it had a non-elitist door policy: those first in line got in. It didn't matter whether you were a frequent celebrity visitor like Boy George, Kate Moss or Björk or the guy at the supermarket checkout. There was a diverse crowd, some dressed in the style of Leigh Bowery, some in drag, some dressed down, but all hugging, dancing and laughing. A great atmosphere – the dance floor was a riot. Such a great stress-reliever. At least we offloaded some before a shitload more arrived.

24 April 2004
*I've been in a state of shock really. We went to London to an
urgent meeting at the Groucho Club with Paul Smith and Barry.
RE-TG has been postponed until April 25th next year.*

Just ten days before we were due to play ATP, the whole RE-TG event was off. Sleazy, me and Chris met Paul and Barry at the Groucho Club. After all the work we'd done, to say we were pissed off would be an understatement. We wanted an explanation as to what the fuck had gone wrong. It all boiled down to basic mismanagement, resulting in ticket sales not covering costs.

It was suggested we put out a postponement notice. That wouldn't do. I'd been thinking of all the things that were affected. We'd each been allocated a merchandise stall for the RE-TG ATP weekend and me, Chris and Sleazy had already paid out for CDs to be pressed, as well as other stock. Where would we sell them now? Me and Chris had even finished the first Carter Tutti album to coincide with the event. When would we release that now? The merchandise, the other bands, the fans travelling from abroad, the new *TG Now* album that was recorded and pressed, the posters, the postcards, the sticks of TG rock, the flags, the film programme for the chalets . . . The list was endless. Financial debt aside, the bottom line was that we weren't prepared to treat TG's fans, the ticket holders, in such a dismissive way.

Me and Chris agreed with Sleazy's damage-limitation proposal of doing a filmed live recording session (like *Heathen Earth*), free to all ticket holders, who could also either get a refund or transfer their tickets to next year's rescheduled RE~TG at ATP. Barry would cover the cost and we'd sell the RE~TG merchandise and *TG Now* album to pay back the Mute studio costs.

I felt so deflated. We three thought the live recording idea was our best option, all things considered, and it assuaged our consciences about letting down the fans. But when we told Gen he (understandably) did his fucking nut and (not so understandably) demanded £5,000 be paid into his bank account or he wouldn't do the gig. That upped the stress levels. Gen got his £5,000, and me, Chris and Sleazy performed for free. I didn't like the precedent that had just been set but we'd been forced into a corner by the cancellation and Gen's demand. TG's democracy and united front had fallen at the first hurdle but at least we could deliver something that compensated the fans.

18 May 2004

Phew! Sunday TG recording session . . . what can I say? All
aspects of it were immense – emotional, logistics troublesome,
'interesting' interrelations, sound so physical and so much more I
just don't know where to start. I'm shell shocked really.

Because we had an early load-in scheduled for 10 a.m. on the day of the show, we'd all arrived in London the day before so we could sign merchandise posters and listen to tracks to agree a running order for the set.

Gen had brought his own merchandise with him to sell at the venue – something we'd all agreed not to do. TG was the focus and only the TG merchandise was to be sold, specifically to recoup as much as we could to pay accrued TG costs. Sleazy started the discussion off, being very diplomatic about it. Silence. I seemed the only one willing to say what we all felt – 'I don't want any of the merch you've done to be sold at the Astoria' – and I reminded Gen that it was agreed in emails before he came that none of us were to sell our own merchandise. Unlike him, me, Chris and Sleazy hadn't received any payment to turn up and were hoping our own merchandise losses could be offset by any shared profit from the RE-TG merchandise sales after repaying Mute. Then Gen told us he'd done a 'Hamburger Lady' T-shirt and a TG badge as a surprise. What happened to working and agreeing TG things together?

He was still a little sulky when we went back to our hotels. I told him not to dwell on the merchandise issues, that we'd sort it out tomorrow. He said, 'OK', but I knew he wasn't OK about it.

The next day, with the help of the crew, we set up our equipment, leaving the stage stark, with nothing fancy and all the house lights up. The camera crew of eight were given their instructions by Sleazy. Chris set up an Alesis twenty-four-track recorder at the side of the stage to be manned by MJ, a technician from Mute. Gen arrived in a miniskirt and low-cut blouse, blowing his 'Hamburger Lady' duck horn, with Jackie keeping her personal distance from us but once again with video camera, recording the soundcheck. None of us wanted to escalate the already compromised atmosphere over merch issues by telling her to stop. Soundcheck done, we went backstage to get something to eat.

After our lunch break, Chris, Sleazy and I went into the empty auditorium to get a feel for the place. At 3.30 Gen appeared on the deserted stage, unplugged his violin and guitar and started sounding off about people being two-faced and how he'd complied to all wishes and done what he was supposed to do, that he was sick of it all, and was now going to do what HE wanted after twenty-five years. I said his walking off wasn't a good thing, with over a thousand people waiting outside for TG to play in an hour.

Kirsten, our trusty assistant, stepped in to prevent a full-on huge row between me and Gen. She took him backstage and I called Paul to let him know what was happening. While Paul and Kirsten tried to calm Gen down, we three waited in the auditorium. Jon Whitney (of *Brainwashed*) was there and casually asked Sleazy when he was going back to Weston. Laughing, Sleazy said, 'In about ten minutes, I think. Taxi for Mr Christopherson, please!'

We were told that Gen was upset and crying backstage. Paul took us to the communal dressing room to discuss what Gen's outburst was about and what to do to make sure the gig went ahead on schedule. There wasn't much time. Paul asked me if I could deal with it. In what way? Could my heart trouble withstand it? Yes . . . but what Paul actually meant was that he thought the situation was really about me and Gen and our history. I was flabbergasted. After twenty-five years? The other thing was that Paul knew I wouldn't compromise over Gen selling his merchandise. I knew we'd live to regret giving Gen the 'sweetener' payment and that submitting to more of his tantrums and demands would give him the wrong idea that he could ride roughshod over the three of us.

Sleazy always avoided confrontation and Chris wasn't getting involved. The event had to go ahead so I said I'd talk to Gen. He joined us, walking in like the injured party. Sleazy apologised for any hurt he may have unintentionally caused and Gen accepted that and thanked him for being so adult – whatever that meant. Then Gen looked at the floor as he talked, avoiding eye contact with me as he said that my telling him last night not to dwell on things was intended to make him do exactly that.

'Whoa, whoa, whoa – stop right there,' I said, 'and look at me when you're talking about me.' I reiterated that my intention was to reassure him. I wasn't into playing games.

Then he mentioned my conversation with one of his friends about the TG T-shirts, saying things that weren't true. It had all the hallmarks of turning into a petty 'he said, she said' argument, so I called his friend in to confirm the truth of what I'd said to him – that I'd not said what Gen had just implied. At that point Sleazy agreed that what I'd said about TG merchandise having to be a joint decision was correct, that the TG house style was the four of us together and that was and is how it should always be. Then, as if a switch had been flipped, Gen giggled and cuddled up to Sleazy.

As we were about to go on stage half an hour later, someone said, 'Group hug.' A tentative attempt was made, with Gen saying, 'We're legends, you know. And it's twenty-three years since we last played together.'

At that moment all I could think was that this would be the last time ever – but walking on stage blew away all the preceding wranglings. The atmosphere was charged with expectation and joy, the place heaving with people thrilled to see us together. It was an immensely emotional moment. After a brief technical hitch we started playing and the place erupted. The musician Susan Stenger had loaned me her guitar strap in the hope that I'd stand and play guitar to make my presence felt. I had a feeling that, if I stood up, Gen would come over to me acting like a rock-star lead vocalist, playing up to my guitar sounds. But this was a recording session and sitting best suited the way I used and abused my guitar. So I stayed seated until I played cornet, when a great cheer went up. That was nice.

I set aside Gen's antics – these people were who mattered. This was TG magic in action. I felt such affinity with the audience as the TG beast was unleashed. When we played 'Discipline', Chris's descending sub-bass sent me and the crowd into raptures . . . and apparently the bar staff shut up shop, fearful that the building would collapse as it was shaking so much.

The session ended in a climactic frenzy, with the audience all but hysterical. One young guy with pink hair directly in front of me was so far gone, his eyes rolling back then staring at me as he head-banged to the rhythm. I sped up the rhythm on my guitar in response. I felt wicked but good too. People went crazy, stripping off, crying and clawing at themselves. The effect we had was extraordinary. It was one of the most intense one and a half hours I'd ever played. We left the stage stunned, with our ears ringing.

14 August 2004
This week has been absolutely terrible. What we may have been guessing for months now happened . . . World Serpent went bust and owe us somewhere in the region of £8,000.

Just as our Carter Tutti album *Cabal* was getting radio play and gigs were coming in, World Serpent collapsed. They'd sold thousands of our CDs and we were to receive nothing. We weren't the only ones. Coil were owed more than us. We'd talked to Sleazy about our World Serpent worries when we were in Amsterdam for a Kink FM gig. The line-up was Carter Tutti, Coil and Whitehouse. An odd mix, considering the animosity Sleazy and Geff had towards William Bennett. But good to see Coil in action . . . even if Geff was slumped out of his head at the back of the stage for most of their show.

The way World Serpent handled things was bad, keeping us hanging on and taking more of our stock at a time when they weren't able to pay us. I'd only spoken to Gibby a few days before he walked out and he gave me no inkling what was about to happen. Alan had left the previous year and now Gibby was gone, leaving only Alison to deal with everyone. She called me to tell me the bad news. She told us she had some of our stock in her garage and we could collect it. We drove there in our car. The garage was at the bottom of her garden and was half falling down with a leaking roof. A lot of other people's stock had been water-damaged but we were lucky that ours was in a dry part. We loaded up as much as we could and slowly drove home with the car so loaded down that the body was nearly touching the wheels. We talked with Sleazy about suing them but the cost and hassle weren't worth the aggravation.

We were panicking about how we were going to get our work distributed. Paul Taylor came to our rescue, suggesting Mute Distribution, and Paul Smith put us in touch with Cargo Distribution. Having lost money on TG and now this, the offers of TG gigs were looking more likely as an option to solve our dilemma. But the TG gig saga was rolling on in the same confused and raggedy fashion, with Gen annoying us all by playing TG tracks 'Discipline' and 'How Do You Deal?' as part of his own band's 'Best of' live set, then Sleazy talking to Barry about TG and confusing Paul Smith's negotiations. That was the point at which Paul started to take on TG managerial duties.

Setting aside the disappointment and chaos, I continued with my own projects and returned to Hull to do a lecture on my work to media technology students. I wasn't sure how I'd be received after so many years. It went well and I was especially pleased Pam had come along with Les. Neither of them really knew the details about my sex-magazine work so I didn't know how they'd take it. Pam had a tear in her eye and said how proud she was of me. From there I went to the Frieze Art Fair, where my work was profiled on the Cabinet stand and duly sold to collectors.

That side of my life was on track and I felt good. I'd completed the second '*Self*lessness' action in the Sandringham woods, the Queen's country estate. Me and Chris had found a secluded area that felt suitable for a short ritual. The piece referenced my historic connection to the Queen: as reigning monarch she owned the building that housed the ICA, the site of the sex-magazine-and-tampons scandal. I'd collected some leaves from the site and used them as a template for leaves made from the cache of my last tampons, which I'd crushed and pulped into papier-mâché. The different sizes, shades of white, spots of pale blue (tampon string) and varied hues of dried red blood looked beautiful. On the day of the action we drove to the Sandringham Estate, parked in the tourist car park and took our video camera, tripod and all my materials to our designated spot. The woods were pretty much empty other than the occasional dog-walker who passed by without noticing us. It was so still, with only birdsong, the rustling of squirrels and other woodland creatures, and the ground gave off a musky, earthy, composting-leaf-mould smell. It felt warm and comforting, evoking memories of my childhood, when I'd sit in solitude among the long grass, feeling at one with nature. I hung my tampon leaves from the branches of the nearby trees and shrubs, which had supplied the leaf templates, and placed some among the layers of fallen leaves. A token, an imprint of my*self*.

~

The TG gig at ATP was cancelled yet again, causing another all-round freak-out in the TG camp. We accepted another compromise from Barry. TG would headline at Jake and Dinos Chapman's curated 'Nightmare Before Christmas' ATP weekend on 3 December.

Sleazy was behind with the TG Astoria video and artworks – Geff had been on a drinking binge again. At 6.30 p.m. on 14 November I received an email from Sleazy to inform us that Geff had died. I shouted downstairs to Chris, 'Geff's dead!'

Not being able to take it in, we both read Sleazy's email again together. After what Sleazy described as 'a three-week dip into the oblivion of vodka', Geff had fallen over the upstairs banister, hitting his head on the hard tiled floor below. He was rushed to hospital but his head injuries were so severe that he was pronounced dead soon afterwards.

We were bereft and kept thinking of Sleazy and how he must feel in that huge house that screamed Geff from every corner. Although Sleazy had left Weston in many ways, going to Thailand at any opportunity, it was still the hub of Coil and supposedly the place where Geff could find himself and be free from his dependency on alcohol. But it had become the site of his death.

I called Sleazy and offered to come to Weston but he had others there and wanted to spare me. I said the TG show would of course be cancelled, but he said he wanted to do it. I kept thinking about when me and Chris walked with Sleazy along the Harrow Road after the TG Mute meeting just eight weeks earlier, when he'd been a bit melancholy about Geff, saying that he blamed himself for Geff's demise, that he didn't think it would be long before Geff would die. That had turned out to be tragically prophetic.

Sleazy was devastated and he understandably couldn't talk about the accident. I doubt that the full story of the circumstances of Geff's death will ever be known. Sleazy refused to discuss it or why Geff's most recent (ex-) lover inherited such a large share of his estate.

Geff's private funeral took place ten days later, with about a hundred invited close friends and family. The small chapel was festooned with flowers, vegetables and fruit, a truly beautiful setting that wasn't too heavy with sadness. Sleazy sobbed uncontrollably at times as he led the ceremony. He said at the beginning that he didn't think he could get through it without tears and that he wanted people to know that they too should feel free to cry. We did. It wasn't reverential or formal, just very, very personal. Geff's soft nature was countered with a reminder by Sleazy that 'Geff could also be a nightmare, bless him.' As much as he had at times been an utter pain with his drinking, I, like Sleazy, remembered the person inside. The sweetness Geff had about him, the fact that he was so lost and desperately trying to find himself. When that got too difficult he drank, and that killed him. I was so sad and angry he was gone.

Sleazy stood beside the open silk-lined wicker coffin and Geff's mother and sister sat beneath a large photo of Geff as a child. The contrast of such innocence and his tragic death was heartbreaking. There were readings and selected recorded and live music, including Coil's 'The Dreamer Is Still Asleep' and their version of 'Going Up', the theme tune to the TV programme *Are You Being Served?* Maybe a weird choice to some but it felt anything but to everyone there. The ceremony was powerful and emotional, especially when we all lit a candle and walked up to say our final goodbye to Geff and lay a token of our love beside him in his coffin. Me and Chris saw it as the greatest and last Coil performance.

The ceremony over, we watched as the black, glass-sided, horse-drawn carriage disappeared into the distance, taking Geff for cremation, his ashes to be scattered under a hawthorn tree.

Sleazy was bent over crying, then let out an enormously loud, heart-wrenching wail as Geff left us forever.

Everyone gathered in a hospitality room for the wake, where a spread of food and fruit was laid out, with a centrepiece of a huge heap of broccoli forming a ring around the largest bottle of vodka I'd ever seen. Everyone noticed it but no one mentioned or touched it. Sleazy entered the room, walked straight up to the table, smiled, grabbed the vodka bottle, poured out a glass and drank it.

Still reeling from the ceremony, I was on stage the next evening playing a solo gig at Spitz club in London. I dedicated it to Geff and did my best to transcend the deep hurt inside. Chris recorded the show but I've never listened to it.

A few weeks later TG was about to kick off again, starting with us all meeting at Mute Studios to run through the set, then drive in convoy to Camber Sands to finally play the ill-fated ATP gig at a Pontins holiday camp. The 'TG family', as it became known, arrived safely and took up residence in chalets, with Sleazy and Gen either side of me and Chris. Sleazy was pretty isolated from us to help him to get through the evening, and was tearful when I was discussing with Gen the idea of dedicating the gig to Geff.

After soundcheck we went back to the band chalet area. Sleazy and Gen were discussing drugs and I made my way to hospitality to get some food. It was dark and the light on the corner was broken so I couldn't see the step. I fell to the ground with such a thump. In a split second, I'd managed to put my hands out to save me from going face-first on to concrete. There was nobody around so I got up and made my way back to the chalet. I was shaking with shock. 'I've just fallen over,' I said to Chris. My wrists and knees had taken the brunt of the force when I fell. Both my wrists were throbbing with pain and swelling up, and my knees were bleeding and felt like they'd been hit with a hammer. Chris called Paul, who came with

Susan and Kirsten to assess the damage and whether I'd be able to play my guitar. A paramedic was called but was useless. I ended up telling him to just leave some support bandages for my wrists and I sat on the bed waiting and hoping it wasn't as bad as it felt.

The decision was made for me to do the best I could within the limitations of my pain threshold. Mitch, our roadie and tech assistant, was wonderful. When we got on stage he put my guitar over my shoulder for me, placed my plectrum between thumb and forefinger and stayed knelt at my side to help me at any time. TG were ready to go even if I was the worse for wear, with my bandaged wrist and aching knees. Sleazy wore his white-fur mirrored Coil costume in memory of Geff and as a tribute to Coil, who should have been performing on the same stage the next night but were now no more. He held his head down to weep whenever he was overcome with sadness. The gig started with Gen's dedication to Geff and we all focused in on the sound. Sleazy managed to transcend his difficulties and I endured the agony with the help of painkillers.

The concert was recorded and mixed by Live Here Now, immediately burned on to CD-Rs and put on sale just ten minutes after we'd finished playing. Sleazy disappeared really fast after the show, throwing all his gear into his bag, retreating to his chalet and dropping acid to enter another world for the rest of the evening. Gen stumbled into his chalet and we didn't see him again. Our room filled with sweet, warm-hearted people helping me re-bandage my wrists and asking if there was anything I needed. We said our thanks and goodbyes and settled in for the night, with Chris having to wash me and brush my hair and teeth for me. I couldn't sleep – the painkillers weren't effective and I was in agony with my wrists, which had ballooned in size. I spent the night propped up, resting my arms on soft pillows.

We left for home early the next morning. Chris drove straight to our local hospital. I was relieved I hadn't broken anything but it took nearly a year and many visits to a chiropractor to put things right.

1 January 2005
I think many of us are thankful that 2004 is over when we think back on all the traumas that it delivered in abundance. But then I have to also consider that it was the most successful and inspiring year we have had in decades.

Our new guise as Carter Tutti had gone so well, with radio play, reviews and live work all tumbling into our laps. My art was forging ahead too, with sales to museums and collectors and forthcoming exhibitions in Europe and America.

I felt so elated and blessed, not least because our music was to be part of the 'Visual Music: Synaesthesia in Art and Music Since 1900' exhibition at MOCA in Los Angeles. I was to give a lecture on 'Synaesthesia' and Carter Tutti were to play at REDCAT, a theatre inside the Walt Disney Concert Hall. Once again I was performing in a Disney space. The theatre was ideal for our audiovisual work, so technologically advanced and versatile, offering a huge screen that filled the wall behind us and a sound system and acoustics we could only have dreamed of. The concert sold out fast and there was a second concert offered for the fans that had missed out, but this wasn't a 'gig' as such – this was a different context altogether.

9 May 2005
I got back from Eindhoven late last night and am still a bit worn out from it all. It was amazing to work there for a week and gradually have everything emerge so beautifully and seem so right in that library setting.

Andrew and I had been going through my sex action works, sifting through the archive to put together the first comprehensive presentation of the material ready to install for the exhibition 'In the Vitrines' at the Van Abbemuseum in Eindhoven, Holland. I was absolutely thrilled and excited, but scared when I thought of how much work was involved. It was the first time I'd fully engaged on such a scale. Re-viewing and analysing my magazine works and all the related letters, model cards and photographs was a strange (but not unpleasant) revisiting experience. Andrew's assistance and informed critical gaze were invaluable and we worked with one of the museum curators, Diana, who was totally committed to helping us bring the show together. We worked in the library reading space for a week, forming coherent readings from the vast amount of material laid out in six vitrines and accompanied by captioned informational text and a four-piece framed magazine work across one wall. We put out a desk with reading matter on it: my *Confessions* edition and a transcript of an email conversation between me and Lucy McKenzie on our work, the exhibition and about being pornographic models – she'd worked exclusively for Richard Kern. It looked serene in its simplicity and so elegant in the quiet setting.

The library itself consisted of two walls of art-related printed material, spanning two floors and twelve shelves high. I had appeared in over two hundred sex magazines and as part of my show I placed my magazines in one stratum of the library shelves. It looked great to see all the colourful glamour covers, my art taking its place alongside so many other printed works on art.

Everything had gone so well, then on the eve of the opening an ICA moment raised its ugly head. One of the museum staff took exception to the framed work in particular as being too confrontational and said that the museum could be closed down by complaints. I couldn't believe that revisiting the 'Prostitution' works had resulted in the same censorship issues. Me and Andrew remained calm but firm and suggested a warning sign stating that the lower-floor area of the library contained pornographic material, and that there was no access to anyone under the age of sixteen. What made the situation worse was that there was a retrospective of a male Dutch artist in the main museum space, which included pornographic collages. There was no demand that he install warning signs for his work. That male/female artist hierarchy prevailed. Just one guy had caused the unnecessary angst. The other museum staff and the director were very apologetic and supportive. The opening went ahead with very discreet signage for my show.

3 July 2005
I was so shattered when we got home from Turin on Thursday, well we all were. It took us until today to feel anywhere near normal.

TG gigs had been offered, assessed and declined or accepted. A gig in Turin was agreed but attached to the deal was what I'd expected – a demand from Gen. He wanted a return business-class air ticket from New York. TG was certainly not a stadium band and the budget was tight. Sleazy was pragmatic and just said, 'He can fly with a coach and horses as long as HE pays.'

Gen's demand (without which he wouldn't play) pissed off all three of us, as well as the promoter who'd recently seen Gen in Spain and knew that he had flown economy and seemed healthy and well. That ran contrary to the health issues Gen had given as the reason for the extra cost. The promoter thought Gen was being opportunistic at his and TG's expense.

Turin was to be a performance with some additional time booked in a recording studio – a chance to do some recording together for a second TG album and finish Gen's vocal and instrumental parts for the album *Part Two: The Endless Not*. Sleazy had come to stay at our house and work in our studio to prepare. We hadn't heard from Gen, either about the album or the gig. He was on tour in the back of a van doing 'Best of' gigs with his band – and, much to our annoyance, still playing some TG songs. He got in touch two weeks before the Turin show to let us know that he was now going on holiday to Mexico. We kept things civil and focused on the bigger picture, hoping that Gen would work 'with' us at some point, as he repeatedly said he wanted to.

The festival organisers had decided TG would play in an 'industrial setting' on an outdoor stage with 'the cement men', all thirty-six of them underneath us throwing cement all over the place as we played. That wasn't going to happen. Paul insisted TG play in the indoor theatre but because it only held 1,500 people, TG would have to play two concerts with an hour's turn-around between sets to get the second audience in. It was Italy, is all I can say.

Back at the hotel for a rest and there was a crisis with Gen. He was jet-lagged and without his usual 'medication'. He was in a bad way and was eventually taken to the emergency room at the hospital to be 'fixed up' with legal pharmaceuticals. TG wasn't top of his to-do list. Rather than being in the studio with us preparing for the show and recording for the new TG album, he was out dining and shopping for a dress to wear for the gig.

The first day in the 'studio' was absolute hell. It was what you'd call a 'project studio', a small space with no air conditioning or fans and the temperature gauge topping forty-two degrees. We were sweating buckets and the gear was turning itself off as it overheated. As arranged, we arrived at 11.30 a.m. with Charlie, our TG sound engineer. Gen showed up at 4.30, did six minutes of vocals, then wanted to leave because it was too hot. By that time so did we, as we'd been there for five hours, so we all left.

Backstage was heaving with people before the shows. John Duncan was there, so glad to see Nick, who was about to see TG for the first time. Sleazy's Coil friends, Massimo and Pierce, were there, as was one hard-core Coil fan who had their logo carved across the full expanse of his back. Gen displayed his breast implants to the room, blurting out to the women present, 'It's all right for you, you're lucky you were born with them. I had to work hard to get these.' But, ever the showman, once Gen had a stage he delivered the goods.

8 August 2005
Well onwards with the new album . . . which sounds great!

Sleazy came back to our house from Turin to work on the *Part Two* album. Having Sleazy stay again was a total pleasure. He slotted in so easily, as if he'd always lived with us. He wanted to get as much done on the album before he got distracted by moving house. He'd sold Weston and was moving to Thailand to set up home there, taking his two dogs, Moon and Pan, with him. Chris was to mix the album, ready for an end-of-year release in time for the next TG gig in Berlin.

One element was missing. All we'd got from Gen out of the two Turin studio sessions was six minutes of vocals and a few minutes of bass and violin. Plus we were all doing a solo track. We three had finished ours but were still waiting for Gen's contribution and for him to record the vocals on the title song, 'Endless Not'. We managed to get that finished but then were informed that the lyrics he'd sung were from a song he'd already recorded with his other band. He didn't seem able to keep his different music projects separate. That attitude came across to us three like a refusal to fully engage and

393

commit to TG, most blatantly displayed by his choice of dress being far from what we'd all agreed, and always placing his other band's logo prominently on the TG stage. That sent conflicting messages to us and our fans. But the most troublesome thing was him (re-) using already published lyrics for TG songs (which happened more than once), even though the TG album was contracted to Mute and Mute Song Publishing. We were left trying to make some sense of his tangled web of confusion, which was becoming very wearisome, as well as having to salvage what Gen material we could from live gig recordings to use on the album as a substitute for the lack of any studio recordings by him. It wasn't easy as we couldn't use vocals from the Turin gigs because he'd sung the wrong lyrics to the wrong songs.

The deadline for delivering the album was getting so close that Chris finished as much as he could (bar Gen's vocals and solo track) and sent a copy to Mute, Paul, Sleazy and Gen. Everyone thought it was fantastic . . . but no word from Gen. I'd been ringing him to try and bring him back into TG reality about the now-urgent deadlines. Then I finally got to speak to him. He sounded pretty ill. He'd been put on medication and a strict diet and advised to rest. It was difficult to figure out whether what he told me was true or exaggerated because the list of ailments was so long: possible cancer, pneumonia, heart trouble, diabetes, arthritis, brittle bones . . . Then he added that he'd broken his shoulder and some ribs when he was pushing his laundry down the street in a trolley a couple of days earlier. That prompted questions in my mind. If he's so ill why isn't someone helping and doing his laundry for him? I guessed we'd only know what he wanted us to. If what he said was fact, then I could understand why he'd not been in touch. He told me he was awaiting test results and said he would be scaling down his activities. But two weeks after our conversation we got an email from him to say he was free of all the possible illnesses, and giving us his feed-back on the new TG album: 'Put bluntly, as it is I am ashamed of it and would never play it to anyone as being anything connected voluntarily with my body of work. Having said that I am prepared to work hard to help it become perfect. Ironically I think it's really close and everyone has done a great job.'

To have that slap-down after all the work we'd done (and the little Gen had done) was too much for Chris, particularly Gen's generous offer to 'perfect' it for us all – he still hadn't sent us his vocals or solo track. To cap it all, he said he'd mislaid his CD of the new unreleased album, possibly in a local studio. That set alarm bells ringing as to whether it would appear on the internet before it was even released.

Chris went ballistic. He'd spent so much time on TG already, having mastered the TG DVD surround mixes of the TG sessions at the Astoria and for Berlin, and two months finishing tracks and mixing the new album. He was blunt in his reply: 'Gen, if you wanted more involvement in this album why on earth didn't you get involved? We asked you to send us a solo track, you didn't. We asked you to send us voice, guitar, violin parts, snippets, ANYTHING we could work with, you didn't. If you wanted MORE voice, violin, bass you should have helped us out a bit more in Turin. What did you expect, a classic TG album with 10% input? I half expected this kind of response. You reacted in a similar way to *TG Now* and you told us (more than once!) you hated all the tracks on *Mutant TG*. Two TG albums that were well received and successful I might add. So I guess your response is par for the course.'

Chris's email tore apart Gen's points of criticism one by one, reminding him that this was one of two albums contracted to Mute, and that, if things couldn't be resolved, he and I were ready to walk away from TG. Sleazy stepped in to try and find a solution, couldn't, then stepped back and left it to me, Chris and Paul, who was so patient and tenacious in his determination to bring us all together again.

It wasn't just the album that was giving us angst-ridden days and sleepless nights. The forthcoming TG Berlin gig, which was to act as promotion for the launch of the new album, took a lot of preparation as it involved two live shows and an exhibition, 'Industrial Annual Report'. That had been another source of friction between us three and Gen, who'd made noises about supplying material from his archive but didn't deliver. After meetings with Paul Smith and Markus Müller from Kunst-Werke in Berlin, me and Andrew (Wheatley) worked on collating the material for the exhibition. Sleazy sent items from his archive and I delved into ours, scanning and supplying print files for enlarged photographic prints of classic TG images to include in the show. Gen had expressed no interest in the exhibition. I forged on, giving only a fleeting thought to whether he'd give a similar 'ashamed' critique as he had with the album.

Me and Chris took the train to London for a meeting. On the station newsstand, Chris saw the cover of *Zero Tolerance* magazine advertising an interview with Gen. Out of curiosity he looked inside, only to read Gen saying, 'I'm committed to my own projects, but I'm not really committed to TG any more. I've written new songs with TG, though – I had to. We had to. It's just not possible to be a caricature of something that you're not any more. The new stuff is more ambient, more peaceful, because with me being the voice, it has to be how I really feel, and that's different now to how it was twenty-five years ago . . .'

That was a body blow but confirmed what all three of us had been feeling about Gen's (non-) commitment to TG. As for Gen being the 'voice' of TG, none of us agreed with that. The overall impression he gave was that TG was secondary and we fit ourselves around him. 'When there's something interesting to do, and I have spare time, then I'll do TG with the others,' he said. It was not only demeaning to us and TG but it was also disinformation and didn't reflect the real situation.

7 October 2005
I feel like I have sold my soul to the devil and he is poisoning my life. I can't see us sitting down and having a talk through our past misgivings because he has continued to be worse than he ever was. Where would you begin and end? He couldn't face it or handle it. He'd shut down immediately. TG would end there and then . . . The fat cheque means nothing to me. At the beginning of all this I said I couldn't be bought but was outvoted. I should have stuck to my guns. I am in the Faustus zone.

As Gen travelled around the world disseminating his views on TG and doing a pretty good job of obstructing and undermining our ongoing hard work in his absence, I was feeling like I'd paid a high price for allowing his malevolent presence back into my life.

There were also great things going on that went a long way to negate the drip feed of Gen's disruptive actions. I was to be included in the Tate Triennial and me and Chris had contributed a sound work, '4:16:16', for European Radio Day: four images converted into four audio pieces arranged to present the linear sound of the visual pixels of the four images. I loved those non-TG activities and the escape afforded by everyday symbiotic moments of gentle beauty, like sweeping up the autumn leaves in the garden joined by a robin redbreast just feet away, picking up the bugs as I unearthed them.

The TG exhibition came together. Word had been sent to us that Gen was too busy with an exhibition of his own. It turned out that he screened the COUM films including me and Sleazy and music by Chris and John Lacey. The gallery apologised as they had assumed Gen had our permission, but he'd not consulted any of us beforehand. One thing after another.

We started calling Gen's emails 'hand grenades', as he'd be silent for months then hurl a 'bomb' of demands or statements of intent (or not) our way. One such hand grenade arrived just a month before the Berlin shows. After a prolonged silence, with our emails going unanswered, which was driving Paul and us crazy, Gen emailed to inform us that he had a new manager and that ALL TG matters must go through his manager first. That included the Mute contract, which had been months in the making and was about to be signed, and which could now face Gen's new manager's amendments – as could the Berlin schedule. He also laid his cards on the table as to his commitment to TG – it would come after everything else he 'may' get offered. Placing TG secondary to as yet non-existent possibilities led us to think that he didn't want to do TG at all.

There was a lot of money at stake. The new Mute deal with TG came with an advance and obligations that had been discussed and largely agreed, including further gigs that Gen's new manager saw as an area of potential conflict. Sleazy lost his will to bother with Gen, even suggesting we work without him in future. He'd been working hard on the TG merchandise and preparing the many component parts for the TG limited-edition Berlin Uber (Super) ticket, to get it all manufactured in time to bring with him. Each ticket came in a red velvet bag containing a silver box, inside which was a 3" CD-R of live tracks from Turin, two 'Endless Knot' badges (gold and enamel), four postcards, four totemic gifts, a signed poster and a lanyard laminated ticket decorated with gold foil.

Paul as ever saved the day and somehow made it all work out for the greater good, and as always was magnanimous towards Gen. Me and Andrew packed the TG exhibition materials, and me and Chris got down to working on TG live material for the gigs.

6 December 2005

Poor Paul Smith, he's worked so hard for TG and Gen has made his life hell. I did warn him and Sleazy at the beginning of all this that Gen would undermine TG and manipulate the situation as an act of revenge but I think they thought I was being bitchy and vengeful.

I was being philosophical about it. Maybe it was a mixed blessing . . . that Gen could have possibly engineered the scenario of Throbbing Gristle's final spurt coming to a sticky end. The release of the album had been postponed, on top of the concerns with the contract, which was now on hold. When we arrived in Berlin it was covered in snow and Christmas decorations, a stunningly festive, welcoming scene. We were staying in a large hotel at the Alexanderplatz in the former East Berlin. A 1970s timewarp. We dropped our bags off in our room and went down to the lounge for quick hellos. Sleazy had flown from Bangkok and Gen and Jackie from New York.

The photographer Paul Heartfield and his partner and assistant, Alix, joined us a few days later to document the whole TG trip. The two shows at the Volksbühne were to be on New Year's Eve and New Year's Day, and the TG Astoria film premiere was to be screened on the 29th, then the TG exhibition. To make best use of us all being in one place at the same time and to fulfil Gen's request 'to be all four in the studio together', we'd booked time in a recording studio.

Breakfast on our first day in Berlin, and the start of what we expected but didn't want . . . Gen wouldn't be at the studio until much later. It was a pattern that continued throughout the ten days in the studio, which was costing us a fortune on top of the extra hotel expenses. Gen's alcohol and drug use had got worse and we were having to work around his highs and lows as best we could, gently but persistently steering him towards producing material for the new second album. There were concerns over his health, as he was drinking a lot in addition to taking what was referred to as his 'arthritis medication'. As well as him being irritable, easily distracted or spaced out, the drink and drugs created a disconnect from us when we were supposed to be working in unity. I found it upsetting to witness.

The studio we'd hired was at Funkhaus Berlin, situated in the former East Berlin and housed in a 1950s building used as the broadcast headquarters of the GDR's state radio. Not only was it a massive complex with purpose-built recording studios for all kinds of genres of music, even for whole orchestras, but it also had the most fantastic foley facilities we were likely to get access to. It was an incredible place, a warren of corridors leading to offices, acoustic rooms, textured floors of every description, cave and cellar spaces, listening booths, with an array of instruments at our disposal. The engineers and technicians were so very nice; it was a great atmosphere to work in.

Rehearsing for the gigs took priority for the first few days. The TG gig set was sorted quickly, then we started working on ideas for the live Derek Jarman soundtrack. Sleazy, Chris and me had bought some new equipment – Sleazy a cheap child-size guitar, and all three of us had a sex toy to use as an instrument. My sex toy was a clear-glass dildo, Chris's dildo was stainless steel, and Sleazy's was a steel vibrating penis probe. I got a really great sound using the dildo on my guitar, and my effects pedal fitted well with what Chris and Sleazy were doing. I was pleased to play that and bring in my sampled sounds and cornet.

Gen had been in the hospitality room while we worked – he didn't seem to know what to do for the soundtrack. He asked to see Sleazy's sex toy. Sleazy handed it to him (switched on), and Gen got an electric shock and jumped, spilling his cup of coffee all down his dress. I rushed him off to clean it, leaving Sleazy laughing. Later he did apologise and Gen took it very well, considering it was his favourite outfit. We all went back to the hotel to wash and rest before the TG exhibition private view at the Kunst-Werke Institute for Contemporary Art.

The exhibition looked wonderful and we received tremendously good feedback. The show focused on the development and strategies of TG and Industrial Records, with newsletters, badges, patches, audio and visual releases, artworks and posters. It was a great night all round, a full house. There was also a viewing room, where the floor was covered in carpet featuring a huge TG flash logo, and where TG live videos were screened. The Mute and Cabinet contingent were on fine form, as was Richard from Cosey Club. We stayed till late. Gen and Jackie stayed about an hour and were sociable and pleasant. Gen didn't comment to me personally about the show. It was a shame he hadn't been involved but that was his choice and he had supplied us with nothing from his archive. People probably didn't notice, other than the absence of his portrait print from the *Heathen Earth* display.

We later found out why he hadn't cooperated. He'd sold his archive to the Tate, including TG tapes, artworks and other related TG and IR items. He never mentioned that he was doing it either before, during or after the time we discussed needing his materials for the show. For me, I'd worked on two TG exhibitions, which had provided the provenance that had no doubt contributed to the value of the TG archive. I felt he took advantage and sold what he held at the opportune moment and before any of us had a chance to question his actions or amalgamate all of our archives to ensure the full TG/IR story was safely stored away for posterity. Once again we all felt deceived.

31 December 2005

Then the New Year's Eve gig . . . it was true theatre I suppose but not as you know it.

The day of the first gig, we had a big interview arranged for *Rolling Stone* magazine. Jackie walked into the room where we were all sat waiting for Gen and announced that Gen wouldn't be coming, that he was too debilitated to take part and that she would be his representative, because, as she said, 'I know enough about the criminal mind to speak for TG.'

Where was Gen's head at – or Jackie's? We were all taken aback, including the journalist. None of us understood what her reasoning was or why Gen would even think it was OK to treat us like that. We all looked at each other as Jackie plonked herself on to a chair. Sleazy looked over at me and nodded his head to signal for me not to go mad, that we'd deal with it. I held back, but the journalist showed his lack of interest in what Jackie had to say by cutting her short whenever she spoke. In spite of being set up by Gen, the interview went well. What was most infuriating was that, for the last fifteen minutes of it, Gen, in what looked very much like a drug-induced state, was leaning against the door smirking and watching us. The journalist left and Paul Smith returned from sorting out things with the PA crew. When he was told what had happened he went to Gen and Jackie's dressing room and had a very heated conversation, which was audible down the backstage corridor. The pre-gig relaxed ambience had taken a battering.

Susan Stenger's band, Big Bottom, with Susan, Mitch, Cerith and Alex Hacke (from Neubauten) all playing bass guitars, performed first to a seated auditorium and I watched them do a great set. When they finished the stage was broken down by the crew and the audience were asked to return in twenty minutes for the TG show.

They came back and took their seats to see no TG, just an empty stage. The red curtains at the rear of the stage were then drawn back, revealing a larger empty space for them to enter that had a high stage at the far end and a thirty-foot black rubber backdrop. That was the TG quad PA zone. We were watching it all unfold backstage on surveillance monitors – people making their way into the quadraphonic zone, with some changing their minds and taking an auditorium seat – and in doing so they became an audience watching an audience about to watch TG. I said that this could all turn very weird if, as we were all watching them, they mounted the stage and nicked everything – then the show would just be a myth because it couldn't take place.

When the audience settled down, we entered the stage to an uproarious cheer and began the set with a trumpet and cornet herald, which was sent to each corner of the space. There were technical problems. I had issues with my mic not being turned up and my monitors cutting out. Then the whole PA cut out, leaving us with only the stage monitors. Halfway through, my gear stopped working altogether and the show was brought to a halt for a good ten minutes until Chris managed to sort it out. Some of the audience thought it was intentional, others not, but it made the gig what it was. The usual TG mayhem. The show was intense and VERY physical, with sounds hitting the stomach and head and being spun around the space.

The response was unbelievable, so much so that Gen suggested we do an encore – which TG had never done before. 'Just "Hamburger Lady",' he said. Me and Chris preferred to leave it as it was but Sleazy was up for an encore too so we said OK – but just the one song. Then, on the way to the stage, Gen announced that he hadn't got his duck horn, which was integral to the song. Kirsten searched but couldn't find it so I had to fill in on my cornet. The

impromptu encore caused chaos for Sleazy because he had to frantically reconnect and start up his laptop again. By the time it was up
and running the encore was over so he actually never did it. I don't
think anyone noticed with Chris on rhythm and synth, me on cornet and guitar and Gen doing vocals.

Another day, another show. We were understandably a little fragile so we all took the morning off before an afternoon soundcheck
for the TG live soundtrack to Derek Jarman's film *In the Shadow of
the Sun*. We'd had a new print of the film made and the quality and
richness of the colours was breathtaking. Projected so large behind
us, it looked fantastic. Sleazy and Chris wanted to be together at one
side of the screen so I shared a large table with Gen on the opposite
side. With it being dark, we also had to make the stage safe for Gen
as he had to get up at some point to play the massive gong we'd
hired for the second half of the film. I made sure the sharp edges
on the gong stand were padded so Gen couldn't inadvertently hurt
himself.

The Jarman soundtrack was to be totally different from the previous TG night and would be a lot more ambient. Me and Chris
had worked on some things before we set off for Berlin and then
got together with Sleazy and Gen in the studio a few days before.
Gen had his customary bottle of wine next to him on the table
– I dreaded him knocking it over and soaking my equipment. I
kept checking on him, that he was OK, as he didn't play much.
At one point he was leaning across the table staring into space and
absent-mindedly flicking his violin with a battery, unaware that it
was making a noise and coming through the PA. When he got up
to play the gong, he knocked a bottle of water off the table and on
to the stage, narrowly missing my guitar pedals. That made for an
unexpected 'sound'. At first the gong sounded amazing, then Gen
really got into it, staring trance-like and hitting it like he was beating

a carpet, not really playing 'to' the film. When he stopped, he came back to the table to sit next to me.

It all worked out tremendously well and everyone adored the evening and was amazed at the transformation in sound that TG could create in comparison to the previous night.

4 January 2006
Our last day in the studio . . . I feel and look so awful and I
have to do extra photographs today. I told Paul H he'd have to do
some serious photoshopping on me to get anything decent.

By the time the day had come to a close, we'd managed to record some of Gen's bass, doodling piano and two lots of vocals. In the sound booth, with a bottle of wine to hand, Gen tried out different vocals for some of the new album tracks we'd put together during the week, descending at one point into a Beefheart impression and exorcist screaming. He emerged pleased with himself, saying how he'd brought the track together for us – like we'd needed his magic touch to get the job done. I said nothing and left the room thinking that we still had a long way to go as far as the second album was concerned.

There'd been ongoing talks about a TG/Kraftwerk/Aphex Twin '5 Cities' project. A venue had been suggested: an old power plant in Berlin that was due to be renovated (now called Atonal). The first '5 Cities' performance would also be the inaugural event for the newly repurposed building. We were invited to look around, to get ideas for the show. Gen said he didn't like Kraftwerk and wasn't interested in coming along.

The power plant was phenomenal, an immense derelict space, the epitome of 'industrial', and could provide a fitting end to the TG regrouping. That evening all TG personnel and friends had a last

TG supper together in a nearby restaurant. Gen and Jackie turned up late with glazed eyes and puffy faces. Gen was slumped across the table or leaning on Jackie's shoulder. He didn't offer anything in the way of conversation or discuss the TG events or the business at hand – that Markus wanted to tour the TG exhibition. In the end, Markus directed his proposals to the three of us and Paul. Gen and Jackie left, saying they had an early flight, so we said our goodbyes. At breakfast the next day Sleazy said he'd had a slurred, 'out of it' call from Gen at 1 a.m. to thank him for everything . . . A parting morsel of niceness.

17 January 2006
The Nico project seems to have become the possible last album of TG. We have Robert Wyatt and Antony in mind to ask for vocals alongside Chris, Sleazy, me and Gen . . . Hoping to get this done in a live situation built around the ICA plan in June. None of us wants to go into a studio with him again.

TG in Berlin had been something to behold. There was so much – maybe too much – going on. Every day had been full-on, with rehearsals, the exhibition, the film premiere and 'in conversation', gigs, photo shoots, interviews and behind-the-scenes challenges. But it was the best New Year's Eve I'd had and I've got treasured memories of it and everyone who made it so special.

On balance the trip as a whole was positive, with many offers and interesting projects to consider. The best of which came from Sleazy while we were all in a taxi together: 'What do you guys think about TG doing a cover version of a whole album?' He said it would be totally not TG, which ironically made it very TG. 'How about Nico's *Desertshore*, my favourite album?' he said.

3 February 2006

Well I'm in Art Tate mode now as I'm printing new text pages ready for dry mounting, the shippers have just collected the box of Cosey works and I'm beginning to get excited.

The theme of the Tate Triennial, 'New British Art' (curated by Beatrix Ruf): appropriation of cultural material. My sex-magazine actions were selected and I was working like crazy and travelling back and forth to London for meetings with Beatrix, Andrew and the Tate's associate curators. I stayed in London for three days, installing my works and carefully writing the captions, with assistance from Andrew. My work had a large room to itself, and much like the show at the Van Abbemuseum, the presentation was kept simple, a perfect backdrop for the heavily loaded pornographic imagery and text.

Being in London and away from other distractions, I was able to focus on my art and be with Andrew and Martin for extended lengths of time rather than my usual swooping visits between other projects. Having that precious uninterrupted time to talk with them in depth about my work was so important and inspiring. They made me feel good about working in the art world again.

Nick came to the private view with us. It was a fun evening that went on into the early hours. We returned home feeling elated. The press had reported positively on my 're-emergence' in the art world. The *Evening Standard* front page announced: 'Tate to show porn star 30 years after ICA outrage – A classic of British art? Welcome back Cosey Fanni Tutti'. And in my hometown newspaper, the *Hull Daily Mail*: 'I'm back, decades after the scandals'. Maybe that was what triggered another Gen 'hand grenade'.

9 March 2006

I've had enough. I can't see how I can share air space with
someone who quite clearly seems hell bent on causing mayhem
in pursuit of his own needs . . . but we need to discuss TG
contractual obligations and anything else necessary for the benefit
of TG.

A few days after the official opening of the Tate Triennial, Gen sent an email to the Tate press office claiming my magazine works as his own, saying, 'Cosey was only the supplier of my work by default'; that 'All Cosey did, at my request, was legitimise them as "art" by signing the corners'; that 'She was embarrassed and uncomfortable about it for a long time and appalled when it became public knowledge via the ICA.'

Gen had also asserted that he'd secretly bought the magazines and had them framed himself, in silver high-art frames. But it was common knowledge that the magazines had been put into clip frames. Contrary to what he said in the letter, there I was, well documented for all to see in newspapers and magazines (and in my own diaries): NOT embarrassed, NOT uncomfortable, NOT appalled, but stridently confident, modelling for years and collecting my sex magazines, and being photographed smiling on the box of CLIP-framed magazines in the ICA in 1976.

I saw his sending the letter as a vindictive and malicious ploy to demean me as an artist. Everyone was incredulous when they read it. There were so many lies in it that I thought he'd finally lost the plot. But I took it as him trying to rewrite history, an attempt to exclude me, to place himself in the limelight to be credited for works he hadn't done. It was beyond reason as to why the hell he thought he could do that when the truth was so well documented as art-historical fact. His claim of 'appropriation' in his letter was not quite in the same spirit as that of the works in the Tate show. His denigrating me as subordinate to the 'male artist' (him) who (he claimed) used me to make the magazine works smacked of a male chauvinistic attitude and suggested he wasn't quite the supporter of feminism or egalitarianism he purported to be. In my opinion, as someone 'now transgendered', his spurious claims and actions against me (a woman) didn't cut the mustard as far as true 'sisterhood' was concerned.

I had support from every quarter. The Tate replied to Gen on my behalf. I didn't respond to him. I gave him and his delusional email the attention it deserved. None. I didn't want to work with him again. For me, the TG regrouping was over.

Sleazy corresponded with Gen about the consequences of his letter on TG. What had made matters worse was that Gen had also sent a (slightly amended) version of the letter to the editor of *Art Monthly* magazine – which was published. His letter went public. TG fans (rightly) started suspecting unrest in the TG camp, asking how Gen could insult me at a time when he was supposedly working with me and expect me to just accept it as his opinion. Sleazy at first put it down to Gen being disruptive. Monte said, 'Gen just can't bury the hatchet plus it's another way to get publicity . . . I just think he has lots of animosity.'

Gen eventually made a statement on his website which wasn't very helpful but revealed his mindset towards TG. There was no apology to me, just further indirect belittlement in the form of a 'get over it' attitude, with him stating, 'Just because a minor point was made in a letter to a magazine . . . Thee [sic] idea that ANYONE should COUMhow [sic] exponentiate a minor letter to a major issue is ridiculous.' He didn't see that his letter should affect TG at all: 'We do not need to agree, love each other, speak to each other, or respect each other for TG to still remain a force to be exalted.'

I was again dumbfounded. How do you work with someone who doesn't feel respect for you, or who feels that speaking to you is not important as far as sharing personal space and the creative process is concerned? I sensed an undertone in the to and fro of emails that I was overreacting, which in turn put me in a defensive position (to prove Gen wrong) when I was the one who had been 'attacked'.

I sent Sleazy my 'evidence'. He was seething that Gen had misled him on a number of counts, while the public nature of Gen's dissing of me brought back his and Geff's own past experience of being on the receiving end of Gen's public maliciousness. He fired off a tirade of facts about both my and Gen's accounts of 'Prostitution' in the *Wreckers* book, contradicting what Gen had said in the Tate letter: 'your email to the Tate contains lies, fabrications or at the very least a deliberate distortion of the facts on your part. Presumably intended to be malicious and/or extend your own perceived role.' That email hit a nerve with Gen. He replied in passive-aggressive mode, turning the situation around to him being the victim – we were all 'having a go at Gen'. But he did want to carry on with TG and would give it his best, accepting a 'code of conduct' we'd all adhere to that would enable TG to carry on.

15 April 2006
I don't want to lose anything TG could achieve because of one malicious little man so I would hope he does the right thing.

The timing of the latest Gen chaos wasn't good, as Paul was negotiating for TG to play the Turbine Hall at the Tate Modern and we still hadn't agreed the TG/Mute contract.

I should have seen the writing on the wall back in 2003, when Gen did an interview with the *Independent* about his gallery show in London and talked about how 'he' had made my magazine actions into art by placing them in a gallery. His retrospective view of COUM and omitting me was also reinforced by a statement on his website. I'd been careful to include and credit him when supplying COUM material for exhibitions. He didn't afford me the same courtesy. That had infuriated me but I didn't rise to the bait or ruffle feathers as it was so early on in the TG regrouping. I wanted an apology, or at least a conversation so he could explain his actions. Sleazy felt that this was 'the bottom line', and that Gen's excuses were 'only believable if followed with a conscientious desire to make good'. There didn't seem to be any such desire. For the benefit of TG/Mute and other obligations, the dust was left to settle. Communications between me and Gen ceased.

17 March 2006
Where would you begin to try and fathom (if you wanted to bother)? All that angst, insults and wasted time.

We'd reached stalemate with the TG/Mute contract. Another ten points had been added by Gen's manager – one being that there could be no TG release within three months on either side of any of Gen's solo releases. That was unacceptable as it effectively meant Gen alone could control the timing of TG releases. His manager said he just wanted to make sure Gen got a fair deal for all the time and artistic effort he'd put into the TG project . . . No comment.

But then, out of the blue, Gen asked for the TG/Mute contract to be sent ASAP for him to sign. After months of arguments over Gen and his manager requesting unrealistic amendments, Gen had OK'd the original contract. The release of the TG album *Part Two* was pencilled in by Mute for October, but Gen informed us that he'd decided to release his own band's new album around the same time. Not only was that a clash but we also discovered one of their tracks had lyrics from a TG song. In light of potential copyright issues and other promotional considerations, the TG album release was moved to 2007 . . . keeping the fans waiting even longer.

> 17 May 2006
> *Hello new day! Exploding heads and all else that challenges us when we wake to perhaps enjoy natures glories.*

Carter Tutti melodies were flowing – soft and melodic, rather laid-back, a little bit jazzy. Recording the new album, *Feral Vapours of the Silver Ether*, was our haven, an untainted stress-free zone where we could fully immerse ourselves in making evocative, uplifting music.

Our Carter Tutti and Chris & Cosey work was hardly ever mentioned or acknowledged by Sleazy or Gen. It was as if it didn't exist, an irrelevance of no interest to them. TG continued to interrupt our other activities. Chris was mastering the audio and Sleazy the videos for the TG DVD box set, *TGV*, and there were emails and phone calls between them, with me raiding my archive for photos and relevant images for the accompanying booklet. There was still the unresolved issue of that Tate letter. Sleazy saw potential in TG working together and was sad but resigned that it may come to an end. I was happy to be working on more of my own exhibitions and to let TG live performances slip away, even though the Tate was supposedly about to confirm a 2007 TG show.

> 8 July 2006
> *I haven't written for ages because of all the work piling up. I do so many emails too so I tend to exorcise things in them and not in my diary.*

After the Tate Triennial show, I'd been selected to be part of an exhibition at Migros Museum in Zurich, 'It's Time for Action (There's No Option)' – the title being a quote from a Yoko Ono song. There were censorship problems about the pornographic material – internal politics that Heike the curator worked hard to overcome. The selection process had to be revisited. I was determined to take the problem as something to run with rather than fight. The biggest issue was that, like Andrew had said, we had established (via the Tate and other institutions) the magazines were art and not pornographic. They were my art-sex actions, and as such their presentation in a gallery resisted their original context. That was key to the concept of the magazine actions. It seemed acceptable for Jeff Koons to do a hard-core pastiche like 'Made in Heaven' using the porn star Cicciolina and her reputation, but as a female artist who revealed all, my work was still a problem. Sensitivities seemed unrelenting but had inadvertently made things turn out for the better. The final material encompassed all aspects of my work and made a great exhibit. I included the first presentation of the '*Self*lessness' Disney action, 'The Kiss' magazine work and my music in the form of the *Time to Tell* album special edition.

15 December 2006
I have had morose thoughts of thinking I would sooner die than go through that again. Life is too painful and my pain threshold has been breached.

I had a feeling of dread about the whole thing. Nick had been ill and I'd been calling him for five days to check on how he was. From the symptoms he had, I suspected it was appendicitis or, worse, peritonitis. I'd told him to go to A&E but he held on, just saying it was probably food poisoning as his doctor had said. After

413

more anxious phone calls and him being in such pain and vomiting, I finally got him to go back to the doctor, who told him to take a taxi immediately to A&E. I waited for Nick to call me to let me know what was happening. In the meantime I followed my instincts and made up his bed and got ready in case we had to rush off (he was seventy-five miles away at uni in Nottingham). I didn't hear from Nick so I called Nottingham City Hospital and was told that he'd been admitted and would be going in for surgery as soon as possible. My instinct had been right.

As I rushed around locking up the house and telling Chris to get ready to drive to Nottingham, I got a phone call. It was a surgeon from Nottingham City Hospital, informing me that Nick was being taken straight into theatre. My stomach turned over; my throat almost closed up. 'Is it peritonitis? How serious is it?' I asked.

There was what seemed a long silence, then he said, 'Just get here as soon as you possibly can.'

That sounded grim and made me fear for Nick's life. The traffic was horrendous and it took us nearly four hours. We didn't talk much – neither of us wanted to voice our fears. I've never felt such overwhelming relief than when I saw Nick safely out of theatre, doped up but alive. We hugged and kissed him, then left him with his girlfriend, Laura, and drove back home, saying we'd be back in the morning.

When we saw Nick the next day it was obvious he'd gone downhill. He was pale, sweating, in pain and didn't look at all well. I booked into the hospital hotel so I could look after him, with Chris driving back and forth through fog, ice and sleet and keeping everything going back home. I saw the surgeon who'd operated on Nick when he came to do a follow-up examination. He said how pleased he was the operation was successful because it was the worst case of peritonitis he'd seen. The gangrenous appendix had ruptured and they'd had to remove part of Nick's bowel. Nick had only just made it, mainly because he was young, fit and strong. The surgeon marvelled at Nick's pain threshold but said ironically that he'd have been better off it were lower as the appendicitis would have been caught sooner.

A mother's love is cruelly all-consuming. I felt at times I would die from the heartbreak of being so helpless to end Nick's pain, my fears for him and fatigue, but I couldn't show that to Nick. I had to be strong and ooze confidence for his sake. There were nights in the hospital hotel when I thought I would die, my heart was racing and skipping so much.

Christmas was approaching fast and Nick didn't want to stay in hospital – he wanted to come home. I wanted him home too but knew he wasn't really ready to leave hospital. He was discharged. I arranged for a district nurse to attend to Nick's wound at home, hoping that they still worked over the Christmas period. The journey back home was agonising for Nick and by the time we arrived his wound had opened up. I called the doctor, who sent our assigned nurse, the most wonderful Nurse Dot. As fate would have it, she'd been a surgery theatre nurse and specialised in wound dressing – and had worked at St Joseph's Hospice in Hackney, opposite Beck Road, at the time I lived there. We got on so well and she was fond of Nick and cared. I saw the surgery wound for the first time – a long cut above his groin that opened into a cavernous hole – as Dot flushed it with sterile water then packed the cavity with special dressing. I tried not to react but I was taken aback. It was an education seeing her work so gently and expertly, administering drugs that didn't make him throw up and adjusting antibiotics at each stage of the healing process. We were so lucky to have her. I believed two people had saved Nick's life: the surgeon and Nurse Dot.

6 April 2007
There's a whole load of shit involving Gen that bores even me.

A change of scene and sunshine can work wonders. I went off on another solo trip to Los Angeles, installing my work at MOCA in the exhibition 'WACK!: Art and the Feminist Revolution'.

While I was away, Chris and Sleazy had been talking about whether TG could carry on in light of the problems we were having internally as well as with the 2007 TG live schedule that was in place. There were TG crisis calls with Paul Smith, as he'd received emails from Gen's manager to say that Gen was not available for the TG schedule we'd all agreed months earlier, that he was only able to do Donaufestival at Krems in Austria, despite the other TG shows at the Tate and the *Desertshore* recording sessions at the ICA in London having been confirmed.

We were thrust into another maelstrom of contradictory information, unreasonable demands and unnecessary aggravation from Gen and his manager. Sleazy and Paul repeatedly tried calling him but got no answer. Eventually Sleazy got through and had a long conversation, which Gen insisted was 'off the record' – which wasn't much use. Then Gen's manager went over Paul's head and called the Tate saying Gen wasn't doing the show, contradicting the TG confirmation. Appeals to Gen about addressing the conduct of his manager went unanswered. Then, just as the TG album *Part Two* was released, Gen sent a long email informing us that we must discuss his availability for TG only with his manager and not with him.

That email was followed by one he sent to the Tate, allegedly demeaning Sleazy's film work as 'not art'. Sleazy swallowed the insults and replied pragmatically that, because Gen was no longer available for the TG shows, we three would honour the agreements and perform them without him. The venues agreed.

TG was falling apart. We prepared a statement for the website. Time was getting tight and Sleazy was flying to our house in two weeks to start working with me and Chris on the material for the shows. We gave Gen a deadline to confirm before we announced his non-attendance in TG. Gen confirmed he would do Krems. All that crap had largely spoiled any enjoyment we could have had from the release of the first TG full-length studio album in over twenty-five years.

19 May 2007
I've been in a 'neutral zone' while TG has taken place. It's the only place to be to limit damage from unwanted energies . . .
Suffice to say Gen was as polite as he needed to get his money . . .

The two TG shows in Krems had taken months of work by Chris, Sleazy and me, with our sound engineer Charlie jumping on board to facilitate a recording of the ambisonic performances. We'd also co-opted Hildur Guðnadóttir, a brilliant Icelandic cellist, to write a piece for a choir as part of our live Derek Jarman film soundtrack. The choir was to perform alongside TG, with her conducting them. There was a lot to cope with on each gig day, soundchecking a twenty-piece choir as well as TG and ensuring the eight-channel ambisonic PA system worked as we'd imagined it could. Hildur did an amazing job – she and Sleazy had worked closely together and he signalled to her across the stage when to bring the choir in and out as we all played. It was something totally new and left-field for TG, but worked so well.

In the dressing room afterwards, Gen asked what Paul thought of the show. Paul said he thought it was beautiful. Gen smiled and replied, 'That's because I wasn't playing. I stopped after fifteen minutes and just watched the film. Easy money for me.' Even though we knew it to be true, Gen voicing his joy at getting money for doing little after all we'd gone through to get him there wasn't an easy thing for any of us to hear.

The TG show itself differed slightly from previous TG gigs, in that me and Sleazy did vocals – he on 'The Old Man Smiled' and me on 'Hot on the Heels of Love'. I was getting levels at soundcheck when Gen came over to me to offer me advice on using a microphone . . . Did he not know I'd been singing live C&C vocals for over twenty-five years? I let it pass.

20 May 2007
Well this extended TG period is proving weird . . . preparations for TG have been horrendously draining but great also in regard to the work we three have created. It's been wonderful and Sleazy has been an absolute pleasure despite him missing his home so terribly. Gen meanwhile only asks about his hotel and ticket – no word on what we are doing, have done or he is expected to do.

Sleazy came back to stay with us after Krems. There was a lot to do for the Tate Turbine Hall show as we were playing a live soundtrack to another of Derek Jarman's films and having Hildur perform with a choir again – plus the *Desertshore* live recording sessions at the ICA were to happen just a week after the Tate. We'd made site visits to both venues and there was to be new related TG merchandise on sale at both the Tate and the ICA. Sleazy went into 'merch mode' once we'd discussed what to do. He sat at his laptop putting together artworks, sourcing items and generally ordering me and Chris about to get quotes from local printers, to upscale images for posters, etc. He was a sight to behold, seemingly inexhaustible once he had his merch hat on. The Tate poster was based on the TG 'Death Factory' poster, replacing the original death factory with the Tate Modern building (art factory).

26 May 2007
In fact this Tate performance is the nearest to what I had hoped we'd do when we re-grouped.

The Turbine Hall was ram-packed, with hundreds unable to get in and people stood like zombies from *The Living Dead*, pressing themselves against the glass entrance doors to feel the sound. We knew that the Turbine Hall would be particularly challenging, with its extended reverb. The sounds we used had to take that into account. As we played and sent the sound out, it returned many seconds later. The room became our reverb unit. We started with a tone that matched and enhanced the constant hum from the old turbine. The sounds resonated throughout the building, travelling up into the vast cathedral-like space and vibrating throughout the upper floors. It was overwhelmingly emotional, with the choir and the physicality of the sounds we used and the massive projected visuals of Derek's films.

At the end we came off stage and were immediately taken to the green room – when we noticed Gen wasn't with us. He'd stayed behind on stage to take a final bow during what we were told was a ten-minute standing ovation.

The after-show party proved eventful. We had to pack the gear and didn't get there until 12.30, by which time some of our friends had gone home thinking we weren't bothering. Andrew was there, waiting and looking ecstatic, and gave us huge hugs. So many happy, congratulatory people. We were pretty tired but sat enjoying some well-deserved downtime. I saw Gen briefly, then he seemed to disappear into the night.

After about an hour, Paul came over and discreetly told us we had to leave immediately as there'd been an incident with Gen that he didn't want us to get involved with. Within minutes the security alarms went off, echoing all around the Tate – the next stage would be lockdown. We were quickly taken out of the building to where a taxi had been ordered for us. We'd got out just before they locked the Tate doors and we stood and watched as police cars arrived. It was 3 a.m. when we finally got back to the hotel and Paul filled us in on what had happened.

The story was that Gen had been dancing around and accidentally knocked a Warhol painting off the wall, damaging one edge of it. Apparently he and his friend were leaving the building, got lost and wandered into a gallery where the Warhol paintings were hung. The CCTV footage didn't really fit that version of events. Gen was arrested, held for questioning and charged with minor criminal damage, to appear in court that week. Paul looked after him. Jackie thought she and Gen could get some great publicity from it – which would be the worst thing for everyone concerned. The situation had to be handled carefully as any publicity could have an adverse impact all round and also jeopardise the forthcoming ICA event.

As far as I was concerned, Gen had spoiled what was a tremendous coup for TG. Tate curators Will and Stuart and so many others were overwhelmed with enthusiasm and glory for what we did. Gen had ruined that euphoria and TG's achievement.

27 May 2007
We arrived home at 1.30, Chris went straight in and threw up and retired to bed with a severe migraine. Sleazy and I watched a mundane 1980s Agatha Christie while we had toasted cheese and salad sandwiches then went to bed. Nice quiet evening with the cats.

We took a few days to rest from the Gen drama at the Tate and to allow Chris's migraine hangover to clear, then set about the final preparations for the ICA 'Desertshore Installation' live recording sessions, which were to be twice a day for three days – 12–2 p.m. and 7–9 p.m. – and take place in the ICA Theatre, with Charlie as sound engineer. We'd had an area sectioned off for Gen to do vocals and had sent him Sleazy and Chris's rudimentary reference backing tracks to practise singing to before he came. He did really well to get vocals done for every song from *Desertshore* over the three days. Some of the audience requested I do some vocals too but I could do those at home – the priority was getting Gen's done.

Providing Gen with a stage and audience worked far better for getting some recordings from him than a studio setting – which had failed to provide us with much material to work with and cost us a small fortune in the process. Right from the beginning the concept of the album was Sleazy's – for TG to rework Nico's songs and use a number of guest vocalists. As Sleazy described to me back in April of 2006, 'For this I expect to use mostly vocalists other than Gen, by all means including you if you like, but Chris or I should prepare just a few backing tracks with just sufficient information for Gen to sing over as before that we can THEN make those songs into something completely different for the actual record.'

We all suggested guest vocalists but the music was crucially important too. The ICA setting provided us with the means to jam together and get some recorded instrumentation from Gen, and jamming together was a means to collectively explore ideas for the Nico backings.

Like the historic *Heathen Earth* recording, we kept the setting informal, a very relaxed atmosphere instead of the required silence signalled by a red recording light. Unlike *Heathen Earth* we had

Desertshore merchandise, including a poster and T-shirt that were a 2007 reworking of the original ICA 'Prostitution' poster – a reference to our last 'installation' there in 1976. TG had a large running buffet to one side of the stage, with hot and cold drinks supplied on demand. When we ended the sessions we chatted with the audience and signed posters or albums that they'd brought along. I was sat at the merch table when a young guy asked me to sign his 'Death Factory' poster. I glanced at it and said, 'My signature's already on it.'

'Yes, I know,' he said, 'but that was Gen. He signed your name.' He looked embarrassed to have to say it.

I scribbled out what Gen had written and signed my own signature. 'There. You have the genuine Cosey now.' He seemed happier.

We didn't know at the time but the ICA recording sessions were the last time all four of us would record together. The ICA was the site of the launch of TG and also hosted the last TG working group gathering. The whole three days of sessions were recorded on video but will probably never see the light of day. As a document of the creative process of recording *Desertshore*, we produced a limited-edition twelve-CD wallet set of the entire three days.

24 June 2007
So I'm up in the office while Chris tweaks our cover version of 'Lucifer Sam'. Sleazy comes back on Thursday to do the 'TGV' 5.1 audio and to collect his degree. Then we are free of TG until whenever, seeing as Gen has said he can't do Frieze and Bologna.

From the ICA to Nottingham Trent University to see the final degree show. Nick had graduated with a BA Hons in fine art and me and Chris went to see his final work – a sound installation. We had no trouble finding him: we just followed the low bass rumble. He'd taken over a small space and made it into a science laboratory, with his research materials, electrical components and writings scattered on a desk and a whiteboard above it covered in his notes and various schematic diagrams. He'd borrowed an amp and speakers from us, as well as the original TG audio generator and oscilloscope. Dressed in a white laboratory coat with clipboard in hand, he was questioning people as they came into the space, adding their responses to his work. A week later we and half the family attended his degree ceremony. It was such a fantastic emotional moment for us. We were all smiles watching him receive his degree and so proud he'd done it in spite of his surgery and other difficulties he'd faced along the way.

Nick wasn't the only one to graduate: Sleazy had been offered an honorary degree for his work with Hipgnosis. He asked us if he should take it. I remembered the incident with Gen's Tate letter about Sleazy's film work not being 'art' and Skot saying, 'Gen was always using me to make Sleazy jealous. Sleazy was ashamed of how commercial his art output was, and Gen tortured him about "real artists" (using me to belittle him).' I think that had an effect on how Sleazy valued his work.

'What? Hell yeah, you should. You've been recognised for all your incredible work. So take it!' I said. He immediately broke out into a giggly wriggle of joy.

He went to the ceremony and was conferred, and had his official portrait taken as a souvenir. He came back to stay with us for a while longer so he and Chris could finish the *TGV* surround-sound audio. He'd been away from home for months and could hardly contain his excitement when he set off back to Thailand. He was due back in the UK for TG's October shows at the London Frieze Art Fair and in Bologna to continue promoting the new album. They'd been timed to coincide with a major TG article in *Wire* magazine, along with us on the front cover, but Gen decided to do a tour with his own band to promote their new album instead and the TG shows were cancelled. That left the three of us in the lurch and disappointed, but at least we could get on with our own projects and pick up with proposed TG live events in 2008.

> 13 September 2007
> *There's always many things running in parallel but I find it invigorating and exciting – new territories and experiences are pure nectar.*

Our studio was once again reverberating with Carter Tutti sounds and I was working on a collaborative project for the Raster-Noton label for release in 2008. The new Carter Tutti album, *Feral Vapours of the Silver Ether*, was mastered and put into production, and was due to be delivered to our distributor, Cargo UK, and through Sleazy we'd secured a US release with John Deek of Divine Frequency. We were relaunching our CTI mail order system and sorting out promotion in readiness for the release of the album. The reflective mood of the music and songs was heavily influenced by the emotionally charged events that had dominated our lives in the preceding few years. Some tracks were more obviously deeply personal, like 'Woven Clouds', which was about us nearly losing Nick. We were so pleased about the positive feedback for the new album. It meant such a lot to us. I could safely say that if, for whatever reason, we didn't do another Carter Tutti album, we'd be happy that *Feral Vapours* stood as testament to our work.

> 23 September 2007
> *The whole TG situation is getting fragmented and fractured to boot. Sleazy hasn't contacted us for over a month. We were busy with our own album and needed space from TG . . .*

We resisted getting embroiled in anything TG-related but then a series of unexpected events thrust us back into the centre of it. Having cancelled the TG shows to prioritise his own band's gigs, Gen's tour collapsed due to what they claimed on their Myspace page to be 'mismanagement and agency incompetence', blaming and sacking Gen's manager, who in turn claimed it was lack of fans and ticket sales.

Then, just over a week later, on 9 October, Gen's wife Jackie died. Everyone was so shocked and rallied round Gen. Paul and Susan met up with him in New York to provide support. Me, Chris and Sleazy sent our heartfelt condolences and offered our help. We were all empathetic and sensitive to his needs at such a terribly sad time.

I was torn by my feelings of sadness for Gen and guilt at wanting to enjoy the reviews and great reception our new album was receiving. It was hard to reconcile Gen suffering at a time when things were going so well for us. Chris had started a new solo project, *Chemistry Lessons*, and was building sound-making gadgets. It was great to see him lit up with excitement again, beavering away with his wiring and electrical tools scattered on his worktop.

25 October 2007

This has made me feel that it seems grief as ever is touching us all and I can't help but think of 'what if'. Each day I keep thinking I must hold and kiss Chris just in case. It's no way to live but at the moment the events are constant reminders of one's fragile mortality.

Gen's sudden loss brought me up sharp and I felt lucky me and Chris were still together. Sleazy was affected in a different way, as Jackie's death was within a month of the anniversary of Geff's fatal fall. He always found that time of year hard to deal with and every anniversary since Geff had died Sleazy would go away for a week – 'up country', as he called it – indulging in such wildly excessive hedonistic drug-fuelled sexual activities we feared he'd never return. As worried as we were for him, such a frightening prospect held a perverse appeal for him.

Talking of perversity . . . Me and Chris went to Rome. I was doing an 'in conversation' with the writer Daniela Cascella at the British School at Rome, a prestigious archaeology, history and arts research academy housed in the beautiful British Pavilion, where we were accommodated. Not far from the pavilion was a park with an enchanting grotto where we'd take afternoon walks. On one of those walks we noticed a man staring our way. We moved on – there he was again, stood still, fixing his gaze on us both. It felt weird. It *was* weird. He slowly opened his raincoat to reveal his semi-erect cock. He was naked from his waist to his knees, with a shirt and braces that held up the cut-off trousers. He was dressed in what was a classic flasher's outfit you'd see on a Benny Hill show. I looked at Chris, he at me, and we both laughed in disbelief, wandering off to have coffee, with me commenting on why flashers and perverts seemed so attracted to me.

I also wondered how many women had had more than one encounter, like me. There was my childhood incident of the flasher in the woods, but others too. When I was about eleven, me and Jo went to a football match in Hull. As we were leaving, squashed in the crowd I felt a hand slowly moving up my inner thigh. I looked down, thinking it was a small child holding on as best they could, but it was a little middle-aged man, about four foot high, smiling up at me with his hand up my skirt. He'd already had a feel of Jo. We both pushed our way out of his reach. I've never been to a football match since.

Short skirts are most definitely not an open invitation to sexual assault but mine appeared to be irresistible to opportunistic perverts, like the one who put his hand up mine as I waited in the bus queue in Hackney. I had my dancing bag with me, which was pretty heavy. I swung it at his head, shouting, 'You dirty bastard!' at him and knocking him stumbling across the pavement. The people around me hadn't seen what he'd done and looked at me as if I were mad. 'He put his hand up my skirt,' I explained. The bus pulled up and he tried to get on it, but no one would let him.

But by far the worst case was on the Tube in London when I was travelling home one day. A man was sat opposite me with a newspaper on his lap, which started moving rhythmically, then a spurt of semen shot down the front of the seat. Before I could react, the train pulled into the next station, he got off and a woman sat in his vacant seat with her long coat soaking up the wet patch he'd left behind.

22 January 2008
I've just returned from the doctor as I'd been getting more ill by the day.

I'd had a bad cold and didn't seem to be recovering. I was listless and easily exhausted. While standing cooking the evening meal, I got a sudden high-pitched tone in my left ear, then went deaf. I called my GP and got a locum, who told me it was nothing to worry about, but the next day, when the deafness was still there and I had numbness on that side of my face, I went to see my preferred GP.

He recognised the symptoms and acted immediately. I had shingles in my left ear canal, with an added complication of a condition called Ramsay Hunt Syndrome that causes paralysis of the facial muscles. He put me on a regimen of bed rest and specific medication to try and limit any nerve damage. When I was told that recovery could take between three and sometimes up to eight months, with full recovery from facial paralysis and deafness being unlikely, I was speechless. I went on to the internet to see what information there was on self-help and found facial exercises that 'may' assist in regaining some facial-muscle control, and practised them three times a day, monitoring any slight improvement in a log I kept. I'm glad I did because, when I eventually went for my follow-up assessment months later, the consultant was impressed by the extent of my recovery.

Chris had been incredible at looking after me, so encouraging and lovingly attentive to my many needs. I couldn't have got through it without him. I was a physical wreck, impaired by the illness and the different side effects of the drugs I'd had to take. So many negative thoughts flooded my mind about what degree of recovery I would have, whether I'd have the facial problems and be deaf forever. If so, my public life could well be over, and my work in music would be affected. I certainly couldn't blow my cornet and wondered if I'd ever be able to again, and I couldn't sing either, as even pronouncing some words was impossible.

With TG live gigs in the pipeline I had to break the news that I was too ill to do them. Paul, Sleazy and Gen wished me well and everyone awaited my availability for TG.

21 June 2008
Well where do I begin with all this 3 weeks of activities? My brain is buzzing with it all . . . The inner circles are shifting and they slip into deliberate acts of celebrity and opportunism and we pull back even more in disgust.

It took me three months to feel anywhere near well enough to consider working. The facial paralysis and deafness had improved slightly. I was determined to play my cornet again but I just wasn't able to pucker up my lips enough to deliver the powerful blast of air needed. To help my rehabilitation I bought a small 'pocket' cornet, which was used by beginners. During my recovery, TG plans went ahead largely to assist Gen's financial situation in the wake of Jackie's death. It was all hands on deck to help Gen at such a sad time.

Then we learned of him going on tour with his band around the time of the TG shows – the usual debates over clashing with TG dates hadn't abated. Nevertheless we provided support for him and made allowances based on him still grieving. He said he was feeling fragile and wasn't sure about being able to deliver vocals for TG. That was understandable under the circumstances so we reassured him that the TG set-up was based on the more instrumental *Second Annual Report*.

Sleazy came to stay with us to get ready for the two TG shows – one at the Primavera festival in Spain and one in Paris at Villette Sonique. We were going to play (and record) the performance as *Thirty-Second Annual Report*, a reference to the release of TG's first album, *Second Annual Report*, thirty years ago. We designed merchandise: TG pocket knives, a numbered limited-edition poster and large banners to drape on each of our stage tables.

The TG outing was strange. It was the first time we'd seen Gen since Jackie died. He seemed to be coping well; he had a film-maker friend with him making the documentary they'd started prior to Jackie's untimely death. There was a difficult moment when he asked for the TG gig and backstage to be filmed for inclusion, as well as for Sleazy, me and Chris to be interviewed on film about our working experience with Gen. As I was still struggling with the aftermath of my illness I wasn't comfortable being filmed with a partially paralysed face, so I declined. Chris said no. Sleazy accepted. As much as we sympathised with his personal loss and how Gen chose to cope with it, it seemed like business as usual – his extracurricular activities planned around our two TG shows seemed more important to him than the TG shows themselves and smacked of opportunism, using TG as a platform to further his own activities, with us three as facilitators doing the lion's share of TG work. We also screened our film *After Cease to Exist* and were told that the castration scene with me and Chris had caused fainting and vomiting among at least six members of the audience, and ambulances had been called.

Barcelona had been a rather restrained TG concert in comparison to Paris. I think it may have had something to do with me, Chris and Sleazy recording the contemplative music for the TG audio sculptural collaboration with Cerith (Wyn Evans) – a work entitled 'A=P=P=A=R=I=T=I=O=N'. Chris worked hard on the concept, which was based on using multiple highly directional speakers that he'd reviewed for *Sound on Sound* magazine back in 2004. He and Paul researched further options, finally deciding on the thin, flat, circular panel Audio Spotlight speakers invented by Dr Joe Pompei, founder of Holosonics. TG was going to use them in a live show but it never panned out, so they were suggested as the basis for the work with Cerith. He was to design the huge sculpture (requiring a space 9×9×10 metres high), using the speakers as part of a suspended 'child's mobile'-type structure. TG composed the audio, with Cerith providing Gen with the lyrics. Chris, me and Sleazy spent a week at our studio recording the sound.

Chris took another two weeks to complete the audio, editing, manipulating, adding further recordings of additional parts from me and Sleazy, time-stretching some of Gen's vocals, and he finally mixed the material to a length of nearly three hours. Sleazy was happy to have the piece on stereo 'playback' through the speakers, not wanting to spend too much time on it, but Chris and I saw the obvious potential to use all sixteen speakers and sub-bass speaker

430

in a more interesting and innovative way. Chris developed a multi-channel complex playback method using Ableton Live that would, as he described it, 'simultaneously move each individual channel of the TG multitrack audio "through" each of the sculpture's Audio Spotlights every three to five minutes in a sequential and relatively seamless process'.

He, Paul and I took all our parts and audio gear to the fabricators for a trial run with Cerith, where we brought the sculpture together with the sound. It worked beautifully. The speakers were finished in highly polished aluminium, with mirrored backs that not only looked amazing but also added another interactive aspect. When fed through the speakers, the directional sounds shifted slowly, reflecting off the speakers' mirrored surfaces, the sounds constantly moving from one suspended speaker to another as they slowly rotated. It all contributed to an indefinable, ethereal experience, with the sounds seemingly hovering in the air and each person's experience being unique to them and never the same twice.

Gen didn't 'get it' and wasn't interested. His only involvement was recording Cerith's lyrics, which took five minutes. But us persisting in getting him to take part paid off. He received an equal share of the substantial amount of money when White Cube Gallery sold it to the Pompidou Centre.

26 July 2008
We've really pushed ourselves this year and after a month 'off' we're only just getting the hang of relaxing. We're promising ourselves that we won't take on so many projects again . . . but we get so excited by things that we can't resist them. But our illnesses have been due to fatigue and stress so it's not a choice option anymore really.

There were still unfinished TG matters to deal with – like the official reactivating of Industrial Records Ltd that we'd discussed during our last TG get-together. I wasn't keen as, after a brief period of Sleazy managing the payments and not being reliably contactable, it was looking more and more like me and Chris may have to step in. Sleazy and Gen told us that being directors of a UK limited company could complicate their status in their adopted countries. As UK residents, me and Chris were proposed to be the registered directors. I didn't want the responsibility and I knew I would incur the workload of doing the accounts and Chris the other admin connected with running a record label.

But, with the eventual agreement of all four of us, the decision was made to go ahead. IR Ltd was registered in August 2008 and the first release was to be a framed, limited (777-copy) edition of *Thirty-Second Annual Report*. I was giving a talk at Frieze Art Fair and Cabinet were including the TG release on their Frieze stand in October, and we wanted it released in time for Christmas that year (in commemoration of the thirtieth anniversary of *The Second Annual Report*). Gen suggested we all did 'a mix' but, it being a live album, it wasn't that kind of 'remix' project and we only had three months to get masters and artworks done.

~

It was Halloween. Gen wasn't in the UK when we had a TG meeting at state51 in London. We were all sat eating bags of chips when Paul and Susan arrived. Paul's face looked grey and he'd been having chest pains and trouble breathing as he came up the stairs. We were all concerned, particularly Susan, but he's not someone to fuss and dismissed our worries for him.

Meeting over, we went off to a nearby pub to meet S.C.U.M., a very young band that me and Chris had initially seen play at Mute's Harrow Road closing party in March 2007. The band were interested in TG and wanted us to remix one of the new tracks they were working on. They had a good restless presence about them and seemed to know a lot about TG. Having all said our goodbyes, with promises to be in touch, me and Chris headed home to do a final run-through of our Carter Tutti set for a gig we had in Poland.

I was still worried about Paul and before we left I emailed him to see how he was. He said he was going to see his doctor, but before he could he had a massive heart attack, followed soon after by successful bypass surgery. We nearly lost him and it shook us up badly, and more so poor Susan.

11 February 2009
I gave Chris a big hug and kiss of appreciation from Sleazy . . .
the audio is consuming us and I didn't want to have to think
of anything else being added to the already overwhelming TG
workload on top of our non-TG lives.

Paul was irrepressible even after his heart surgery, and we each received an email from him outlining TG live offers for the USA in April and Europe in June. Gen had been in touch with Paul asking if there were any TG shows in the offing. Sleazy could be persuaded out of his Thailand paradise. Me and Chris had many things on the go but TG had only ever played two shows in the USA, back in 1981, and an opportunity to play there again was appealing, especially as Paul had secured the elusive, expensive work permits for us.

We'd had emails from Gen informing us that he was not only incapacitated through ill health but also very busy and had another new manager, who we must discuss all TG matters with. We saw this as hopefully avoiding previous problems and lapses in Gen's memory (which appeared rather selective as far as TG was concerned) – especially as Gen was now going on holiday to Nepal for a month and wouldn't be available.

The TG gig sets and merchandise (to help finance the USA tour) had been mostly agreed but needed to be designed, sourced and ordered. Sleazy, me and Chris put all the essentials together. Chris did all the live TG rhythms and single-handedly put together the *Third Mind Movements* album using multitracks from the TG ICA jam sessions. That in itself was a substantial project and ended up being the final TG studio album.

Paul coordinated and sourced the enamel badges, T-shirts and CD pressing for collection in New York. It was a frantic few months as Chris was also corresponding with an American guy who was reproducing the legendary TG Gristleizer effects unit. We got my original Gristleizer unit out of the archive cupboard for Chris to run some tests on it. We didn't get far. I turned it on, it spluttered, then stopped working altogether. My first and only Gristleizer had died. A sad, sad moment.

I, meanwhile, was trying to meet the continuing demand for my art, giving a talk with Andrew at the Stanley Picker Gallery in London and preparing work and catalogue material for a large exhibition called 'Pop Life: Art in a Material World' that was opening at the Tate Modern later in the year.

17 April 2009
Last night's show was full on like the Astoria. Phew! Felt good amongst all that positive energy.

The first TG New York show, at the Masonic Temple in Brooklyn, set the bar for what the USA audiences would be like. Their

434

excitement was palpable and beyond anything we could have anticipated. I'm sure that contributed to the overall amicable feelings between us all as we flew from one state to another over the two weeks. Old fans and new filled the venues each night and we fed off their energy, driving into full-throttle TG mode then pulling back for the live film soundtrack performances we were all doing alongside the regular shows. We were a small team: Paul, Susan, Charlie and the four of us. I'd been worried about the stress having an adverse effect on Paul so soon after his heart surgery, but he was incredibly efficient and everything went so well, considering the mammoth task and all that came with a TG gathering. There were some annoying and unnecessary moments when Gen gave Paul a hard time, only talking to him 'through' Susan. Paul was as professional and pragmatic as ever, and got on with the job at hand. The gig that had made the whole tour possible was next: the Coachella Festival in Palm Springs.

19 April 2009
Jet lagged in Palm Springs awaiting the show tonight. Cure, Paul McCartney, Yeah Yeah Yeahs etc . . . VERY hot indeedy.

We were driven by minibus from the swish hotel to the huge sprawling Coachella Festival site. On arrival we were directed to the artists' gate to be dropped off. We moved on through security into the artists' dressing-room area. It looked like a holiday camp, full of caravans and trailers, each with a white picket fence. There were fairy lights everywhere and a central chill-out zone, where occupied hammocks swung gently amid the heavy smell of hash.

Our dressing-room caravan was cute and had been decorated specially for us, with gifts laid out on a table of drinks and food. But the air conditioning unit didn't work and the heat was stifling – then got worse under the lights of the film crew who were interviewing us. We were slowly getting more red-faced and sweaty, so when my and Gen's make-up started to slide down our faces we called a halt to the interview and headed out to our little fenced garden for some fresh air.

As night fell the atmosphere changed. The heat, stillness and the distant sound of music, bangs from fireworks and being in the open air created a sense of detachment, which was further enhanced when we were transported to the stage by a golf cart, passing uniformed armed security guards with guns at the ready, keeping a keen eye on the 'payment' office where the band fees were dispensed. Sitting opposite each other in silence as the cart trundled along, we all looked around, then at each other, sat there like unwilling victims being delivered to a place that was alien and assaulted our sensibilities and principles. It felt like the Playboy Bunnies scene from *Apocalypse Now*, where acts are dropped in to play and transported out again.

'What the fuck are we doing here?' we all muttered. We knew, but this was so very un-TG . . . An industrial-factory approach to entertainment production, yes, but not 'industrial' as we perceived it.

The band before us were still playing when we arrived at the back of the stage. A riser was awaiting us, with a table each to set up our gear on. We were to just get a line check, and not a proper soundcheck. There's a first time for everything, I guess.

I hadn't expected anyone to come to Coachella but Sasha Grey had said she'd try to come along so we could finally meet. We'd been in touch for a while, discussing, among many things, our sex-industry experiences. I was plugging everything in when Sasha arrived with her then partner, Ian. I was so, so happy to see her. Not the best place for a first meet but she lifted me out of the weird Coachella-zone mood. It was like we'd known each other years – there was a mutual unspoken understanding between two strong, driven women and it was wonderful to meet someone new and young who had such strength, spirit, warmth and humour. We talked as I set up and arranged to meet for lunch.

As the band finished, their risers were moved back and ours pushed forward. It was time to go . . . Chris tweeted we were about to play and within a split second a huge cheer of 'YES!' went up from the audience as they held up their phones in answer. The audience dispersed any reservations we had about being there. The gig was mad in every which way, and we smiled throughout, hugging each other at the end, wet with sweat as we all were.

22 April 2009
LA was a blast last night. Now we've just settled into our hotel room in SF and looking forward to a night off – shattered after a late night and early start.

TG moved on to San Francisco. Refreshed from our relaxing tiki evening, we arrived midday at the venue. The ballroom was a very old but beautiful building and held just over two thousand people. While the video crew set up, we put our gear on stage ready for soundcheck and were shown to our dressing rooms. We had one each and Sleazy's was up four narrow steps. I was walking behind him when he suddenly stopped after the second step. He was out of breath and panting quite badly.

'Are you OK?' I asked.

He took a deep breath and replied, 'Yeah, I'm fine.'

He clearly wasn't and I thought first of how similar it was to Paul before his heart attack, and then about the way Sleazy had been walking so slowly through the airport, lagging behind us all. I'd thought it was him being cool and casual, in preference to being on the 'hurry up', but it must have been because he wasn't well. He wouldn't talk about it. I knew he'd been on warfarin for deep vein thrombosis some time ago but he never mentioned illness unless it actually impacted on his plans. I kept a discreet check on him from then on.

The ballroom was full to capacity and the welcome cheer as we appeared on stage was as fiercely enthusiastic as at all the other shows so far. Although Gen's ex-wife Paula lived nearby, she didn't come to the show (as requested by Gen), but their younger daughter, Genesse, did. We didn't see her until she appeared in the middle of the set, when Gen brought her on stage to introduce her to the audience and wish her happy birthday. That was a 'What the fuck?!' moment for the three of us. Gen hadn't told us beforehand, he'd just thrown Genesse into the TG performance mix. We wouldn't have begrudged her a happy birthday at all, but would have appreciated being told and having some say as to when it would happen. TG run on the fly, creating music very much in the moment, so to have that connection between us interrupted by a 'Happy Birthday' announcement wasn't the best thing to do. What could we do but smile and wish Genesse well?

4 May 2009
What a weird 4 days it's been since I got home. The jet lag, fatigue, TG head cold and euphoria combined to put me in another space for a while – between sleep and consciousness. I'm gradually coming round and assimilating the magnitude of the experiences I had in the US. The shows and audiences were overwhelmingly wonderful.

During the USA tour, sales of the merch CD *Third Mind Movements* started to trail off pretty quickly. Then we found out why.

Someone had put the whole album up for free download. The merch sales made up a big slice of the overall income to cover costs for the tour, so although it was considered 'de rigueur' and cool to offer everyone a new TG album for free, it felt like we were being well and truly fucked over. It should always be the decision of the artist whether to give their work away or not. I didn't agree with it then and I still don't.

On top of that we'd recorded all the TG USA shows and were planning to release them, much like the TG live shows of old were made available, but the mindset of those who host torrent sites and provide other people's work for free scuppered our plans, and robbed TG fans of an official USA live 2009 box set.

Having been bootlegged to oblivion over the years, we did a bit of lateral thinking . . . What could we release that wasn't easy, or was nigh impossible, to bootleg or give away for free? Happenstance stepped up with the solution. As pre-TG gig ambience, Charlie had been playing his little FM3 Buddha Machine – a small, iPod-sized, battery-operated loop player with built-in speaker. Chris tweeted about it and the inventor of the FM3, Christiaan Virant, got in touch with him. Then Chris, Paul and Sleazy asked Christiaan if he'd be interested in a 'TG Machine' version. He agreed to collaborate with us and we began work on the 'Gristleism', a self-contained, looping playback unit embedded with TG sounds – a physical object that was unbootleggable.

Christiaan suggested an exchange and pooling of ideas and a meet-up in July. In that time, me, Chris, Sleazy and Christiaan discussed different adaptations to the Buddha Machine that were more suited to TG. Gen was away but kept in the loop (no pun intended). Things were happening so quickly and we wanted Gen's input. Selecting the right sounds to meet the technical specifications of the unit was challenging – limitations of the chip technology dictated what frequencies and length of sounds could be used. Longer sounds had lower quality, shorter sounds higher quality, so it was a trade-off and it took months of work to compile something for a concept that seemed so simple.

As with all TG releases, and for Christiaan, the sounds had to be registered with our publisher for copyright reasons. That flagged up a problem when Gen sent his loop suggestions. We didn't recognise the sounds or track titles he'd sent us. It turned out that they were from a bootleg release. How ironic that he'd sent bootleg material and had missed the point that the concept of the project was all about countering TG bootlegs. Why would we include them? He took our reasoning as to why we couldn't use them as a personal slight and wrote a tirade of spurious accusations about me and Chris bootlegging TG. A fiery email exchange followed. To get things back on track, we stuck with the official registered TG sounds.

With Gen and Sleazy living abroad and Christiaan travelling to and from the UK at that point, as well as time factors related to factory slots in China (where the Gristleism was being made), me and Chris were the ones who worked closely with Christiaan and brought the project to fruition. Chris and Christiaan put together the final audio loops and worked out all the other necessary technical considerations. It was a complex but terrifically fulfilling experience working with Christiaan, who was so incredibly gifted and a stickler for detail.

The Gristleism packaging was an equally exciting and intricate process, with Christiaan (working in conjunction with Jonathan Leijonhufvud) coming to our house to discuss designs and us making tweaks and further suggestions. It was decided that the Gristleism would come in three TG-related colours – red, black and chromed silver – as would the outer packaging, which was in two parts: a spot-varnished solid inner sleeve with a wraparound outer sleeve die-cut with the 'Endless Knot' design. Both sleeves had spot-varnished text and designs so if you had more than one unit, the sleeves could be interchanged. We had 'messages' included on the inside of the units as part of the mould itself – to be changed with each subsequent production run. We purposely made it easy to disassemble to encourage modification, hacking and experimentation. We wanted people to be inventive, to get inside, where they'd discover our messages. In its simplest form it was an interactive TG release but it had potential for so much more. It was a beautiful object that people could carry around with them, have in their home or workplace to create a TG ambience – which many found strangely relaxing.

As well as the single Gristleism we produced a Tri-Colour edition of one hundred, presented in a bespoke, dark-red, silk-covered box with an embroidered gold 'Endless Knot'/flash that included all three colours, enamel Gristleism badge and card with numbered authentication certificate. Gristleism was later included in one of the broadsheet colour supplements' recommended Christmas gifts of the year, but by then it (and the limited edition) had sold out and the next single Gristleism production run was under way.

6 June 2009
I'm feeling pretty damn good and energised again. Lots has been happening in other areas of my work/life . . . Mainly in the art world with being in the Tate Modern exhibition . . . music projects are coming together now which will take up all my time for the rest of this year. It's all VERY exciting and fulfilling especially working with new people. For now, I'm back in the studio working on the upcoming TG shows.

Sleazy arrived at our house to work on the TG European shows. There was a new set to put together. We were performing a TG set and a live soundtrack to Cerith's short film *The Sky Is Thin as Paper Here* at Tramway in Glasgow, then taking the soundtrack concert to Statens Museum of Art in Copenhagen, culminating in two TG shows at Heaven in London, where Cerith would do a DJ set. Cerith was to travel with us. He didn't cope too well with the pace of an on-the-road schedule. He was still drinking heavily, so we had double the usual alcohol problem to deal with, as well as both him and Gen vying for the spotlight. Susan and Paul managed things wonderfully well.

The hotel in Copenhagen seemed to cause the biggest upset for Cerith. It was in the 'boutique' style. Each room had a different theme, which was quirky, to say the least. Paul and Susan were lucky – they got the modern room that was perfectly adequate. Gen got the bridal suite, which suited him just fine. Sleazy had the grandiose Napoleon Room, which was so perversely Sleazy. He flopped happily on to the huge four-poster bed and sank into the pale-blue satin bed cover. Me and Chris moved on to our room quite excited at what we'd find. We were on the top floor of the hotel. Our hearts sank when we opened the door. We'd got the Hansel and Gretel room. Everything was child-size. The bed was only two foot off the floor – it looked like they'd sawn off the legs. Likewise the chairs and table. The ceiling, being part of the roof gables, was low and sloped at one end, the wood was all dark brown, and the curtains, bed linen, cushions and towels all red-and-white gingham. We dumped our bags and left the room not really wanting to go back, but there were no other rooms available for us. Poor Cerith felt worse than us – we heard his shouts of protest and horror. He'd been put in the 'Boys' Room', which was decorated with huge images of monster trucks and had a bunk bed to sleep in. He wasn't having any of that and an alternative was offered – a boxing-gym-themed room, which we thought might

442

be more up his street. We all had a go on the enormous punch-bag that hung in the middle of the room. He was still upset. We showed him how bad our room was and he felt better.

By the time we got back to London, Cerith wasn't at all well. His skin had broken out into what I suspect was a stress rash from the hectic schedule. He didn't make it for his DJ set at Heaven. Paul got a call to say Cerith had collapsed and was extremely ill in hospital. That was upsetting news.

TG were back in Heaven, to play two shows where Derek Jarman had filmed us playing way back in 1980. That link in our history wasn't lost on us or on all those who came to the gigs. It felt good too. Being a rare TG London show, Heaven was heaving, both shows sold out. The matinee gig with S.C.U.M. as support was more restrained than the evening gig, which was furiously intense and I loved every minute of it.

We had an army of friends backstage afterwards. The atmosphere was fantastically 'up', with so much laughter and love in the room. Sleazy was very tipsy and jolly but slumped on the sofa unable to get up without great effort or a helping hand – which made me think he still wasn't well. His friend expressed his worries about Sleazy's health, asking if I could help in any way, that maybe Sleazy would listen to me. Sleazy had put on a lot of weight. That aside, I loved rubbing his Buddha belly, and I'd already tried to find out what was wrong with him, but he refused to talk about it to anyone. Sleazy was as Sleazy did. He wasn't into being 'fit' – he preferred a less-than-healthy, very indulgent lifestyle, and, finances allowing, nothing would stop him pursuing further excessive pleasures.

5 July 2009
Feeling pretty chipper after an extended time out after the TG

activities. I've been relaxing (alas with interruptions) . . . Too
much to do really what with all the mundane stuff as well. I
need a Cosey clone to do the mundane and keep me sane.

Having the summer off from travelling and performing gave me the chance to ground myself by getting into the garden and down with nature, growing vegetables and spending love time with Chris, Nick, Les, family, friends and all our precious cats. Chris, the cats and our garden were my saviours during the madness of being on the road and meeting demands that, at times, seemed insurmountable and unreasonable.

I looked on a trip to Tramway Glasgow for the showing of 'A=P=P=A=R=I=T=I=O=N' as more of a summer break than a work obligation. Paul and Susan were going along, as was Cerith. He was out of hospital and feeling better, but facing some hard lifestyle changes. The sculpture looked and sounded wonderful. It was the first time we'd seen it since the fabricators' test run. Sleazy had gone to Yokohama when it was shown there and sent photos saying how awesome it was. He was right: you had to experience it to appreciate its beauty and uniqueness. I was so proud of it but especially of Chris for persevering with his concept of a complex multichannel audio feed. It was sad some years later to be told that Cerith had produced works very similar to 'A=P=P=A=R=I=T=I=O=N' off the back of our hard work. We felt betrayed and ripped off, particularly Chris.

13 September 2009
I'll be installing my work for the Tate exhibition 'Pop Life' in 2
weeks time then going for the PV with friends. I'm really looking
forward to the show . . . As it gets cold outside I'm longing to
get back to recording in the studio. I'm itching to get cracking.

There's three sound projects in progress and all so very different to each other.

Summer was receding. I always looked forward to autumn – it's one of my favourite seasons. I love the riot of colour that leaf-fall brings and watching as the farmers and gardeners go through their routines of putting the land to bed for the winter. Then there's the added pleasure of hot, buttered crumpets and snuggling up to watch some good films. As autumnal gardening jobs ended, it gave me more time to work in the studio.

There's nothing more frustrating than being in the studio on a glorious summer's day – which was where we always seemed to be. We have to run with the creative spark and ideas when they emerge, as moments of inspiration know no seasons or boundaries. I went to stay in London to spend two days with Andrew, installing my work at the Tate Modern. The exhibition 'Pop Life', curated by Catherine Wood, was to run until January 2010 and included some great works. The show was about 'Art in a Material World', using Andy Warhol's provocative statement 'Good business is the best art' – I don't agree, but that provided a great platform for discussion on art as art and/or art as business.

The artists in the show had engaged with the market in different ways. It was a theme that had legs, as far as I was concerned, bearing in mind the 'engagement' with art and business courtesy of White Cube Gallery. There were advisory notices for three rooms, which all contained works of a 'sexual nature' – including mine. For once I wasn't the target of press porn outrage. It was Richard Prince's portrait of a very young Brooke Shields that instigated a police visit to the Tate.

Context is everything, no more so than with the selection of the five-frame *Knave* magazine work I showed, 'And I Should Be Blue'.

It comprised the whole magazine, which included my action of a set of lesbian photographs of me and another girl, naked and painting each other red and blue, with the caption, 'When they're finished their colourful claspings, our two artistes will still be left with the problem of the wall. If they're smart, they'll leave it as it stands, and try and palm it off on the Tate for vast sums of money.' Priceless – in a manner of speaking. How wonderfully serendipitous that the sex action was now hanging in the Tate as part of a show on 'art as business'. But I was (and still am) open to further exploring and extending the interesting contexts which the magazine actions continue to present me with. The inclusion of the *Knave* magazine work in 'Pop Life' provided such an opportunity. I received an invitation, instigated by Skot, to do the artist 'guest lecture' for the next ('Sex and Art') issue of the Los Angeles art magazine *Artillery*. I wrote an accompanying text for the *Knave* images that were published – extracting centrefold sex-magazine images and transposing them as the centrefold of an art magazine.

7

21 February 2010

*This year seemed to have a weird stop start feel to it with
projects hovering around then falling away. Now focusing in is
possible as confirmed exhibitions and events move ever closer.
My recent lectures and in conversations have been so enjoyable
and thought-provoking – new ideas placed to one side while I
pay full attention to present works. Those restless undercurrents
of creativity are bringing a fantastic feeling of expectation and
excitement.*

The jerky start to 2010 was mainly due to the future of TG. After
the USA tour all seemed well for a while, then an increasingly
acerbic tone appeared in Gen's emails to us about Paul's role as
TG manager, basically saying he didn't want Paul involved any
more, suggesting his own manager take over TG managerial
duties.

Gen sent a long email, which prompted an equally long reply
from Sleazy directly addressing Gen's conflicting personas and attitudes towards us, that his emails showed a lack of concentration on
TG matters, a tone of mistrust, paranoia and bitterness towards us.
The regrouping was teetering on the edge but Sleazy wanted to continue for a while longer, like me and Chris – we'd moved on from
TG of old and were excited about Gristleism and a whole load of
other gadgets we'd been working on that could bring new TG works
in their wake: 'a new thrust', as Sleazy put it. Paul was more than

a manager to TG: he added ideas into the mix, sought out suitable shows. He'd worked hard with us on 'A=P=P=A=R=I=T=I=O=N' (exceeding Gen's own input), so for Gen to conspire to sack him was crazy talk.

Things settled down – then Paul was forwarded a newsletter Gen had sent out (but not to any of us), announcing that Gen was 'retiring from touring in any and all bands including TG to concentrate on art, writing and music'. Not surprisingly, people assumed TG had ended again – even we felt the need to contact Gen, thinking he'd left, particularly as we were all working on options for TG shows and new material.

5 March 2010
We've been feeling really good lately – mood has changed here at the School House. From wallowing and drifting to sharp focus and many ideas. I think it was the final 'no live TG this year' that closed one door and opened the flood gates. There's nothing worse than wanting to do something but having a 'maybe' hanging over you.

Paul's many efforts to secure TG shows had faltered for one reason or another. It wasn't easy to coordinate four very active people's schedules. I'd been busy with more public speaking on art and music, doing a lecture at UCA Farnham, a filmed interview for a new online series, *Sound & Vision*, for the Tate's website, a talk and Q&A for the Red Bull Music Academy in London, and me and Chris were part of a panel discussion for 'Parallel Voices' at the Siobhan Davies Studios, curated by Carsten Nicolai, that had us plus Carsten and Blixa (from Neubauten) speaking about our experiences in music and exchanging fun anecdotes and serious opinions on each other's histories.

After our talk, Carsten and Blixa played a short set which included some recordings of our voices from the conversation we'd just done – and Blixa doing his 'voice of *The Mummy*' scream, sending glass-shattering frequencies bouncing off the walls and making people recoil – except the ninety-year-old lady sat in the front row, who was partially deaf and loved it.

The whole day had been enlightening, not only for having the pleasure of meeting Sue (Siobhan) and hearing Blixa's scream, but also because of the afternoon interview between me, Carsten and Sue. We all analysed why we did what we did, how we did it and our feelings about the process, performance and reception of our work. It was deeply personal at times and revealing for us all. Sue was one of the few people I've felt immediate affinity with, an incredible talent and spirit.

30 March 2010

It's taken me 2 days to come down from the euphoria of 'Cosey Complex'. Well that and sleeping after the intense day of events then Cosey Club evening that went into the wee hours of Sunday. I do feel so privileged that so many creatively gifted and wonderful people took part in 'Cosey Complex'. The day's events were outstanding for so many reasons, not least for the opportunity to hear and see such diverse inspired and inspiring works in an atmosphere free of pretension and loaded with the spirit of generosity.

'Cosey Complex' was a special one-day event at the ICA, conceived by the writer Maria Fusco, who at the time was director of art writing at Goldsmiths, London. The event had been in the planning for nigh on a year. I'd first met Maria in 2007, when she interviewed me for the first *Happy Hypocrite* journal. The theme of that issue, and the starting point for our talk, was 'Linguistic Hardcore'.

We discussed my name, 'Cosey', how I got it, and what it meant to me. Maria pointed out that 'Cosey' seemed to have a life separate from me. She was right. To me, 'Cosey' had become a concept that represented what I was as well as what I did – it was more than just a name. I suppose that might have had some subconscious influence on our changing from Chris & Cosey to Carter Tutti beyond the more simple reason we'd given.

Getting together with Maria and having such an unbelievably open and energised conversation planted a seed that grew slowly into what became one of the best concepts for an event in both my 'name' and the innovative repurposing of it. Maria approached the ICA – it being synonymous with my name from the 'Prostitution' scandal and as such a prime example of how 'Cosey' had become something 'other' than just being my name. The ICA commissioned the event and Maria worked with the curator, Richard Birkett. After many exchanges and meetings, Maria selected fourteen participants, some invited and some from open submission, all to create works by responding to 'Cosey' as methodology – or, as Maria so beautifully and succinctly put it, 'By shifting Cosey from noun to verb'.

'Cosey Complex' wasn't about me or my work. That was a tough concept to get your head around. I adopted a hands-off approach so that 'Cosey Complex' could remain true to Cosey as methodology and unfold without any intervention by me (Cosey as noun). I thought long and hard about whether to participate myself but came to the conclusion that I already was, by virtue of my role in the event as verb, as a concept for others to explore as methodology: 'to further interrogate the implications of Cosey's work, without direct reference to the work itself . . . to put research directly into practice', as Maria described it. I felt that any presentation by me could complicate things, go against the whole notion of 'Cosey Complex', and simply wasn't necessary. Instead I wrote a short introduction to

450

open the event, particularly highlighting the fact that the concept was challenging for me because I didn't subscribe to methodology (how it's usually defined), it being anathema to my improvisational working practice – my work being my*self* and therefore inseparable. Where would I locate a methodology in my own work? Maria's idea had provoked many questions about whether I actually did have my own methodology. I decided my creative freedom overrode any subconscious methodology that could be hidden deep within my approach, that ultimately 'I just am and my work is – Cosey'.

Me and Chris arrived in London the day before 'Cosey Complex' to have a meal with Maria, Richard and many of the artists, including Chris Kraus and John Duncan. If anyone got me and what I did as Cosey, it was John. Everyone was so friendly and relaxed and very much looking forward to the next day. I had no idea what to expect from everyone and was so overwhelmed at them being there to present new works. As well as the live presentations, 'Cosey Complex' had a publication, *The Reader*, designed by Zak Kyes, which would be available on the day. The week leading up to the event, the ICA's Reading Room was converted into a design and print studio, open to the public so that they could see *The Reader* being brought together. The publication included an introduction by Maria and her original interview with me, an overview by Zak, 'Notes' by Clunie Reid, and I'd contributed a sequence of images spanning my various works, from the magazine actions, old and new press cuttings, model cards and '*Self* lessness', which were placed as 'citings' throughout the book. But what formed the core of *The Reader* were transcriptions of fascinating and diverse discussions on issues around methodology that had taken place between different research groups at the beginning of May. The whole project was so powerful in its completeness. Maria had produced an incredible work in 'Cosey Complex'.

The daytime programme ran from 1 p.m. through to 6 p.m., with readings, slide shows, a play and video works by writers, artists and theorists – Maria, Richard, Martin Bax, Clunie Reid, Anthony Elms, Daniela Cascella, Chris Kraus, Corin Sworn, Diedrich Diederichsen, Gerard Byrne and Rob Stone. The writer, actor and producer Graham Duff wrote and read out a satirical and hilarious fictional piece about him interviewing me for an art and culture magazine, analysing my work and ending in my producing a new work, 'Restraining Order' (against Graham), that had run into its third year. His consummate delivery of his piece had some people belly-laughing all the way through – although some of the more academically inclined didn't much like the piss being taken out of the art world. It was refreshingly enjoyable and what I would have expected as he's a genius when it comes to strange scenarios that go off at oblique and most bizarre tangents, like his amazing TV series, *Ideal*, and his work with Steve Coogan and Mark Gatiss.

It didn't seem like the day could get any better but the evening took celebration and joy up quite a few more notches with Richard's Cosey Club, which, to all intents and purposes, had already taken up Cosey as methodology. Cosey Club ran from 9 p.m. until 3 a.m., with Andrew Weatherall, Fixmer/McCarthy, a great duo called Eve Black/Eve White and a new band (to me), Factory Floor. Paul was their manager at the time so we'd heard good things about them, Chris had done a remix for them and we were both keen to hear what they sounded like live. Nik Void, Gabe Gurnsey and Dominic Butler played a stomping set that had me dancing by the mixing desk and took me back to the early days when there was a more raw, free approach to music. That introduction marked the start of future collaborations. I was blown away by it all. The day and evening were truly 'Cosey as methodology' in action.

28 April 2010

We are now back in the studio recording for an audiovisual
presentation in Italy at the end of May. I'm playing at Tate
Modern's 10th anniversary weekend. So I have lots of work to do
in the coming weeks.

On the tenth anniversary of the Tate Modern, I performed in the
Turbine Hall along with Thurston Moore, DJ Spooky and others.
Knowing what that chasm of a space was like for sound, I kept
things ambient and played a live solo soundtrack to the projected
collage of video and still images from my various art actions. Chris
oversaw the front-of-house sound for me – I trusted his technical
skills more than anyone else's.

Szabo was in my life again. After his funeral in 1982, the mourners
had gone back to his wife Tris's flat for the usual tea and sandwiches.
Tris played Szabo's favourite jazz records – to hell with whether they
were to anyone else's taste, they were a part of Szabo and made her
and me smile. She came over to sit and talk with me. I could be
wrong but I got the sense that only we two knew and understood
Szabo and the very full life he'd led. She leaned over and picked
something up. 'I want you to have these,' she said. 'Szabo wanted
you to have them.'

She handed me a stack of over three hundred and fifty transparencies that he'd taken of me, all from the collaboration projects we'd
worked on together – except those he'd sold to magazines. I was so
touched by her kindness. When I got home and looked through
them all I started thinking about my time in Szabo's living-room
studio, recalling our last sessions together when he'd commented on
my body having changed since I'd started dancing. It wasn't something I'd even thought about but he had a discerning eye when it
came to the female form, and mine had apparently become firmer

453

and more muscular. As soon as I saw the slides, mainly in red, black and white, all laid out in sequence, I knew it was a work just waiting to be realised. It took a long time to formulate.

Over the following years, I visited and revisited the images before I arrived at the final form the work would take. I called it 'Szabo Sessions Volumes 1–4'. Each volume consisted of selected frame-by-frame sequences of different poses, showing the slight adjustments to angles of my body, hand positions and facial expressions, and revealing the process of our co-creating the exacting aesthetic needed to meet market demand. I'd spent months scanning all the slides, doing endless test prints until I got the colour balance that matched the depth and richness of the slides, and then printed them myself on to A3 supergloss archival photographic paper. They looked beautiful, a lasting testament to Szabo's exceptional talent and our brief but wonderful and creative friendship. 'Szabo Sessions' was exhibited for the first time at the A Palazzo Gallery in Brescia, Italy, as part of the exhibition '120 Day Volume' curated by Cabinet Gallery.

Carter Tutti were also part of the group show in Brescia. We'd been wanting to do something different in a live situation. The invitation to Brescia initiated a new way of working with sound. We prepared an audiovisual piece called 'Harmonic Coaction', the first in an ongoing series of live audiovisual performances that represented the assimilation of person, place and time, created live in situ using field recordings and visuals from and inspired by the site itself. In the case of Brescia, we used the exhibition and gallery space as source material. The exhibition-associated images we'd put together were projected on a huge scale from four corners of the room, intersecting with one another, the walls, ceiling, floor, exhibits and audience, integrating all within the space as we manipulated the many recorded sounds. The performance was recorded and immediately installed as a work – a soundtrack of the exhibition contained in a tall, black, monolithic speaker column.

16 October 2010

I'm in the grip of preparations for upcoming TG shows right now with most exhilarating moments in the studio trying out new sounds AND Chris just finished making a new sound box for me.

For over six months our time and attention were taken up with all things Carter Tutti and our solo projects. 'Harmonic Coaction' had resurfaced in Ancona, Italy, and we'd mastered the early Chris & Cosey albums ready to release on vinyl through our trusted colleagues at Cargo. Chris had gone to the STEIM centre for electronic music in Amsterdam, to do a 'Dirty Electronics' experimental electronic music workshop and performance with John Richards. He'd already done one at De Montfort University, Leicester, and had designed his own touch-sensitive random sound instrument called Dirty-Carter. It was this and all the other off-the-wall hand-built units and the Gristleism that had launched me, Chris and Sleazy into that 'new-thrust' zone for both our individual music work and for TG – which had sprung back on to our schedule for some more live shows.

Sleazy had commissioned a number of strange noise-making objects to be built for him, consulting with Chris on the practical possibilities over and above his fantastical ideas. Sleazy brought them over to use for the TG shows – and Chris rebuilt them so they actually worked, resoldering joints and reconfiguring where necessary. He also built me a Tutti Box, an awesome noise-generator made from spare electronic parts built into a retro wooden radio, battery-powered with a flashing plasma display triggered by the audio signals. It was outlandishly grungy and very noisy. I couldn't have asked for more.

It came with a cost attached, though. When Chris was drilling the case he drilled through his fingernail. He almost passed out. I got him straight into the car, where he *did* pass out, waking up as we arrived at A&E. It was excruciatingly painful. But he isn't one to do things by halves – a few days later he broke a finger on the other hand when he trapped it in a folding table. He was splinted on both hands but ready for the TG gigs.

Despite the drilled and broken fingers, we couldn't wait to get out there and blast our new instruments through a big PA. The problem we had was: what would Gen do? We wanted to include him. Specifically with that in mind, we'd worked with an inventive but secretive electronics guy (who had previously built Chris some small handheld synth boxes) on developing a simple, interactive, long 'ribbon strip' instrument (similar to a theremin), which would provide Gen with the means to join in with us and our new TG-type material. Alas the ribbon project didn't quite work out, so at the last minute TG hastily bought Gen a handheld Korg Monotron to use and put through his effects pedals. Anything a bit different and 'outside the box' was better than nothing, and we hoped he'd embrace our enthusiasm for the new, more experimental TG live experience.

We all arrived in London and met up for a talk at the Hoxton hotel on the gigs and releasing TG back-catalogue vinyl re-releases and the Nico *Desertshore* album on Industrial Records through Cargo. Gen kept closing his eyes throughout the meeting and we couldn't tell whether he was bored or genuinely tired, as he was lucid at pertinent points in the conversation. I ordered him some food to perk him up.

After the meeting came to an end we all retired for the night, ready for a rehearsal the next day, the day before the TG Village Underground gig. We'd booked a rehearsal space in Hackney from 10.30 a.m. till 6 p.m. The place was damp, cold and noisy, with heavy-metal bands in the adjoining rooms thrashing away at full volume. It felt alien to our usual preparation space but needs must, as they say. It was a strange day. We three arrived on time with Charlie, and got word that Gen wanted some extra sleep and wouldn't be joining us until 2 p.m. Sleazy rolled his eyes, put his head down and then started setting up and testing his new gear. We had a table each, ours laden with our additional sound gadgets. We jammed together, demonstrating what our new noise-making equipment could do and generally slamming out sounds to make mental notes of what seemed to fit together – or not. Charlie had set up a table and microphone for Gen so he could join in as soon as he arrived. We were anxious that he got a feel for the freer approach and new sounds. But he didn't turn up until around 3.30, moaning about his hotel and ranting about Paul.

Sleazy totally ignored him, looked over at me and flicked his head as if to tell me to take Gen outside to sort it out. I did. I called Paul, who was busy with last-minute gig business and had already managed to book Gen five days in the four-star Crowne Plaza Hotel in St James (an extra TG cost) – while Sleazy was staying on a friend's floor to help keep the TG budget on target. The rehearsal time was fast running out and we were pissed off that Gen had yet again fucked up the opportunity to be 'with' us. We had a gig to get ready for but he never mentioned that or the music we were supposed to be making together. Sleazy closed off completely.

By the time we left the rehearsal space, both Sleazy and Gen's moods had become ominously sombre. We all walked out into the street. We'd gone from the isolated bubble of the rehearsal room into the hubbub of London at its busiest time, and yet me and Chris felt strangely removed from the chaotic scene as we stood there watching Sleazy and Gen walk away from us in different directions towards the Tube, Gen limping badly and Sleazy with his slow, heavy stride.

Neither of them looked at each other or back at us, even when we called out to them to go and have a meal together. They were each in their own world, disappearing into the distance. Me and Chris looked at one another. We knew that TG was over.

That night me and Sleazy got numerous emails from Gen, complaining about Paul and saying that he may have to cut his losses and find a way home. Sleazy was furious with Gen about possibly leaving and explained that we three would incur substantial financial losses if he left. He told Gen that his version of events regarding Paul was a fantasy: 'Please do not rewrite history or the circumstances so you feel justified in blaming Paul for everything, as this is not how it happened . . . stop thinking you are victimised in some way . . .'

When we all arrived at the Village Underground to set up and soundcheck, Gen's mood had changed. He was in the private area at the side of the stage drinking wine and seemed a little merrier – he was even lovey-dovey with Paul, leaning on his shoulder and laughing.

The gig was a transitional point for TG and started out like an experimental sound workshop with us all sat at our workbenches, none of us knowing, or feeling the need to know, who was creating which sounds, just working our way through them. There was an off-the-wall moment that took even Gen by surprise, when a naked guy jumped on the stage drugged up to his eyeballs. He proceeded to do a stage dive and threw himself into the audience, expecting to be caught by them, but they parted and he hit the concrete floor with a loud splat. Gen was drinking more wine and bowing his violin, sometimes staring into the audience giving the impression he was uninterested in what we were doing. I certainly got the feeling he didn't like it and found it uninspiring, especially when the audience applauded and he said to us three, with cynical bemusement, 'They actually like all this shit.'

458

Yes, the new material had gone down well, the audience were ecstatic, so were we three, and we'd just played the longest TG gig ever. Gen's attitude and contribution to the gig appeared to reflect the undertone of his recent emails – that he wanted out of TG. Those suspicions were to be confirmed.

26 October 2010
So many people there and I was a bit phased with the sound and playing for 2 hours. We're kicking back before going to Prague on Friday. Sleazy's on UK time now and feeling a lot brighter. Lots of talking going on about many things . . . I just sent a 'hello' email to Gen saying see him Friday etc.

There's always a bit of a post-mortem that goes on the morning after a gig and after-show party. Shattered as we were, we had a group breakfast meeting at the Hoxton hotel, going through the TG schedule and details for our trip to Prague in five days' time, before me, Chris and Sleazy headed back to our house to work in the studio for a few days while Gen stayed in London. On the Wednesday, Sleazy went off to visit friends while me and Chris worked on a promo video clip for our Chris & Cosey re-releases. We were all to meet at the airport for the flight to Prague. I'd done interviews for Prague and Porto to help publicise our shows there, and the Prague air tickets were booked and paid for.

The day we received copies of our first two re-released, remastered Chris & Cosey vinyl albums, *Heartbeat* and *Trance*, we also received an email from Gen to inform us that he was quitting the TG 'tour'. Our elated mood crumbled. Chris's face dropped. He was fuming. 'What?! That's it! I've had enough. I knew he'd try and destroy TG . . . What the hell are we going to do – the fans, the money everyone's paid out . . . Doesn't he feel any responsibility to anyone?'

The reason Gen gave us for leaving was Paul being TG manager and that apparently his own 'conscience' wouldn't allow him to continue with the rest of the TG 'tour'. It was clear that Gen's moral compass and conscience differed from ours – they centred around him and he didn't appear to feel what he did was morally wrong. I couldn't help but think that this had all the hallmarks of the very first regrouped TG gig at the Astoria – Gen threatening to walk out over money. His quitting would impact hugely on thousands of people. We were frantically trying to think of a way of preventing what would be a catastrophic and very costly end to TG.

As texts and phone calls were frequently going unanswered, I emailed Gen at 8.15 a.m. the next morning to say how serious the situation was and would he reconsider, and if not to let me know as we had to make other arrangements urgently and I needed a reply from him before 3 p.m. to enable us to sort things out with everyone affected. He replied at 4 p.m. He was already at the departure gate waiting to board the plane back to New York. That short timeline between contacting us and his departure made us suspect that he'd bought a ticket before he sent us the 'I'm quitting the tour' email. He said that he felt it was impossible for him to suffer any financial shortfall. That was particularly galling as it implied that he thought it possible and agreeable (to him) that we three suffer a huge financial loss, as well as having to cope with the hellish mess that he left behind. But he did say he 'loved TG, our music and us', which didn't make any sense in view of what he'd just done to us. As Sleazy wrote to him, 'We are glad to hear you still love TG, the music we are making now, and us personally, but your actions and attitude do not seem to reflect this, which IS sad, and leaves us not knowing what you really think. To be honest we are more inclined to believe that your actions reflect your true feelings.'

We hastily contacted the venues to offer a solution and limit damage as much as possible. The three of us offered to play as X-TG at Bologna and Porto. They agreed. Alas, Prague was cancelled altogether as Gen's sudden walk-out had left us no time to prepare a replacement show for them. We put out a statement informing venues and fans that TG would not be performing because Gen wasn't willing to perform in TG for the confirmed sold-out shows. We three and Paul had to deal with the backlash as best we could, and attempt to avoid us and Gen being sued for vast sums of money.

I didn't believe that Gen's reason for quitting was because of Paul and neither did Chris or Sleazy. From years of dealing with Gen, we thought his quitting was another possible hollow threat. He never apologised or gave us or our fans the real reason for leaving. We couldn't help but wonder if the TG regrouping had all just been about the money for him. I thought back to all the instances where money had cropped up and it seemed it most likely had been, with Gen saying during the working out of this last 'tour' that, 'in terms of what we [his new terminology for 'I'] get out of it, the fee is key'. The quitting drama rolled on, email after email, as we tried to figure out what had made Gen do this and where we were to go from here.

TG live performances had been problematic in so much as me, Chris and Sleazy embraced the original ethos of TG being musically flexible, innovative and improvised. We were fired up about the prospect of working together again and had invested in different hardware gadgets, effects units and software to give us as large a palette to work from as possible. We were like kids in a candy store when our research bore fruit and we got a new piece of gear. Every TG gig saw a different equipment set-up for the three of us. We wanted to create new works and not just perform TG's 'greatest hits' – much as many fans and promoters wanted us to. TG as a whole could gel incredibly well on old songs but we were now incompatible with Gen when it came to venturing into new territory. We three would be soaring off into sound oblivion and Gen would be on the sidelines despite our efforts to include him. I guess no matter what Gen wrote to us in emails about working 'together' like in the old TG days, it never became a reality simply because he was in a different musical mindset from us three. Inevitably, even though Gen said he wasn't comfortable with performing old TG tracks, we ended up playing them because the alternative (new material) was more uncomfortable for him.

The democratic foundation of TG should have prevented the situation Gen put us all in. But Gen had ignored that and acted independently by leaving without first consulting us or giving us the chance to discuss his problem – but then he played the democracy card to demand that, whatever we three decided to do in response to the awful predicament he'd created (playing without him as X-TG), we must have his agreement. That wasn't democracy. The fans and promoters happily and gratefully accepted X-TG. As far as TG was concerned, there were other commitments we had to fulfil, but those would have to wait until we returned from Europe.

1 November 2010

Very excited that the re-released Chris & Cosey vinyl albums will be out!! I can't see much time to rest between now and next May as there are so many other big projects in the pipeline. A lot of recorded material awaiting final mixing and release. What more can I say? Life is gloriously rich in so many ways.

It was so good to have the joy of the Chris & Cosey re-releases and the prospect of playing the old C&C tracks live again in the new year was something positive to really look forward to. Plus X-TG was feeling and sounding great. Gen's quitting email had been a

Gen hand grenade too many for Sleazy, and one he was thankful for as it signalled an end to all the aggravation we'd endured. It was as if a heavy weight had been lifted from Sleazy's shoulders. We three had the opportunity to explore and experiment together, and Sleazy bombarded me and Chris with ideas for X-TG logos, sounds and future plans. Me and Chris felt the relief too and wholeheartedly embraced our new X-TG collaborative relationship.

Sleazy was so chipper about it that he accidentally sent his honest opinion of Gen quitting TG to Gen by mistake, saying, 'My first impression is that it could be exactly what we want . . . I personally am not inclined to try to change his mind.' It became known as the 'LOL' email – the term Sleazy used as his apology to Gen for the slip-up. With the Bologna show just four days away, we had to work fast to get a new X-TG set together. We worked right up to – and on the day of – the first performance.

X-TG and crew arrived in Bologna, checking into a very swish hotel. Sleazy came to our room and flopped on to our bed, munching our snacks and generally making himself totally at home. He was happy and relaxed. We'd put together material not only for the shows but more that we could use for a future X-TG album. Sleazy was keen to do vocals and asked if I minded. I didn't object. We had no intention of including conventional vocals, and we were open to change as we went along. No limits, no egos to hinder us.

Sleazy had his new vocal instruments to use: a touch-sensitive, circular spoked wheel with light fixed to his microphone; an air tube running through an effects unit; as well as a regular microphone that he used to feed vocal sounds through an audio processor. When we walked on stage in Bologna, the place was crammed with people. We were greeted with applause, much affection and an atmosphere of excited expectation. The gig was extreme, loud, sonically overpowering, and how I imagined the soundtrack would be to some hellish journey into outer space. I was in my element, my whole body seemed melded with the sound, and the audience response was just as intense and glorious.

A day off in Bologna was a treat we all deserved and we had no unexpected dramas to deal with. The only problem was that I'd pulled a muscle in my back, or so I thought. I tried walking to relieve the pain and we went out for coffee, Sleazy having a beer and musing on doing more X-TG gigs. He'd been sleeping for up to fourteen hours a day, which didn't sound right or healthy, but he was so upbeat and I put it down to him catching up on rest after the frantic two weeks we'd just had. The day we flew to Porto was my birthday. Chris had secretly brought cards and presents with him to make my day as special as he could. I loved him for that. I received lots of emailed birthday wishes too – and one from Gen. The first in over thirty years. Was he serious? I was in agony with my back, but still out gigging, trying to recoup money from his fucking off and leaving us in the shit.

The venue for Porto was the ultra-modern Casa da Música concert hall and we waited outside the hotel for our pick-up to the gig. A car drew up and the driver leaned out: 'Taxi for Pulsing Crystal.' Fabulous name – we knew he meant Throbbing Gristle. My back was painfully uncooperative and I couldn't get into the car. I had to walk the thankfully shortish distance from the hotel to the venue, with someone carrying my bag. In light of the already revised line-up for the gig, there was no way I could pull out. The gig was sold out, a blast – it felt as good as Bologna, and a success with the audience too.

9 November 2010
We're back from two successful shows as X-TG. Full house and great response so we're all very happy about the start of the transition.

The return flight and train journey home made my back worse. It had locked up completely by the time I tried to get out of bed the next morning. Chris took me to the doctor's clinic at our local hospital. The assessment examination was painful. I was sent home with muscle relaxants and painkillers that knocked me out for a couple of hours. When I woke up I couldn't put any weight on my left leg – the pain was excruciating. It was like someone had run me through with a sword from the sole of my left foot up the centre of my leg to my lower back. I just made it to a chair before I passed out.

Chris rang for an ambulance. The paramedics were there in twelve minutes. I was hooked up to a heart monitor and drifting in and out of consciousness. Poor Chris must have thought he was in for a re-run of the Papworth cardiac crash. The paramedic asked me, 'What's your pain on a scale of one to ten, ten being childbirth?'

I replied, 'Nine.'

He didn't believe me, but not having gone through natural childbirth like me, how would he know and who was he to judge my pain tolerance? I ended up being taken to A&E, where they gave me more drugs that gave me little relief. I was by now shaking uncontrollably, sweating, throwing up and intermittently losing consciousness. It turned out that I'd had a reaction to the pain meds – I was intolerant to opiates. I hadn't pulled a muscle at all, I'd herniated a disc in my lower back and had a pinched sciatic nerve. The treatment was to keep mobile, relaxed and no lifting or stretching for six months.

17 November 2010
Things have been a bit full on lately but as one door closes another opens. We three will be exploring our ideas now as X-TG. The stress of it all took its toll and Chris and me are in that post adrenaline phase after making good the TG

commitments to fans and promoters. We had some dramas on our
return but the worst is over.

Sleazy was back in Thailand and intent on making X-TG work. He'd left a lot of his gear in the UK and his desk set up in our studio ready for his return in a few weeks' time. In place of what would have been the scheduled TG performance, we were booked to play ATP Festival in Minehead as X-TG on 3 December. Sleazy was gathering together possible stage presentation ideas, new audio and visual instruments and talking of a 2011 X-TG tour of the USA, Japan, Canada and the UK, with an album and DVD release, and putting up an X-TG website. He saw X-TG as a new project for him. He wanted to put out a statement to the effect of 'Now we have fulfilled the obligations of Throbbing Gristle's live shows we will be moving forward as X-TG with all-new material for 2011 . . .'

There was no guarantee against a repeat performance of what had just happened with TG and we didn't want to revisit that amount of stress again. TG live was over but contracts for TG releases were still on the table so we had to find a way back for Gen, regardless of how we all felt about him. He excused his erratic behaviour and the consequential chaos it caused us by proclaiming, 'I'm the chaos element' – as if making our lives and TG regroupings difficult and hellish was a fun, prankster thing to bring to TG. Him walking out had been a shock. Sleazy emailed him: 'I had not imagined this happening this soon but you seem to be fulfilling your role as "chaos element" with aplomb, as usual.' How could TG come back from this?

25 November 2010
Bee called and I was sobbing. He was very sweet and reassured

me Sleazy died peacefully. We spent all day just wandering
around not knowing what to do, crying and unable to speak for
choking up. Chris spoke with Paul, he is so shattered by the news.

If we and others thought the Gen-quitting episode sealed the ending of TG, everyone had grossly overestimated his importance to the whole TG equation. It was Sleazy's unexpected and untimely death that ended TG forever. Something none of us had anticipated would happen.

When I got up on the morning of the 25th, I saw the red light flashing on the answerphone. There were three messages from Sleazy's friend Bee in Thailand. I pressed 'Play'. Bee's soft voice said, 'Cosey, please call me as soon as you can.' His tone told me all I needed to know. I rang him and he answered quickly. 'Darling . . .' he said.

'No, no, no. Please don't say it,' I sobbed. I wanted him to say anything but that Sleazy had died. I couldn't bear the thought.

As I cried uncontrollably, Bee gently told me what had happened. That Sleazy died in his sleep next to his lover and in his beloved Thailand home was a comfort I clung to as I tried to hold back the tears to talk to Bee. Knowing the TG situation, he asked if I wanted him to tell Gen. I said that I would tell him. It seemed the right thing to do. Chris had been stood in front of me with a look of shock and disbelief on his face as the awful reality of the phone conversation hit him. He came over and held me in his arms and we wept together. The sense of loss and grief was beyond any we'd felt before. Our hearts were broken. We'd lost Sleazy, our dearest, adored, loving, fun friend of thirty-six years, our fellow collaborator, experimentalist and explorer of life.

Thailand was six hours ahead of UK time. Sleazy had died the evening of 24 November (UK time), just hours after my last email exchange with him about the ramifications of Gen's walking out and how best to proceed – he'd just received an email from Gen and was vitriolic about him. Gen had still not apologised, which irked Sleazy as much as the financial shortfall incurred by Gen's quitting: 'The loss he caused came very close to me losing my house, possibly even my ability to stay in Thailand, which is true. He needs to understand his actions hurt his so-called friends.'

Sleazy had been forced to cash in a life insurance policy to stave off the unthinkable scenario of leaving Thailand. It was Gen's callous behaviour that hung foremost in my mind as I tried to deal with my despair at Sleazy dying and spending part of his very last day dealing with the aftermath of Gen quitting TG. So many 'what if's and 'why's.

Grief is a strange thing: you have a need for an answer to what caused someone to die so suddenly. It was hard for me and Chris not to connect Sleazy's heart attack with the immense stress levels of the past month and that day's revisiting of them, which could likely have had some influence on his seeking escape from the TG mess in recreational indulgences. His lifestyle was at times excessively and dangerously hedonistic. I suspect that was a contributing factor to his death, which came sooner than he or anyone would have thought.

The announcement of Sleazy's death brought an enormous outpouring of shock, sadness, love, respect and condolences. Everyone was stunned and grief-stricken. Paul and Skot were a huge support to me and Chris through it all. Sleazy's death was going to take a long time to get over.

Chris was racked with sorrow – he couldn't sleep and kept crying. It all seemed so unfair that Sleazy, who was such a warm and tender person, had been ripped from us all. His equipment table in our studio was still set up for his return for ATP. We couldn't bring ourselves to take it down. That seemed too final an act. We preferred to kid ourselves that he was just off in Thailand and we'd see him soon. His presence lingered from when he stayed with us, which was both a comfort and a reminder that he would never be returning to make magic with us again. We'd shared so much excitement about X-TG. Sleazy had gone home with lots of new goodies and now they were just sitting abandoned in Thailand. That thought made us so very sad. Sleazy really hadn't been ready to leave us yet.

Two years after Sleazy's death, I was asked to write a memoir of him and Geff for *England's Hidden Reverse*. I decided not to have it included. This is an extract:

> From the moment I first met Sleazy at the Oval House in 1974 he was 'family' to me, no matter where we were or what we were doing, separately or together. We had an unspoken connection on so many levels. I don't think either of us fully understood why, considering some of our differences, but we embraced the longevity and intimacy of our relationship, particularly during the regrouping of TG. We were both older and wiser then and the wounds of life have a way of making you treasure love in its many guises. His work with COUM and TG gave voice to his interests over and above what he could do with his creative ideas for Hipgnosis. Together we were incorrigible explorers of the unorthodox – the film *After Cease to Exist* being a prime example. That was a wonderful day. A near-derelict building, a willing 'victim' (Chris), the scene was set and we three were on a symbiotic roll. That key and precious unspoken connection between us all was there to the very end.

4 December 2010

Sleazy was cremated this morning (UK time) so we have had a contemplative morning. Amid many tears I wrote our farewell words to Sleazy last night to read out at the cremation. His ashes are to be taken out in boats by his friends and scattered into the sea. I'm still in a weird place with all this.

I'd emailed Gen immediately after speaking with Bee to tell him about Sleazy. I hadn't been able to enter into a dialogue with him. Maybe that was wrong of me but my feelings towards him were still so negative, my emotions over Sleazy so very raw. We had yet to assess the TG losses, the deepest unimaginable loss being Sleazy. Gen had been in touch about the future of TG. There was a lot to sort out as we'd been on the verge of signing assorted agreements with Cargo, White Cube and state51. Sleazy was so far away, being cared for and having all his funeral arrangements made by his Thai friends.

His cremation took place the day X-TG would have played ATP. It had happened so quickly, before we really fully had time to consider travelling to Bangkok. It was odd that we and his biological family weren't in Thailand with him. His 'will' was even odder, but that's a whole other story.

11 January 2011

The ending of 2010 was so sad and cruel but now I'm just beginning to feel the resurgence of positive energies and it feels good. There are so many plans for this year, some that were laid last year and some new exciting projects that we're utterly thrilled about . . . I have a LOT of work to do for the C&C ICA show . . . a shift in time to our earlier works . . . fun!

If we'd needed something to lift our spirits, nothing could surpass the Chris & Cosey live performance and reception of the vinyl re-releases. We'd had a second bite of the cherry with TG and now with C&C. We were feeling more than blessed. The reinvigoration that Chris & Cosey brought, courtesy of Richard Clouston, was the antidote to the many losses of the past ten years. We wanted to celebrate our lives and those we'd lost, not mourn what we couldn't have any more.

The reactivating of Chris & Cosey propelled us into the realm of happiness and positivity again. We knew that C&C tracks were played regularly by DJs but hadn't fully appreciated how much people still loved them. Richard had been asking us for years to play a Chris & Cosey live show for Cosey Club and we'd refused, wanting to concentrate on new work. With the C&C vinyl albums about to be released it seemed the perfect time and Richard asked again. We relented with a casual 'OK', thinking we'd do one show and that would be it.

But we stumbled on a problem as soon as we started putting the set together. All the old C&C material we'd selected to play live relied on equipment we no longer had or sounds that were stored on old optical drives. It all needed to be digitally transferred. A combination of forensic editing, resampling and sourcing sounds and vintage equipment took over six weeks. That was more work than we'd assumed it would take but in a way it was a good thing because we hadn't wanted to re-present the tracks with a thin 1980s sound. The old live video material was re-edited and remastered and synchronised live to the music. It was a neat but complex set-up that had taken weeks of programming and run-throughs until we were happy. We'd put together a set of songs that we'd loved playing live, starting slow, then building into 120 b.p.m. through to the end, finishing with 'Dancing on Your Grave', with the option for our classic 'October (Love Song)' as an encore.

The C&C show was announced, billed as 'Carter Tutti plays Chris & Cosey', and sold out immediately. We seemed to be the only ones surprised. Also on the bill were Factory Floor and DJ sets from Trevor Jackson and Richard. We were a little apprehensive about performing our first C&C gig in ten years, the first gig since X-TG, and it being at the ICA in the same room we'd worked with Sleazy on the *Desertshore* sessions. We were with good people, though: Nick, Paul, Susan, Charlie, Terry, Richard and other friends. We dedicated the show to Sleazy.

As soon as 'Sleeping Stephen' struck up, we were away on the crest of the C&C wave with everyone alongside us. I was singing, playing guitar, cornet, melodica and drum pads, and dancing as Chris drove the rhythms, sequencers and melodies. The atmosphere was intoxicating, the audience jubilant, and I was enjoying myself so much I almost forgot to play. I was so deliriously happy I thought I'd burst. We had to do an encore and the iconic first notes of 'October (Love Song)' sent the whole place shooting off the Richter scale. I'd never experienced that amount of love towards us both before.

20 May 2011
*Materials from Gen's archive and 'a private collection'??? Is my
name not allowed to be mentioned in public alongside Gen's
regarding his archive? I find this very odd if indeed this 'private
collection' is referring to my framed pieces and the polaroid.*

The mastering and artworks for the TG re-releases had to be finished and delivered, as did a remix for S.C.U.M. (finally) and Billie Ray Martin, Tate Britain business and a gig for Mute's 'Short Circuit' event at the Roundhouse in London. The Tate had a great exhibition – 'The Scene Is Set' – which was to include COUM and use works from both my and Gen's archives. I'd received the text referring to COUM, and my loaned works had been acknowledged as from 'a private collection'. As my magazine works and the Polaroid of me sitting on them at the ICA were being loaned to give context to Gen's archive, I wasn't pleased that my name had been omitted. I was effectively an anonymous 'collector'.

Gen's tendency to make me all but invisible in COUM was a continuing irritant to me and others, and I took exception to what would seem a small, insignificant oversight to most people. Context is everything, that's why my work was there, and I wasn't going to be a silent facilitator. I was so glad that I'd insisted on the text amendment after the meeting to view Gen's archive materials. I was to assist in providing information on the various letters, photographs, etc. that related to my own exhibits. When I looked at what the Tate had bought from Gen I was shocked and upset to see some of my personal letters, the photographs I'd taken and printed myself in my darkroom, and other personal objects laid out before me. Anger resurfaced and I wanted to reclaim them. It felt so wrong that what I considered to be mine could be sold by someone without my permission. I read and looked through them and reminisced, making affectionate comments about the stories behind them and thinking how sad it was that COUM had become marred by Gen's increasing tendency to not give due credit to those involved in the co-creation of many shared past works.

6 May 2011

We had a pleasant 10 days after we returned from Europe with visits from Nick and Tatis, then Rose and Vicki. Now we're behind on our preps for the Mute Roundhouse gig next Friday!! Nik arrives on Monday to go through the set with us then we're all off to London for the show. It'll be exciting to play live with someone new.

As Mute label artists, me and Chris were asked to take part in the Mute 'Short Circuit' event at the Roundhouse in London. I looked on it as a celebration of their refound independence. They suggested we, like some of the other Mute artists, could collaborate with someone on the label. Our adrenaline started surging at the thought of a one-off gig where we could do anything we wanted, no expectation, no strings, just freedom to 'play', and with the idea of pursuing 'Carter Tutti +' as an additional outlet for further musical adventures.

We decided against the more obvious choices and asked Nik Void. We knew from the Triptych Festival that she'd been on Mute as a member of KaitO and liked what she did with Factory Floor, and Chris really liked the idea of being flanked by two women on guitars. I sent Nik an email to see if she was interested. She wrote back straight away, thrilled by the idea. To keep things totally open to chance and our own ideas having free rein, we said we'd prepare the leanest of guide rhythms and run through them just twice in our studio to see how we all gelled before leaving to perform live together. Nik came to our studio for three days. Our compatibility was no problem at all. We were all caught a bit off guard by how intuitive it felt.

The last time I was at the Roundhouse had been in 1974 for the COUM performance 'Miners Catastrophe', inspired by the volatile political climate of the time, with two general elections in quick succession after the first resulted in a hung parliament, and also the three-day week imposed due to industrial action by the miners. Since then the Roundhouse had been renovated and looked nothing like I remembered it in its 'bare bones' performing-arts-venue days. There were now two performance spaces, a large one and a small studio theatre. We were in the studio theatre with NON, Richard Kirk, Komputer and Balanescu Quartet.

Richard's set-up time had overrun due to problems with his equipment, so soundcheck was running later than late. We set up pretty quick, with Charlie doing PA sound for us. Fitting us all on to the stage was difficult, but we pulled together to make it work. All was going well until Balanescu Quartet turned up and demanded that the stage be cleared for them. After all the careful plugging in and placing of everyone's gear we were all completely thrown by what they said, but more so by the way they said it – as if they were headlining and we were all just novice support acts that didn't know how to play 'real' music. Their disrespectful attitude had affronted and angered artists and sound engineers alike. The situation started to escalate when one of the women performers with the quartet told Charlie to shut up, more or less saying he was of no importance to the discussion. I was ready to give her a verbal bollocking for being such a rude, arrogant bastard. Charlie was already red in the face and shouting at her. There were comments suggesting that someone should point out to the quartet that at least we all wrote and played our own music and our reputations weren't founded on doing cover versions of Kraftwerk. The whole situation had to be calmed down.

Everyone withdrew to the communal dressing room, where the atmosphere was warmer and more party-like, where friends, artists and Florian Schneider of Kraftwerk had no such delusions of grandeur. Nik had gone off to get her old guitar for Boyd to use with his electric drill, and me and Chris took a walk round the building, stopping off at the Dirty Electronics workshop and then the Schneiders Buero, who had a stand stacked with modular synths. Chris got 'hands-on' and I took a detour, leaving him to explore and no doubt place an order or two.

We were due to perform after Komputer and Boyd (NON). The studio theatre was full, with a long line of very disappointed people stuck outside unable to get in. It was a shame the room was so small but the upside of it was that the sonic overload we created had more impact. It was good to see some familiar faces at the front, including our Nick, his girlfriend Tatis, Andrew, Joe Ahmed, Phil (P6), DIL23 and others, all grinning away and up for whatever we were to do. It was a wonderful feeling; the audience were so receptive and embraced the idea of us doing something new. Chris was centre stage, with me and Nik either side. He provided a constant 4/4 beat with extra rhythmic elements, which briefly and accidentally included his metronome tick-tocking away. The whole room locked into the unceasing rhythm, the metallic, forceful thrusting of my and Nik's guitars and the random bizarre sounds that cut across the pulsing beats or locked into them, driving them furiously forward. From the get-go the audience were totally with us. What we'd thought was a one-off show had unintentionally created a demand for more, as well as another grouping configuration as Carter Tutti Void.

Two months after Mute's 'Short Circuit' we were back at the Roundhouse. This time it was Chris playing with Factory Floor to fill in for Dom, who was on paternity leave. Chris had already played at the Primavera festival for them as well. We met up with Nik and she introduced us to her new boyfriend, Tim (Burgess), and we all sat down to have dinner together, chatting away. Watching Chris play was a treat for me as I hadn't seen him perform without me since pre-TG days.

Me and Chris stayed over in London as I was taking part in an informal discussion at the Royal College of Art about the medium of pornography. I had to do a quick mindset change as I headed off from there to the ICA for a seminar based around the issues raised by Simon Reynolds' new book, *Retromania*, about the trend for bands re-forming, the demand for retro music and what the future held for music and art. It was appropriate for me, having regrouped with TG and my now revisiting Chris & Cosey music.

There was still much to do on the TG back catalogue re-releases – artworks for five separate albums on vinyl, CD and
download meant fifteen lots of mastering and artworks. Their
release had been agreed back in 2010, before Sleazy died. Sleazy
had announced the re-releases via his blog: 'I can confirm that
TG will continue to complete all existing contracts, sales, ongoing negotiations and the recording/delivery obligations already
in place.' So me and Chris were to proceed with the production
and deliver to Cargo.

Gen had emailed Cargo to reassure them that, despite him quitting TG, he would fully support the deal with press and PR. We
felt that our working relationship with Gen was no longer tenable.
Even so, we involved him, but through Paul. The format for the TG
packaging was agreed, including an eight-page colour booklet of
unpublished photos, TG interviews, reviews and ephemera relating
to each album, all taken from my and Chris's archive. We'd asked
Gen to contribute to the booklet and he'd offered material, but we
received nothing. The albums were finally released at the end of
October and got fantastic reviews.

9 October 2011
Far too much going on here that I've had to retreat to remain
sane and healthy. The memorial for Sleazy has proved far more
emotional than expected having been in contact with his brother
and sister. Coil world is a tangled web as expected.

We talked mostly with Paul about the best way to make Sleazy's
memorial a celebration and the happiest of gatherings, as far as
possible, considering the sadness and everyone's sensitivities. Sleazy
had led a compartmentalised life and kept his different worlds separate. We decided that all his family and his collaborators in music

and film should be brought together, much as that would have freaked him out.

The memorial took place at the Horse Hospital in Bloomsbury, London, founded by Roger Burton – a most befitting and intimate venue as it had historic links with 'the underground', be it film, readings, writing, art or fashion. Me and Chris arrived in London mid-afternoon and made our way to a pub close by the Horse Hospital. We were meeting Paul, Susan and Terry to set up the space in time for everyone arriving at 7 p.m.

One of Sleazy's close friends, Jenks, had recently got in touch with us. He was from Manchester, a fellow plain-speaking Northerner. Meeting him for the first time brought me and Chris some comfort and peace as he told us first-hand what had happened to Sleazy. I felt at ease with him. He joined us all as we prepared the room, placing the photo books I'd made on a long table, hanging strings of blue, white, red, green and yellow Tibetan Buddhist prayer flags. The photos were also projected on to a large screen so Sleazy was there for us as a constant visual presence. To one side of the screen, Paul and Susan had set a small table with a large photo of Sleazy, a candle and two vases of flowers.

We knew it would be an emotional day as we hadn't seen some of our friends since that fateful event. There were lots of tears but also so many smiling faces as everyone recounted their often hilarious and crazy Sleazy experiences to one another, to the accompaniment of Sleazy's iPod music library – which included the usual suspects and some not so usual, like 'It's Raining Men' by the Weather Girls. It was heartwarming to see his sister and brothers, who were sat with one of the books, going through the photos one by one, piecing together the parts of Sleazy's life they hadn't known about. It was clear that they all adored him, so anyone who had suggested he was ostracised from his family and doubted my inviting them had been totally wrong. For one thing, had his sister Anne not come along, we would never have known the extraordinary revelation that she had lived next door to Susan in Buffalo and bought some of Susan's music books from her mother when Susan moved to the UK. They were both astounded at that coincidence. Meeting his family and other friends of Sleazy's filled in so many gaps for me and Chris too. No matter what had transpired concerning Sleazy's affairs since his death, I wanted them to suspend their differences for those few hours.

I took the prayer flags home and hung them in our garden to blow in the Norfolk winds, as a symbol of Sleazy's passing, peace and harmony.

12 February 2012

We're gradually working our way through the TG 'Desertshore' recording. Only a quarter way into it and wondering what reception we are condemned to receive for our efforts. One day we don't give a damn what people say and the next we wonder if we're wasting our time, ideas and energies. I guess we're ultimately driven by our obligation to Sleazy to fulfil this project for him. Be good to finally push the TG boat out to sea from the 'Desertshore' and wave a final farewell.

The *Desertshore* project conceived by Sleazy was unfinished when he died. With Gen having walked out, and then losing Sleazy, TG in its original form was no more and we felt that it would be a fitting memorial to Sleazy to complete his project and release it on Industrial Records as the final Throbbing Gristle album. Me and Chris made a commitment to that end – we'd had numerous email and Skype conversations with Sleazy about how it would finally sound so we could carry on from where he left off, using his files and remaining true to how he had envisaged it. That caused us problems because Sleazy had moved a long way from the ICA recordings and was no longer using the backing tracks from those sessions. He'd always regarded them as a reference and he was about to start recording guest vocalists, as he had originally intended back in 2006. He wasn't going to use any of Gen's vocals – they were to be consigned to history, or, as he said, 'I'm not having that cunt anywhere near *Desertshore*.'

Knowing how Gen wanted his vocals included on the album, me and Chris were in a difficult position, torn between realising Sleazy's last work as he had wanted it and Gen's feelings at not being on it. Gen wanted to work with us on *Desertshore* but we no longer felt a creative relationship with him was possible, especially as we were still trying to resolve outstanding issues from him quitting. But we were willing to finish the project, especially as Sleazy had always intended that Chris do the final production on it for him.

We were given an ultimatum by Gen: he said that if his ICA vocals weren't on the album, we couldn't release it using the name Throbbing Gristle. *Desertshore* discussions turned into being all about his vocals and my and Chris's right to use the name of TG, and not about the most important thing of all – that *Desertshore* was a memorial work to Sleazy. We wanted to honour Sleazy's wishes but it looked like we'd have to make compromises and so proposed that we work some of Gen's vocals from the ICA into one or more of the songs alongside the guest vocalists.

Gen didn't like that idea and said that, if we removed his voice, altered the music without his consent, or if we used other vocalists, we couldn't release it as a TG record. He was fixated on the ICA version of *Desertshore*, wrongly thinking that we were reworking those recordings, and seemed convinced we were plotting to exclude him from the final album. *We* weren't. Sleazy already had. The ICA version was a completely separate piece to what Sleazy had worked towards and wanted as the final release. Gen wasn't on any of Sleazy's latest *Desertshore* audio files, which we were working from, so we couldn't 'remove' his voice or music – simply because they weren't even there to remove.

We were getting nowhere and the deadline for delivering parts was looming, so as Gen wouldn't agree to us including him in a way that suited the project we made a last-ditch attempt to use the TG name for Sleazy. We offered Gen royalties, even though he wasn't on the record. He was immovable. It was his presence on the album or nothing.

We could have gone ahead and used the name Throbbing Gristle – to all intents and purposes we were the only remaining members and had the required majority vote – but that would have caused havoc and tainted what was supposed to be a tender, loving gesture to our dearest friend. To prevent more stress and arguments, and to avoid submitting to Gen changing Sleazy's wishes, we decided to release *Desertshore* as X-TG. After all, that was more reflective of the reality of the TG situation at its end, and we could keep *Desertshore* as the work Sleazy had wanted it to be.

Throughout 2011, me and Chris had spent much of our spare time compiling all the audio parts and recording the guest vocalists from Sleazy's list, ready for mixing and mastering *Desertshore*. We had to make sense of his idiosyncratic electronic filing system, which took a while, as did learning to use some of the equipment he'd bought specifically for the album. I'd already recorded and sent Sleazy my vocals for 'All That Is My Own' and 'My Only Child', so our next step was to approach the guest vocalists, Blixa Bargeld, Antony (Anohni), Sasha Grey, Marc Almond and Gaspar Noé. Everyone graciously agreed to contribute without hesitation. Blixa recorded his vocals in Germany as we liaised via phone throughout the day. He was incredibly generous and recorded amazing vocals for all the tracks bar 'Le Petit Chevalier', gallantly apologising that he didn't consider his French good enough.

Gaspar had agreed to do the French vocals for 'Le Petit Chevalier'. He was the only guest vocalist who came to our studio to record, the only one who had never sung before, and it was to be the first time we'd all met. We only knew him through emailing and from him using our music in his films. Having seen his work, we wondered what he'd be like. Maybe he thought the same about us because of our history. We picked him up from the train station in our car and by the time we got to our house we were talking about everything from conspiracy theories to sex and beyond. When it came to recording he was a little nervous, but we looked on him not having sung before as a plus. He could do whatever he wanted and he had a great low, gravelly voice that suited the nuances of the French language so well, and was the opposite of Ari's ten-year-old little-boy voice on Nico's original version of the track.

We got all the great material we needed surprisingly quickly and had a relaxed and great day together into the bargain. Sasha lived in LA, so recorded her vocals to 'Afraid' to a guide track we gave her and sent us a heartfelt vocal interpretation that was so different from everything else we'd received so far and reflected the sparse arrangement we had in place. Anohni's vocals for 'Janitor of Lunacy' were incredibly beautiful and sent shivers down our spines when we heard them. They were so inspiring that they took the final track in a different direction entirely. The same happened with Marc's vocals on 'The Falconer', which were heartwrenchingly emotional, and he'd also given us extra harmonies and vocal parts to work with.

The last track on the album was to be 'Desertshores', a spoken farewell from Sleazy's close friends, saying to him, 'Meet me on the desertshore.'

Everyone had been so kind, obliging and supportive. The final arrangements and mixing of each track took a shockingly short time. It was as if we were conduits for some unseen force channelling ideas for marrying sounds with emotions, as if magic were involved. We'd look at one another, big smiles on our faces and wide-eyed in amazement that it was finding its form so readily – as if it was meant to be.

~

Mute had recorded the Carter Tutti Void performance at the Roundhouse using a high-end mobile recording studio. The quality and sound were superb and there were immediate calls for us to release it. With so much else going on, we decided to put it out on Mute and had OK'd the test pressings, having delivered audio masters and artworks back in December. The title was *Transverse* – as in the interaction of both the sounds cutting across one another and Nik cutting across the bow of Carter Tutti.

We all wanted the cover to be entirely different from what any of us had done before and had exchanged ideas as we each travelled between our separate gigs. I liked the idea of the cover representing indefinability: it fitted the concept of the live performance but I also thought it would be good to have something that 'moved' amid the other CDs and vinyl albums in the racks. We chose a black-and-white graphic that created the optical illusion of the cover being three-dimensional and appearing to move.

We'd done interviews to help promote the album and the reviews were starting to appear, and they just kept on coming. I've never been one to bother about reviews, but the sheer number was staggering, as was the positive consensus. Booking enquiries started coming in for CTV to perform. We'd all been caught unawares by the reaction, just as me and Chris had been by the revisiting of Chris & Cosey.

7 April 2012
The day went so well. Such a joyous relaxed atmosphere. Informal after wedding gathering at a nearby bar/restaurant was just such fun. So many of Nick's friends came along and that really really made me happy to see and hear the genuine love and affection they had for each other.

The party of sixty family and friends gathered at Islington Town Hall, London, for Nick and Tatis's wedding. It was a sunny day, if a bit blustery, and we waited for Tatis to arrive. She looked beautiful in an elegant, tailored, ivory-coloured, below-knee-length dress, looking worried as she was a bit late. Nick was in a cobalt-blue suit, as Tatis's traditional 'something blue'. They both looked stunning and glowed with happiness – even the ladies officiating the ceremony were cheery and happy.

The reception as such was at a bistro bar called Browns, just around the corner but too long a walk in high heels. Me, Chris, Nick, Tatis and two of Nick's friends piled into a black cab. 'Browns, please.' But we seemed to be going a long way round. 'You're going the wrong way, mate,' Nick said.

'Browns, right?' the cabbie said.

Then it clicked. He was taking us to Browns the lap-dancing club, which some wedding parties went on to after their ceremonies. I knew it as the Horns from my stripping days. Definitely not the place to go or be reminded of on Nick's wedding day. We'd arranged a buffet and put a tab on the bar. Nick's best man, Chesney, did the usual brief speech, which was humorously and boisterously shouted down after a few minutes. I noticed Tatis go outside to call her mother. Her family couldn't travel from Colombia and I felt for her on such a special day.

The wedding day had gone well – there'd been no drama to speak of. That was to happen two days later, when I broke my foot. This was now the fourth time I'd broken the same foot and it was certainly the most painful. Previous breaks, once in a cast and supported, were hardly troublesome as far as the level of pain was concerned. No one had told me I'd also damaged tendons, ligaments and muscles, which each brought their own separate long-term challenges as they healed.

21 April 2012

Today is the first day my broken foot feels any better. The swelling has gone down a bit and the throbbing too. I've felt quite ill with it – whether that's shock to the system or not I don't know but it really depressed me. That and being totally dependent on Chris. A single-storey dwelling is looking more and more attractive.

A downstairs bathroom suddenly made an appearance at the top of our to-do list. This latest break had given us both a wake-up call about possible mobility problems in our older years. Neither of us liked the idea of going up and down the stairs on our backsides or installing a stairlift. We had images of it breaking down halfway, like in *Phoenix Nights*.

The plastic cast the hospital gave me was a fantastic bit of kit. It had airbags that you inflated and deflated to adjust the support. Seeing as I was to be in it for up to twelve weeks, I bought another, shorter version to do the forthcoming French gig in. I'd broken my foot just in time to avoid the no-fly window. Lucky me. The gig could go ahead.

My injury, though inconvenient and uncomfortable, paled into insignificance compared to what Xeni Jardin was going through. She'd been diagnosed with breast cancer and was undergoing chemotherapy treatment. I'd liked Xeni from our first meeting in LA for the TG interview with *Boing Boing*. She had a vibrancy and zest for life that was now being put to the worst test. We'd written to one another over the years and through Twitter – which was where she chose to document her experience. Our personal email exchanges were deeply moving. I offered what support I could from so far away. Out of the blue she sent me and Chris a recording of the chemo machine from her last session. She likened the machines to an eight-track tape recorder and was recording each chemo treatment as reference for writing about it later when her brain was less compromised by the drugs.

The same day as Xeni's email, I'd received one from the ICA inviting me to contribute a twenty-minute audio work for 'Soundworks', based on the theme of time and the immateriality of audio recordings, which was to tie in with the Bruce Nauman exhibition 'Days' – seven voices randomly reciting the days of the week.

The installation was about the passing and measure of time, something that Xeni was connecting with at such a deep level with her recordings of the chemo timeline, the repetitive rhythm of the machine as it fed her drip after drip of precise doses of toxic chemicals that caused a strange feeling, as if time were morphing. Xeni's machine-noise recording had such depth – it held within it the potential for life, an extension of time, and the timing of the emails was too serendipitous to ignore. But I was sensitive to Xeni's feelings. I wrote to her and explained my idea of creating a work based on her chemo-machine recording. I didn't want to come across as intrusive. Xeni's response was exceptional: she'd hoped I'd do something with the recording and embraced the prospect of creating a work from her ordeal. She sent me further recordings to work with and I also used the documentary photos she'd taken of herself, inputted into software to transform them into sound. My approach was to attempt to evoke the feelings she'd described to me of being submerged in another time zone.

I sent the finished piece to Xeni. I was worried that it may depress her in some way, remind her of suffering the nausea and pain. She listened to it over and over and wrote to me to say that I'd captured the feeling so well and how happy she was that her intimate, painful experience had made its way into my art, become something beautiful and a source of strength for her. I felt privileged to have been able to bring some light to her darker days. The piece was called 'Bioschismic' and released to the world on the ICA website.

4 October 2012
TG business has been so bad that whenever I get a chance NOT to discuss it I take it . . . When you try and try to make things amicable for the sake of TG legacy and Sleazy's memory and to no avail, it's exhausting. Then you get slagged off on the internet and accused of things you haven't done . . . this year has been mammoth crazy.

The *Desertshore* official release date of 25 November was announced in September. It was a double album release, *Desertshore* and *The Final Report*, recordings we three as X-TG had made together in our studio. The artwork echoed back to TG's first album, *Second Annual Report*, being white and simple. The two albums were represented in the artwork as well: the vinyl and CD front and back covers were divided in two (top and bottom), one half matt with the title *Desertshore* in spot varnish, and the other half in gloss varnish with a matt *The Final Report*. The accompanying booklet was likewise divided in two, each half giving information on one album, and included a postcard as a nod to the first termination of TG. We produced a special limited edition on white vinyl in a two-tone grey slipcase with a photograph of X-TG signed by me and Chris.

Desertshore had been a mammoth task, emotionally and practically. The production costs were very high but to us it was a labour of love so profit didn't really feature. Now that it was an X-TG release too any loss wouldn't affect Gen.

Negotiations for a settlement of the 2010 TG 'tour' losses were still hovering in the background like a black cloud, and were not helped by an interview with Gen back in February in which he was reported as saying he was suing me and Chris over the TG re-releases, that we hadn't had his permission for them or paid him. He omitted to say that there were thousands of pounds' worth of outstanding TG 'tour' losses that he'd refused to accept any responsibility for and which we hadn't reconciled yet.

In consideration of that and Gen's objections over *Desertshore* we'd done all we could to avoid any possible unnecessary disruption to what was, for us, a lasting token of remembrance for Sleazy. But within hours of the announcement being posted, Gen took to social media to publicly whinge and repeat his previous unfounded accusations. But what was worst of all was his call for people not to buy Sleazy's memorial album: 'DESERTSHORE is NOT a legitimate TG release. BOYCOTT it.' Why would anyone do that? It was clearly an X-TG album. We and so many others had done this for Sleazy. I was upset and angry that Gen had portrayed himself as a victim. Not a word about Sleazy. It was a selfish, contemptible and disrespectful thing to do. Gen followed up his boycott tweets with an email to Cargo advising them not to release the album and that he was preparing a legal letter.

We released the album for Sleazy.

8 December 2012

We still can't believe this year's successes. We have two albums that have been in 2012 albums of the year (some at times listed together) and CTV got in top lists for cover design. I guess it would be a good time to bow out, i.e. if we didn't already have more to do. The amount of press we've had has been staggering. CTV is up to 81 reviews that we know of and the TG re-releases and X-TG are climbing up there too. Previously you'd be happy to get 3 or 4.

Our last gig of the year was performing as Chris & Cosey at Berghain club in Berlin. Nick came with us, and Richard and other friends made the trip to watch us, which made it very special, like a birthday treat. Berghain is regarded as one of the world's best nightclubs, famous for its excellent sound system, events that go on into the next day, its rigorous door policy, its historic gay fetish club roots, and much debauchery and hedonism – a larger and more industrial version of Heaven in London. It was perfect for us.

The Tuesday after my birthday, me and Chris were in London doing a CTV interview with Nik and signing *Desertshore* photos. The promotion for the X-TG album was in full swing and going strong, even making the front page of the *Guardian* as their album of the week. I was thrilled for Sleazy and everyone who'd contributed and supported us.

A live Q&A we did at Rough Trade East gave us a measure of how our work on Sleazy's behalf had been received by the many hard-core TG fans that attended. The audience were so very grateful that we'd gone ahead with the album. It was good to talk about Sleazy with a lighter heart, having fulfilled our promise to him. The whole process of creating the tracks had served to put to rest a lot of the pain of losing him. At first we'd choke up or cry when we heard his voice, especially the last message he left on our answerphone, then we started smiling and laughing more at his endearing mannerisms. He would have laughed his head off with glee and disbelief that the album made the UK charts at no. 40 and was in numerous 'Albums of the Year' lists. With such an unbelievably great reception and reviews, we felt our decision to complete and release the album had been fully vindicated. I toasted Sleazy with the last of his bottle of vintage port that had sat in our kitchen since 2010, when he'd left for Bangkok and never come back.

8 January 2013
We're going to rationalise our schedule for this year. Talk of us performing in the USA again but we will push it to spring 2014. We have much recording we want to do and too many live gig offers. We're at the stage of needing the money live work brings, loving them but not having the energy of youth. Sigh.

There comes a time when, whether you like it or not, your body tells you to slow down. Much as everyone hates that moment, it's a reality we all face. But to reach a point of physical limitation is tough when you so want to carry on and do more. We weren't alone: other artists we worked with at festivals were reaching burnout point – and some of them were twenty years younger than us. The schedules for playing live can be unforgivingly physically demanding. Trouble is, there's nothing that can compare with when you're on stage, lost in the magic of music with an audience that is with you all the way.

The other conundrum was that, while we were gigging, we weren't recording, and that really bothered us. We had a stack of unreleased material and files of ideas.

An interim measure presented itself. I was cooking in the kitchen and Chris was in the studio going through our Carter Tutti ideas. The studio door was open and I heard a rhythm and melody clip. 'That's it! That's it!' I shouted at him, and rushed into the studio. 'Don't change a thing. That rhythm and melody is it – it's awesome,'

We worked for the rest of the day building a track from a small rhythm clip and hint of melody, as well as sampling an old metal (Coolicon) lightshade, like the one Delia Derbyshire had used for sound in the 1960s when she worked at the BBC Radiophonic Workshop. The track became our Carter Tutti single 'Coolicon'. That would serve as a taster for our next Carter Tutti album and we'd play it live as the last song of our 'Carter Tutti plays Chris & Cosey' gigs – and to signal that we would be moving on from performing the older Chris & Cosey material.

We took the train from King's Lynn to King's Cross for a lunchtime meeting with Paul to discuss our 2013 schedule. We met at the usual place, Costa Coffee in York Way, affectionately known to us as 'the TG office'. It was where we held most of our meetings, it being so conveniently close to King's Cross station.

We'd had some great offers for gigs and projects and we hated having to turn them down, particularly Phil Collins (the Turner Prize artist), who wanted us to collaborate with him for his show in Cologne. Clashing dates and deadlines can be so aggravating. From our first live performance of our 'Carter Tutti plays Chris & Cosey' material back in February 2011, we'd been inundated with gig requests and spent the best part of that year and 2012 performing at sold-out shows and music festivals around the world. It looked likely that 2013 would be the same.

Working non-stop doesn't leave a lot of time for a social life either. What little spare time we had we used for quiet time together and seeing family. Not being able to go to see Pam Hogg's collection at London Fashion Week was a huge disappointment for us. We would have loved to be there, especially to see the English National Ballet dancing to Carter Tutti Void music.

Sometimes we get lucky, though, and timing is on our side. David from KOKO club, a friend of Richard's, got in touch on behalf of an old friend of ours, Scumeck Sabottka. We'd known Scumeck since the 1980s, when he'd tour-managed us for C&C gigs in Germany. Reading his name again triggered such fond memories of fun times.

Scumeck was now the agent and coordinator for Kraftwerk's live performances and he invited us to the Saturday-night *Man-Machine* show and after-party at the Tate Modern. I'd intended to get tickets as a birthday treat for Chris but they were like gold dust. Scumeck really made our day. Having played that space, we knew how tricky the sound could be, but they nailed it, helped by the twenty-four or more speakers around the hall. The show was perfection. Immaculate presentation, and the synchronised 3D visuals were mind-blowing. The entire audience stood in 3D glasses, staring and looking up, watching and listening to such influential master craftsmen of sound. It was mesmerising. We had a fabulous evening and saw loads of friends and music colleagues. The Kraftwerk show will forever be etched in my memory and I doubt, for me, that it could ever be bettered.

12 July 2013

I got the confirmation from Andrew that Tate Britain ratified the acquisition of three of my works. Yeah!! I'm very happy it's all finally gone through . . . I'm hoping that as we wind down the live performances I can get more focused on the art projects I have listed on my much neglected 'to do' list! We'll be poorer without the gig money but fulfilled in the most meaningful ways.

My work had been acquired by other museums and respected private collectors but I was particularly pleased to get confirmation that three of my works were now in the Tate Britain permanent collection: two of my 1970s magazine actions ('Alpha No.5', 'Exposure Vol. 2 No.7') and the recent 2010 work, 'Confessions Projected'. Not that being 'accepted' was or is a goal with any of my work; neither is acknowledgement or 'success'. I always think that, once released, it will find its place in culture at the right time – over thirty years, in my case. At least, unlike some, I've lived to see that happen.

On a lighter and earthier note, who would have thought my vegetable-growing would be of interest to the wider world, but apparently it was. *The Quietus* was doing a documentary series of 'At Leisure' films with, amongst others, Stephen Morris of New Order with his military vehicles, Tim Burgess, Steve Ignorant of Crass on his lifeboat duties, and me talking about growing vegetables organically. Films about what we all did in our downtime from music, art or other public activities. Getting down and being at one with nature is how I unwind. To help generate life from seed and soil is a gratifying feeling. A mutually beneficial collaboration. Luke Turner, who interviewed me, knew a little about plants and enough about me to make it interesting.

Our garden was a popular film location – me and Nik had been interviewed by Red Bull Music Academy sat at our picnic bench. It was for the publication *For the Record*, fifteen conversations between artists who they felt had influenced the way people listen to music. I was initially approached after my Red Bull talk in London and I was supposed to discuss the physicality of music with Stephen O'Malley of Sunn O))). Disappointingly, he couldn't do it. I proposed Nik. Todd, who was moderating, provided some good comments for our conversation. It was enlightening listening to Nik talk at length about her approach to making music.

The summer of 2013 was shaping up to be the sunniest ever, metaphorically speaking – and for the most part literally. We released 'Coolicon' as a 10" vinyl single, which sold out, forcing a re-press. The reviews were so good and affirmed the direction we wanted to go in for our next Carter Tutti album. I just kept wondering how everything could be going so well – and when I'd be brought down to earth.

4 September 2013
Yesterday we got a signed-for 7 page legal letter from a UK solicitor working on Gen's behalf claiming against IR, and me and Chris as individuals for copyright infringement and damages regarding the TG re-releases. We are advised to make a 'substantial response with a satisfactory settlement offer' by 5pm on 16th September. It's all so unnecessary and especially nasty suing me and Chris individually . . .

The doorbell rang. Our friendly postman stood there smiling. 'One to be signed for today. Looks official.'

I wondered what it could be. As I opened the envelope and saw the first few lines I called Chris from the studio. 'It looks like that legal letter Gen was preparing last year has finally arrived.'

There's nothing like a signed-for legal letter to get your attention. We both read through the pages, our jaws dropping at Gen's temerity to accuse us of copyright infringement over the TG re-releases. Considering how many copyright infringements we'd suffered in relation to those past TG bootlegs, Gen's legal letter was risible. Documentation existed that he knew about which supported the TG re-releases. We'd wondered why he'd been quiet for so long about reconciling the impasse over the TG 'tour' losses. Now we knew. All we'd had from Gen in the past months was a polite request for paperwork he said he needed for the IRS. I could be forgiven for thinking that may have been him garnering information for his lawyer.

We talked to Paul and took legal advice. Gen's legal letter contained inaccuracies and omitted pertinent information that would cast doubt on the claims of so-called copyright infringement. But his legal letter did include confirmation that Gen had left Throbbing Gristle in 2010. Finally his leaving TG was officially confirmed. We supplied supporting documentation in a thirty-page response, refuting all the accusations Gen made against us. Paul suggested and arranged a follow-up meeting with Gen's lawyer, both to save a lot of time and because we and Paul weren't sure that the lawyer possessed many of the relevant facts about the claims Gen had made.

Paul met the lawyer at the firm's office in London but it didn't go very well. Paul left the offices saying all further communication should be in writing. It had been a brief meeting and it was the last we heard from the lawyer.

Coincidentally and ironically, Spydeee was in correspondence with Gen about why Gen had infringed *his* copyright, after Gen had released a COUM album that included Spydeee without informing him or acquiring his permission to do so. It was Spydeee's run-in with Gen that brought me and Spydeee back together. He'd emailed Gen asking for an explanation and then wrote to me to ask for my advice on Gen's response . . . which I understood hadn't been very helpful.

16 January 2014
I'm more or less back on UK time . . . hope I haven't spoken too soon! Dexter is pleased as punch that we're back. He's being very vocal and all over us. I've got a ton of emails to answer but I'm taking it easy this week.

We returned from playing our final 'Carter Tutti plays Chris & Cosey' USA shows in New York and Chicago, having had to add more dates as the scheduled concerts sold out. 2014 was already mapped out. First thing every morning I'd consult our appointment diary and year planner to see what was next on the horizon. I had two weeks before we were off to perform in Holland – possibly enough time to get over any residual effects of jet lag and my cold, but worrying that my sore throat may affect my ability to sing. It didn't – the shows went smooth as silk.

Once home, we had a three-month stretch where we weren't travelling that we'd earmarked for doing remixes, remastering my 1986 video *Pussy Got the Cream* for an exhibition at Tate Liverpool, and preparing a new live audio/video piece, *Impulse Response II*, for our Carter Tutti concert at the J. G. Ballard-themed Only Connect Festival of Sound in Oslo.

I was in the grasp of a 'loop', in a state of heightened tension, constantly aware of a tightening coiled spring in my chest that was only relieved by being outside the 'loop' – quiet time with Chris away from the studio and in the company of close friends and family. Not for the first time the notion of maintaining a sense of balance and perspective in my life had entered my thoughts, probably helped by Les and Pam, who had been telling me to slow down.

We took a weekend break and went to Graham Duff's fiftieth birthday bash in Brighton. Before we went in to the party we took a stroll along the seafront opposite the club. I've always loved the sea at night: it has a dark, eerie beauty that I find scary and captivating in equal measure, not knowing what lurks beneath the hidden depths of the vast, endless expanse of undulating blackness that disappears into the distance. I can stand for hours entranced by its movement and sound, breathing like a brooding ecosystem or powerful unfathomable monster.

My face smarted from the cold sea breeze, and I could hear the cheery voices of Graham's partygoers and music punch the air then disappear in rhythm to the opening and closing of the club door. We turned and walked over to the club, got checked off the doorman's list and went inside.

The room was full of Graham's guests and friends from his world as a screenwriter and actor. We could just see Graham over the heads of everyone, looking the picture of happiness. We had birthday love hugs and Chris and I tucked ourselves away next to the table full of birthday gifts, adding ours to the growing pile. Standing at the side and taking in the crowd, we could see familiar faces, then realised that some were familiar to us, having just watched them acting in *Game of Thrones* or other films and TV programmes. Ben Wheatley was there, the director of one of our favourite films, *A Field in England*. Chris and Ben had had a brief back-and-forth on Twitter over a limited-edition poster from the film. From across a very crowded room he gave us a 'hello' smile and raised eyebrow, and a rolled-eyes look about the guy talking to him. He looked a bit peeved, like he'd been hijacked by an ambitious networker.

Maybe we should have rescued him but it wasn't long before our would-be 'safe zone' was invaded and people started coming over to thank us and tell us what our work meant to them. I never know what to say in reply. 'Thank you' always seems inadequate. Mal, our old friend from Cabaret Voltaire, was with us when one guy came up, bowed down low to me and Chris and said, 'You are my heroes' – then ran off.

Mal was smiling. 'You two have a strange effect on people.' It seemed so.

We were happy to melt into the background and took a seat at the side of the room to watch Graham's favourite band, Wire, perform and then see Graham, dressed in a bright-blue velvet suit, ushered up on stage and handed a guitar to join in. What a fantastic birthday present.

> 30 April 2014
> *I've begun collating info for my autobiography . . . It will be a strange journey into the past. So much so that I'll have to do it in stages and not at a time when I'm being creatively active on new works. It was a BIG decision to bite the bullet and get started.*

I'd been revisiting my past for some time, firstly through the exhibiting of my magazine works and COUM actions, then the regrouping of TG and the reworking of our 1980s Chris & Cosey songs, and I'd begun working with Andrew on sifting through my archive in preparation for an exhibition that would include my work as COUM. That was under way when, in November 2013, Hull was announced as the winner of UK City of Culture for 2017 and Andrew Dixon, who had led the bid for Hull, tweeted me saying, 'Look forward to welcoming you back in #2017hull to do new work.'

I was thrilled that Hull had triumphed, and at the idea of possibly being involved. There were calls on social media to include myself and COUM in the Hull 2017 programme. I started getting tweets and emails, and so did past COUM members Spydeee and Les. It was great that so many people were championing the COUM cause but it was very early days and would need a lot of careful thought. Andrew and I continued working on my archive, letting the idea of returning to present work in Hull simmer gently in the background.

A combination of what seemed unrelated factors had come together, fulfilling all the necessary conditions for me to begin work on writing my autobiography. I'd come full circle: from

Hull, the place where my life and my art began, and where my book would begin, and now back there, marking where my book will end as I enter into a new dialogue with Hull, in recognition of my life and art.

Acknowledgements

First and foremost, my thanks go to my lover and creative collaborator Chris, without whom this book and so much in my life would not have been possible. Writing this book was tough and I couldn't have done it without his unwavering support and belief in me.

Thanks to our dearest son, Nick, and daughter-in-law, Tatis, for their encouragement and for bringing such joy into my present life as I waded through my past.

Special thanks to my longest-standing, dearest friend, Les, who has been and continues to be a constant loving presence in my life – who never ceases to amaze me or make me laugh like no one else can.

Thank you all at Faber, especially my editor, Lee Brackstone, who wrestled with my huge word count and won, and managed to make the process as painless as possible. Dan Papps for his enduring enthusiasm. Silvia Crompton, Luke Bird, Jack Murphy and Dave Watkins.

Big thank you to Matthew Hamilton, my literary agent, for his encouragement and support from the very first time we met.

A big thank you to Luke Turner for introducing me to Lee Brackstone and thereby instigating the chain of events that led to the completion and publication of this book.

Thanks to those who gave me advice and encouragement to write about my life: the astounding Maria Fusco, Jack Sargeant, my wonderful generous friend Paul Buck, who is always ready to help, John Doran, and Graham Duff, a man of huge talent who took the time to offer me advice and friendship – always with great humour.

Thanks to the Newby family: especially Mum, who tried so hard to make things work, and my dear sister, Pam; Debbie, Simon, Lily, Danny, Uncle Mike and his inspiring guitar-playing, Edwina, Beryl, Ken and Barbara.

The Carter family, especially Rose and Albert – Rose for being my much-loved surrogate mother – Nan, Shud, Pat and Ernie, the Fosseys, Phillips and Drapers.

A huge thank you to all my friends and collaborators for being a part of my life, enriching it beyond measure – especially dearly loved but sadly departed Sleazy and Geff – and with apologies to those whose names aren't included for whatever reason. You are far from forgotten.

Thanks to Spydeee for bringing light where there were shadows, dearest sweet Fizzy Paet, Ian Goodrich, Anna Stillmaker, Foxtrot Echo, John Lacey, Menzies Brook, Alan Worsley, Tim Poston, my close friend and confidant Skot Armstrong, James Tallon, the extraordinary and lovable Monte Cazazza, Alex Fergusson, Alaura, Fred Giannelli, Sasha Grey, Marc Almond, Blixa Bargeld, Anohni, Gaspar Noé, Robert Wyatt, John Duncan, Olga Gerrard, Barbara Rogers, Steve Montgomery, Chris Connelly, Brian Williams, Tracey Roberts, Robert Crouch, Richard Chartier, Bob Eckhardt, Jo Ahmed, Bobby Bonbon, Andria Degens, Ossian, Steve, Todd Snow, Chesney Phelps, the effervescent, lovely Terry McGaughey, and Jenks, whose visits bring peace and a dash of down-to-earth northern common sense. Peter Edney, Nik Void, Tim Burgess and my godson Morgan, Pam Hogg, Suzan and Robert Swale.

Thank you, Jill Drower, for permission to quote from your excellent book, *99 Balls Pond Road: The Story of the Exploding Galaxy* (London, 2014).

~

For those who supported me in my music and art:

Thank you Andrew Wheatley and Martin McGeown of Cabinet, London.

Thank you Rough Trade, Peer Music, Mute Records, Mute Song, PIAS, Wax Trax!, Nettwerk, Cargo UK, Heike Munder, Catherine Wood, Anthony at Baba Yaga's Hut. Especially Daniel Miller, Paul Taylor, David McGinnis, John McRobbie, Zoe Miller, Darren Crawford, Phil Hill, the remarkable Paul Smith, brilliant musician, artist and friend Susan Stenger, the master of live sound Chris Fullard, and fabulous TG family and crew: Mitch Flacko, Kirsten Reynolds, Ashley, Charles Poulet. The marvellous, once-met-never-forgotten Andrew Weatherall, friend and DJ extraordinaire Richard Clouston of Cosey Club, JD Twitch (Optimo – Keith McIvor), Gavin Toomey, André Stitt, Xeni Jardin and John Grant.

Extra-special thanks, love and respect to all the Throbbing Gristle, Chris & Cosey, Carter Tutti and Carter Tutti Void fans around the world.